# Preschool Children with Special Needs

# Preschool Children with Special Needs

## Children at Risk and Children with Disabilities

### SECOND EDITION

**Janet W. Lerner**

*Northeastern Illinois University*

**Barbara Lowenthal**

*Northeastern Illinois University*

**Rosemary W. Egan**

*Northeastern Illinois University*

Boston • New York • San Francisco
Mexico City • Montreal • Toronto • London • Madrid • Munich • Paris
Hong Kong • Singapore • Tokyo • Cape Town • Sydney

KH

**Executive Editor:** *Virginia Lanigan*
**Editor in Chief:** *Paul A. Smith*
**Editorial Assistant:** *Robert Champagne*
**Marketing Manager:** *Taryn Wahlquist*
**Editorial-Production Administrator:** *Annette Joseph*
**Editorial-Production Coordinator:** *Holly Crawford*
**Editorial-Production Service:** *Lynda Griffiths, TKM Productions*
**Photo Researcher:** *Katharine S. Cook*
**Composition Buyer:** *Linda Cox*
**Electronic Composition:** *Omegatype Typography, Inc.*
**Manufacturing Buyer:** *JoAnne Sweeney*
**Cover Administrator:** *Kristina Mose-Libon*
**Cover Designer:** *Suzanne Harbison*

For related titles and support materials, visit our online catalog at www.ablongman.com

Between the time Website information is gathered and then published, it is not unusual for some sites to have closed. Also, the transcription of URLs can result in unintended typographical errors. The publisher would appreciate notification where these errors occur so that they may be corrected in subsequent editions.

CIP data not available at the time of publication.
0-205-35879-9

Printed in the United States of America

10   9   8   7            RRD-IN   07

**Photo Credits:**   pp. 1 and 137: National Lekotek Center 1-800-366-PLAY; p. 13: Lori Adamski Peek/ Getty Images Inc.; pp. 16, 22, 46, 69, 87, 103, 112, 129, 156, 168, 172, 212, 229, and 248: Will Faller; p. 30: Robert E. Daemmrich/Getty Images Inc.; p. 36: Lori Morris/Photoquest, Inc.; p. 56: AP/Wide World Photos; p. 65: Pearson Learning; p. 83: Mark Richards/PhotoEdit; pp. 94, 98, 185, 195, and 215: Will Hart; p. 116: Laura Dwight/PhotoEdit; pp. 145 and 269: Robert Harbison; p. 162: © Rifton Equipment; p. 181: Mary Kate Denny/PhotoEdit; p. 200: Tony Freeman/PhotoEdit; p. 216: Myrleen Ferguson/PhotoEdit; p. 239: Jim Pickerell; p. 254: Corbis Digital Stock; p. 276: Michael Newman/PhotoEdit.

08/26/08

*This book is dedicated to the families of young children with special needs,*
*who are ultimately responsible for the child.*
*It is with love and dedication that the families are involved*
*with their youngsters every day.*

# Contents

Preface      xiii

PART ONE • *Overview*

## 1    *Preschool Children with Special Needs*      1

*Children with Special Needs*      2

*Early Intervention*      6

*Two Age Groups: Programs for Infants and Toddlers and Programs for Preschoolers*      8

*The Number of Young Children with Disabilities Who Are Receiving Special Services*      9

*Educational Environments for Young Children with Special Needs*      10

*Cultural Diversity*      13

*Theoretical Foundations of Early Education*      15

*Summary*      20

*Key Terms*      21

## 2    *Changing Policies and Laws*      22

*Historical Perspectives*      23

*Studies of Early Childhood Intervention*      26

*Legislation and Programs for Young Children with Disabilities*      28

*Legislation and Programs for Children at Risk*      36

*Current Trends and Issues*     39

*Summary*     45

*Key Terms*     45

**3**     *Family Systems*     46

*The Family*     47

*Parent/Family Reactions to Having a Child with Special Needs*     52

*Participation of the Family in Early Intervention: A Partnership*     54

*Special Issues*     59

*Summary*     67

*Key Terms*     68

**PART TWO • *Assessment, Learning Environments,
and Curricula***

**4**     *Assessment and Evaluation of Young Children*     69

*Purposes of Assessment*     70

*Eligibility for Special Services*     74

*Stages of the Assessment Process*     75

*Types of Assessment Instruments*     80

*Alternative Assessment Methods*     82

*Special Considerations for Assessing Young Children*     90

*Summary*     92

*Key Terms*     93

**5**     *Environments for Learning*     94

*Types of Settings*     96

*The Law and Settings for Learning*     97

*The Process of Integrating Young Children with Special Needs
with Typically Functioning Children*     99

*Early Intervention Teams*     103

*Service Coordination*     105

*Interagency Collaboration*     107

*Summary*     110

*Key Terms*     111

**6**     *Curriculum Development*     **112**

*Defining the Curriculum*     114

*Curriculum Routines and Schedules*     117

*Types of Early Childhood Curricula*     120

*The Role of Play in the Curriculum*     128

*Establishing the Physical Environment for Learning*     130

*The IEP and the IFSP and the Curriculum*     130

*Summary*     135

*Key Terms*     136

**PART THREE • *Intervention***

**7**     *Motor Development and Medically Related Problems*     **137**

*Normal Motor Growth and Development*     139

*Atypical Motor Development: Delays and Disabilities*     144

*Characteristics and Types of Motor and Physical Disabilities*     146

*Medically Related Disabilities*     151

*Intervention Strategies for Children with Motor Delays and Physical Disabilities*     157

*Special Issues in Motor Development*     164

*Summary*     166

*Key Terms*     167

**8**    *Adaptive Behavior and Self-Help Skills*    **168**

     *Adaptive Behavior in Early Childhood*    **169**

     *Principles of Adaptive Behaviors*    **171**

     *Toileting Skills*    **173**

     *Eating Skills*    **176**

     *Dressing Skills*    **180**

     *Grooming Skills*    **182**

     *Summary*    **183**

     *Key Terms*    **184**


**9**    *Social and Emotional Development*    **185**

     *Defining Social and Emotional Problems*    **187**

     *Theories of Social and Emotional Development in Young Children*    **188**

     *Types of Social and Emotional Problems in Young Children*    **197**

     *Intervention Strategies for Young Children with Social and Emotional Difficulties*    **206**

     *Summary*    **210**

     *Key Terms*    **211**


**10**    *Communication and Language Development*    **212**

     *Definitions of Communication, Speech, and Language*    **214**

     *Stages of Language Development*    **215**

     *Theories of Language Acquisition*    **219**

     *Linguistic Systems of Language*    **222**

     *Language Difficulties Associated with Specific Conditions*    **223**

     *Intervention for Children with Language Problems*    **228**

     *Summary*    **237**

     *Key Terms*    **238**

**11**  *Cognitive Development*    **239**

> *What Are Cognitive Skills?*    **241**
>
> *Theories of Cognitive Development*    **242**
>
> *Intervention Strategies for Teaching Cognitive Skills*    **247**
>
> *Early Literacy*    **253**
>
> *Using Computer Technology*    **262**
>
> *Tips for Teachers: Strategies for Building Early Literacy Skills*    **264**
>
> *Summary*    **267**
>
> *Key Terms*    **268**

**12**  *Transition*    **269**

> *Overview of Transition for Young Children with Special Needs*    **272**
>
> *Factors Affecting Transitions*    **278**
>
> *Planning for Transitions*    **282**
>
> *Stages in a Coordinated Transition Plan*    **284**
>
> *Summary*    **286**
>
> *Key Terms*    **276**

**APPENDIX A**  **Tests and Assessment Instruments**    **288**

**APPENDIX B**  **Selected List of Test Publishers**    **293**

**APPENDIX C**  **Developmental Milestones: Infancy to Age Six**    **295**

**APPENDIX D**  **Individualized Family Service Plan**    **301**

**Glossary**    **315**

**References**    **325**

**Author Index**    **351**

**Subject Index**    **357**

# *Preface*

Accumulating evidence shows how crucial the childhood years are for all children. This is the time of rapid brain growth and overall development that lays the foundation for all learning. For young children who have special needs in terms of physical, behavioral, developmental, or learning characteristics, these years are even more critical. The early years offer a unique opportunity to open the door to a child's future. The purpose of this book is to provide a current, research-based, and functional resource for professionals and families who nurture and intervene with preschool children who have special needs. The target audience involves preservice and in-service teachers and family members.

Part One provides an overview of the book. Chapter 1 describes preschoolers who have special needs, both children who are at risk and children with disabilities. Chapter 2 reviews changing policies and practices, including recent laws that affect young children with disabilities. Chapter 3 discusses the family systems approach, an approach that analyzes the child in the context of the family. The family-centered approach is evident in this chapter and throughout the book—in recognizing the cultural and linguistic diversities of families, in emphasizing respect for the significant roles of families in the development of their children, in understanding family priorities, and in recognizing differences in family structure.

Part Two deals with assessment, learning environments, and the curriculum. Chapter 4 concentrates on assessment and evaluation techniques, which involve formal, informal, and alternative assessments (such as play-based, authentic, and dynamic assessments). Chapter 5 focuses on appropriate learning environments, including the growing practice of inclusion and integration in early childhood settings; components of the individualized education program (IEP) and the individualized family service plan (IFSP); and the need for service coordination, interagency collaboration, and interdisciplinary teamwork. Chapter 6 describes current models of preschool curricula, developmentally appropriate practices, and recommendations for best practices.

Part Three deals with intervention and teaching. Chapter 7 discusses sensory motor interventions and medical conditions of children with motor problems. Chapter 8 focuses on interventions for adaptive behavior and self-help skills. Chapter 9 deals with social and emotional development and intervention techniques for preschoolers who need help in this area. Chapter 10 describes communication and language development, which is a problem area for many preschool children who are at risk or who have disabilities. Chapter 11 focuses on cognitive development and thinking skills with intervention methods to help children in cognitive development and in early literacy learning. Chapter 12 involves transition, the process of helping young children and families as they enter into new programs.

The appendices provide useful information for readers. Appendix A lists and describes tests and assessment instruments. Appendix B contains addresses of selected test publishers. Appendix C describes typical developmental milestones from infancy to age 6. Appendix D provides a sample individualized family service plan form. A glossary of important terms used in this text is also included.

*Preschool Children with Special Needs* incorporates several pedagogical features. Each chapter has an opening outline, an introduction to the chapter, an early childhood "snapshot," a summary of major points, and a list of key terms.

An Instructor's Manual with Test Items is available for this edition; please contact your local Allyn & Bacon sales representative to obtain your copy. In addition, we have prepared a companion website as a helpful resource for readers of our text, which contains summaries, practice tests, weblinks, and key terms for each chapter of the text. The website may be found at www.ablongman.com/lerner2e.

We gratefully acknowledge the many students who have taken our courses and provided valuable feedback. We also have learned from speakers at conferences and seminars that we have attended over the years. The published writings and research of our colleagues have been extremely valuable. We also are grateful to Northeastern Illinois University for providing conditions to complete this work. In addition, we thank the following scholars who reviewed this book in manuscript form: Ruth Ann Ferrante, Columbia College; Rebecca Oekerman, University of Texas of the Permian Basin; Daryl J. Wilcox, Wayne State College; and Gloria Wolpert, Manhattan College.

It is our hope that this book will be an inspiring and useful resource for teachers, related professionals, and families who work daily with preschool children who are at risk and with children who have disabilities.

*Preschool Children
with Special Needs*

# 1

## *Preschool Children with Special Needs*

## *Chapter Outline*

*Children with Special Needs*
   Children with Disabilities
   Children Who Are at Risk

*Early Intervention*
   Benefits of Early Intervention
   The Effects of Early Intervention

*Two Age Groups: Programs for Infants and Toddlers and Programs for Preschoolers*
   Infants and Toddlers (Birth to Age 3)
   Preschoolers (Ages 3 to 6)

*The Number of Young Children with Disabilities Who Are Receiving Special Services*

*Educational Environments for Young Children with Special Needs*
   Environments for Preschool Children
   Environments for Infants and Toddlers

   Transition to New Placements

*Cultural Diversity*
   Ethnic and Cultural Diversity of Preschool
      Children with Disabilities
   Appropriate Practices in Serving Culturally
      Diverse Children and Families

*Theoretical Foundations of Early Education*
   Developmental Theories
   Cognitive Theories
   Behavioral Theories
   Social Theories
   Family Systems Theory
   Combining Theories in Practice

This book explores ways of meeting the challenges of preschool children who have special needs by providing these children and their families with an environment that will help them develop and learn. The text concentrates on the special needs of preschoolers, ages 3 to 6. The information is essential for all prospective and current teachers and others who work with preschool children who are at risk or who have disabilities as well as for teachers in general education preschool classes.

Society is finally recognizing the importance of the early childhood years and of the need for early identification and intervention for infants, toddlers, and preschoolers who have special needs. Several factors contribute to this growing realization: strong research support for early education, evolving social policies on early education, expanding legislation for young children, and increasing numbers of early intervention programs for young children with special needs.

This chapter provides an overview of the field by reviewing the various populations of young children with special needs, the importance of the early childhood years and intervention, the age groups of infants and toddlers and of preschoolers with disabilities, the number of young children with special needs receiving services, the learning environments for young children with special needs, cultural diversity, and the theoretical foundations of early education.

## *Children with Special Needs*

The term *special needs* includes two populations: (1) children with disabilities who are identified under special education law and (2) children who are considered to be at risk

*Early Childhood Snapshot*    TINA: A PRESCHOOLER WITH SPECIAL NEEDS

Tina went with her mother to their neighborhood school during the school's early childhood screening session. In the course of the school's preschool screening program, Tina was identified as a child who needed further assessment and observation. Tina was 3 years, 9 months old at the time of the testing. Her performance on expressive language tests and social measures was poor.

The school obtained additional information about Tina through an interview with her mother. Tina was born 6 weeks prematurely. She weighed a little over 4 pounds at birth and also had trouble breathing. During her first two years, she frequently suffered from colds, and between the ages of 2 and 3, she had at least eight serious ear infections. Motor development seemed to be normal; she sat up, walked, and crawled at the same age as her older siblings. Her language development, however, was slower than theirs. Tina seemed to understand language when others spoke to her, but she could not use language well enough to make her wants known. She did not use any words until the age of 2 and even now only uses very short sentences, such as, "Me want pizza," or "Him break cup." She often uses the wrong word or sim-ply points to what she means. She still has temper tantrums, which seem to be triggered by her inability to communicate what she wants.

Her mother described Tina as an "overactive" child compared to the other children. She would "tear the house apart," break the crib, and take all her toys apart. She never sat down, except to watch television, and that usually lasted for only a few minutes. When she turned 3, her mother tried to enroll her in a small play school, but after a few days the director said Tina could not stay because of her extreme hyperactivity. She would grab toys from other children and hit or scratch her classmates without provocation.

Tina's mother said she suspected that Tina was different but that everyone had told her not to worry—that the child would outgrow her disruptive behavior. Tina's mother said she would be relieved to have her daughter in the special preschool program. At last someone else recognized Tina's problem and would be working to help her. The hours Tina would be in school would offer her mother the first break in child care since Tina was born, and she was looking forward to receiving help from the school on home behavior management.

for school and learning failure. Although these two populations differ, they have much in common in terms of assessment, curriculum, and intervention practices. What research reveals about one of these populations is often useful in serving other young children with special needs, enhancing the ability of educators to serve all young children and their families (Keogh, 2000).

## Children with Disabilities

The first group of young children with special needs is children who have identified disabilities, such as physical, behavioral, cognitive, language, or learning disabilities. They need early intervention and related special education services under special education law, the Individuals with Disabilities Education Act of 1997 (PL 105-17). This act incorporates features of the earlier laws regarding early childhood special education, PL 99-457 and PL 102-199. The many features of the law that covers preschool children with disabilities are discussed in Chapter 2.

### Children Who Are at Risk

The second group of children with special needs that are the concern of this book are young children at risk. It is estimated that one-third of the children in the United States are at risk for school failure before they even enter kindergarten. Problems begin in their early childhood years—from birth to age 6—which are pivotal years for learning. It is during these formative years that rapid and critical brain development occurs. A study conducted by the Carnegie Corporation (1994) paints a bleak picture for some these children. The study shows that millions of this nation's infants and toddlers are so deprived of medical care, loving supervision, and intellectual stimulation that their growth into healthy and responsible adults is threatened.

Early childhood programs for children in low-income homes, considered environmentally at risk, include Head Start, state-provided prekindergarten programs, federally funded child-care programs, family support, and family preservation programs.

The research indicates that early childhood programs for children at risk can have substantial effects on their lives years after their involvement in the programs. The benefits include enhanced school achievement, higher earnings, and decreased involvement with the criminal justice system. Appropriately designed programs help parents strengthen their parenting skills and move toward economic self-sufficiency (Keough, 2000; Gomby, Larner, Stevenson, Lewit, & Behrman, 1995).

The *at-risk* population of young children has three subgroups: those who are at (1) environmental risk, (2) biological risk, and (3) established risk (Zervigon-Hakes, 1995). Specific conditions that fit into each of these at-risk subgroups are shown in Table 1.1.

- *Environmental risk factors.* In today's society, many children are regarded as at risk for academic failure because of their economically and socially impoverished environment. These children are likely to experience school failure and the causes are rooted in poverty and social class factors. The intellectual and emotional development of these youngsters is threatened by disintegrating families, persistent poverty, high levels of child abuse, substance abuse, inadequate health care, and child care of very poor quality. These conditions increase the likelihood that the children will do poorly in school and have significant problems with achieving even the most basic level of literacy (Chira, 1994).

- *Biological at-risk factors.* In addition to children at risk for environmental reasons, certain infants have biological risk factors. For example, a premature birth or low birth weight are biological risk factors, which possibly may result in disabilities or in school difficulties. These children must be carefully observed and provided with rich opportunities and experiences for learning. (Biological at-risk factors are discussed in Chapter 7.)

- *Established risk conditions.* Established risk conditions include genetic and biomedical causes of developmental delay and disability. These conditions include chromosomal disorders, inborn errors of metabolism, congenital malformations, sensory loss, and injuries. It is known that these conditions will result in developmental differences. Many

**TABLE 1.1**  *Risk Conditions for Young Children*

| Environmental Risks | Biological Risks | Established Risk Conditions |
|---|---|---|
| • Teen mother without high school diploma | • Medically complex or technologically dependent | • Congenital/genetic disorders |
| • History of abuse and neglect (self and sibling) | • Illness or trauma associated with delays | • Neurological abnormalities |
| • Legal guardian not established | • Drug exposure | • Atypical developmental disorders |
| • Shelter or foster care environment | • Chronically ill mother associated with delays | • Very low birth weight. Less than or equal to 1000 grams |
| • Parent unable to perform essential parenting functions consistently | • In NICU (neonatal intensive care unit)or graduate of NICU | • Delay in cognition, physical/motor, speech and language, psychosocial, or self-help skills |
| • History of abuse or violence in the home | • Low birth weight—1001 to 2500 grams with complications | |
| • Migrant or homeless family | • Factors impinging on developmental progress | |
| • Family exposure to poisons or toxins | | |

*Source:* Zervigon-Hakes (1995), p. 186. Reprinted with permission of the Center for the Future of Children of the David and Lucile Packard Foundation.

of these conditions will meet the criteria of a disability. (Established risk conditions are discussed in Chapter 7.)

Growing evidence shows that children at risk dramatically improve when early intervention and work with families are provided. For example, low-birth-weight infants significantly gain in cognitive and behavioral function when they receive comprehensive early intervention consisting of home visits, parent training, parent group meetings, attendance at child development centers, pediatric surveillance, and community referral services (Richmond, 1990).

Research also shows the critical effect of the infant's environment on the early development of the brain. During the early months and first years of life, the synapses in the brain (the interconnecting links between the neurons) grow at a phenomenal rate. The brain increases rapidly in size and becomes more effective. Environmental influences and the child's experiences during the earliest years of life play play a major role in brain development, affecting intelligence and the ability to learn (Keogh, 2000; Gopnick, Meltzoff, & Kuhl, 1999; Huttenlocher, 1991).

To maximize intellectual growth, efforts must begin during the first three years of life. The child's environment and experiences in the earliest years influence the development of brain cells and the connections between the cells. The opportunity to build a better life exists only in the first few years of life. A happy, nurturing, and stimulating atmosphere can actually help a child become more intelligent. Early brain development research (Carnegie Corporation, 1994) shows the following:

- Environment affects the number of brain cells, the connections among them, and the way the connections are wired. Brain development is much more vulnerable to environmental influences than was previously suspected.
- Brain development before age 1 is more rapid and extensive than previously realized.
- The influence of early environment on brain development is long lasting.
- Early stress has a negative impact on brain function.

## Early Intervention

The critical learning that occurs during infancy and during the toddler and preschool years is now recognized by many professionals. Psychologists, educators, occupational and physical therapists, speech and language pathologists, medical researchers, and others understand the importance of providing intervention during these very important early years.

The early childhood years are crucial for all children, but for the child who has special needs in terms of mental, physical, behavioral, developmental, or learning characteristics, these years are especially critical. Research from several disciplines confirms what early childhood educators have long observed—that the early years of life are crucial for establishing a lifelong foundation for learning and emotional development. If the opportunity for children to develop intellectually and emotionally during these important years is missed, precious learning time is lost forever (Keogh, 2000; Gopnick, Meltzoff, & Kuhl, 1999; Guralnick, 1997).

### Benefits of Early Intervention

Perhaps the most promising success stories in education today are the reports of special programs for young children who have disabilities or who are at risk. The underlying premise of early childhood special education is that early intervention makes a significant difference in child growth and development. When a child's problems are recognized early, school failure can to a large extent be prevented or reduced. Early childhood special education programs (1) *identify* young children who have special needs and are likely to encounter difficulty in developmental and academic learning and (2) then *provide an immediate early intervention program*. Research shows that early comprehensive and intensive intervention is beneficial for children with disabilities, for their families, and for society:

- *Early intervention helps children with disabilities.* Early intervention accelerates cognitive and social development and reduces behavioral problems. Many conditions can be alleviated, other disorders can be overcome to a large extent, and some problems can be managed so that the child have live a better life. Early intervention can avert the occurrence of secondary problems that compound the original difficulty.

- *Early intervention benefits the families of young children with special needs.* The family-centered approach accepts the family as a critical element of the intervention process. The family takes on a prominent role in the process of teaching the child and improving child-adult interactions.
- *Early intervention benefits society.* Early intervention programs offer a substantial financial savings for the community by reducing the number of children needing special education services.

In summary, early intervention accomplishes the following (American Academy of Pediatrics, 2001; Guralick, 1997; Schweinhart, Barnes, & Weikart, 1993):

- Enhances intelligence
- Promotes substantial gains in all developmental areas (physical, cognitive, language, psychosocial, and self-help)
- Inhibits or prevents secondary disabilities
- Reduces family stress
- Reduces dependency and institutionalization
- Reduces the need for special education services at school age
- Saves the nation and society substantial health-care and education costs

## The Effects of Early Intervention

The underlying premise for all young children with special needs is that early intervention makes a significant difference in growth and development. Over the past 35 years, there have been many efforts to meet the needs of young children and their families. For example, the Head Start movement began in the 1960s, targeting children of low-income families, in which children had limited access to traditional early childhood services. Now more than 35 years old, Head Start is the largest program providing comprehensive educational, health, and social services to these children and their families in this country and is an important player in the early childhood service delivery system (Buscemi, Bennett, Thomas, & Deluca, 1996). Also, in the late 1960s, services began to be provided for children with identified disabilities. During the 1980s, distinct programs existed for young children considered at risk because of economic and social conditions as well as young children with identified disabilities. By the 1990s, the special education movement broadened its scope beyond school-age children to preschoolers with disabilities. It became apparent that there were many similarities in intervention strategies and philosophical perspectives between serving young children at risk and young children with disabilities. Today, service coordination, collaboration, restructuring, and inclusive environments allow young children with special needs to be integrated with their typical peers. Bridges are being built to accommodate what these populations of young children have in common and what the distinct constituencies have to offer each other to enhance our ability to better serve all young children and their families (Johnson, 1992).

Child development experts recognize the tremendous significance of the rapid rate of learning that occurs during the years from birth to age 6. Children should be ready for academic learning when they start school. By the time they enter first grade at age 6, a significant amount of learning should already have occurred.

Research demonstrates quite conclusively that early intervention is beneficial and provides children with a better life. Early intervention brings forth positive results in cognition and social skills, as well as in the reduction of behavioral and social problems (Barnett, 1995; Gallagher, 1989; Gomby et al., 1995; Guralnick, 1997; Yoshikawa, 1995). In addition, research shows that teaching parents to work with their children leads to improvement in the children's schoolwork and to strengthened parent-child interactions (Harbin, Gallagher, & Terry, 1991).

Intervention during the crucial early childhood years produces gains in many other areas (Barnett, 1995; Fletcher & Foorman, 1995; Foorman et al., 1997; Gomby et al., 1995; Guralnick, 1997; Smith, Fairchild, & Groginsky, 1995, Yoshikawa, 1995). In summary, the overall research evidence shows that early intervention:

- *Helps children who are at risk and children with disabilities.* Early intervention accelerates cognitive and social development and reduces behavioral problems. Many conditions can be alleviated, other disorders can be overcome to a large extent, and some problems can be managed so that the child can live a better life.
- *Promotes substantial gains in all developmental areas.* Research shows that when young children with special needs are identified and provided with appropriate and timely intervention, they improve in physical, cognitive, language and speech, psychosocial, and self-help domains.
- *Inhibits or prevents secondary problems.* When young children receive comprehensive and intensive services early, many behavioral and learning problems will not develop or will be significantly lessened.
- *Reduces family stress.* In the family-centered intervention approach, the child is viewed as part of a family system. When the parents are empowered to be an integral part of the intervention process, the family becomes an essential element in the processes of teaching the child and improving child-adult interactions.
- *Offers advantages for society.* Early intervention programs offer a substantial financial savings for the community. It reduces dependency and institutionalization. It lessens the need for special education services at school age. It saves the nation and society substantial health care, institutional, and education costs.

## Two Age Groups: Programs for Infants and Toddlers and Programs for Preschoolers

### Infants and Toddlers (Birth to Age 3)

Biological problems may be evident at birth or in the first few years of life. The infant/toddler years are also critical ages for children at risk for academic failure. Current scientific knowledge about brain development points to the need for programs that focus on the years from birth to age 3 for children subject to poverty, abuse, and inner-city violence (Gopnick, Meltzoff, & Kuhl, 1999).

Early intervention professionals need to know about the critical issues and unique services for infants and toddlers and their families. When infants and toddlers are deprived of such help, their future is jeopardized. A family focus is particularly important during the infant/toddler years. Special legislation for infants and toddlers is included in Part C of the 1997 reauthorized special education law PL 105-17 of the Individuals with Disabilities Education Act (IDEA). This law and the earlier laws, and PL 99-457 and PL 102-119, are further discussed in Chapter 2.

### Preschoolers (Ages 3 to 6)

The preschool years continue to be a vulnerable time for children with special needs and their families. Children ages 3 through 5 are served through Part B of the law (IDEA-1997). Meeting the needs of these children calls for early identification, assessment, and intervention to increase their chances to become healthy, productive members of society. A variety of models for providing intervention services are effective with preschool children with special needs.

## The Number of Young Children with Disabilities Who Are Receiving Special Services

The number of young children with special needs is increasing. About 4.8 percent of the general population of 3- to 5-year-old children currently receive early special education services through the schools. The percentage varies across states, ranging from 1.3 percent to 9.4 percent. In terms of age, 45 percent are 5-year-old children, 34 percent are 4 years old, and 21 percent are 3 years old. About 1.7 percent of infants and toddlers and their families receive special education services (U.S. Department of Education, 2000).

For children who are considered economically and environmentally at risk, it is more difficult to know how many children are receiving services. Programs for these children are scattered through a variety of other programs, such as Head Start, state or

### *Early Childhood Snapshot*  CHILDREN AT ENVIRONMENTAL RISK

One teacher described the experiences and behaviors of preschool children who were environmentally at risk (Quindlen, 1991).

Some had never owned a toy. Some had never held a book. Some had never sat at a table or used a fork. This teacher had to abandon her initial plan to read stories to these children because they had not acquired basic social skills. The children in this class had been born and raised in welfare hotels, where there were no tables and chairs. They had eaten all their meals with their hands. (They had the quickest hands you've ever seen.) These children had virtually no language. They hit and kicked and spit at anyone who tried to touch them.

These children lacked the basic experiences needed for preschool learning. They were not ready for traditional school learning.

municipal prekindergarten programs, child-care programs, Chapter 1 programs, and family support programs. Research shows that children from low-income families improve greatly from preschool education, but the number of low-income children benefitting from these programs is limited. These children are less likely than children from middle- and upper-income families to enroll in preschool programs because of the costs (Behrman, 1995; U.S. General Accounting Office, 1995).

## Educational Environments for Young Children with Special Needs

*Educational environments* refer to the site of primary service delivery for young children with disabilities. The educational environment for preschoolers (ages 3 through 5) differs from the environments for infants and toddlers (ages birth through age 2).

### Environments for Preschool Children

Data collected by the U.S. Department of Education (2000) show that preschool children with disabilities, ages 3 through 5, are served in four basic environments: general education classes, separate classes, resource rooms, and other (separate schools, residential, and home/hospital). Figure 1.1 shows the percentage of preschool children served in these various environments.

***General Education Classes (Inclusive Settings).***    In the past, most young children with disabilities were served through special classes. Today, more young children are

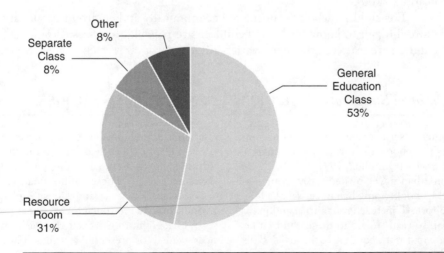

**FIGURE 1.1**   *Educational Environments for Preschool Children with Disabilities*
*Source:* U.S. Department of Education (2000).

in general education classes or inclusive settings. A goal of early childhood special education is to integrate young children with disabilities with their peers. The movement toward inclusive environments for young children is growing. Over half (53 percent) of preschool children with disabilities are placed in general education classes (U.S. Department of Education, 2000). The *least restrictive environment (LRE)* feature of the federal law IDEA-1997 requires that the IEP or IFSP team consider a placement that provides the child with disabilities with experiences with children who do not have disabilities. The IEP refers to the individualized education program and is used for children ages 3 through 5. The IFSP refers to the individualized family service plan and is required for children ages birth to 3 years old.

An immediate challenge in providing inclusive environments for preschoolers with disabilities is that most public schools do not offer programs for 3- and 4-year-olds children, although they do have kindergartens for 5-year-olds. Children with disabilities are placed in a variety of environments that serve as integrated settings: nursery schools, Head Start classes, child-care centers, and other kinds of public early childhood programs. The position on inclusion taken by the Division for Early Childhood (DEC) of the Council for Exceptional Children is shown in Figure 1.2.

**FIGURE 1.2**   *DEC Position on Inclusion*

---

Inclusion, as a value, supports the right of all children, regardless of abilities, to participate actively in natural settings within their communities. Natural settings are those in which the child would spend time had he or she not had a disability. These settings include, but are not limited to home, preschool, nursery schools, Head Start programs, kindergartens, neighborhood school classrooms, child care places of worship, recreational (such as community playgrounds and community events) and other settings that all children and families enjoy.

DEC supports and advocates that young children and their families have full and successful access to health, social, educational, and other support services that promote full participation in family and community life. DEC values the cultural, economic, and educational diversity of families and supports a family-guided process for identifying a program of service.

As young children participate in group settings (such as preschool, play groups, child care, kindergarten) their active participations would be guided by developmentally and individually appropriate curriculum. Access to and participation in the age appropriate general curriculum becomes central to the identification and provision of specialized support services.

To implement inclusive practices DEC supports: (a) the continued development, implementation, evaluation, and dissemination of full inclusion supports, services, and systems that are of high quality for all children; (b) the development of preservice and inservice training programs that prepare families, service providers, and administrators to develop and work within inclusive settings; (c) collaboration among key stakeholders to implement flexible fiscal and administrative procedures in support of inclusion; (d) restructuring and unification of social, educational, health, and intervention supports and services to make them more responsive to the needs of all children and families. Ultimately, the implementation of inclusive practice must lead to optimal development benefit for each individual child and family.

---

*Source:* Division for Early Childhood of the Council for Exceptional Children (1998). Permission to copy not required—distribution encouraged.

*Resource Rooms.*   The resource room is an educational setting that provides services for a portion of the day to children with disabilities. For the most part, they are in a general education setting for the rest of the day. According to the U.S. Department of Education (2000), 31 percent of preschool children with disabilities receive services in the educational environment of a resource room. This number is decreasing as the number of children in the inclusive setting of the general education class increases. The resource room offers more intensive intervention programs for preschool children with disabilities.

*Separate Classes.*   A separate class offers children with disabilities the opportunity for more intensive, highly individualized services. About 8 percent of preschoolers with disabilities are served in this environment (U.S. Department of Education, 2000). The severity of disabilities of these children require the kind of services that a separate class can provide.

*Other Settings.*   About 8 percent of preschool children with disabilities are served through other settings, such as residential facilities, homebound instruction, or hospital environments (U.S. Department of Education, 2000).

## Environments for Infants and Toddlers

Regulations for infants and toddlers (birth through age 2) are included in Part C of the Individuals with Disabilities Education Act. Part C states that early intervention services for infants and toddlers are "provided in natural environments, including the home, and community settings in which children without disabilities participate" [Section 632 (a) (16b)]. This often means home-based services or community settings for infants and toddlers through center-based services (Dunst, Bruda, Trivette, & McLean, 2001; Dunst, Horby, Trivette, Raabl, & Bruda, 2000).

In *home-based services*, the interventionist comes to the child's home and works individually with the child and family. Visits are scheduled weekly or bi-weekly as needed. The parents learn from the interventionist how to provide services to their child. In *center-based services*, children are transported to centers where professionals from many disciplines can provide a variety of services, such as physical and occupational therapy, speech and language instruction, psychological services, medial diagnosis, social work, and early childhood special education. These types of services are discussed more fully in Chapter 5.

## Transition to New Placements

*Transition* involves transferring or moving the child from one type of organized program to another. Transition for infants and toddlers (birth through age 2) requires moving from Part C of the law (IDEA-1997), the infant and toddler program, to Part B of the law, the preschooler program. Transition for preschool children with disabilities requires moving from the Part B program to general kindergarten and first-grade programs or different special education programs. Going to a new placement can be a traumatic experience for young children and their families; therefore, transition should be carefully planned, coordinated, and monitored. It is important to take steps to ensure a smooth transition through family and professional collaboration (La Para, Pianta, & Cox, 2000; Fowler, Donegan, Lueke, Hadden, & Phillips, 2000). A detailed discussion of the transition process is included in Chapter 12.

## Cultural Diversity

Many children and families who participate in the programs are from diverse linguistic and cultural backgrounds. *Cultural and linguistic diversity (CLD)* refers to (1) children and families who have a language other than Enlgish spoken at home and (2) children and families who have values, beliefs, understandings, and practices that differ from those in the general population (Barrera, 2000). Today's teachers and child-care workers must be attuned to differences in language, values, attitudes about child development, and attitudes about disabilities. All of these factors affect how children and their families react to early intervention practices.

Families from diverse cultures differ in child-rearing practices, parent-child interactions, values, perceptions of a family unit, perceptions of problems, acceptable

*Many children and families come to programs from diverse linguistic and cultural backgrounds.*

solutions to problems, and attitudes toward seeking help. Professionals who work with families with diverse cultural values must have the ability to communicate with family members in a way that is respectful and clear (Barrera, 2000).

In today's culturally diverse society, an increasing number of children come from homes in which a language other than English is spoken. Some 320 different languages are spoken in the United States (National Center for Educational Statistics, 1994). More than 15 percent of the students in the United States are identified as Hispanic, and this percentage is expected to grow. It is anticipated that by the year 2020, 25 percent of the students in the United States will be of Hispanic descent and one-third of the students in U.S. schools will come from homes in which the primary language is not English.

## Ethnic and Cultural Diversity of Preschool Children with Disabilities

The U.S. Department of Education (2000) reported data on the race/ethnicity of young children with disabilities for the first time in its Twenty-Second Annual Report. The percentage of preschoolers with disabilities is as follows:

| Race/Ethnicity | Percent |
| --- | --- |
| White | 68.9 |
| Hispanic | 12.0 |
| Black | 15.7 |
| American Indian | 1.3 |

The report notes that the percent of disabilities within each group is similar to the race/ethnicity percent found in the general population.

## Appropriate Practices in Serving Culturally Diverse Children and Families

Early childhood professionals should be aware of a number of issues that may arise as they work with families of diverse cultures. They should recognize their own cultural values and biases, have knowledge of diverse child-rearing practices, understand the different cultural perspectives of disabilities, and recognize the diversity of communicative styles. If cultural values are not taken into account, the interventions proposed by the professionals may be considered inappropriate and will often be resisted by the families. Early childhood professionals, then, need to

1. Recognize their own cultural values and beliefs, as well as biases.
2. Promote effective communication by understanding the culture of the families they serve.
3. Recognize that every family, regardless of its cultural, linguistic, or ethnic heritage, is unique in its ways of functioning and in its degree of identification with a particular culture.
4. Keep in mind both the individual families as well as their common cultural backgrounds when planning interventions and services.

The following guidelines for honoring cultural differences of young children with special needs and their families are provided by Barrera (2000):

- *Recognize the pervasive influence of culture and cultural dynamics.* It is important to become open and respectful to diverse behaviors, even when these are outside of one's areas of familiarity.
- *Increase access between families and services.* One effective way of disseminating information orally is to contact significant persons in neighborhoods, such as clergy, respected community leaders, and staff from other agencies.
- *Recognize the importance of establishing rapport.* Rapport is the relationship between the family and the staff person marked by conformity, accord, or affinity. It is most easily established when the family feels that the staff person understands the family's point of view.
- *Support families' efforts to deal with diverse cultures and languages.* One effective method is to develop "Parent Partners," volunteers who are from the same culture who can help the parent during key times, such as home visits, clinic visits, assessments, and meetings with staff.
- *Develop reciprocal "additive" responses to families and children.* "Additive" responses are respectful of the family's current behaviors. In other words, the family does not have to eliminate or drop old behaviors but expand their responses.
- *Address the need for cultural and linguistic mediation.* Language-culture mediators are persons who can interpose between two or more languages or cultures. Their role is to buffer differences, explain the unfamiliar, and make one comprehensible to the other.

## Theoretical Foundations of Early Education

Several theories play a part in guiding assessment and intervention practices for young children with special needs. The richness of this field is created by the many disciplines that contribute critical ideas and practices including early childhood education, special education, the psychology of learning, and counseling. Intervention methods and curriculum models are based on several different theories of learning; they include developmental, cognitive, behavioral, social, and family systems theories. In this section we briefly describe these theoretical perspectives. (The applications of these theories in the curriculum are discussed in Chapter 6.)

### Developmental Theories

Developmental theories provide the foundation for many programs in early childhood education, kindergarten classes, and preschool programs. The theories are based in developmental psychology, which reflects a maturation view of child development and provides a foundation for the field of early childhood education. Key to this concept of education is the natural growth sequence of the young child. The premise is that under favorable, open circumstances, the child's own inner drive and need to learn will naturally emerge and develop. The role of the teacher is to enhance this natural growth

*The teacher should enhance the natural group process by providing opportunities in an environment that is enriching, encouraging, and nurturing.*

process by providing learning opportunities within an environment that is enriching, encouraging, and nurturing.

The "whole child" theory, which encompasses all aspects of a child's growth—physical, emotional, language, social, and cognitive development—is based on developmental theories. According to this comprehensive philosophy of the young child's education, the curriculum offers the child a variety of experiences and many enrichment opportunities.

The developmental early childhood enrichment classroom typically contains special activity areas—for example, an area for play with large blocks, a center for dress-up and playhouse materials, a quiet play section, and a creative arts area. Enrichment programs typically have periods of the day assigned for both outdoor and indoor play. A priority for the enrichment class is to stimulate child exploration. Communication and language activities are encouraged through story telling and conversations. Field trips are designed to broaden children's experience levels in the larger community. For example, they may visit museums, the post office, stores, and parks. Although the teacher arranges a general but flexible schedule for the day, activities are often child selected. The teacher capitalizes on opportunities for incidental and informal learning.

## Cognitive Theories

The cognitive approaches to child development are based on the ideas and theories of Piaget (1970), who studied the way children develop cognitive or thinking abilities. Cognitive skills include memory, discrimination, problem solving, concept formation, verbal learning, and comprehension. One of Piaget's ground-breaking insights is that children do not think like adults but rather pass through distinct stages of development that are characterized by particular types of thinking. The cognitive emphasis curriculum encourages experiences and actions that help build thinking skills. One such program designed for at-risk preschool children is the Perry Preschool Project. The report by Schweinhart, Barnes, and Weikart (1993) shows that benefits of a cognitive early intervention curriculum for at-risk children continue, even after 27 years.

***Constructive Learning and Problem Solving.*** An important concept of cognitive theory is that learning is a constructive process. Knowledge cannot be given directly to a child; instead, each child must actively construct or build his or her own knowledge. Learning depends on what the child already knows and the building of new knowledge. For example, in learning mathematics, the early number ideas of young children are developed as the child builds or constructs number meanings. Children naturally invent and rely on their own arithmetic procedures, such as counting, because these methods allow them to cope with the environment in a meaningful manner. Children should be encouraged to develop and use invented mathematics for solving problems because these experiences will help them build mathematics mental structures (Resnick & Klopfer, 1989). For example, children in a preschool class could be asked to solve this problem: Are there enough cookies for each child in the class? The principle of constructive learning can be summarized succinctly in this Chinese proverb:

Tell me and I forget,
Show me and I remember,
Involve me and I understand.

## Behavioral Theories

Many special education practices are based on theories stemming from behavioral psychology. Behavioral psychology helps us understand how learning behavior is shaped and how teachers can guide the learning of skills. The underlying concepts of behavior management theories were first initiated over 50 years ago by B. F. Skinner, who is considered the father of behavioral psychology. Principles of behavioral psychology have significantly influenced teaching practices for young children who are at risk and for children with disabilities.

The behavioral approach focuses on direct instruction and teaching the specific skills that the child must learn. Goals and objectives are selected by the teacher. Materials and activities are carefully designed to develop these selected abilities. The role of the teacher is to plan and structure learning experiences to build specific kinds of social, motor, cognitive, or language skills.

In applying behavioral theories, teachers first determine the behaviors that the child should learn, and they become goals to be achieved. The steps leading to the desired behavioral goal are determined, and each step is then directly taught to the child. Children learn behaviors through techniques such as reinforcement, modeling, and shaping. The behavioral approach can also be used to modify behaviors that occur at home, in child care, as well as at school. Behavioral methods can be used by teachers, parents, and others who interact with the child.

***The Concept of Reinforcement.***   Reinforcement is a key concept in behavioral psychology. A *reinforcer* is an event that follows a behavior and causes the behavior to be repeated or discontinued. Commonly used *extrinsic* reinforcements for young children include cereal, stickers, verbal praise, computer time, and smiling face stamps. An *intrinsic* reinforcement would be the satisfaction of accomplishment. Reinforcement can be either positive or negative. For example, if Sarah puts away her building blocks at the end of the free-play period, the teacher gives *positive* reinforcement for her behavior by saying, "Good work, Sarah," or by giving her a hug. If Jennifer shouts out an answer to get attention, her behavior is ignored, which is *negative* reinforcement.

## Social Theories

The social context in which learning occurs also significantly influences the learning process. The social interactions between the child and others (parent, teacher, caregiver, other family members) are a needed ingredient in learning. Vygotsky (1962) is a Russian psychologist who emphasizes the social nature of learning and the critical role that interpersonal relationships play in promoting learning. Learning is an interpersonal, dynamic, social event that depends on at least two people, one better informed or more skilled than the other. Human learning occurs as a transfer of responsibility, whether it is learning to play, learning to share, or learning to smile. All of these learning skills pass along the interpersonal dimension through a reciprocal interaction with adults and peers. The transmission of skills requires the teacher, the parent, or a peer to provide a scaffolding or support that helps the child learn. Teachers and parents take an active role in encouraging young children to attempt new things, using verbal interactions, and even to learn from failure. When the child attempts a task, the adult provides support, encouragement, and enlargement (Sameroff & Fiese, 1990).

The role of social interaction is evident in learning how to play. For example, 4-year-old Nina had not learned how to play spontaneously because of her cognitive delays. Through experiences in a social situation, she first observed others playing at the water table with boats. After a while, another child invited Nina to join him at the water table. With some encouragement from the teacher, Nina was soon engaged in social play with another child.

## Family Systems Theory

"A family of five is like five people lying on a waterbed. Whenever one person moves, everyone feels the ripple" (Lavoie, 1995). The family systems theory represents a shift from focusing on the child in isolation to the child within the family system. It is based on the belief that no single member of a family functions in isolation from other family members. Thus, an intervention for the child affects other family members, and an intervention at the family level directly or indirectly affects the child (Dunst, Trivette, & Deal, 1994; Sameroff & Fiese, 1990).

The family system consists of the child, parent(s), caregivers, siblings, and extended family members, such as grandparents, neighbors, relatives, friends, and others that impinge on the child's life. These relationships are interdependent; that is, what happens to one member of the family has an effect on other members of the family.

The birth of a child with a disability affects all members of the family system, and an event that happens to a parent or a sibling will affect the child. Day-to-day living can be stressful from the start. As infants, these children may be irritable, demanding, and difficult to soothe, making parents feel incompetent, confused, and helpless. As the child enters group situations, the parents may have feelings of guilt, shame, and embarrassment. As they become frustrated, they may blame each other for the child's problems. Siblings and other family members are also affected when a child in the family has disabilities. Often, siblings are embarrassed or feel angry or jealous if parents pay more attention to the child who has special needs. A fundamental goal of family systems theory is to enable and empower the families to make decisions for themselves (Dunst, Trivette, & Deal, 1994).

Beyond the family, a broader network of community resources can offer many support systems. Community resources to support the family include a network of extended family, friends, neighbors, and community organizations and programs, such as child-care centers, religious groups, libraries, businesses, recreational programs, and self-help groups (Lowenthal, 1996; Umstead, Boyd, & Dunst, 1995). Teachers must be cognizant of the family's interaction with the broader community system.

## Combining Theories in Practice

Most programs for young children with special needs do not follow a single theoretical model but combine elements from several. Most provide some open experiences that are child selected, encourage active learning and cognitive problem-solving activities, offer some directed teaching of specific skills, teach in social settings, and involve the family.

Preschool children with special needs require a comprehensive curriculum that offers stimulation and practice in many areas. Young children who lack preacademic or readiness skills need help in preparing for later academic learning. The curriculum in most programs for young children with special needs includes:

1. *Adaptive behaviors and self-concept development activities.* Children must learn to care for themselves through activities such as dressing, eating, and personal hygiene. Learning self-help skills promotes the development of a positive self-concept and feelings of independence (see Chapters 8 and 9).
2. *Gross motor activities.* Gross motor skills require the use of the large muscles used to move the arms, legs, torso, hands, and feet. Activities to help children develop

gross motor skills include walking, crawling, climbing, jumping, throwing, and rolling movements (see Chapter 7).

3. *Fine motor activities.* Fine motor skills involve the small muscles used to move fingers and wrists as well as eye-hand coordination and coordination of the two hands. Activities to promote fine motor skills include puzzles, finger games, cutting and pasting, painting, buttoning, and lacing (see Chapter 7).

4. *Communication activities.* The ability to use language to communicate thoughts is central to learning and includes the verbal skills of listening and talking, as well as sign and augmentative communication. Language includes the ability to understand the language of others, to respond to instructions, to initiate communication, to explain, and to engage in interactions (see Chapter 10).

5. *Visual activities.* Activities to help children develop visual discrimination, visual memory, and visual-motor integration, as in eye-hand coordination, include recognizing differences and similarities in pictures, shapes, and letters (see Chapter 7).

6. *Auditory activities.* An important prereading skill is the awareness of the sounds in words (phonological awareness). Activities to help children practice auditory identification of sounds, auditory discrimination of sounds, and auditory memory include word games, rhyming games, and word memory games (see Chapters 10 and 11).

7. *Cognitive activities.* Activities to help children practice thinking skills, learn relationships, identify differences, classify, compare and contrast ideas, and solve problems include many play activities (see Chapter 12).

8. *Social activities.* Activities to help children develop social skills include learning to interact and get along with others by forming age-appropriate relationships with other children and with adults and learning to play cooperatively (see Chapter 9).

## *Summary*

- Young children with special needs includes children with disabilities and children who are at risk.
- Early intervention is effective. The early years are critical in a child's development. For young children with special needs, early identification and intervention have been successful in helping children, helping families, and benefitting society.
- Programs are classified by two age groups: infants and toddlers (birth to age 3) and preschoolers (ages 3 to 6).
- The educational environments for young preschool children with disabilities include the inclusive setting of the general education class, the resource room, separate classes, and other environments. The educational environment for infants and toddlers with disabilities include the home-based setting and the center-based setting.
- Cultural diversity is an important consideration. Many children and families who participate in programs are from linguistic and culturally diverse backgrounds. Preschool educators must be attuned to differences in language, values, attitudes about child development, and attitudes about disabilities.

- Several theoretical foundations guide instruction and intervention practices.
- Developmental theories emphasize a child-centered curriculum and allow the child to develop through his or her own selected activities.
- Cognitive theories emphasize the development of thinking and problem-solving skills in young children.
- Behavioral theories are teacher guided and specific objectives are set for the learning of skills.
- Social theories of learning emphasize that learning occurs in a social environment through reciprocal interactions with adults and peers.
- The family-centered focus emphasizes the crucial role of the family system in working with a child who has special needs.

## Key Terms

behavioral theories
biological risk
children at risk
children with disabilities
cognitive theories
developmental theories
developmental delay
early intervention
educational environment
environmental risk
established risk

family systems theory
Head Start
inclusive settings
infants and toddlers
integration
linguistic and cultural diversity
preschoolers
reinforcement
social learning theory
transition

# 2

## *Changing Policies and Laws*

## Chapter Outline

*Historical Perspectives*
    Early Childhood Education
    Early Childhood Special Education
    Children Who Are at Risk
*Studies of Early Childhood Intervention*
    Early Studies
    Recent Longitudinal Studies
*Legislation and Programs for Young Children with Disabilities*
    Public Law 99-457 and Public Law 102-119
    Individuals with Disabilities Education Act (IDEA) of 1997

The Early Education Program for Children with Disabilities (EEPCD)
Other Special Education Laws
*Legislation and Programs for Children at Risk*
    Head Start
    Other Compensatory Programs
*Current Trends and Issues*
    Assistive Technology
    Natural Environments
    Partnerships with Families
    Sensitivity to Cultural Diversity

This chapter offers a historical perspective and discusses how laws and policies affect programs and services for young children with special needs. It reviews how three separate fields laid a foundation for understanding these children: early childhood education, early childhood special education, and children at risk. Also, some of the key studies of early childhood intervention are discussed. In addition, the laws that play a critical role in the provision of programs and services for young children with special needs are reviewed. The chapter concludes with a discussion on several current trends and issues in the field.

# Historical Perspectives

Tremendous changes have taken place in our thinking about the education of all young children over the years. The philosophies that guide programs for young children without disabilities have been evolving for a long time, and the historical roots for early childhood education philosophies go back several hundred years. Concern about young children with disabilities and children who are at risk is more recent. The historical perspectives from each of three different fields of study (early childhood education, early childhood special education, and young children who are at risk) contribute to our knowledge base. What is discovered through practice and research in one of these fields influences the thinking in the others.

## Early Childhood Education

Society, parents, and educators did not always recognize that early education is beneficial for young children. Jean-Jacques Rousseau (1762) contributed to the study of the early education of young children and observed that children have stages of development,

*Early Childhood Snapshot*    USING MEDIATION TO RESOLVE DISPUTES

The initial process of trying to resolve a dispute between the school and the parents is called *mediation*. Under the Individuals with Disabilities Education Act of 1997, mediation is offered at no cost to the parents. In the following example, mediation was used to resolve a dispute.

Jennifer is a 4-year-old girl in a preschool special education program. She has spina bifida, and as a result, she uses braces and has a neurogenic bladder, which prevents her from emptying her bladder voluntarily. She must be catheterized every three or four hours to avoid injury to her kidneys. She needs a clean intermittent catheterization (CIC), a procedure involving the insertion of a catheter into the urethra to drain the bladder.

Jennifer's parents have asked the school to provide a trained person to provide the catheterization as a related service in her individualized education program (IEP). The school refused to include this as a related service, claiming it is a medical service and not the school's responsibility.

Jennifer's parents have asked for *mediation* as an initial process to resolve this dispute. The mediation meeting was held at a time convenient for the parents and was conducted by a qualified and impartial individual who was on a list of persons maintained by the state.

At the mediation meeting, both the parents and the school presented their perspective on this issue. During the meeting, the mediator referred to case law (*Irving Independent School District* vs. *Tatro*) in which the U.S. Supreme Court held that catheterization is a related service that the school must provide. As a result of the mediation, the school and parents agreed to include the catheterization in Jennifer's IEP as a related service.

which he viewed as a natural unfolding. In the 1800s, Johann Pestalozzi (1990) wrote that children can learn through self-discovery and that mothers were their children's best teachers. Friedrich Froebel (1896) contributed to the philosophy of the education of young children by establishing the first kindergarten in Germany in the early 1800s. *Kindergarten* is a German word meaning "garden for children." Froebel's philosophy emphasized the value of play and concern for the emotional and social development of the *whole child*. Margaret Schurz immigrated from Germany and established a kindergarten adapted from the Froebel model, in Watertown, Wisconsin, in 1856. Four years later, the first English-speaking kindergarten was established in Boston by Elizabeth Peabody. In 1873, the first public school kindergarten in the United States was started in St. Louis, Missouri. It took many years before kindergartens became established practice in the public schools.

The establishment of nursery schools and day care was also very slow in getting started. The slow but steady growth of interest in the development of young children is due to changes in the beliefs and values of society, changes in attitudes toward children, and growing knowledge about the process of child development.

Others have contributed to early childhood education. For example, extensive longitudinal studies—such as those of Gesell and Ames (1937), Bergman and Escalona (1949), and Bayley (1968)—provided data for establishing the normative stages of child growth. Dewey and Dewey (1962) stressed the value of early experiences, as well as environments that offer active learning. Montessori (1967) demonstrated the value of preschool programs with the use of her didactic materials. Piaget (1970) was influential in the field of early childhood development with his writings about the cognitive development of young children.

Today, many types of services exist for young children, including child-care centers, nursery schools, kindergartens, and Head Start programs. With the spiraling cost of living, two incomes have increasingly become necessary to adequately support households. Many children are from single-parent families, which necessitates that the parent work outside the home. Recognizing that their employees have young children, many large businesses have established suitable facilities so parents can see their preschool children at various times of the day. Mothers may feel more comfortable about leaving their young children in the care of others on the premise that the *quality* of time parents spend with their children is more significant than the *quantity* of time.

## Early Childhood Special Education

Included in the term *special needs* are both young children with disabilities and children who are considered at risk. The research findings from both fields are often intermingled: Theories about children with disabilities have implications for children at risk; good practices for children at risk have applications for children with disabilities.

Until the mid-1960s, few programs served young children with disabilities. All that could be found were a few private agencies or clinics and some state institutions. Virtually no public school programs were available for parents or their preschool child. The first special education programs and services did not include children below school age with disabilities. Although some states provided services for preschool children with disabilities, many did not. Today, the special education law is quite explicit: preschool children (ages 3 through 5) with identified disabilities have the right to early intervention services (PL 105-17). There are also special programs for infants and toddlers with disabilities and their families. The laws for children with disabilities are described later in this chapter.

The term *early intervention* is generally used to describe services for infants and toddlers who have disabilities (Kleinhammer-Tramill, Rosenkoetter, & Tramill, 1994). Specialized early intervention programs can include both home intervention and center-based programs. Parent participation is required in planning and meeting educational goals.

## Children Who Are at Risk

One of the early and important contributors to thinking about young children who are at risk was Maria Montessori, a physician who lived in Italy. In the early 1900s Montessori (1967) opened a school for young children who lived in the poorest and most crime-ridden section of Rome, Italy. Central to the Montessori method is the idea of a *prepared environment*, which includes an array of organized and coordinated materials that promote learning. An early nursery school for at-risk children in England was established by Rachael and Margaret MacMillan in 1910 (Whitbread, 1972).

In the United States, programs for at-risk children were considered compensatory programs. In other words, they were intended to compensate for the lack of early experiences and education found among disadvantaged children from low socio-economic environments. One of the largest programs for young children who are at risk is the Head Start program. Head Start is designed for young children who are identified as coming from families with low income. The Follow-Through programs have studied the early childhood education intervention efforts and the resulting cognitive gains made by Head Start graduates.

The Individuals with Disabilities Act of 1997 increases the funding to the states based on preschoolers living in poverty. Part C of the law encourages states to expand opportunities for children under 3 years of age who are at risk for developmental delay *if* they do *not* receive intervention services.

## Studies of Early Childhood Intervention

Several experiments set the stage for later work by demonstrating that the intellectual functioning of young children can improve dramatically under stimulating environmental conditions.

### Early Studies

An early theory that was widely accepted, as set forth by Goddard (1916), was that intellectual functioning was largely inherited and that training would not affect a child's intellectual ability. Goddard's theory was challenged by researchers who conducted experiments to show the crucial importance of the early childhood years in all areas of development, especially of thinking skills and cognitive growth.

In his seminal work, *Intelligence and Experience,* Hunt (1961) disputed the notion that intelligence or cognitive ability is a fixed entity. He argued that a person's intellectual level could be changed by environmental experiences. Bloom (1976) supplied further evidence to show how critical early years are to cognitive growth. Finding that 80 percent of the child's cognitive development is completed by age 4, Bloom warned that waiting until a child is 6 years old to begin school is perhaps too late.

A number of research studies have demonstrated improvements in the cognitive abilities of retarded babies who were placed in favorable environmental conditions. These studies provide additional evidence of the positive impact of early intervention. Skeels and Dye (1939) conducted an experiment in Iowa in which 13 children under 3 years old were removed from an orphanage and placed in an institution for "mental defectives." These infants were placed only one to a ward, with adolescent girls in the institution who were identified as mentally retarded. The girls provided much attention and training for these babies. A comparison group of babies remained in the orphanage but received no special training or care. Just 2 years later, both groups were tested, and the babies who had received a great deal of attention and stimulation from the girls with mental retardation increased in their intelligence test scores an average of 27.5 points. The babies who remained in the orphanage in an unstimulating environment experienced an average decrease of 26.2 points in their intelligence test scores. In follow-up studies 3 years later, the children who had received special attention and care retained their accelerated rate of development in foster homes, and the comparison children from the orphanage with no special care and attention retained their decreased intellectual performance (Skeels, 1942). In a follow-up study conducted 21 years later (Skeels, 1966), all of the 25 adults were located. Of the 13 children in the experimental group, all were self-supporting. Not one of them was in an institution. Of the 12 children in the contrast group, 1 had died and 4 were wards of institutions. In terms of education, the experimental group had completed a median of twelfth grade; 4 of them were college educated. The contrast group had completed a median of third grade.

Another important study was conducted by Samuel Kirk (1958, 1965). Kirk conducted an experiment to determine the effects of preschool education on the mental and social development of young children who were identified as mentally retarded. Two preschool groups were organized—one group received a preschool education in the community, and the other group was placed in an institution and received no preschool education. Children who received the two years of preschool education increased in both mental and social development and retained this increase to age 8. Moreover, after instruction, the children scored at the second-grade level in arithmetic and at the first-grade level in reading. Those who did not receive preschool education had a decrease in both their IQ (intelligence quotient) and SQ (social quotient).

### Recent Longitudinal Studies

Several longitudinal studies show impressive long-term effects of early intervention for at-risk children. These studies demonstrate that early intervention for at-risk preschoolers is effective in improving cognitive skills, behavior, attitude toward school, and academic achievement. In terms of cost-benefit analysis, the schools and society get their money back with interest because there is less need for special education services and a decrease in the retention rate, thereby reducing the time that children spend in public school. Further, upon completion of schooling, the graduates are more likely to be gainfully employed—to be taxpayers rather than tax receivers, and to be citizens who contribute to society.

Two follow-up studies in particular have received wide publicity: the Head Start longitudinal study (Lazar & Darlington, 1982) and the Perry Preschool Program study (Schweinhart, Barnes, & Weikart, 1993; Schweinhart & Weikart, 1988):

1. *Head Start longitudinal study.* An unusual opportunity to investigate the impact of early intervention on cognitive growth and later adjustment came with the Head Start programs. Head Start was funded by the federal government in 1964 as part of the War on Poverty. The intent of Head Start was to provide compensatory educational experiences for preschoolers who might otherwise come to school unprepared and unmotivated to learn. Over 800 children who had taken part in Head Start or similar programs were evaluated some 15 years later. The data collected in this follow-up study revealed impressive and very encouraging information. The analysis demonstrated that

early intervention is effective (Lazar & Darlington, 1982). The following questions were asked to evaluate the early intervention experience after a long period:

   a. Was the student placed in special education class during schooling or in a regular class?
   b. Was the student retained a grade or more?
   c. Did the student finish school by the age of 18?

The follow-up data showed that Head Start participants did significantly better on all these measures than did the control children. Moreover, the study showed that Head Start programs were cost effective. That is, society saved money by providing preschool education because the investment reduced costs for special education and grade retention later.

   **2.** *Perry Preschool Program longitudinal study.* Another important longitudinal study, the Perry Preschool Program, was carried out by the High/Scope Educational Research Foundation of Ypsilanti, Michigan (Schweinhart, Barnes, & Weikart, 1993). The preschool children selected for this project had test scores showing low cognitive ability and came from the bottom 20 percent of the population in terms of economic income. The Perry Preschool Program had a cognitive-emphasis curriculum. When the participants were tested at ages 15 and 19, the positive effects were impressive. These students were more committed to school and doing better in school than peers who did not have the preschool experiences. Scores were higher on reading, arithmetic, and language achievement tests at all grade levels. Moreover, there was a 50 percent reduction in the need for special education services. These students also had less deviant and delinquent behavior, and parents of children in the study reported they received greater satisfaction from their children.

# Legislation and Programs for Young Children with Disabilities

Lawmakers are finally recognizing the special needs of young children who have disabilities. Several recent laws are designed to protect the rights of young children with disabilities and to provide early intervention services for these children. A summary of the legislation that affects young children who have disabilities or who are at risk is shown in Figure 2.1.

## Public Law 99-457 and Public Law 102-119

Two laws that strengthened the federal government's role in providing services to young children with disabilities are PL 99-457 (passed in 1986) and PL 102-119 (passed in 1991). They are now incorporated in the Individuals with Disabilities Act of 1997. These laws were written to provide comprehensive services to preschool children with disabilities and their families through a number of significant features. We discuss these early childhood laws in several chapters as they apply to dimensions of the field: legislation (this chapter), families (Chapter 3), assessment (Chapter 4), and learning environments (Chapter 5).

**FIGURE 2.1**   *Selected Legislation Affecting Young Children Who Are at Risk and Children Who Have Disabilities*

1965   **Project Head Start.** Office of Economic Opportunity Act. Established early education programs for 4-year-old children from economically disadvantaged homes.

1966   **HCEEP Handicapped Children's Early Education Act.** PL 89-750. This law provided funding for establishing experimental and model programs for early education programs (now known as EEPCD—Early Education Programs for Children with Disabilities).

1972   **Head Start.** PL 92-424. Economic Opportunity Act Amendments. This law established a preschool mandate that required that not less than 10 percent of the total number of Head Start placements be reserved for children with disabilities.

1974   **Education Amendments.** PL 93-380. Established a total federal commitment to the education of children with disabilities. Provided funds for teacher training and was a precursor to PL 94-142.

1975   **Education for All Handicapped Children Act (EHA).** PL 94-142. Department of Education. Considered landmark legislation. Provided that all children with disabilities have a free, appropriate public education with related services. Part B of EHA established the categories of disabilities and mandated special education services for children 5 through 21 years old.

1985   **The Education of the Handicapped Act Amendments.** PL 98-199. This law provided financial incentives for states to extend service levels to children at birth.

1986   **The Education of the Handicapped Children's Act Amendments.** Amendments to EHA. PL 99-457. Extended PL 94-142 (EHA) Part B to full services for 3- through 5-year-olds. Established Part H, added a new grant program for establishing a comprehensive system of early intervention services for infants and toddlers with disabilities and their families.

1990   **Individuals with Disabilities Education Act (IDEA).** PL 101-476. A reauthorization of the earlier law, PL 94-142, passed by Congress in 1975. It is designed to assure a free, and appropriate public education for children and adolescents with disabilities, and it is the basis of the assessment, placement, and teaching for children and youth with disabilities. Reauthorization and renaming of PL 94-142 (EHA).

1990   **The Head Start Expansion and Quality Improvement Act.** PL 101-501. Reauthorized Head Start.

1991   **The Early Childhood Amendments to IDEA.** PL 102-119. Department of Education. This law amends PL 101-476 with regard to young children with disabilities. Amends Part H for infants and toddlers and Part B for preschoolers with disabilities.

1994   **The Technology Act.** PL 101-218. This law recognizes the need for persons with disabilities, including young children, to assess and use assistive technology devices and provide services to support assistive technology.

1997   **The Individuals with Disabilities Education Act of 1997.** PL 105-17. This law updates the 1990 Individuals with Disabilities Education Act (PL 101-476). It includes Part C, Infants and Toddlers with Disabilities, and it makes several changes in the preschool programs for children with disabilities. It also incorporates features of the earlier early childhood laws (PL 99-457) and (PL 102-119).

2001   **Leave No Child Behind Act (LNCB).** Creates strong standards in each state for what every child should know and learn in reading and math in grades 3 through 8. Student progress and achievement will be measured for every child, every year. Reauthorization of the Elementary and Secondary Education Act.

The following are some of the important features of PL 99-457:

- A national policy for early intervention establishes incentives and assistance to states for the extension of existing special education services from school-age children to infants, toddlers, and preschoolers.
- New ground was broken in recognizing and acknowledging the critical impact that families have on children's development.
- The application of a variety of models, other than traditional education models, is required, employing a team of multidisciplinary professionals to serve very young children with disabilities and their families.
- The rights and protection of the Individuals with Disabilities Education Act (IDEA) is extended to preschoolers (ages 3 through 5) with disabilities.
- Financial assistance is offered to states to develop and implement a statewide, comprehensive, coordinated, multidisciplinary, interagency program of early intervention services for infants and toddlers with disabilities, birth through age 3, and their families.

PL 102-119 added early intervention services (such as assistive technology), personnel (such as family therapists), and the concept of serving children in "natural environments."

*The law recognizes the critical importance of families in child development.*

These early childhood special education laws categorize the preschool population into two age groups, with different provisions for each group: (1) *Part B* covers preschoolers with disabilities (ages 3 through 5), extending the provisions of IDEA for preschool children with disabilities. (2) *Part C* covers infants and toddlers (birth through 2 years) and addresses the needs of very young children with disabilities and focuses on the child's developmental and medical needs as well as the importance of the family. The differences between Part B and Part C are summarized in Table 2.1.

***Part B: Preschool Children with Disabilities.*** Part B of the law adds a mandate to the major special education legislation, IDEA. It requires each state to provide a free, appropriate public education, along with related services to all eligible children with disabilities, ages 3 through 5. Some of the important dimensions of Part B (PL 105-17, 1997) are:

- It extends full rights and protection to children with disabilities, ages 3 through 5, by mandating services for children with disabilities in this age group.
- It permits the noncategorical reporting of children ages 3 through 9. Schools may elect to identify children with a noncategorical term, such as *developmental delay*, or to identify them by the category of disability.
- It provides that children ages 3 through 5 have full provisions of the law. This includes the development of either an *individualized education program* (*IEP*) or an *individualized family service plan* (*IFSP*). Preschool children with disabilities are

**TABLE 2.1** *A Comparison of Part B and Part C*

|  | *Part B* | *Part C* |
|---|---|---|
| *Age Range* | 3 through 5 | Birth through 2 |
| *Purpose* | Extends IDEA for 3 through 5 | Assist states to develop plan for birth through 2 |
| *Eligibility* | Category of disability or developmental delay (for ages 3–9) | Developmental delay (optional at risk) |
| *Plan* | IEP or IFSP | IFSP |
| *Law* | Mandatory | Permissive |
| *Lead Agency* | State education agency | Agency appointed by governor |
| *Primary Goal* | Developmental learning | Family/infant interaction |
| *Transition* | To general or special education program | To Part B program or regular preschool |
| *Personnel* | Early childhood special education teacher | Service Coordinator |

also afforded due process, confidentiality, and placement in the least restrictive environment.
- The state education agency working through local education agencies or other contracted service agencies is responsible for implementation of Part B.
- Appropriate service delivery models are left up to individual states.

**Part C: The Early Intervention Program for Infants and Toddlers with Disabilities.**    Part C of the IDEA-1997 addresses the provision of services for infants and toddlers with disabilities. Because of recent advances in medical technology, neonates with very low birth weights and substantial health problems are surviving. These fragile babies often need highly specialized medical attention, yet they and their families also require services that medical professionals cannot provide. Infant specialists and infant/toddler service providers are needed as key members of the interdisciplinary team in neonatal intensive care units and in child-care centers.

Unlike Part B, which mandates services for children ages 3 through 5, Part C authorizes financial assistance to the states through state grants to address the needs of infants and toddlers with disabilities and their families. The state grants support coordination across agencies and disciplines to ensure that comprehensive early intervention services are available on a statewide basis. These services are designed for children below the age of 3 who meet the state's eligibility criteria for "developmental delay" and their families. States are encouraged to strengthen collaborative efforts related to children at risk (PL 105-17, 1997). The purposes of Part C of the law are as follows (U.S. Department of Education, 1995, 1996):

- It enhances the development of infants and toddlers with disabilities and minimizes their potential for developmental delay.
- It reduces the educational costs to society by minimizing the need for special education and related services after infants and toddlers reach school age.
- The likelihood of institutionalization of individuals with disabilities is minimized, and the potential for their independent living in society is maximized.
- It enhances the capacity of families to meet the special needs of their infants and toddlers with disabilities.

Many of the delivery and intervention services to be provided to infants and toddlers with disabilities and their families under Part C are different from traditional special education services. Some of the important features of Part C of the law are listed in Figure 2.2. The provisions for Part C include:

- "Assistive technology services" is provided to infants and toddlers in Part C programs.
- With the permission of the family, a transition plan is formulated and meetings are held for children who are going into preschool (Part B) programs at least 90 days before the child's third birthday.
- Parents may withdraw consent for the provision of a particular early intervention service after initially agreeing to its provision.

**FIGURE 2.2** *Features of Part C of the Law*

These features apply to infants and toddlers, but many are often used for preschoolers, as well.

**1.** *Noncategorical identification.* Each state must define the term *developmental delay* for identifying infants and toddlers for service.

**2.** *Lead agency.* The governor of each state must designate a lead agency and an Interagency Coordinating Council to implement Part C and serve infants and toddlers, and their families. For Part C, some 19 states or territories chose their education agency as the lead agency. The majority, 22 states or territories, chose a health agency, 11 chose other lead agencies, including the Departments of Health, Mental Health, Mental Retardation, Human Services, and Public Welfare; and 2 states chose the Interagency Coordination Council (U.S. Department of Education, 1994).

(As noted, preschoolers with disabilities are provided services under Part B of the federal law. For Part B the lead agency is the State Education Agency in all states.)

**3.** *Multidisciplinary services.* There must be a comprehensive multidisciplinary evaluation for the infant/toddler and family. Other services may include family training and counseling, home visits, special instruction, speech/language pathology and audiology, occupational and physical therapy, psychological services, diagnostic and evaluative medical services, early identification screening and assessment services, and health services necessary to enable the infant or toddler to benefit from the other early intervention services.

**4.** *Individualized family service plan (IFSP).* Under Part C, an individualized family service plan (IFSP) is required (instead of an IEP) for infants and toddlers with disabilities and their families. This requirement underscores the significant role of the families. Each IFSP must include present levels of functioning, a statement of family strengths and needs, expected outcomes, specific services provided, projected dates of initiation and duration of services, name of the service coordinator, and steps taken to support the transition to the preschool program. Under Part C,

family members other than the child with a disability may be receiving services. The primary recipient of the services may be a parent through parent training and counseling. The IFSP must be reviewed, at the least, in six-month intervals.

**5.** *Service coordinator.* Part C requires that a service coordinator be named who will give guidance to the family and be responsible for the implementation of the IFSP. This professional coordinates the efforts of the various agencies and serves the family directly. The problems with infants and toddlers are often complex, as many different agencies and professionals often become involved. A service coordinator's duties are to work closely with the family, to coordinate the efforts of the various agencies and disciplines, and to oversee the transition to a new placement.

**6.** *Interagency coordination.* This is another important feature of Part C. The lead agency is responsible for entering into formal interagency agreements to provide comprehensive services to infants and toddlers with disabilities and their families. The law requires coordination of services at local, state, and federal levels. The Federal Interagency Coordinating Council (FICC) includes a broad range of federal agencies involved with policies, programs, and services to infants and toddlers with disabilities and their families and to preschool children with disabilities (U.S. Department of Education, 1994).

**7.** *Eligibility.* To be eligible for the infant/ toddler program, children must be experiencing developmental delays as measured by appropriate diagnostic instruments and procedures in at least one of five areas:
- Cognitive development
- Physical development, including vision and hearing
- Communication/language and speech development
- Social or emotional development
- Adaptive development

Also included are children whose diagnosed physical/mental condition has a *high probability* of resulting in developmental delays.

- The individualized family service plan (IFSP) includes, to the extent appropriate, strategies to secure funding sources for non-entitlement services that may be needed by the child or family.
- Complaint procedures between public agencies and the lead agency will be clarified.

## Individuals with Disabilities Education Act (IDEA) of 1997

The IDEA-1977 (PL 105-17), which was passed by Congress in 1997, incorporates the features of PL 99-457 and PL 102-119. Before IDEA-1997 were the Individuals with Disabilities Education Act of 1990 and the 1975 Education of Handicapped Children Act (PL 94-142). IDEA-1997 covers assessment and intervention procedures, the rights of children and parents, and other pertinent matters related to early childhood.

***Developmental Delay: A Noncategorical Classification of Young Children with Disabilities.***    IDEA-1997 permits states and schools to use a noncategorical classification such as *developmental delay* for preschool children with disabilities. The diagnostic classification of children with disabilities is not a simple process and presents some major concerns. First, there may be potentially harmful effects from labeling children at an early age. Further, since children do not mature at the same rate, the lack of developmental skills in a young child may be only a matter of timing; the child's developmental lags may disappear by the time he or she is ready for formal schooling. Finally, it is difficult to diagnose with certainty a 3-year-old's category of disability, especially since there is a lack of confidence about assessment procedures for young children (Lerner, 2003). For example, a speech delay in a 3-year-old may be due to one of several disabilities: a speech/language impairment, learning disabilities, mental retardation, a hearing disability, or an emotional problem. Through further observation and work with a child over a period of time, the nature of the disability is clarified.

Because of these classification dilemmas, IDEA-1997 permits a noncategorical classification, such as *developmental delay* for children ages 3 through 9. Thus, schools may report the number of 3- through 9-year-old children by either the category of *disability* or noncategorically as *developmental delay*. Infants and toddlers must be classified under a noncategorical term, such as *developmental delay* (PL 105-17, 1997).

A common definition of *developmental delay* is a delay in one or more of the following areas: cognitive development, physical development (which includes fine motor and gross motor), communication development, social/emotional development, or adaptive development. Many states have quantified the delay in terms of standard deviations (SD), either 1.5 SD or 2.0 SD below the mean, using standardized developmental assessment instruments and professional observation (Harbin, Danaker, Bailer, & Eller, 1991). A survey of how states classified preschool children showed that some states still use categorical Part B classifications, some states use a noncategorical classification, and some states use both (U.S. Department of Education, 1994).

***Mediation.***    Another feature in the IDEA-1997 is mediation. States and schools are encouraged to use the initial process of mediation to resolve disputes. There is no cost to parents. The process is conducted by a qualified and impartial mediator. The states maintain a list of mediators. The meeting must be held at a time convenient for parents. Discussions are confidential and *cannot* be used as evidence in any subsequent due process hearing or civil proceeding.

***Categories in IDEA.***    IDEA creates 12 separate categories of disabilities. As noted earlier, programs for preschoolers (ages 3 through 9) have the option of reporting children by categories or noncategorically (such as developmental delay). The 12 categories of disabilities in IDEA-1997 (PL 105-17) are:

| | |
|---|---|
| Specific learning disabilities | Orthopedic impairments |
| Speech or language impairments | Other health impairments |
| Mental retardation | Visual impairments |
| Serious emotional disturbance | Autism |
| Multiple disabilities | Deaf-blindness |
| Hearing impairments | Traumatic brain injury |

## The Early Education Program for Children with Disabilities (EEPCD)

Many early childhood special education demonstration and model projects are supported by the Department of Education under the EEPCD (Early Education Program for Children with Disabilities). The precursor of these programs were the HCEEP studies (Handicapped Children's Early Education Programs). The HCEEP varied widely in purpose, curriculum, disabilities served, age groups, and activities. The programs used a variety of theoretical approaches, age groups, and settings (urban, suburban, and rural). The HCEEP studies stimulated the development of many early childhood special education programs in the public schools.

The Department of Education continues to support model and demonstration projects, outreach projects, experimental projects, and research institutes under the EEPCD (Early Education Programs for Children with Disabilities). Over the years, the EEPCD programs served the nation and the field of early childhood special education well. The model demonstration and outreach projects establish state-of-the-art practices and techniques in the field of early childhood special education programs. They demonstrate a wide variety of curriculum approaches for many different types of disabilities in a variety of rural and urban settings (U.S. Department of Education, 1995).

## Other Special Education Laws

Two additional laws affect preschoolers with disabilities. Section 504 of the Rehabilitation Act requires that accommodations be made for individuals with disabilities in institutions that receive federal funds. A child may qualify for the protection of Section

504 if the child requires special education or related services. Some children who are not eligible for services under IDEA may be eligible for accommodation under Section 504. The Americans with Disabilities Act (ADA) protects people with disabilities from discrimination in the workplace.

## Legislation and Programs for Children at Risk

Children who are at risk may not at present be eligible for services under the law but they are at high risk for becoming a child with a disability and for having substantial developmental delays if early intervention services are not provided. States may choose to serve children who are at risk, but they are not required by law to serve these children. The law urges states that do not include children at risk in their eligible population to establish interagency policies and procedures to assure referral to special education in a timely manner when these children may be eligible for services.

Under Part C of IDEA-1997, each state has the option to include infants and toddlers who are at risk for developmental delays if services are not provided. Infants and toddlers can be considered "biologically at risk" or "environmentally at risk." A population that will have a significant effect on Part C is composed of children who

*Head Start serves children who may be at risk as well as children with identified disabilities.*

are exposed prenatally to cocaine and other substances. The funding and policy implications of such decisions are enormous.

## *Head Start*

Head Start, now over 35 years old, is the largest program providing comprehensive educational, health, and social services to young children and their families with low income, and it is an important player in the early childhood services delivery system (Buscemi, Bennett, Thomas, & Deluca, 1996). Head Start falls under the jurisdiction of the Department of Health and Human Services. As noted earlier in this chapter, project Head Start was one of the initiatives of Lyndon Johnson's "War on Poverty" within the Economic Opportunity Act of 1965. Its purpose was to break the cycle of poverty by providing education and social opportunities for children from low-income families. In 1972, legislation required Head Start programs to include children with disabilities to the extent of at least 10 percent. A major focus was to integrate children with disabilities into classrooms with children without disabilities. In the year 2000, 13 percent of the Head Start enrollment were children with disabilities.

The Head Start program services children who may be at risk as well as children with identified disabilities. These disabilities include the 12 categories discussed earlier: mental retardation; hearing impairments, including deafness, speech, or language impairments; visual impairments, including blindness; serious emotional disturbance; orthopedic impairments; autism; traumatic brain injury; other health impairments or special language disabilities; and others who need special education and related services (Head Start Bureau, 2000). Other information regarding this program is discussed next.

### *Some Facts about Head Start (Head Start Bureau, 2000)*
- About 52 percent of Head Start families have annual income of less than $9,000 per year, and 69 percent have incomes of less than $12,000.
- Head Start programs are encouraged to use non–Head Start resources in their communities for Head Start children and their families. Some 62 percent of Head Start children are enrolled in the Medicaid/Early and Periodic Screen, Diagnosis and Treatment (EPSDT) program, which pays for their medical and dental services.
- In 1965, 561,000 children were enrolled in Head Start. In 1999, 826,016 children were enrolled in the program.
- The ages of the children served through Head Start are:

  | | |
  |---|---|
  | 5 year olds and older | 5% |
  | 4 year olds | 58% |
  | 3 year olds | 33% |
  | under 3 years | 4% |

- The racial/ethnic composition of Head Start children are:

  | | |
  |---|---|
  | American Indian | 3.4% |
  | Hispanic | 27.8% |

| Black | 35.1% |
| White | 30.5% |
| Asian | 2.1% |
| Hawaiian/Pacific Islander | 1.0% |

***Early Head Start Programs.***    An Early Head Start program was established in 1994 to serve children under age 3. These programs offer effective service integration between Part C programs for infants and toddlers with disabilities and Early Head Start to serve children in natural environments (Summers et al., 2001).

## Other Compensatory Programs

Other compensatory education programs created by the federal government to intervene in the lives of young children considered to be at risk for development delay or underachievement are notable. They include Parent and Child Centers, Follow-Through, Home Start, and Head Start/EPSDT Collaborative Projects (Peterson, 1987). A strong case for federal support of early intervention programs is the study of the long-term improvements of children who were in the Perry Preschool Project (Schweinhart, Barnes, & Weikart, 1993; Schweinhart & Weikart, 1988).

***Title 1: Compensatory Education Programs.***    Title I programs are intended for at-risk children at the primary and elementary levels. Title I legislation is one of the amendments to the Improving America's Schools Act (a reauthorization of the Elementary and Secondary Education Act), which was passed by Congress in 1994. The purpose of the Title I legislation is to supply compensatory education for children from families with low incomes. Research shows that children from low-income environments tend to be at risk for reading failure; these children often lack the stimulation and literacy experiences of middle- or high-income environments. The National Adult Literacy Survey (Kirsch, Jungeblut, Jenkins, & Kolstad, 1993) shows that adults in the lowest level on the literacy scale were more likely (44 percent) to live in poverty than those in the highest level (4 percent).

Students are eligible for Title I services when their academic performance is below grade-level criteria (as determined by the state or local education agency) and if the school they attend has the prescribed number of children from families with low income in attendance to warrant funding. Schools that are eligible for Title I funds can provide compensatory instruction to improve students' skills in the areas of reading and mathematics. Over 75 percent of the children receive reading instruction. These students receive between 2½ to 3½ hours of weekly supplementary reading instruction.

Title I programs currently serve six million children. Recent revisions of Title I rules require that programs develop written policies to include parents in the school's planning and implementation of the Title I services. The programs use a variety of methods, strategies, and organizational plans; there is no single prescribed methodology.

# Current Trends and Issues

This section discusses several of the major trends and issues in early intervention for young children with special needs. The focus is on assistive technology, placements in natural environments for teaching, establishment of family partnerships, and family diversity.

## Assistive Technology

It is important that assistive technology be considered for every child as the IFSP and IEP are being developed. Technology applications should be examined across the following areas to enhance child development and to provide natural learning opportunities and the typical curriculum: motor development, cognitive/perceptional learning, communication/language development, social interaction, adaptive behaviors, daily life skills, play, and precursors for academic learning (Stremel, 2000).

Today's young children are being raised in a computer society that is changing rapidly as a result of the influx of new computer-based technologies. Early childhood programs must prepare children to meet these dramatic changes of the past decade so that all students can fully participate in today's exciting new computer world and compete in the increasingly complex technological workplace.

Society readily recognizes the benefits of computer-based technologies for typical young children. However, there are even greater benefits that computer-based technologies may afford young children with special needs. Computer applications can help level the playing field for young children with special needs by helping them to succeed in the general education environment. For many young children with special needs, using computers is an area of strength, helping the children overcome other areas of severe difficulty, such as abilities in language. Research shows that young children with special needs often have a special facility with computers (Stremel, 2000; Hasselbring & Glazer, 2000; Raskin & Higgins, 1998).

**Technology in the Law.** *Technology* for students with disabilities is defined in federal law as "any item, piece of equipment, or product system, whether acquired commercially off the shelf, modified, or customized, that is used to increase, maintain, or improve functional capabilities of individuals with disabilities" (Individuals with Disabilities Act, 1997).

*The Technology Act.* The Technology Act was passed by Congress in 1994 (PL 103-218, 1994). This law recognizes the need for persons with disabilities to access and use assistive technology devises and provides funding to support assistive technology. *Assistive technology devices* enable users with disabilities to move, play, communicate, write, speak, and participate in many activities that would be impossible to them without a computer. Assistive technology can help students overcome barriers in print, in communication, and in learning. Students who have problems with reading and writing, for example, can use assistive devices such as taped books, devices that read printed books aloud, and "talking" computer programs. Students who have difficulty with written communication can use word-processing programs, spelling and grammar aides for editing help, programs that help writers organize their thoughts during the planning stage of the writing process, and voice input devices to dictate the written message (Lewis, 1998). The use of computer technology to teach cognitive skills is discussed in Chapter 11.

## Natural Environments

The *natural environment* refers to a placement the family chooses (such as child-care centers, homes, and preschools), using play and other developmentally appropriate activities as learning opportunities. It is a setting in which the child would spend time had he or she not had a disability (Sandall, McLean, & Smith, 2000). The Individuals with Disabilities Education Act of 1997 explicitly calls for delivery of services in "natural environments" for young children with disabilities. To the maximum extent appropriate, early intervention services are to be provided in a natural environment for infants, toddlers, and preschoolers, as well.

A goal of placement in natural environments is to reduce separate placements and isolated therapy and to increase integrated or inclusive placements. The natural environment view reflects a significant trend in intervention for young children with special needs. To increase the effectiveness of placing young children with special needs into natural or inclusive settings:

- The philosophy of natural environments must be accepted and valued by families of young children with and without disabilities and by community members (Dunst & Trivette, 1994; Howard, Williams, Port, & Lepper, 1997).
- Children with disabilities must have opportunities to become continuing members of their peer groups (Sandall, McLean, & Smith, 2000).
- More research must be conducted to find specific pedagogical practices that will increase the success of a variety of natural environments and inclusive placements (Guralnick, 1994).

Natural environments and inclusive settings are not just places where young children with special needs are in physical proximity to their typical peers. To successfully meet the needs of individual children, the appropriateness of the placement must be considered. An appropriate inclusive setting provides the necessary resources, special services, quality personnel, and curriculum that is both age and individually appropriate to achieve objectives on IEPs and IFSPs (Bredekamp, 1993; Bredekamp & Copple, 1997; Carta, Atwater, Schwartz, & McConnell, 1993; Howard, Williams, Port, & Lepper, 1997).

The policy of delivering services in the natural environment involves integrated and inclusive settings. An issue of current discussion is whether integrated regular preschool settings and day-care placements can effectively provide the services needed by children with special needs (Odom & McEvoy, 1990; Winton, 1993).

It is important that early interventionists should support the rationale of the natural environment and the philosophy of the integrated service delivery model. However, they should also be able to function effectively in separate classes and individual settings. Skills in teaching both separate classes and in inclusive settings are needed (Widerstrom & Bricker, 1996; Wolery, 2000).

## Partnerships with Families

A major goal for early interventionists is to develop strong partnerships with the families they serve. The family must see the purpose of the intervention activities and these activities should be aligned with the family's cultural values, child-rearing practices, and perception of the child's disabilities. The early childhood professional works with families to provide the supports and resources that the family needs. Figure 2.3 shows the DEC recommended family practices.

The individualized family service plan (IFSP) emphasizes a family-centered approach to the intervention. The development of a partnership between the family and the early interventionist is essential. Partnerships with families can offer the resources and supports necessary for families to have the time, energy, knowledge, and skills to provide their children with the learning opportunities and experiences that promote child development. When intervention is done in a family-centered manner, it strengthens the family and gives them feelings of control and competency (Trivette & Dunst, 2000).

Research indicates that when family partnerships are used in working with families, there are positive consequences in terms of families valuing the support and help they receive from early intervention providers. The provision of resources and supports to parents and families enables them to provide for the development of their children. Early childhood professionals must strengthen the will of families to support the development of their children in a manner that increases families' sense of parenting and competence. The early interventionist, of course, must respect the racial, linguistic, cultural, and ethnic diversities among families, and services for them should be responsible to the family concerns (Trivette & Dunst, 2000).

## Sensitivity to Cultural Diversity

To gain cultural sensitivity, early childhood professionals should be alert to a number of issues that may arise as they work with families of diverse cultures. Early childhood professionals should be aware of their own cultural values, have knowledge of diverse child-rearing practices, understand the different cultural perspectives about disabilities, and recognize the diversity of communicative styles.

Awareness of one's own culture is a first step in recognizing the cultural diversity of others. Interventionists should examine their own beliefs about different cultures, races, linguistic differences, and family structures. Many Anglo American families value independence, self-help, control of one's life, individual achievement, equality, and informality in their relationships with people (Au & Kawakami, 1991). It is easy to assume that these values are similar in other cultures, but the beliefs of other cultures could be quite different. For example, Native American individuals are judged by their contributions to the group and the community rather than by their individual achievements (Nelson, Smith, & Dodd, 1991). A sense of mistrust could be created if early interventionists are unaware that the values of the families are different from their own. If cultural differences are not taken into account, the interventions proposed by the professionals may be considered inappropriate and resisted by the families.

**FIGURE 2.3   *DEC Recommended Practices: Family-Based Practices***

The Division for Early Childhood (DEC) has developed some guidelines for developing partnerships with families (Sandal, McLean, & Smith, 2000), which are summarized here:

1. **Families and early childhood professionals should share responsibility and work collaboratively.**
   • Families and early childhood professionals should jointly develop appropriate family-identified outcomes.
   • Families and early childhood professionals should work together and share information routinely to achieve family-identified outcomes.
   • Early childhood professionals should fully and appropriately provide relevant information to parents so they can make informed choices and decisions.
   • Early childhood professionals should use helping styles that promote shared family/professional responsibility in achieving family-identified outcomes.
   • The family and professional relationship should be accomplished in ways that are responsive to cultural, language, and other family characteristics.

2. **Intervention practices should strengthen family functioning.**
   • Practices, supports, and resources should offer families with a participating experience and opportunities to make choices and engage in decision making.
   • Practices, supports, and resources should encourage family participation in obtaining desired resources and supports to strengthen parenting competence and confidence.
   • Intrafamily, informal, community, and formal supports and resources should be used to achieve desired outcomes.
   • Supports and resources should provide families with information, competency-enhancing experiences, and participatory opportunities to strengthen family functioning and promote parenting knowledge and skills.
   • Supports and resources should be used in ways that are supportive and do not disrupt family and community life.

3. **Intervention practices should be individualized and flexible.**
   • Resources and supports are provided in ways that are flexible, individualized, and tailored to the child's family's preferences and styles, and that promote well-being.
   • Resources and supports should match each family member's priorities and preferences.
   • Practices, supports, and resources should be responsible to the cultural, ethnic, racial, language, and socioeconomic characteristics and preferences of families and their communities.
   • Practices, supports, and resources should incorporate family beliefs and values into decisions, interventions plans, resources, and support mobilization.

4. **Intervention practices should use the family strengths and assets.**
   • Family and child strengths and assets should be used as a basis for engaging families as participants in experiences supporting parenting, competence, and confidence.
   • Practices, supports, and resources should build on existing parent competencies and confidence.
   • Practices, supports, and resources should promote the family's and the early childhood professional's acquisition of new knowledge and skills to strengthen competence and confidence.

*Source:* Adapted from "Recommended Practices in Family-Based Practices" by C. Trivette and C. Dunst, in *DEC Recommended Practices in Early Intervention/Early Childhood Special Education* (pp. 45–46), ed. S. Sandall, M. McLean, and B. Smith. Denver, CO: Division for Early Childhood. © 2000 by The Division for Early Childhood. Reprinted with permission.

***Child-Rearing Practices.***    In Anglo American society, children often are encouraged to be as independent as possible. Child-rearing practices reflect this perspective in the emphasis on early toilet training and self-reliance. However, in some cultures, dependence is expected in childhood. For example, in traditional Cuban cultures, there are fears that if too much independence is promoted, children will be at risk for physical harm. From this cultural perspective, autonomy in children could be a sign of poor parenting (DeSantis & Thomas, 1994).

Native American families traditionally have been permissive and accepting of their children. Adults give the same respect to the children as they do to one another (Bearcrane, Dodd, Nelson, & Ostwald, 1990). Among African American families, the custom is to indulge the children, encourage them to be assertive, and to identify strongly with their peers (Phillips, 1994). In order to assist diverse families, the interventionist must learn their beliefs, values, and child-rearing practices so that the goals for the children are compatible with family customs.

***Cultural Beliefs about Disabilities.***    The ways in which families from different cultures perceive disabilities and the causes of disabilities are important because it affects their attitudes toward their children with special needs. In some cultures, a disability is viewed as a form of punishment (Groce & Zola, 1993). The affected child and her or his family is believed to be cursed by God, and the disability is a punishment for past sins. Support for family members is minimal, as community people may wish to distance themselves from the "evil" family.

Another belief in a number of African and Carribean societies is that witchcraft is the cause of the disability (Groce, 1990). An individual who is disabled is thought to be bewitched. Close association with a child with a disability is thought to put others at risk for the evil witchcraft. The affected child and family members are avoided by community members. The responsibility for the disability as well as its cure is placed on the child and the family (Chan, 1990).

The consequences of these beliefs can affect the way that families treat their children with special needs. Family members may feel ashamed, and they may neglect these children. These families may be too embarrassed to accept the help of an interventionist in obtaining needed services. They may keep the child at home, unseen by others, as a way of coping with the disability. Even when family members may be aware of the need for intervention to assist the child, they can be reluctant to accept help because of the fear of being disgraced when the disability is publicly known (Lequerica, 1993).

In order to serve diverse families who have children with disabilities, it is essential for interventionists to understand the perceptions the families have about the causes of the disabilities and the value of intervention. The stress and discrimination that family members incur can be unrecognized by service providers. These families deserve clear explanations in their own languages about the reasons for the interventions and services proposed for themselves and their children. In addition, the family members need to know how they can participate with the professionals in making culturally sensitive decisions.

***Diversity of Communication Styles.***    Two issues concerning communicating clearly with families of diverse cultural and linguistic origins are (1) the use of interpreters and (2) the recognition of different interaction styles.

*The Use of Interpreters.*   Effective interpreters on the early intervention team should have the following skills and abilities: proficiency in the languages spoken by the diverse families and the service providers, knowledge of the cultures of both the families and the early interventionists, proficiency in cross-cultural communication, and the ability to keep information confidential (Lynch & Hanson, 1992). Brandenburg-Ayres (1990) suggests that ideal interpreters will be culturally sensitive informants who can explain diverse customs, beliefs, and styles of communication to the early intervention teams of professionals and paraprofessionals.

*Recognition of Different Interaction Styles.*   The second issue in cross-cultural communication is that different cultures can have diverse interaction styles. The values of some cultures emphasize that children are to be "seen but not heard." Behaviors such as talking assertively to adults or making direct eye contact with them are regarded as disrespectful, reflecting poor manners. Turning the eyes downward to the speaker implies one is listening intently in some Asian, African, and Native American societies (Williams, 1994). Some Asian families caution their children not to ask questions of authority figures. Questioning is thought to be disrespectful (Chan, 1990). Differences in interaction styles also can be reflected in the length of time it takes to build relationships with family members. Some families focus on long-term relationships and need time to develop trust with the interventionists through many visits (Allen & Majidi-Ahi, 1989). Anglo American families tend to be informal in their interactions and want to establish quick relationships with professionals. In many societies, there are cultural differences in communication involving personal space, eye contact, wait time, tone of voice, facial expressions, and touching that early interventionists should recognize (Saland & Taylor, 1993).

*Culturally Responsive Interventionists.*   Culturally responsive interventionists are essential in our increasingly diverse U.S. society. To meet the challenges of culturally diverse families and be culturally responsive, early childhood professionals need several competencies (Bruder, Anderson, Schutz, & Caldera, 1991; Chan, 1990; Mallach, 1993). Early childhood professionals need to:

- Recognize their own cultures and beliefs.
- Understand the culture of the families they service for effective communication with them.
- Recognize that every family, regardless of its cultural, linguistic, or ethnic heritage, is unique in its ways of functioning and in its degree of identification with a particular culture.
- Keep in mind both the individual families as well as their common cultural backgrounds when planning interventions and services.

To assist interventionists in acquiring these competencies, university programs need to include coursework in the following areas: diverse family structures, styles of communication, service coordination, transdisciplinary teamwork with other professionals and families, and ethnic-cultural diversity. The practica for students should provide direct experiences in forming partnerships with families, service providers, and paraprofessionals of different cultures (Mallach, 1993).

# Summary

- Research and the success of several programs have changed our thinking about the education of young children. There has also been a transformation in our understanding of young children who are at risk or who have disabilities and in effective intervention practices for these children. Recently, society, parents, and educators have realized that early education is beneficial for young children.
- The term *special needs* applies to both young children with disabilities and children who are considered at risk. The research findings from both fields are often intermingled: Theories about children with disabilities have applications for children at risk; good practices for children at risk can be applied to children with disabilities.
- Several recent laws are designed to protect the rights of young children with disabilities and preschoolers considered at risk for failure and provide early intervention services for these children.
- Two laws (PL 99-457 and PL 102-119) amended the special education laws and strengthened the federal government's role in providing services to young children with disabilities. These laws are incorporated in the Individuals with Disabilities Education Act of 1997 (PL 105-17). The law divides the preschool population into two groups by age, with different provisions within the law for each group: (1) Part B covers preschoolers with disabilities and (2) Part C covers infants and toddlers (birth through 2 years).
- Head Start is an early childhood program for 3- to 5-year-old children from families with low income. In 1972, Head Start legislation was amended to require Head Start programs to include children with disabilities to the extent of at least 10 percent. A major focus is to integrate children with disabilities into classrooms with children who have no disabilities.
- Current trends and issues include assistive technology, natural environments, partnerships with parents, and family diversity.

# Key Terms

| | |
|---|---|
| assistive technology | least restrictive environment |
| center-based program | mediation |
| cognitive emphasis curriculum | natural environments |
| directed teaching curriculum | Part B |
| early Head Start | Part C |
| family partnerships | PL 99-457 |
| Head Start | PL 105-17 |
| home-based program | service providers |
| IDEA-1997 | transition |
| lead agency | |

# 3

## *Family Systems*

## Chapter Outline

**The Family**
Changing Definitions of a Family
Recognition of the Family in the Law
The Family Systems Perspective
Assessment of the Family

**Parent/Family Reactions to Having a Child
with Special Needs**
Stages of Acceptance and Grief
Challenges to the Stage Theory

**Participation of the Family in Early
Intervention: A Partnership**
Working with Parents When Making a
Referral for a Child's Assessment
Empowering and Enabling Families

Informal Sources of Support
Assistance through Family Support Programs

**Special Issues**
Abuse and Neglect
Ethical Dilemmas
Divorce and Custody Issues
Serving Culturally Diverse Families
Poverty and Families
Fathers
Siblings
Respite Care
National Organizations and Support Groups
for Families

The role of the family is critical in terms of the intervention policies and practices for young children with special needs. This chapter discusses (1) the changing concept of what constitutes a family, (2) the reaction of parents to having a child with a disability, (3) ways that families can participate in the intervention, and (4) several special issues that involve families—namely, abuse and neglect, ethical dilemmas, the roles of fathers and siblings, and the effects of cultural and linguistic diversity.

# The Family

It is highly desirable to include the parents and the extended family members in all aspects of the assessment process and intervention practices. To consider the impact of the family, one should (1) examine the changing ideas about what comprises a family, (2) look at the how the law supports a family focus, (3) analyze the family as a system, and (4) explore the assessment of families and family members.

## Changing Definitions of a Family

The notion of a *family* has undergone radical change in the past 25 years. We no longer expect the family unit to consist of a mother, father, and child or children. Today, we recognize many variations of the family unit. For example, many families in today's world consist of a single parent and a child or children. Often, a grandparent or other relatives or friends are an integral part of the family unit. The reality is that the *family* has expanded from the traditional family unit to one that includes persons who are

## *Early Childhood Snapshot*    A FAMILY FOCUS

The Hernandez family consists of Mr. and Mrs. Hernandez and three children. Their two older children, Jose (age 6) and Carmen (age 4), have had a normal developmental course. Their youngest child Maria, (age 3), was born with Down syndrome. Having recently moved to the United States from Guatemala, the family has only a few close friends and no available extended family members. Mr. Hernandez works as an assembler in a factory, Mrs. Hernandez currently is a homemaker, although she had worked part time before they moved.

Their neighborhood school arranged an initial consultation with Maria's parents, which included a school representative, a translator, and a mentor parent. During this meeting, the team set a date for assessment.

Using a play assessment format, the assessment was conducted with the family, translator, mentor parent, and a bilingual psychologist and speech therapist. The team decided to place Maria in a bilingual early childhood special education class in the morning and a bilingual preschool program in the afternoon. At present, this arrangement seems to be working well, and the family continues to collaborate with the schools regarding Maria's goals and services provided under her IEP.

legally responsible for a child's well-being and also those who care for the child as a parent would. One definition of a *family* is

> two or more individuals, at least one of whom is an adult and the other a child, who are legally bound to each other through birth, adoption, or legal guardianship. The family represents a complex set of bonds, dynamics, relationships, systems, and subsystems, in which each individual is developing and at the same time interacting with and adjusting to the family. (Widerstrom, Mowder, & Sandall, 1991, p. 116)

During the past several decades, there have been substantial changes in the structure of the family. These changes can be attributed to variability in social arrangements for raising children. Increasingly recognized are alternative social patterns and other societal and research shifts (Paul & Simeonsson, 1993). Moreover, the changing family structure has direct relevance for interventionists or teachers who work with the families of young children.

Early childhood interventionists must accept as a family unit whomever the child's parents or guardians consider to be the child's family. Since all members of the family are affected by the child's special needs, they all need to be involved in the intervention plan to some degree.

Despite the changes in family composition, one aspect of raising a child has remained constant over time. In order to flourish, each child needs someone in his or her life who loves and cherishes the child deeply. Early childhood researchers and child development specialists elaborate on the child's need for a loving adult (Bronfenbrenner, 1979; Erickson & Kurz-Reimer, 1999). This need is expressed by Bronfenbrenner (1979, p. v), as cited in Berns (1993):

> A child needs the enduring, irrational involvement of one or more adults in care and joint activity with the child. Public policies and practices are required to provide parents and

other key adults in a child's life with the opportunity, status, resources, encouragement, and above all, time, to be involved with the child both within and outside the home.

## Recognition of the Family in the Law

As discussed in Chapter 2, PL 105-17 and earlier early childhood legislation (PL 99-457 and PL 102-119) recognize the family as a critical component for young children with special needs. Prior to PL 99-457, educators, medical specialists, and therapists tended to focus solely on the needs of the child. The contributions that families could make were often not fully appreciated, and the personal needs of parents were generally ignored. Although, in some cases, social workers or psychologists served parents, these services were not typically integrated in the child's educational program.

With the creation of Part H in the 1986 PL 99-457 (now Part C in the reauthorized IDEA), there was a tangible change in the recognition of the role of parents and family members in the total picture. Further, PL 99-457 encouraged each state to establish a comprehensive system of early intervention services for infants and toddlers that included their families. Harbin, McWilliam, and Gallagher (2000) state that the revised law is intended to increase the number of children receiving services as early as possible, and to improve services for children and families by making those services more family centered. PL 99-457 served not only to increase attention for providing assessment and intervention for families but also for the types of involvement and practices that are most beneficial to families (Dunst & Deal, 1992). Several models of family involvement are discussed in this chapter.

## The Family Systems Perspective

The application of a systems approach to working with families is a relatively new mode of thinking in this field. A systems approach for viewing families has its roots in a structural framework called *systems analysis*, which is generally credited to the work of von Bertalanffy (1968). The theory of systems analysis is based on the notion that whatever happens to one part of a system affects all other parts. Moreover, the effects are not linear, but each component of the system interacts with other components. From a systems perspective, the whole is greater than the sum of all of the parts (Becvar & Becvar, 1993).

The application of systems analysis theory to families was proposed by Bronfenbrenner (1979). In the family systems framework, families and agencies are viewed as components of an "organized whole." The "whole" is a hierarchical and orderly system of interrelated and interdependent components, with constant adaptation within the system. In applying the theory of systems analysis to the family, the family is viewed as a system. As a system, all members of the family unit are interdependent, and each member of the family has interactive effect on all other members of the family system.

The family is also viewed as a social unit, embedded within other formal and informal social units (Becvar & Becvar, 1993; Shea & Bauer, 1991). The ramification is that any intervention with one family member will inevitably affect all of the other family members. Moreover, there are so many possible interconnections among family members that the total interactions add up to more than the number of people in the family.

*A Family Systems Model.*    In expanding on the systems theory concept in its application to working with families, Bronfenbrenner (1979) described an ecological environment as a nested arrangement of structures, each contained within the next. Figure 3.1 illustrates the family system. The four nested levels of the environment are (1) microsystems, (2) mesosystems, (3) exosystems, and (4) macrosystems. The *microsystem* consists of the home, child-care center, school, peer group, and other family settings. The *mesosystem* includes relationships between two or more of the child's microsystems,

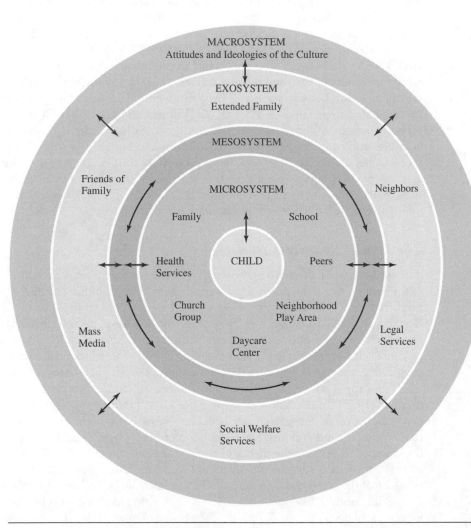

**FIGURE 3.1    *A Family Systems Model***

*Source:* Bukatko, Danuta, and Marvin W. Daehler, *Child Development: A Topical Approach*, First Edition. Copyright © 1992 by Houghton Mifflin Company. Used with permission. Originally adapted from Garabino, 1982.

such as between parents and interventionists, doctors, or other professionals, and professional-professional relationships. The *exosystem* includes societal structures in which the child may not be an active participant, such as school boards, agencies, community organizations, neighborhoods, and churches. However, these settings may directly affect the child in one of his or her microsystems. The *macrosystem* consists of the child's society and subculture—for example, the legislative and cultural contexts in which the other three systems operate. These contexts might include the child's socioeconomic level, ancestry, and whether the child lives in a rural or urban setting.

Recognition of the family macrosystem in the early childhood context is found in PL 99-457 and PL 102-119. Lambie (2000) presents the foundations of family systems concepts for school professionals. Gilkerson and Stott (2000) stress the importance of the parent-child relationship as a tool for child change within the context of Part C from an infant mental health perspective. It is important to cast the concerns and issues experienced by individual families into the context of the larger systems.

## Assessment of the Family

The assessment process should include family assessment, in addition to assessment of the child. For the family assessment, it is critical to consider the family's priorities. Information should be gathered from the family and through other assessment procedures to identify the family's strengths and needs in regard to the child and to support the family members in achieving their own goals (McWilliam, Lang, Vandiviere, Angell, Collins, & Underdown, 1995).

PL 99-457 indicates that the family assessment must be voluntary, be carried out by appropriately trained personnel, be based on information provided by the family through a personal interview, and incorporate the family's description of their strengths and needs as they relate to enhancing the child's development. Kelly and Barnard (2000) emphasize the implications of assessment of parent-child interactions on the outcomes of early intervention and suggest measures appropriate for these evaluations, such as the Maternal Behavior Rating Scale by Mahoney.

Also, for infants and toddlers the *individualized family service plan* (*IFSP*) must be used instead of the *individualized education plan* (*IEP*). For preschool children, schools often use the individualized education plan (IEP), which does not require a family assessment and intervention component. However, the Reauthorized Individuals with Disabilities Education Act of 1997 (PL 105-17) permits states and local education agencies also to use the IFSP for preschool children up to the age of 6.

Turnbull and Turnbull (2001) are highly respected scholars and practitioners who work with families and conduct research at the Beach Center on Families and Disability at the University of Kansas. They emphasize the importance of making the family assessment as "family-friendly" as possible. Although there are many formal family assessment instruments, Turnbull and Turnbull recommend informal assessment. Families and practitioners prefer an informal approach that is open ended and conversational rather than the completion of structured interviews or paper and pencil inventories. Turnbull and Turnbull recommend clinical methods that utilize personal interviews. (This method is described in Appendix B of Turnbull & Turnbull, 2001.)

Several instruments for the assessment of families' strengths are (Deal, Trivette, & Dunst, 1988):

*Family Strengths Inventory* (Stinnett & DeFrain, 1985)
*Family Strengths Scale* (Olson, Larsen, & McCubbin, 1983)
*Family Hardiness Index* (McCubbin, McCubbin, & Thompson, 1987)
*Family Functioning Style Scale* (Deal, Trivette, & Dunst, 1988)

(These instruments are described in Appendix A.)

Work with families will be most productive if (1) the family itself is viewed as a major resource for meeting its own needs and (2) families are accepted as active participants in the process of identifying their own needs and developing and implementing methods to meet their family needs. Dunst, Trivette, and Mott (1994) emphasize that all families have strengths, even though they are not apparent at first:

It must be recognized that all families have strengths and capabilities and if we take the time to identify these characteristics and build on them rather than focus on correcting deficits or weaknesses, families are not only more likely to respond favorably to interventions but the chances of making a significant positive impact on the family unit are enhanced considerably. (p. 122)

## Parent/Family Reactions to Having a Child with Special Needs

When parents are first told that their child has a disability or developmental delays, they often react in a similar manner as people who are grieving. Moses (1987) observes that, in fact, these parents are grieving; they have lost their dream of a healthy, normal child, and they are grieving this loss. Instead of the anticipated "typical" child, parents are confronted with a child who is sick, who needs special care, and who may need care for the rest of his or her life. The patterns of acceptance and working through this loss are based on the theories of Elisabeth Kübler-Ross (1969), who explored the stages of grief around issues of death and dying.

### Stages of Acceptance and Grief

There are approximately seven sequential stages of grief in the parents' reactions to their child's disability: shock, disbelief, denial, anger, bargaining, depression, and acceptance. These reactions are influenced by the family's culture, the many different traditions about raising a child who has a disability, and the emotions evoked during these stages. Each of the stages is normal when an individual is working through grief and loss, and they should not be considered pathological.

**Shock.**    Shock is a numb, distancing feeling that engulfs the parent when bad news is being delivered. Parents often report that they "didn't hear a word the doctor said," or that they never understood what the diagnosis meant.

*Disbelief.* During this stage, parents do not believe the diagnosis given for their child. They are convinced that the professionals are wrong and that their child does not have a disability.

*Denial.* Parents may refuse to even consider that their child has a disability. During this stage, they may "doctor shop" for another professional who will recant the original diagnosis. In some cases, the doctor shopping is an appropriate reaction to an inaccurate or incomplete diagnosis; however, in other instances, it is not in the best interests of the child and postpones the inevitable conclusion that the child has a disability.

Professionals often become frustrated with parents who are in denial. Often, students in early childhood special education training programs want to know how they might "hurry" the parent along through this phase. The only approach that works is for the interventionist to listen to the parent and accept their emotions, validate them, and be available for support when the parents conclude that their child does indeed have a disability.

*Anger.* As denial breaks down and the child's condition becomes more real and apparent, parents begin to experience angry feelings. "Why did this have to happen to me?" "This isn't fair. I've done nothing wrong." Interventionists often are frightened by the intensity of the parents' anger, especially from parents who previously did not show much emotion. The parents' frustration and bottled-up anger may explode during sessions with the child. Again, it is helpful for professionals to recognize anger as a potentially positive sign that the parents have begun to accept the child's condition.

*Bargaining.* In bargaining, the parent makes a mental wager with a higher power and/or decides that dedication to a task or work will somehow alleviate their child's condition or negate it altogether. The parent becomes very "busy" during this stage, and this leaves little time for interactions with professional personnel.

*Depression.* For beginning interventionists, this stage will be very difficult to manage. Parents will make statements like, "What's the use? Why even bother to come to the center anymore—nothing is going to change." "I feel so dragged out and tired, there isn't any point in asking me to continue this therapy." Part of what causes the depression is that the parents have moved through some parts of the previous stages and are now confronted with the child's disability for the rest of their lives, and they may be worried about what will happen to their child after they die.

*Acceptance.* The stage of acceptance is often misunderstood by professionals and parents alike. Acceptance means that the parent can look past the disability and accept the child as the child is. It does not mean that the parent would not change the situation if it were possible but rather that the parents can envision a life for themselves and their child, in spite of the disability.

The use of a sequential paradigm for grief may appear to somewhat reduce the complexity of parental reactions. No parent follows the model exactly, nor do the stages proceed in sequential order. In addition, various "anniversary dates" and events may propel a parent back into a previously resolved stage of grief. Birthdays, starting a new program, the birth of a sibling, and other events may cause the parent to reexperience strong emotions. The purpose of studying the model for grieving and acceptance is to help interventionists become aware of these stages and, thus recognize and understand what may be happening when a parent acts distraught, angry, or depressed. Another stage theory has been suggested by Miller (1994). Those stages include (1) surviving, (2) searching, (3) settling in, and (4) separating (both emotionally and physically) from the child.

### Challenges to the Stage Theory

Although many theorists and practitioners are familiar with and validate the model of grief and acceptance on the part of parents of children who have disabilities, others do not agree with the paradigm nor with the premise that parents often go through a grieving process.

There have been challenges to Kübler-Ross's initial stage theory, including short-comings in the rigid manner in which some have adopted the stages and the limitations of the method used to gather data for establishing stages. Kastenbaum (1986) addresses these issues, including the fact that the "resources, pressures, and characteristics of the immediate environment can also make a tremendous difference" (p. 113).

Berry and Zimmerman (1983) present a revision of the stage model for acceptance on the part of parents of young children who have developmental delays. They state that parents vary tremendously in their approaches to acceptance and that professionals can best help by being good listeners and respecting the struggles that parents endure.

Dyson's (1997) research indicates that although families of children with special needs show higher stress when compared to families with so-called typical children, there are minimal differences in the actual family functioning. Families show resiliency in adapting to the needs of their child with special needs.

Grieving and the grief process often take place within the context of the educational intervention. Professionals are of assistance to parents during this time when they validate the parents' feelings and remain patient and understanding. Using active listening techniques to encourage the parent to verbalize feelings and knowing how and when to make a referral for further support from a counselor or social worker are important skills for the service provider.

## Participation of the Family in Early Intervention: A Partnership

Ideally, the relationship between early interventionists and parents is one of a partnership, with each contributing information and planning together for the benefit of the child (Bricker, 1986). However, this partnership may at times be fraught with difficulties. Several obstacles to forming a partnership include conflicts in values, parental stresses, and the zeal with which interventionists approach working with the child

(Raver, 1991). It is important for parents to decide in what way and to what degree early intervention will be involved in their lives. Parents also need to develop competency in making decisions regarding their child and the early intervention process.

Teachers may expect that all parents would be able to fulfill the role of equal partner in working with their children. Frequently, if parents do not take on this role, interventionists will blame themselves or the parents for failing in their duties (Karr & Landerholm, 1991). It is important for teachers to consider the pressures and stresses that the parents experience and to determine ways that parents might participate in their child's education in a less intense and stressful manner. For example, parents may attend field trips or join support groups. Additionally, it is recommended that parents be given a menu of choices from which they may select activities in which they want to participate. Parents initially may feel comfortable participating in support activities, or they may eventually move to educational program or leadership activities. The mutual feelings of support and understanding between parents and teachers that develop as a result of this type of selective participation enhances the parent-teacher relationship and also benefits the child. However, hasty and intense demand for parental involvement when the parents are not ready may produce a negative result.

One study of parents' perceptions of early intervention services revealed that parents obtained and valued the support from providers (Wehman & Gilkerson, 1999). However, parents in this study requested more home-based services and extended hours, in addition to assistance with their child's intervention program.

## *Working with Parents when Making a Referral for a Child's Assessment*

Early childhood teachers who teach general early childhood classes sometimes are required to plan a conference with parents when the teacher suspects that the child has a developmental delay and would like to make a referral. Abbott and Gold (1991) offer several suggestions for planning this type of meeting. The conference should be especially well planned; the site should be private and comfortable; and sufficient time should be allocated for discussion. They suggest the following steps in preparing for the conference:

1. Collect samples of the child's work.
2. Have dated anecdotal records available that lend support to the position presented to the parents.
3. List the modifications already made for the child in the current program.
4. List the names of other professionals who have assisted in referring the child for additional assistance.
5. Have the names, addresses, and telephone numbers of local agencies for referral. Also, consult Child Find and the local education agency (school) that provide diagnostic and/or counseling services. Have available the names of three or more referrals for psychologists whose reputation is known to the staff if the parents request a private psychologist.

*It is highly desirable to include parents and extended family members in all aspects of the assessment and intervention.*

During the conference, it is important that the teacher start the meeting by asking the parents how the child has been doing at home and if there have been any changes in behavior. Teachers should be prepared for strong emotional responses from the parents. Sometimes, there are tears or parents become angry. It is helpful for the teacher to listen to the parents' concerns by using active listening techniques and to stress the tentative nature of the concern. The referring teacher should be prepared to provide information to the professionals who will be conducting the assessment.

In addition, it is useful for teachers to share checklists with parents that depict a continuum of typical development and behavior to use as a guide for anticipatory guidance. This approach also is useful so that parents are able to compare their child's developmental level with that of typical children.

## Empowering and Enabling Families

Empowering families means giving the family a real stake in the decision-making and leadership roles in their child's life. The concept of empowerment and enablement of families stems from earlier social competency models in which clients seeking therapy are encouraged to take an active role as to whether they wanted treatment and then participate in the decision-making process of selecting among various possibilities. Figure 3.2 provides guidelines for early interventionists and related services personnel (help givers) to encourage the empowerment of families.

One model that seeks to empower the family in early intervention is the Family Enablement Project (Dunst, Trivette, & Deal, 1994). This empowerment model is fluid, the early interventionists continually evaluate and operationalize the model every time they interact with the family. In this model, the empowerment process encompasses four steps:

1. Families identify their needs and aspirations.
2. The family system is examined to determine how the family copes with life events and what aspects of the family system are operating well.
3. The personal social network of the family is analyzed to identify existing and potential sources of aid and assistance that may be mobilized to achieve the identified needs and aspirations.
4. Professionals help the family achieve their identified goals.

The Family Enablement Project model has been widely disseminated through federal training and technical assistance given to states and early intervention programs.

---

**FIGURE 3.2** *Guidelines for Encouraging Family Empowerment*

Help for encouraging family empowerment is

- most useful when the help giver is positive and proactive.
- more likely to be favorably received if the help giver offers help rather than waits for it to be requested.
- more effective when the help giver allows the locus of decision making to rest clearly with the help seeker.
- more effective if the aid and assistance provided by the help giver are normative and do not infer deviance or undue variation.
- maximally effective when the aid and assistance provided by the help giver are congruent with the help seeker's appraisal of his or her problem or need.
- most likely to be favorably received when the response costs of seeking and accepting help do not outweigh the benefits.
- more likely to be favorably received if it can be reciprocated and the possibility of "repaying"

the help giver is sanctioned and approved but not expected.

- more likely to be beneficial if the help seeker experiences immediate success in solving a problem or meeting a need.
- more effective if the help giver promotes the family's use of natural support networks and neither replaces them nor supplants them with professional networks.
- more likely to promote positive functioning when the help giver conveys a sense of cooperation and joint responsibility (partnership) for meeting needs and solving problems.
- most likely to be beneficial if the help giver promotes the help seeker's acquisition of effective behaviors that decrease the need for help.
- more likely to be beneficial if the help seeker perceives improvement and sees him or herself as the responsible agent for producing change.

---

*Source:* Adapted from Dunst, Trivette, and Deal (1988), pp. 94–98.

The evaluation of this project showed that users reported that multiple training opportunities were more effective than brief one- or two-day workshops. More information about the project and a quarterly newsletter may be obtained by contacting the Family, Infant and Preschool Program, Western Carolina Center, 300 Enola Road, Morganton, NC 28655, (704) 433-2877.

Additional methods for assisting parents include videotaping parents as they interact with their children. Erickson and Kurz-Reimer (1999) videotaped parents with their children and then provided opportunities for guided viewing. They found that this system enhanced parental sensitivity to their child and assisted parents in understanding their child as a unique human being with special characteristics and feelings.

In an expansion of Bronfenbrenner's (1979) ecological model, Turnbull, Turbiville, and Turnbull (2000) present the collective empowerment model, which they state surpasses a singular family focus. Their emphasis is on the context in which families and professionals collaborate.

## Informal Sources of Support

Families need informal support as well as professional support. When intervention consists of only the provision of a specific professional therapeutic or educational treatment, it is very limiting and constricted. It is important for early interventionists to recognize the potential positive effects of informal support.

Research shows that the effects of informal support are so great that these influences cannot be ignored as a major form of intervention. According to Dunst, Trivette, and Deal (1988), "To the extent possible, family needs should be met by promoting the use of informal rather than formal support sources" (p. 32). Potential sources of informal support include spouses, in-laws, co-workers, social organizations, and friends and neighbors. In addition, churches and synagogues provide families with social/emotional and direct support in the form of counseling and child-care during services.

In their study of urban African American single mothers, Olson and Esdaile (2000) indicated that it is essential for practitioners to understand the context in which mothering occurs. They found that when mothers' needs for social support are addressed, mothers are better able to participate in meaningful and effective interventions for their children.

## Assistance through Family Support Programs

Basic to family resource and support programs is the building of trust and caring relationships between several groups: staff and participants, participants and participants, and the program and its surrounding community. Weissbourd (1993, p. 409) identifies five principles that help effect this type of trust and collaboration:

1. Collaboration and shared decision making between professionals and parents
2. Cooperative relationships and linkages with community institutions and organizations
3. Nurturance and facilitation of peer support networks

4. Designing programs to meet the needs of parents and to enhance family and individual strengths
5. Planning programs to ensure sensitivity and relevance to the values and culture of the families served

The process of developing family programs raises many questions. The resolution of these questions should reflect a deep commitment to the beliefs that healthy families are essential to a healthy society and that good programs make a difference in the lives of children and families (Weissbourd, 1993).

# Special Issues

This section discusses several key issues related to families: abuse and neglect, ethical dilemmas, divorce and custody issues, serving culturally diverse families, fathers, siblings, respite care, and organizations and support groups for families.

## Abuse and Neglect

Instances of abuse and neglect of young children have increased over the past decade (Lowenthal, 2001). In 1990, the Children's Defense Fund estimated that at least 2.2 million children are abused each year, which is a 48 percent increase in the last five years alone (Zigler, Hopper, & Hall, 1993).

Infants and toddlers represent a disproportionately large percentage of abused children. Whipple (1999) cites national statistics showing that of the 1,046 children who died as a result of abuse in 1996, 77 percent were under 5 years old. Premature and low-birth-weight infants, irritable and colicky infants, and young children with special needs appear to be particularly vulnerable (Devlin & Reynolds, 1994). Although there is no way to predict which parents will abuse their children, there is a strong link between family stress and child abuse (Zigler et al., 1993).

The definition of abuse is clear and definitive. Lowenthal's (2001) book on child abuse cites the definition of child abuse from federal law (PL 93-247). Child abuse is

> the physical or mental injury, sexual abuse, negligent treatment, or maltreatment of a child under the age of eighteen by a person who is responsible for the child's welfare under circumstances which indicate the child's health or welfare is harmed or threatened thereby. (p. 1)

Early interventionists are in a unique position to identify abuse in young children since they often work with entire families and have a trusting relationship with the children they serve. Teachers, early interventionists working with young children, and other professionals may have to deal with instances of suspected or actual abuse. The law is clear about who must report instances of suspected abuse (Lowenthal, 2001). Teachers and early interventionists and related services personnel are mandated reporters and therefore must report cases of suspected abuse. However, reporting suspected abuse can be an emotionally difficult experience, both for the mandated reporter and for the family. The identification of possible child maltreatment requires reporting the suspected abuse, and procedures for reporting may be unclear in some settings. A lack of structured methods for dealing with suspected abuse may leave the early interventionist confused and anxious.

***Dealing with Suspected Abuse.***    In all instances of suspected abuse, a report should be made to the appropriate agency, as required under law. If a situation arises for which it becomes necessary to report suspected abuse, interventionists are encouraged to confer with appropriate persons in their agency or school. Counselors and social workers may be of assistance, and administrators need to be advised that suspected abuse is going to be reported. Interventionists differ on the issue of whether parents should be informed by teachers or staff that suspected abuse has been or will be reported.

Supportive family interventions have been effective in lowering instances of child abuse in targeted populations. In order to help children who are abused, teachers need to try to continue to support and work with the family as they seek help. In order to foster this type of cooperative relationship, the school or facility should inform families at the start of the year that teachers and related services personnel are mandated to report instances of suspected abuse.

With this information presented early in the program, parents may not feel quite as betrayed by the interventionist if reporting becomes necessary. Most importantly for the child, the parent then may have access to school or agency social workers and psychologists to attempt to resolve the issues that led to the abuse. Researchers have provided suggestions for breaking the cycle of abuse when the parents participate in treatment (Lutzker & Newman, cited in Turnbull & Turnbull, 1997).

Some researchers advise caution once suspected abuse has been reported. Cook, Tessier, and Klein (1992) suggest that interventionists should cease making home visits while the parent is under investigation for abuse. This is seen as a safety precaution for both the parents and the interventionist. They also set forth some guidelines for working with maltreated children. Understanding that the maltreated child needs a predictable and safe environment, they suggest that the child may need a more structured program with a primary provider available to the child on a daily basis in the early intervention center.

***Reporting Suspected Abuse: Immunity for Professionals.***    Each state differs in the regulations, reporting procedures, and agencies to which child abuse must be reported. However, reporting suspected child abuse is mandated in every state. Copies of each state's law may be obtained from law enforcement agencies, the county attorney's office, or a regional office of child development. Berns (1993) indicates that individuals who report abuse in good faith are granted immunity from civil and criminal court action, such as lawsuits, even if the report, when investigated, turns out to be erroneous.

The National Child Abuse Hotline number is (800) 422-4453. It is in operation 24 hours a day, seven days a week. The hotline is answered by professional counselors and trained volunteers who can help in crisis situations and refer individuals to the local agencies in their states that deal with child abuse. Children themselves may call the hotline for help. The Child Abuse Hotline will also provide interventionists with materials and incidence figures on child abuse.

***The Effects of Abuse.*** The effects of abuse may be both intense and long lasting. According to Lowenthal (1999), maltreated children's brains are attuned to danger. These children remain vigilant and at great risk for emotional, behavioral, learning, and physical disabilities. Another implication for risk developing from early abuse is in the area of self-esteem. Children learn self-esteem from their interactions with their parents. Romeo (2000) finds that maltreated children develop feelings of being unwanted and unloved, as opposed to children who grew up in loving, nonabusive homes. Those from loving homes had parents who conveyed that their children were good and valued for themselves.

## Ethical Dilemmas

Interventionists often are faced with situations in which they must decide what is not only the appropriate thing to do under the law but also the right thing to do. In order to make "reasoned, articulated, moral judgements" (Turnbull & Turnbull, 1990, p. 385), interventionists need to consider ethics and morals.

*Morals* involve right and wrong behavior. *Ethics* is the science of thinking about and studying morals. In their book, Turnbull and Turnbull (1990) devote an entire chapter to the discussion of moral and ethical issues. They discuss sources of general moral principles and provide a series of open-ended vignettes for consideration and discussion. They also offer a method for applying an analytical approach to ethical decision making, which includes (1) stating the problem, (2) stating the facts and distinguishing them from moral judgments, (3) stating the ethical issue, (4) considering the alternatives to the considered intervention, and (5) repeating the issue: When is a proposed or alternative intervention moral? Finally, they suggest ways to apply professional and philosophical principles.

Ethical guidelines for teachers and early interventionists are suggested by Reamer (1990) and Bailey and Wolery (1992). These ethical guidelines include an analysis of aspects of service delivery when the well-being of the family is threatened or in instances when the child's right to basic well-being is threatened. The rights of individuals to make crucial decisions for themselves, once they have received information, is another consideration (Reamer, 1990).

In order to obtain guidance on ethics, professionals are referred to the codes of ethics adopted by their individual professional organizations: for special educators, the Council for Exceptional Children; for psychologists, the Ethics Code from the American Psychological Association; and for social workers, the ethical code of the National Association of Social Workers.

## Divorce and Custody Issues

The structure of the American family is constantly changing. The number of children living with both parents declined from 88 percent in 1960 to 68 percent in 1998 (*Fact Sheet: Families and the Workplace*, 2002). Some 23 percent of children under age 18 live with their mothers only, and 4 percent live with their fathers only. Thus, over 25 percent of children in this country live with a single parent. The stereotype of the typical family with a mother, father, and two children, with mother at home all day, has also undergone revision. At present, fewer than 15 percent of American families fit this stereotype of the family (Bukato & Daehler, 1992).

It is important for early interventionists and teachers to understand the implications of divorce among families they serve. Paramount for helping the child is to avoid taking sides when working with parents, although this may be difficult, since there is often much blaming by both sides (Hendrick, 1984). One useful reference for both parents and interventionists is *Helping Your Kids Cope with Divorce: The Sandcastles Way* by Neuman (1998). This book provides activities and suggestions for parents in co-parenting, and illustrates divorce through the eyes of children of various ages.

Another difficult issue in divorce situations is that of custody. Under some custody arrangements, either parent may serve as the child's guardian when decisions are made regarding services and the IEP. However, the terms *joint legal custody*, *joint physical custody*, and *shared custody* vary in meaning. Family law is the area that includes custody and visitation issues. The different definitions of *custody* vary on a state-by-state basis (Fisher & Lays, 1995). Because of differences in meaning of *custody*, it is wise for early childhood teachers to clarify which parent(s) is (are) responsible for educational and medical decisions and to obtain a written, signed list of individuals who may pick up the child from school or who may be contacted should problems or questions arise.

There is also a need for special educators to develop a sensitivity toward single-parent families. On one hand, a divorce may mean that the child loses almost all contact with one parent or may lose his or her residence within the community and close friends due to a move. However, in some cases, finalizing a divorce may produce a more stable and caring environment for the child. Divorce is stressful for all involved, and the most important predictive factor appears to be the way parents are able to communicate and manage the separation and divorce. Koplow (1996) offers suggestions on helping preschool children heal through therapeutic techniques and open-ended play situations.

## Serving Culturally Diverse Families

Demographic studies consistently show that the United States is becoming a richer mix of cultures. The increase in multicultural diversity is especially reflected among young children with special educational needs (Blue-Manning, Turnbull, & Pereira, 2000).

It is estimated that by the year 2010, nearly one-quarter of all children in the United States will be from racial or linguistic minorities. Studies of children in poverty show that the children's poverty rates for African American children is over twice that for Caucasians. Poverty rates for Latino American families fall between the two groups (Edmonds, Martinson, & Goldberg, 1990).

Knowing about the cultural mores and background of children in early intervention programs permits professionals to be aware of potential interactional differences between themselves and the families they serve and to respond in an appropriate and supportive manner. Interventionists need to allow families to take the lead in expressing how their culture is manifested within their family. For example, the use of group action planning may be an effective support for Hispanic American families of children with special needs (Blue-Manning, Turnbull, & Pereira, 2000).

Cultural sensitivity implies a refusal to assign values—such as better or worse more or less intelligent, right or wrong—to cultural differences and similarities (Anderson & Fenichel, 1989; Bailey, Skinner, Rodriguez, Gut, & Correa, 1999; Singh, 2000). "Interventionists must accept that there is no entity such as *the* Native American family or *the* African American family" (Raver, 1991, p. 336). Cultural stereotypes are often counterproductive when interacting with families. As noted previously, all families should be treated individually, whatever their culture.

Families from various cultures display various parenting attitudes. Jambunathan, Burts, and Pierce (2000) provide guidelines for understanding the following cultural approaches to parenting: European American, African American, Hispanic American, Asian American, and Asian Indian American. The results of the study suggested that there are cultural variations in the parenting attitudes of mothers involved in the study and that educators keep in mind the diverse nature of the parenting process when working with families from various cultures. Bennett and Grimley (2001) stress the importance of cultural awareness in considering parenting issues in the context of the global community. In addition to concerns about parenting styles, Marshall (2000) encouraged all professionals who work with children who have language and/or speech difficulties to increase their cultural awareness in order to best provide intervention for young children.

The following suggestions are innovative approaches for serving culturally diverse families (Cook et al., 1992; Edmonds et al., 1990):

- Translate materials and public service announcements into languages appropriate to the community served.
- Use cable television to target culturally diverse families;
- Involve community cultural groups in planning public awareness activities.

Interventionists also need to understand that it takes a long time to establish trust in communities that have populations that are culturally and linguistically different from the service provider. Sometimes, early intervention, which empowers the family, actually offers options for resources to the family and may bear little resemblance to "early intervention" as it is traditionally presented. According to Rao (2000), it is essential for early interventionists to avoid viewing families from different cultures as being "at risk." This attitude has been found to be detrimental to parental participation. Rao also finds that families do not necessarily want a service provider from their culture, but want a genuine sense of caring displayed to them.

It may be necessary to establish systems of service delivery that are less alienating to some families. From the perspective of serving a community, it may be necessary to ask community groups what their needs are before establishing services.

Most importantly, agencies must conduct needs assessments in the native languages of the families served in order to determine the families' needs. Then programs must be shaped to meet family needs rather than fit the families into existing programs that may not meet their needs. In addition to these suggestions, it may be comfortable for families to interact with a professional from their own culture.

Colleges and universities need to address the dearth of minority providers and minority professionals in leadership roles (Edmonds et al., 1990). Training programs should recruit people from diverse backgrounds to be professionals and paraprofessionals in all parts of the service system. Personnel preparation programs also need to train service providers in methods of working with families from a variety of cultures. The suggestion has also been made that preparation needs to move beyond the "cultural awareness" phase, and that actual experience in diverse communities is necessary for professionals in training.

## Poverty and Families

Early childhood professionals should be aware of the linkage between poverty and disabling conditions (Edmonds et al., 1990). Potential prenatal causes of disabilities include poor maternal nutrition, low birth weight, and substance abuse. Postnatally, children who are poor are at increased risk for accidental injury, high lead levels, and the AIDS virus.

The data show that individuals who live in poverty for a period of time frequently lack access to health care and are deprived of preventive medicine. In addition, many impoverished preschool children live with only one parent, usually the mother. Over half of all female-headed families with preschool children are considered *poor*. The likelihood of child support is highest when the mother is legally divorced, is white, or has a college degree. Child support payments are lowest for less-educated, never-married, and minority women (Edmonds et al., 1990).

What is the impact of these data for the early interventionist? Besides the need for knowledge about cultural diversity, interventionists need to be sensitive to the poverty that may accompany persons from either the dominant or culturally and linguistically diverse populations. It is also important to realize that the interventionist's traditional communication and intervention techniques may not be effective when working with families from different cultures.

## Fathers

Much of the literature on working with families of young children who have special needs relates specifically to the mother of the young child. However, there has been increasing interest in the roles fathers play in their children's development and the effects of their interactions with infants and young children. In a review of the literature on father-infant dyads with typically developing infants, Crockenberg, Lyons-Ruth, and Dickstein (1993) state that most of the literature regarding father-infant interaction measured only the *amount* of time spent with the infant rather than the *variations* in father-infant interactions. They determined that fathers typically spent a larger percentage of time with their child engaged in play activities than mothers and that the quality of the father-infant play was primarily characterized by physical movement and associated with increased infant arousal.

How do these findings relate to the father–child interactions when the child has developmental delays? Seligman and Darling (1989) indicate that fathers of children

*Fathers play an important role in their children's development.*

with disabilities tend to be less emotional about the child's disability than mothers are. The fathers' concerns may focus around longer-term issues and the need for economic security. Fathers also benefit from support and self-help groups in which they are encouraged to express and explore their feelings.

Based on their extensive experience in conducting groups for fathers, Meyer, Vadasy, Fewell, and Schell (1985) indicate the value of forming groups for fathers. These authors have produced a poignant videotape that depicts the emotions and daily concerns of fathers of young children with developmental delays: *Special Dads, Special Kids* by Family Support Program, Merrywood School, 16120 N.E. Eighth Street, Bellevue, WA, (206) 747-4004.

Interventionists in training need to consider and validate the role of the father in the individualized education program (IEP) or the individualized family service plan (IFSP). If the intervention is based on *family* involvement and a partnership with the parents, the father needs to be included as much as possible. Besides support groups for dads, professionals can include the father in other ways. If the timing of conferences and IEPs or IFSPs are scheduled so that the father is able to attend, this enhances his participation. In addition, telephone calls may be made when the father is home, and his name should be included on all communications from the school or agency. In cases of divorce, separation, or an unmarried mother, professionals should first determine the legal aspects of any custody arrangements. Then they may make efforts to invite and include the father to participate and become involved in his child's intervention, unless the mother or parent with sole custody does not approve of his attendance. Another method for including fathers is to videotape intervention sessions so that fathers may view them at home.

Crockenberg and colleagues (1993) stress the need for clinical practice and intervention so that families can be informed by research results as well as by theory. They suggest that future research should include the concept that investigators need to become attuned to the probability that fathers who are highly involved in their children's care contribute in significant ways to the children's current functioning as well as to their long-term development.

## Siblings

The roles and contributions of mothers and fathers when there is a child with developmental delays in the family are very important. However, the siblings of a child who has developmental delays are often neglected. Seligman and Darling (1989) note that sibling relationships are usually the longest and most enduring of family relationships. Siblings may go through similar grief stages as their parents do, alternately feeling angry and upset with their brother or sister and experiencing sad feelings that their sibling has a disability. They may feel simultaneously embarrassed about the disability and yet jealous of the attention paid to the child who has the developmental delay. In addition, some siblings report feeling guilty about any negative feelings they might have regarding their sibling who has special needs. Miller (1994) finds that brother/sister relationships in typical families aren't always amicable, and that children with special needs and their siblings may have to make adaptations.

Denier (1993) states that siblings want and need accurate information, particularly as to whether the disability is communicable, how to disclose the disability to their friends, and opportunities for open and frank discussion about the disability. If parents require that the sibling provide extensive care for the child who has disabilities, it can often result in frustration and resentment. It is important that parents recognize that children need time to be children and develop peer relationships. Further, it is important for the sibling to be able to openly ask questions and discuss feelings and anxieties with parents and other family members.

Meyer, Vadasy, and Fewell (1981) have written a comprehensive book for siblings entitled *Living with a Brother or Sister with Special Needs: A Book for Sibs*. In this book, they review their experiences in conducting sibling support groups and speak directly to the issues that trouble children: "Why did this happen?" "Will I catch it?" and "What happens if mom and dad die?" The book, which is clearly written in a style that children can understand, deals directly with the causes and types of disabilities as well as issues of guilt, jealousy, and worry.

Support groups for siblings offer tremendous potential for reducing stress and are sometimes developed locally. For example, a sibling support group in Chicago is located at the Illinois Masonic Hospital. They have organized a regular support group, meetings, picnics, and outings, and they publish a newsletter. Siblings may also avail themselves of the services and referrals provided by the Sibling Information Network. The network may be reached at Sibling Information Network, School of Education, Box U-64, The University of Connecticut, Storrs, CT 06268.

### Respite Care

Families who have a child with special needs often require services to support them in caring for their child and reducing stress within the family. Chan and Sigafoos (2000) review the use of respite care in developmental disabilities services. *Respite care* may be defined as "the use of an organized service that is designed to provide temporary relief from the caretaking responsibilities associated with parenting a child with a developmental disability" (p. 28). Chan and Sigafoos (2000) analyze the severity of disability, level of care needed, and the presence and persistence of problem behaviors as critical factors in the use of respite care. They find that the families' perceived level of stress and absence of other support systems contribute to their stress.

### National Organizations and Support Groups for Families

There are a number of organizations and professional groups dedicated to supporting families. These groups provide group support meetings, group counseling, advice to parents, and serve as advocates for the child and family. A listing of family support groups appears in Appendix B.

## Summary

- It is essential that parents and families be involved in the planning and implementation of early intervention services for their child. Intervention plans for children must be designed and implemented within the family context. From the development of the individualized education program (IEP) and the individualized family service plan (IFSP), through implementation and the entire intervention process, family members need to be consulted and involved in decision making.
- Concepts about the composition of the family unit are changing. Interventionists must realize that there are many different compositions of the family unit today. The family should participate in the early intervention program as partners with professionals.
- PL 99-457 recognizes the importance of the family in all aspects of early childhood intervention. Several features of the law require consideration of the family.
- A family systems perspective highlights the fact that what happens to one member of the family affects all of the other family members. A family systems model emphasizes the interrelations among all family members.
- Assessment of the family involves a collaborative sharing of information between the family and professionals that can help in planning the child's intervention.

Part C of PL 105-17 is for children, birth to age 3, and is most specific about the need for inclusion of the family in assessment.

- Family members often experience strong feelings about the child's disability. These intense emotions are normal when families have to adjust to the birth or later acknowledgment of a child who has developmental delays.
- In some instances, interventionists will have to report abuse of young children. Early interventionists are mandated reporters for suspected abuse. Guidelines for reporting and suggestions for working with these families are presented.
- More families in the United States represent culturally diverse populations. Suggestions for working with families from diverse cultural backgrounds are given.
- The needs and potential contributions of fathers and siblings are often neglected. It is important to include fathers and siblings in planning interventions.

## Key Terms

abuse and neglect
culturally diverse families
custody issues
empowering families
enabling families
ethical dilemmas
family systems

IEP
IFSP
informal family support programs
maltreated children
respite care
stages of acceptance
systems analysis

# 4

## *Assessment and Evaluation of Young Children*

## Chapter Outline _____

**Purposes of Assessment**
    Methods for Obtaining Assessment
       Information
    An Ecological Perspective

**Eligibility for Special Services**
    Young Children with Disabilities
    Children at Risk

**Stages of the Assessment Process**
    Stage 1: Child-Find/Case Finding
    Stage 2: Developmental Screening
    Stage 3: Diagnosis
    Stage 4: Individualized Planning of Programs
       and Interventions
    Stage 5: Performance Monitoring
    Stage 6: Program Evaluation

**Types of Assessment Instruments**
    Tests

**Alternative Assessment Methods**
    Observation
    Checklists and Rating Scales
    Assessment of Multiple Intelligences
    Assessment of Emotional Intelligence
    Play-Based Assessment
    Dynamic Assessment
    Performance and Authentic Assessment
    Judgment-Based Assessment
    Family Assessment

**Special Considerations for Assessing Young Children**
    Special Issues in Testing Preschoolers
    Nondiscriminatory Assessment
    Development of Rapport in Assessment

*A*ssessment is the process of collecting information about a child for the purpose of making critical decisions concerning the youngster. To understand the parameters of assessment, this chapter discusses the ecological view of assessment, determining the child's eligibility for special services, and the stages of the assessment process. Other topics include how assessment leads to intervention, types of tests, and alternate assessment methods. The chapter also discusses family involvement and special considerations for testing young children. Descriptive information about specific tests and assessment instruments are included in Appendix A.

## Purposes of Assessment

The major purposes of assessing preschool children with special needs are (1) to gather information about the child that will facilitate the determination of the child's eligibility for special services and (2) to plan intervention that will assist the child. The assessment information shows whether problems exist, the child's strengths and weaknesses, and how to deal with the concerns.

### Methods for Obtaining Assessment Information

A number of methods for obtaining assessment information are used, including testing, interviewing, observing children, and working with their families. Family members

## *Early Childhood Snapshot*  ASSESSMENT

The following illustrates the assessment process. The assessment in this case uses formal standardized and criterion-referenced instruments as well as observations, interviews, checklists, and play-based assessment. In this case, the family members work with the examiner and other members of the transdisciplinary team to develop an informal evaluation of family resources and concerns. This case was conducted in a local agency, but the names and identifiable information have been changed to protect the confidentiality of the child and the family.

> Name of Child: Juan Lopez
> Address: 780 Forest Street
> Telephone: 462-3550
> Chronological Age: 5 years, 0 months
> Sex: Male
> Parent(s) Names: Maria Lopez

Inventory of Early Development–Revised, the Preschool Language Scale (PLS), the Hawaii Early Learning Profile (HELP, edition for 3- to 6-year-olds), Transdisciplinary Plan-Based (TPBA)—Selected Social-Emotional Guidelines.

### Reason for Referral

Maria Lopez is a single mother, and Juan is her only child. Juan was eligible for the local Head Start program. Ms. Lopez enrolled her son because she felt that he should be with peers and have the stimulation of an inclusive program. She also was concerned with Juan's behavioral difficulties and wanted him to be evaluated by the transdisciplinary team at the Head Start center. Ms. Lopez reported that Juan was a behavior problem in the home, exhibited temper tantrums, and was often aggressive. The mother also reported that he didn't eat well and was uncooperative in dressing. Juan is currently attending the Head Start center 5 days a week. He has since experienced chronic ear infections, pneumonia, and croup. It has also been found that he has an immature esophagus. He is presently being treated for asthma.

### Attitude toward Testing

Juan was a talkative boy who smiled or giggled frequently during the formal testing. When formal tests were to be administered, Juan came willingly with the examiner to the child-sized table and chair in the hallway away from the classrooms. During the initial period of time that he was being tested, he gave his full attention to the examiner. Most of the time he was easily redirected back to the testing if he became distracted. However, ofter after 10 or 15 minutes had passed, he would become restless and his performance would change dramatically. The weather was extremely hot during the times that Juan was tested, which may partially account for the short attention span. Therefore, Juan was tested during several short time periods. In addition, Juan was informally evaluated through observation in the natural settings of his classroom and playground.

### Psychoeducational Assessment

The information contained within this report was obtained through the following methods: interviews with Juan's mother and other professionals on the early intervention team, examiner's observations, TPBA—Selected Social-Emotional Guidelines, the Brigance Inventory for Early Development–Revised (Brigance), Preschool Language Scale–3 (PLS), and the Hawaii Early Learning Profile (HELP), edition for 3- to 6-year-olds.

### Gross Motor

Juan enjoys gross motor activities and was observed on the playground performing at approximately the 5-year age level on the Brigance except for two tasks. These were being unable to hop on his non-preferred foot and throwing a playground ball and tennis ball. He could catch a playground ball with both hands and throw it approximately a distance of 13 feet, which is at the 4-year-old level. Overall, Juan appeared confident when performing gross motor activities and had appropriate strength and agility. The teacher and occupational therapist observed him running down the stairs, jumping off

*(continued)*

## ASSESSMENT    Continued

steps, and climbing playground equipment with good coordination skills.

### Fine Motor

According to Brigance, Juan was at age level in performing fine motor tasks except in the area of copying designs. He was not able to copy designs, such as the cross, square, and triangle. Juan was very restless at the time he was asked to cut shapes with scissors and when drawing a person. Both of these tasks were performed inappropriately. However, when observed in the classroom by the teacher, he could cut circles with scissors at the 5-0 level and made a representational drawing at approximately the 6-0 level. The teacher and the examiner observed that Juan could successfully complete fine motor activities, such as coloring and working on a pegboard puzzle, in the preschool class.

### Personal-Social/Self-Help Skills

Juan has age-appropriate adaptive behaviors according to the HELP checklist. His adaptive behavior is at approximately the 4-7 to 5-0 age level. His teacher reports that Juan was able to adapt to changes in his environment and demonstrated appropriate behaviors at group times (circle time, music, etc.). He exhibited responsible behavior in the classroom by sitting quietly to listen to a story and cleaning up after himself. He can initiate and complete a task assigned to him. On a number of occasions, the examiner observed Juan willingly assisting his peers. However, Juan also resorted to physical means (hitting) within active play with others. He did display age-appropriate behaviors in his interpersonal relationships by sharing toys and comforting a playmate in distress. From other observations, Juan has the ability to undress and dress himself, independently go to the bathroom, and eat.

### Language-Receptive

On the PLS, Juan was able to perform at the 5-year, 10-month level in receptive language. He had no difficulty comprehending left from right, body parts, animal parts, and directional commands. He could successfully repeat taps, count blocks, and add numbers to five. He was not able to understand action agents, which is a 4.5- to 5-year skill. His auditory comprehension quotient

was 117, which is in the bright average range. On observing Juan at play, the speech and language therapist and the examiner saw him readily respond to teacher requests and understand questions asked by his peers.

### Language-Expressive

Juan also performed at the 5-year, 10.5-month level on the PLS section of expressive language. He was able to comprehend physical needs, the senses, remote events, and morning versus afternoon. He was not able to correctly answer all the questions about opposites at the 4- to 4.5-year level. The articulation of beginning and ending consonant sounds was at the 6-year level. His language quotient for expressive language was 117. His total language quotient was 117 and his language age was 5 years 10.5 months. The speech and language therapist reported that Juan could clearly state his wants and needs in the classroom, was very verbal, and his sentence structure and articulation were age appropriate.

### Cognitive

Juan's cognitive skills were generally well above his chronological age. On the Brigance, he placed in the 5-6 age level for receptive and expressive understanding of body parts. The examiner observed Juan's knowledge of body parts when he successfully played a game called "Simon Says" on the playground. He could name colors at the 7-year level when in the classroom playing a color game called "Candy Land." Juan was able to name design concepts and knew what to do in different situations at the 6-6 age level. He was just at age level for correctly knowing uses of objects. The examiner also noticed that Juan had one-to-one object correspondence when setting the table for a snack.

### Trandisciplinary Play-Based Assessment

Selected observation guidelines of TPBA in the social/emotional area were used in a play-based assessment of Juan. The examiner observed that Juan was able to adjust well to new situations in appropriate ways. For example, when a new child entered the class, Juan often was the first class member to include him or her in his play. Most of the time, he appeared persistent in finishing a challenging task, such as a complex puzzle. If he needed help, he would ask another peer or the teacher. His level of play was cooperative. Often, Juan was a leader in free-play activities and appeared popular with his peers. The only time that he exhibited aggression (hitting) was during the stimulation and excitement of the gross motor activities. However, he stopped the aggression promptly upon teacher request.

## Conclusion

Juan exhibited age-appropriate skills for his chronological age of 5 years. His overall development was consistent with his cognitive abilities and his quality of responses during testing and observation. He functioned like an active 5-year-old despite health problems.

Juan's cognitive ability and expressive language were definite strengths. He clearly articulated despite an immature esophagus. He also functioned above age level in receptive language skills.

Fine motor, self-help, and gross motor skills were developing appropriately for his age. He was slightly below age level in throwing a playground ball and a tennis ball, which may be due to lack of experience with this activity.

Juan's short attention span in the one-to-one situation during testing was not observed in the classroom when playing with peers or working in a group. He could become physically aggressive during gross motor activities but was able to control himself upon a teacher's verbal request.

His likeable personality and adaptability were real assets in how well Juan functioned in his environment.

## Family Resources and Concerns

Juan's mother was concerned about his development. In addition to spending time with Juan, she continues to bring him to the Head Start center. The teacher, with the assistance of the other members of the team, including Juan's mother, focus on the behavior management skills that help him control his impulsive, physical actions. Juan's mother also provides experiences that enrich his cognitive growth. Juan and his mother have a strong resource in Juan's maternal grandmother because of her willingness to baby-sit, do household chores, and have a nurturing relationship with her grandson.

One concern for the family is that Juan have a surrogate father as a male model. There is no contact with his biological father at this time. Ms. Lopez also would like to spend more quality and fun time with her son.

## Recommendations

Juan should continue attending the Head Start center in order for him to maintain age-appropriate skills with peers and adults. This will help him focus on tasks and respond to peers with less aggression during gross motor activities. A suggestion for his mother would be to find regular times during the day in which she and Juan could play together and enjoy each other's company. Another suggestion, which may locate a surrogate father, is to ask interested male members of the extended family, friends, and neighbors if they could spend some time with Juan on a consistent basis.

---

are integral to the assessment process and provide needed sources of information. It is important that the assessment process be useful, sensitive, and equitable (Bagnato & Neisworth, 2000).

## *An Ecological Perspective*

The assessment of preschool children with special needs should be accomplished within an ecological framework. This means that all aspects of the child should be considered. Many ecological factors contribute to the functioning of the total child, including the child's culture and background, life experiences, family, and development in adaptive, cognitive, motor, social/emotional, and language areas (Meisels, 1996).

The ecological perspective also emphasizes that assessment should occur in the child's natural settings. Research indicates that children perform better when the environment and tasks are familiar to them (Losardo & Notari-Sylverson, 2001; Gregory, 1997).

# Eligibility for Special Services

Two groups of young children are considered for eligible for services: (1) children who have identified disabilities and (2) children who are at risk for academic failure.

## Young Children with Disabilities

As noted earlier, the Individuals with Disabilities Education Act (IDEA) of 1997 (PL 105-17) incorporates earlier early childhood laws—namely, PL 99-457 and PL 102-119, which address early childhood issues. These laws have provisions for the assessment of both preschool children with disabilities as well as infants and toddlers with disabilities.

***Preschool Children with Disabilities.***    Preschoolers with disabilities may be eligible for special services. They may be identified under any of the categories of disabilities that are specified in Part B of IDEA-1997. (See the list on page 35.)

In addition, preschool children with disabilities can be eligible under a general designation, such as a delay in one or more of the developmental areas: physical, cognitive, motor, communication, social/emotional, and adaptive. The general term can be called *developmental delay*, *preschool delayed*, or any other term the state wishes to use. These terms provide an option that states can use to avoid labeling a preschool child with a specific disability (McLean, 1996).

***Infants and Toddlers with Disabilities.***    Part C of IDEA-1997 defines eligible infants and toddlers as those in need of early intervention services because they are experiencing developmental delays as measured by appropriate diagnostic instruments and procedures. In identifying infants and toddlers, a general term such as *developmental delay* must be used. Part C provides grants to states to serve eligible infants and toddlers who have special needs.

## Children at Risk

Under Part C, children younger than age 3 who are at risk may be eligible for services. At each state's discretion, young children who are at risk for developmental delays may receive early assessment and intervention (Meisels, 1996).

The term *development delay* refers to children who have deviant patterns or delays in their development, with or without a specific diagnosis or identified problem. The evaluation of these young children should be based on reliable and valid diagnostic instruments. Two approaches have been used for the identification of the delays. One method is to compare the child's performance on a developmental instrument to expected age-appropriate performance. Eligibility is then determined by the percentage of delay. The other approach to determine eligibility for services is to use psychometric data based on the amount of standard deviation from the mean on normed, standardized tests. The amount of deviation required for provision of services ranges from 1 to 2 standard deviations, depending on the criteria set by the state.

Children who have a high probability of experiencing development delays include those who could be considered at established risk, biological risk, and/or environmental risk (McLean, 1996) (see Chapter 2). The classification for young children who are at environmental risk is intended for infants and toddlers whose environments do not provide for their basic needs, ranging from adequate nutrition, clothing, and shelter to psychological and emotional security. Children from these environments could be at risk for mental, social, and emotional disabilities. Their environments could be classified at times as being abusive or neglectful. The children who are raised in these settings may have caregivers who have inadequate resources and/or support systems, are teenagers, may themselves have emotional and/or developmental disabilities, or may have experienced inadequate caregiving and nurturing in their own childhood (Lowenthal, 2001). There is some evidence that three or more risk factors are related to later childhood difficulties (Greenspan & Meisels, 1996; McLean, Bailey, & Wolery, 1996).

In addition, young children from families with low income are eligible for certain programs, such as Head Start or other compensatory programs, such as Follow Through. Eligibility depends on their economic status.

## Stages of the Assessment Process

There are several sequential stages of the assessment process for young children (see Figure 4.1). Each stage serves a unique purpose and requires specific procedures (Cook, Tessier, & Klein, 2000; Meisels, 1996; Snell & Brown, 2000).

### Stage 1: Child-Find/Case Finding

The initial step in assessment is to locate preschoolers who might need intervention programs and services—a process called *child-find*. Locating children in the community who have disabilities or who are at risk for having disabilities is a challenging task. Some parents may be unaware that their child is not developing normally. Other parents do not know that services are available for their child. In some cases, because of denial of a problem or cultural tradition, parents are reluctant to admit that their child has a disability.

The goal of child-find is to encourage individuals and agencies to take a comprehensive look at the young children they encounter in order to refer for screening those preschoolers who may need early intervention. The following questions might help to alert parents to the need for initial screening (Bagnato & Neisworth, 2000):

- Is the child developing normally? Is the preschooler achieving developmental milestones?
- Is the child exhibiting appropriate behaviors for his or her age level?
- Are there any factors in the child's developmental history that would be of concern?
- Are there conditions in the home setting that might negatively influence the cognitive, physical, linguistic, and emotional development of the child? Does the child require more stimulation and nurturance for healthy development?

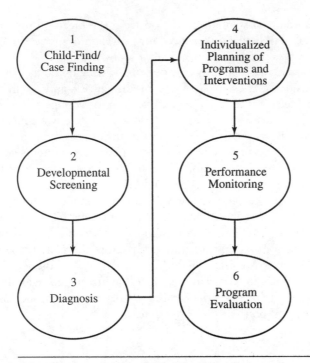

**FIGURE 4.1** *Stages of the Assessment Process*

To locate young children with special needs, the community must clarify the purpose of its child-find program. In some programs, all preschoolers who live in a particular location could be included in the child-find procedure. Other child-find programs target children who are at risk for specific disabilities or who have already demonstrated development delays. Many different strategies, such as the following (Cohen & Spenciner, 1998; McLean, Bailey, & Wolery, 1996; Miller & McNulty, 1996), are used to locate young children in the community who may need special services:

1. *Build community awareness.* Efforts include educating the public about the importance of early identification, alerting people about the services available, and enlisting the help of public agencies and organizations in making referrals.
2. *Set up a system for referral and eliciting referrals.* Strategies involve initiating communication with agencies or individuals who are in contact with young children and encouraging appropriate referrals.
3. *Canvass the community for children who need screening.* Activities involve conducting a systematic survey of young children from a specific geographic area in order to locate those who may need screening.
4. *Maintain local publicity and contacts with sources of referral.* This means keeping the network of agencies and individuals informed about the system for screening.
5. *Use tracking programs.* This means monitoring the development of children who may be at risk but are not eligible for early intervention services.

## Stage 2: Developmental Screening

Developmental screening is a relatively quick way to survey a group of children to detect those who may indicate a developmental difficulty. Screening information is intended to answer the question: Is there a possibility that this child has a problem? The results of the developmental screening assessment are not intended to be used for diagnostic purposes, placement decisions, or providing labels of disabilities. Recommended guidelines for developmental screenings are summarized in Figure 4.2.

The tests used for developmental screening of large groups of children should be brief, inexpensive, and have an objective scoring system. In addition, screening tests must be nondiscriminatory and they should be as reliable and valid as possible (Meisels, 1996). Some selected examples of frequently used preschool screening instruments are listed in Appendix A.

Two possible errors can occur in the screening process: false positives and false negatives. *False positives* identify children as needing intervention when later it is discovered they are functioning within the normal range. *False negatives* fail to identify youngsters who need further diagnosis because they actually have developmental delays. Screenings that result in many false negatives lead to the underidentification of children who need services and intervention. Screenings that result in too many false

---

**FIGURE 4.2** *Recommended Guidelines for Developmentally Appropriate Screening*

1. Screening should be viewed as part of the intervention and not only as a means of identification.

2. Instruments intended for screening should only be used for their specified purposes.

3. Screening requires multiple sources of information.

4. Developmental screening should take place periodically. Revaluation should be conducted at regular intervals.

5. Screening should be viewed as only one way to more in-depth assessment. Failure to qualify for services based on a single source of screening information should not become a barrier to further assessment for intervention if other risk factors are present.

6. Screening procedures should be valid and reliable.

7. Family members should an essential part of the screening process. Information provided by family members is necessary for determining whether to initiate more in depth assessment and for designing appropriate intervention plans. Parents should give their informed consent at each step of the screening and assessment process.

8. During screening of strengths and needs, the more familiar the tasks and the setting are to the child and the child's family, the more likely it is that the results will be valid.

9. All screening tests and methods must be culturally sensitive.

10. Comprehensive training is needed by personnel who screen young children.

---

*Source:* Adapted from Meisels and Provence (1989). Reprinted with permission.

positives identify the wrong children and may take time and resources away from the diagnosis of children who do need further assessment (Cohen & Spenciner, 1994; McLean, Baily, & Wolery, 1996).

When communities provide screenings to identify children with disabilities and children who may be at risk, it is important to give families information about the purposes for screening; to give them options to participate if they desire in the screening program; to inform them about the results of screening; and, if necessary, to explain the next step in the assessment process. It is essential to regard information given by the family about their child as valid and useful in the screening process (Henderson & Meisels, 1994). Once children are identified as having potential problems through the screening process, there should be a follow-up on these youngsters, so children will receive the necessary services. The follow-up process helps minimize false positives and negatives (Bondurant-Utz, 1994).

## Stage 3: Diagnosis

Diagnosis is the next step of assessment and a more intensive procedure than screening. A diagnosis is conducted to determine the nature of the child's problem(s). Observation, interview, case history, informal tests, and standardized tests may be used to obtain information. However, standardized tests should be used with a great deal of caution in the diagnosis of young children, as these instruments often sample limited skills in contrived situations (Wesson, 2001). The Division for Early Childhood (DEC) (2000) recommends that trained professionals choose only norm-referenced tests that are appropriately reliable, valid, and normed with children who are similar to those being tested. The diagnosis should provide information about the severity of the problem and the child's strengths as well as difficulties. This diagnostic information becomes the basis for determining eligibility for special education and services (Wolery, 1996).

The purpose of screening is to ascertain which children may have difficulties; the purpose of diagnosis is to answer questions about the problem and types of intervention that will help this child. To answer such questions, in-depth testing, informed clinical judgment, and information gathered by an interdisciplinary team—including the family—are needed (Brown & Seklemian, 1993; Campbell & Bailey, 1991; Meisels, 1996).

For example, the developmental screening results may indicate that the child performs poorly in language. The diagnosis, however, would provide more in-depth information about the child's language problem. The speech and language clinician may conduct a comprehensive examination and observation of the child's language development in the preschool setting. A specialist in hearing, such as an audiologist or an otologist, may conduct further audiological testing to determine if there is a hearing loss that is responsible for the language delay. A psychologist may evaluate the child to determine how the developmental status of the preschooler may contribute to the language difficulty. The family will be interviewed to determine the child's previous history, language performance at home, and the language that the family uses in their home.

To use an ecological framework in the diagnostic process, it is important to include information from multiple sources, such as teachers, day-care personnel, and caregivers, along with test results. It is also essential to include the child's family on the diagnostic team because the family provides unique and valuable information about the child's functioning in a variety of developmental areas (DEC, 2000). Knowledge of the nature and severity of the dysfunction will assist in planning intervention. Both NAEYC (Bredekamp & Copple, 1997) and DEC (2000) advise that a more holistic assessment of the child's abilities is obtained when multiple measures are used, including an alternative, authentic evaluation.

## Stage 4: Individualized Planning of Programs and Interventions

If the diagnosis indicates a need for early intervention, then the next stage of assessment occurs—assessment for individualized planning of programs and interventions. Usually, criterion-referenced assessment instruments are used to assess the child's mastery of specific skills. In addition, assessment for program planning uses observation of the child, interviews with families and caregivers, and information from other professionals who have worked with the child. It is important that the assessment for planning programs and interventions be closely linked to the actual curricula of the child's early intervention program (Bagnato & Neisworth, 2000; Salvia & Ysseldyke, 1998). In the planning process, the close relationship between assessment and intervention should be highlighted (Puckett & Black, 2000). The assessment results are most useful when they can be immediately implemented to plan goals and objectives for the child. Typically, the instruments used in this stage of assessment are criterion referenced or curriculum based. Some selected examples of criterion-referenced instruments frequently used in early childhood special education are described in Appendix A.

The assessment should provide answers to these questions: What are the areas of the child's strengths and weaknesses? What instructional goals should be set for this child? The goals should focus on family priorities as well as on child-centered objectives. Goals that support family participation, to the extent desired, are more effective in assisting the children to generalize at home the skills taught in the intervention program. The areas considered in the planning process for preschoolers area are as follows:

- Sensory/physical development
- Language and communication abilities
- Fine and gross motor development
- Cognitive abilities
- Self-help adaptive skills
- Social/emotional growth

Often, performance in one developmental domain influences development in the other domains. Therefore, a developmentally inclusive assessment of competence would assist the planning process for preschoolers (DEC, 2000; Meisels, 1996). Following are some general guidelines for assessment for planning programs and interventions (McLean, 1996; DEC, 2000):

- Assess at regular intervals. Understand and revise the goals and objectives with family participation for each child.
- Obtain multiple checks on the child's abilities.

- Report the child's strengths and set priorities for intervention.
- Make sure that assessment is appropriate for each child and the family.
- Assess the child in a variety of natural settings, including the home. Families often report that their child can do tasks at home that the child could not successfully perform during testing in a clinical setting.
- Share the information from the evaluation with the team members and the family.
- Both families and team members collaborate in implementing assessment Results and in planning interventions.

### Stage 5: *Performance Monitoring*

Once the child is in an intervention program, progress should be monitored frequently. Monitoring progress requires multiple checks through observations, developmental checklists, and rating scales. Activities for performance monitoring include (Cohen & Spenciner, 1998; Wolery, 1996):

- Collect data on a regular basis about the areas of concern.
- Analyze the data to determine the mastery of targeted skills.
- Note progress the preschooler has made in accomplishing the stated goals and objectives on the individualized education program or individualized family service plan.
- Judge the effectiveness of the intervention. Should instruction be modified? Note if the child can generalize the learned skills to other settings when needed.
- Use this information to make decisions about further intervention and services.
- Make changes that are needed in the intervention plan.

### Stage 6: *Program Evaluation*

An important purpose of assessment is to evaluate the intervention program itself. Program evaluation is an objective, systematic procedure for determining the progress of the children and the effectiveness of the total intervention program (Bricker, 1996). The program might be improved through certain changes and modifications.

A major reason for evaluating a program is to assess the effects that the program is having on the children and their families (Bondurant-Utz, 1994; Cohen & Spenciner, 1998). Good program evaluation should multidimensional, taking into account both child-centered goals and family objectives. The program evaluation should include both *formative* evaluation (done during the operation of the program) and *summative* evaluation (done at the completion of the program to implement needed changes).

## Types of Assessment Instruments

Multiple measures and methods are used to obtain information about young children. This section of the chapter classifies assessment instruments and methods into (1) tests and (2) alternative assessment methods. The tests include norm-based instruments, criterion-referenced curriculum-based tests, and tests with adaptations for disabilities.

(Selected examples of commonly used instruments are described in Appendix A.) Further information about early childhood tests can be found in Cohen and Spenciner (1998), Lasardo and Notari-Sylverson (2001), and McLean (1996).

## *Tests*

***Norm-Referenced Instruments.*** Norm-referenced tests compare a child's performance to an appropriate referent group of children. For example, in a language test, the child's language performance is compared to that of children of similar age who do not have a disability (a norm group). Performance results are provided in terms of derived scores, such as age scores, grade scores, standard scores, developmental quotients, and percentiles. Thus, in the case of a language test, the results of the test might indicate that a 5-year-old child with disabilities has the language skills of a "typical" child of age 3 years, 6 months. Information obtained from norm-based instruments can be useful for diagnosis, placement, and evaluation of progress. (Some commonly used norm-referenced instruments are listed in Appendix A.)

Norm-based information, however, is not sufficient for program planning for a specific child. The use of items from these norm-based instruments for instruction purposes is not a recommended practice (Bailey & Nabors, 1996; DEC, 2000; Meisels, 1996). Two precautionary questions in using norm-based measures should be considered (Sattler, 1992):

1. Was the normative group representative of the child's characteristics, including age, gender, socioeconomic background, ethnic/cultural background, language, geographical location, and similar disabilities or at-risk status?
2. Was the size of the normative group large enough to ensure adequate reliability and validity?

In using norm-based tests, it is essential to know about the reliability and validity of the test. Researchers are concerned that many of the norm-referenced tests currently being used for early childhood assessment may lack sufficient reliability or validity (Bailey & Nabors, 1996; McLean, Bailey, & Wolery, 1996).

*Reliability* refers to the consistency of the test. It is the degree to which the subject's score is a true score in that there is little or no error in the measurement process over time (Salvia & Ysseldyke, 1998). There are several ways to measure the reliability of an instrument: (1) Test-retest reliability is estimated when the identical test is administered twice. (2) Alternative-form reliability is estimated through administering equivalent forms of the same test. (3) Split-half reliability is obtained by dividing the total number of items on a test in half, forming two tests. Then each test is administered to the students, and the scores are correlated. (4) Interscorer reliability is a measure of the extent to which two or more raters agree on how a test should be scored (Cohen & Spenciner, 1998). Many young children can be inconsistent in their test performance but attempts need to be made to ensure as much reliability as possible in the assessment process.

*Validity* of the test refers to what the instrument measures and how appropriate it is for the examiner to make inferences on the basis of test results (Puckett & Black, 2000). Does the test measure what it is supposed to measure? For example, administering an intelligence test that requires many verbal responses from a language-impaired preschooler would not suitably measure the child's potential.

Types of validity include content, predictive, and construct validity. *Content validity* refers to whether the test items are representative samples of the behaviors they are supposed to measure. *Predictive validity* refers to whether performance on test items can predict actual achievement on other tests of the same skills or future performance (Cook, Tessier, & Klein, 2000). For example, will a reading readiness test given in kindergarten predict a child's reading achievement in first grade? *Construct validity* refers to the extent to which the test measures a particular psychological trait or construct, such as intelligence.

*Criterion-Referenced/Curriculum-Based Instruments.*   These tests are useful for program planning because they link assessment data to curriculum objectives. Early childhood educators are encouraged to use this type of assessment because of their relevance to classroom activities (Bredekamp & Rosegrant, 1997). Unlike norm-based tests that compare the child with a normative group, criterion-referenced instruments measure the skills the child has learned and those not yet mastered. Curriculum-based tests are forms of criterion-referenced instruments in which the curricular objectives act as the criteria for identifying instructional goals and for assessment progress. Both of these types of tests are useful for identifying intervention objectives, tracking progress, and providing feedback for further instruction (Wolery, 1996).

These instruments demonstrate the close link between assessment and intervention (Fox, Hanline, Vail, & Galant, 1994). Curriculum-based or criterion-referenced tests can be commercially produced but also can be constructed by teachers. Sometimes they are in the form of checklists or rating scales. Teams of family members and professionals can use these instruments as a common base to share results, plan interventions, and evaluate progress. (Selected examples of these tests are in Appendix A.)

*Tests with Adaptations for Disabilities.*   Some tests allow for special adaptations, such as alternative sensory or response modes for the child with special needs. The purpose is to obtain valid assessment results by circumventing the disability. Goals for instruction can be identified as well as strategies for learning that would be appropriate for a specific child (Bagnato & Neisworth, 2000). Certain instruments give the examiner choices for the items to administer that would be appropriate for the child. Other tests provide guidelines on how to alter the task for a specific disability. Other tests are specifically standardized on children with specific disabilities. (Selected examples are in Appendix A.)

## Alternative Assessment Methods

The previous section discussed a variety of formal measures used in the assessment of preschoolers. It is also important to use alternative assessment methods, which are informal measures that stress observation of the children in their natural, everyday environments (Losardo & Notari-Sylverson, 2001). This type of assessment is also called

*To obtain information about young children, observe them in their natural environments.*

*ecologically based evaluation* because it views the child as interactive with the environments (Cavallaro, Haney, & Cabello, 1993). The interplay between the environment and the child is important because a change in one causes a change in the other (Hanson & Lynch, 1995).

A combination of multiple measures and observations of the child in natural settings is necessary for a holistic and complete evaluation. Alternative assessment methods include observation, checklists and rating scales, assessment of multiple intelligences, assessment of emotional intelligence, play-based assessment, dynamic assessment, performance and authentic assessment, judgment-based assessment, and family assessment.

## Observation

A powerful technique for obtaining information about young children is to observe them in their natural environments. Observational methods can include anecdotal records, running records, specimen descriptions, event sampling, checklists, and rating scales.

An *anecdotal record* is simply a written description about a child's behavior that helps assist examiners gain information about a child's behaviors. Antecedent events occur *before* the behavior; and consequent events occur *after* the target behavior is performed.

One disadvantage of using anecdotal records is that there are no built-in safeguards against possible examiner bias (Kostelnik, Soderman, & Whiren, 1999; Sattler, 1992).

A *running record* is a written observation made at regular times (such as every half hour). This method offers more complete information than the anecdotal record. The more detail the record is, the more useful it becomes for understanding the child's behavior. A *specimen record* is another type of observation that is more structured than a running record because the examiner needs to identify the subject, setting, time, and event at the beginning of each observation. *Event sampling* is used to record events as they happen. First, the desired behavior is identified, and then it is recorded when it occurs (Puckett & Black, 2000). For example, creative activity is recorded when the child paints a picture.

### Checklists and Rating Scales

*Checklists* are lists of skills that are usually presented in developmental order. The child is asked to perform the tasks, and the examiner records whether the child is successful. *Rating scales* are used to make judgments about the child's behavior in different settings (McLean, Bailey, & Wolery, 1996). For example, rating scales can give the examiner a chance to rate the attention span and activity level of the child in a particular environment, such as at preschool or at home. (Selected examples of checklists and rating scales appear in Appendix A.)

### Assessment of Multiple Intelligences

An additional assessment technique that requires systematic observation is derived from a theory developed by Howard Gardner (1993). The theory of multiple intelligences suggests that people have several different types of intelligences that include, but are not limited to, linguistic intelligence, logical-mathematical intelligence, spatial intelligence, musical intelligence, bodily/kinesthetic intelligence, interpersonal intelligence, and intrapersonal intelligence (see Figure 4.3). Recently, Gardner (1999) has proposed one more type of intelligence, that of naturalistic intelligence. (See Table 4.1 for examples of these intelligences.)

In terms of assessment, this theory can be used as a basis for discovering the strengths of children and analyzing their weaknesses. Through systematic observations, a profile can be built of the child's strengths and weaknesses that is then useful for planning functional interventions and useful enriching activities. Gardner (1999) believes that every child has strengths, and these should be nurtured. The weaknesses can be strengthened through the use of hands-on activities and supportive methods of instruction.

### Assessment of Emotional Intelligence

A different type of assessment that requires close observation is the evaluation of emotional intelligence. The concept of emotional intelligence was developed by Daniel Goleman (1995), who contends that this type of intelligence can be more important

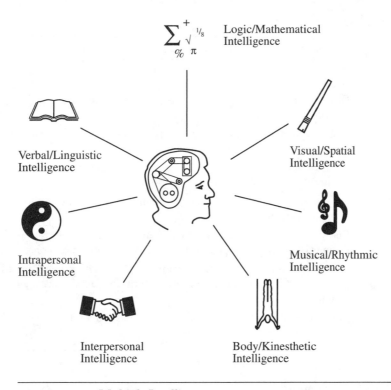

**FIGURE 4.3**  *Multiple Intelligences*

*Source:* Adapted from *Multiple Intelligences* by Howard Gardner. Copyright © 1993 by Howard Gardner. Reprinted by permission of Basic Books, a member of Perseus Books, L.L.C.

than the conventional IQ in determining an individual's happiness and success in life. Some of the components of emotional intelligence are self-awareness or recognizing your own feelings; the ability to manage these feelings, such as finding constructive ways to handle fears, anxieties, anger, and sadness; personal decision making, such as realizing whether thoughts or emotions and ruling your decisions; the ability to handle stress through exercise and relaxation; empathy or understanding other people's feelings; communication, such as the capability to be a good listener and questioner; self-disclosure and acceptance, or the abilities to trust and see yourself in positive ways; and the capabilities for cooperation, assertion, negotiation, and conflict resolution.

Goleman (1995) believes that children who lack a number of the components of emotional IQ will have a difficult time learning and achieving at school. He also believes that the components of emotional intelligence can be observed, taught when necessary, and modeled to young children with and without disabilities to give them important foundations for learning and success. The observers must be familiar with the children in order to assess these components of emotional intelligence and consult with others to verify their conclusions.

**TABLE 4.1**   *Examples of Multiple Intelligences*

| Type of Intelligence | Examples |
|---|---|
| Linguistic | Enjoyment of stories, poems, songs, word games, and conversations. |
| Logical-Mathematical | Enjoyment of numbers, measurement, calculations, classifications, and logical relationships. |
| Spatial | Enjoyment of arts and crafts, patterns, colors, shapes, lines, and forms. Good sense of directions and distance. |
| Musical | Enjoyment of rhythm, melody, songs, musical instruments, and tapes. Sensitivity to sounds in the environment. |
| Bodily/Kinesthetic | Enjoyment of sports, movement, dancing, outdoor play, and the creative use of manipulatives. |
| Interpersonal | Enjoyment of people, social activities, and friendships. Sensitivity to the feelings of other people, body language, and facial expressions. |
| Intrapersonal | Enjoyment and sensitivity to emotional and aesthetic experiences. Deep awareness of inner feelings and introspective. Prefers to learn alone rather than in groups. |
| Naturalistic | Enjoyment of nature, such as plants, flowers, and animals. Sensitivity to the events in nature. |

### Play-Based Assessment

Play-based assessment offers a useful, natural method for evaluating young children who have disabilities or who are at risk. Since play follows a regular developmental sequence during childhood, the child's play activities can provide a measure of maturity and competence. Play is developmental, transdisciplinary, holistic, and dynamic. Therefore, play-based assessment is suitable for any functioning child between the ages of 6 months through 6 years (Linder, 1990). Play-based assessment permits observers to obtain information on the child's developmental skills as well as patterns of interaction with others. This information is very useful for planning intervention (Segal & Weber, 1996).

A model of play-based assessment called *transdisciplinary play-based assessment* (TPBA) has been developed by Linder (1993). In using TPBA, a team, consisting of families and professionals, observes the child for approximately one hour during play activities with the parents, peers, and a play facilitator. The environment for play-based assessment can be any play setting. The toys in the setting need to be selected so that they sample various developmental areas, such as the cognitive, motor, language, self-help, and emotional/social domains. Since the content of the play assessment, the questions asked, and the structure of the play session will vary for each child, play-based assessment procedures will be unique for each preschooler. Linder (1993) describes the following phases in a play-based assessment:

> Phase I is begun in an unstructured manner with the child initiating the play activity.

Phase II incorporates aspects of play not spontaneously initiated by the preschooler.

Phase III has a peer join the target child to enable observations of the interaction between the two children.

Phase IV has the parents play with the child while the team observes the interactions.

Phase V is the final stage, and a snack is served to the target child and the peer.

This approach to assessment can be time consuming but it often gives more valid results through the cooperation and information sharing by the team and the family.

## Dynamic Assessment

Dynamic assessment is an ecological approach that evaluates the child's ability to learn in a teaching situation rather than what the youngster already knows in a testing situation (Lerner, 2000). This type of assessment emphasizes the child's strengths and closely links assessment with intervention. Evolving from the concepts of Vygotsky (1978a), Feuerstein (1980), Luria (1980), and Palinscar and Brown (1994), dynamic assessment is an approach that actively involves the child in the assessment process. Through teaching the child, the teacher determines how the child learns, what seems to be interfering with the child's ability to profit from instruction, and how the child responds to intervention. A process called *scaffolding* is used during dynamic assessment. The teacher provides appropriate support to enable the youngster to master tasks that

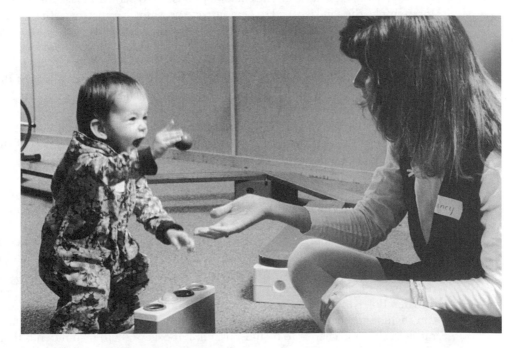

*Play-based assessment is observing a child at play.*

previously were too difficult. The learning potential of the child can then be estimated (Kostelnik, Soderman, & Whiren, 1999).

In dynamic assessment, the teacher first teaches the child a specific task and watches the child's reactions to the instruction. During the interactive teaching situation, the teacher observes the child's performance and determines how many prompts or supports are necessary for the child to learn a particular skill. Dynamic assessment has these benefits:

- It provides insight into the child's learning strategies and suggests ways to modify instruction so that the youngster is successful (Lidz, 1991).
- It provides a nonbiased method of assessing young children from culturally diverse backgrounds (Hoy & Gregg, 1994).
- It is useful for assessing children with severe disabilities because it permits adaptations and modifications, such as allowing more time to finish an assessment task (Losardo & Notari-Sylverson, 2001).

Two examples of dynamic assessment are the Mediated Learning Program (Osborn, Sherwood, & Cole, 1999) and the Preschool Learning Assessment Device (Lidz, 1991).

### Performance and Authentic Assessment

Performance and authentic assessment are types of assessment that reflect a child's learning. In *performance assessment*, the child may be asked to perform a task that is contrived—for example, the child is asked to demonstrate brushing her teeth at different times than usual. Performance assessment requires multiple observations of the same task in natural settings before conclusions are made about the child's abilities. *Authentic assessment* is similar to performance assessment, but the skill is performed in a real-life situation when needed (Puckett & Black, 2000)—for example, the teacher observes the child's skill in zipping a jacket when getting ready to go outside.

*Portfolio assessment* offers another example of authentic assessment that provides a broad picture of the child's strengths and weaknesses in a real-life or authentic context (Meyer, 1992). Rather than using tests, the assessor looks at a collection of the child's work that is arranged into a portfolio. The purposes of the portfolio are to demonstrate efforts, progress, and achievement over time; to demonstrate the processes used by the student in work or play; to show the development of various projects; to communicate to families and teachers; and to evaluate programs (Arter & Spandel, 1991; Kostelnik, Soderman, & Whiren, 1999).

For young children, contents of portfolios could include artwork, such as drawings and paintings; photographs of creative constructions, such as block buildings; and videotapes or audiotapes describing play activities and illustrating the child's development in the language, cognitive, self-help, social/emotional and motor areas (Guidry, Van den Pol, Keeley, & Neilson, 1996). In addition to the children's work, portfolios also can include teacher and caregiver observations, such as checklists, anecdotal records, rating scales, and charts. To be most useful, LaBoskey (2000) recommends that portfolios be organized into sections according to the types of information included. The advantages of portfolio assessment are the child participates in the assessment process, portfolios can reflect a child's ownership of the learning process, portfolios are open ended and flexible, and portfolios emphasize meaningful learning experiences (Diffily & Fleege, 1993; Wetherby & Prizant, 1996).

## Judgment-Based Assessment

Judgment-based assessment uses clinical judgments from multiple sources to collect information about children. This type of assessment supplements the data obtained from norm-referenced tests and criterion-referenced instruments (Losardo & Notari-Sylverson, 2001). It is often difficult to obtain information about the capabilities of children with severe disabilities because of their response limitations on formal and informal tests. Judgment-based assessment provides additional data about the youngsters' strengths and needs. In judgment-based assessment, input from families, teachers, and professionals assists in making clinical judgments about the development and the abilities of the preschoolers. This information is used in planning appropriate interventions. One example of a judgment-based instrument is the *System to Plan Early Childhood Services* (*SPECS*) (Bagnato & Neisworth, 1990), which provides a format for team decision making about functional objectives for a child with special needs (Bagnato & Neisworth, 2000).

## Family Assessment

The recent legislation for young children with special needs (i.e., IDEA-1997, PL 99-457, and PL 102-119) call for a family-focused approach. This means that the service should meet the needs of the family, as well as the needs of the young child. An individualized family service plan (IFSP) is required for young children, birth to age 3, which will include appropriate, voluntary, and noninstrusive assessment of the family's strengths and concerns. The federal legislation allows, but does not require, an IFSP for preschool children over the age of 36 months. For children over age 3, the IEP is used by many states, but the assessment of family resources, priorities, and concern is still important for preschoolers and their families.

Although a variety of techniques for family assessment can be selected, some cautions for the early interventionist in the use of these techniques need to be stressed (Lowenthal, 1991). The instruments and methods must be employed carefully in order not to intrude on family privacy. PL 99-457 is clear that the identification of family resources and concerns is voluntary, and no child can be refused services because the family did not participate in an assessment (McLean, Bailey, & Wolery, 1996).

Identification of family strengths and concerns should not be conducted by the early intervention program until the program is ready to use this information either to assist in the attainment of the child's goals or to assist families in reaching their own prioritized objectives. Only information that can be directly applied to enhance the family's functioning should be gathered. It is important not to ply the families with irrelevant or redundant questions. When families have participated in an assessment of their priorities, resources, and concerns, they have a right to expect that the information will be used for their benefit.

Some useful information that can be gathered as a part of family assessment can be categorized as follows (McLean, Bailey, & Wolery, 1996):

- Child needs and characteristics likely to affect family functioning (e.g., temperament, responsiveness, consolability, regularity, motivation, and persistence)
- Parent-child interactions
- Family concerns (e.g., medical and dental care, respite, finances, information about child development, time to spend with the rest of the family and friends, and future services)
- Critical stressful events or crisis times
- Family strengths, including personal resources (e.g., a positive outlook, a sense of mastery and empowerment over life events, religious or philosophical beliefs)
- Social/emotional support within the family, and an outside support system (e.g., extended family, friends, neighbors, professionals, church groups, and other organizations within the community)

The availability of sources of support is important for optimal family functioning (Dunst, Trivette, & Deal, 1994b). The ability of the family to function and cope effectively, regardless of the number of stressors present, depends on the way the family perceives the stressful events and the support system accessible to it. When assessing family resources and concerns, the interventionist should be a facilitator working in partnership with the family to identify possible resources and needs for assistance.

Three basic techniques are used when conducting a family assessment: tests, observations, and interviews (Winton & Bailey, 1994). An appropriate goal for the use of these techniques is to empower the family to access the resources they require for optimal functioning (Dunst, Trivette, & Deal, 1994b). (Selected examples of family assessment measures can be found in Appendix A.)

In summary, family assessment emphasizes the importance of family involvement, to the extent desired, as equal partners on the interdisciplinary team. The assessment process needs to be family centered and focused. A recommended practice in early childhood special education is to include the family, to the extent desired, in decision making about assessments and interventions for their child (DEC, 2000). The family members are valid and unique sources of information in assessing and making clinical judgments about their preschooler's performances in a variety of functional areas (Cohen & Spencinier, 1998). When the family members are included in the assessment process, it not only ensures their input but it also assists them in identifying their priorities, goals, and objectives for their preschoolers. The best assessment decisions can be made when the family, to the extent desired, and the other team members collaborate (McLean, 1996).

## Special Considerations for Assessing Young Children

Some special considerations in assessing young children are (1) special issues in testing preschoolers, (2) nondiscriminatory assessment, and (3) the importance of establishing rapport between the child and the examiner.

## Special Issues in Testing Preschoolers

The assessment procedures for preschool children should reflect the wide range of normal development characteristics of this age group (Bredekamp & Copple, 1997). Evaluations should be conducted by a transdisciplinary or interdisciplinary team with the family participating as team members to the extent they desire. Experienced and qualified clinicians in early childhood development and other related specialists should be additional members of the assessment team. Team members need to use a wide selection of standardized tests, informal instruments, and natural setting techniques, setting the most appropriate tests and methods for each preschool child. The ecological perspective requires that information from each of the child's relevant environments be collected and considered. Care should be taken to test in the child's native language or primary means of communication. The diagnosis should be based on all this information, as well as on clinical judgment.

Preschoolers who are evaluated for mild delays should be monitored closely, and recommendations for appropriate interventions need to be made collaboratively with the family. After these interventions have been tried, a reevaluation should take place if the delays have become more chronic and are interfering with the child's developmental progress. Preschoolers who are already diagnosed as having disabilities will need further evaluations at regular intervals to determine their status in early intervention programs and services.

## Nondiscriminatory Assessment

It is important to assure that tests and testing procedures do not discriminate against children who come from culturally and linguistically diverse backgrounds. Errors in the assessment process could occur when a child's performance is unfairly judged because of the child's gender or ethnic, cultural, linguistic, socioeconomic, or religious background (Bailey & Wolery, 1992). Team members should make every effort to be aware of and sensitive to diversity and how testing instruments may be discriminatory. The following strategies are recommended to ensure that assessments will be as nondiscriminatory as possible (Bailey & Wolery, 1992; Gregory, 1997; Lynch & Hanson, 1998).

1. Administer tests in the child's native language or preferred mode of communication.
2. Use multiple measures, including alternative assessment, and gather information in natural settings to gain a holistic picture of the child's performance.
3. Make sure the test provides information for appropriate use with children from diverse cultural-linguistic backgrounds. Culturally relevant tests should be used. Examine test items to make sure that they are nondiscriminatory.
4. Be aware of cultural differences in communication styles that could have an impact on children's responses to test items.
5. Check the validity of test data by comparing it with information provided by significant people in the child's life (e.g., caregivers, teachers, therapists, etc.).
6. Encourage the family, to the extent they desire, to be partners in the assessment process. Gather information about their concerns.

7. Perform the assessment at a time and place that is appropriate for the family.
8. A trained cultural guide or interpreter may be helpful during the assessment process when the family is from a diverse background.

### Development of Rapport in Assessment

One of the most common errors made by examiners of preschoolers is to underestimate the importance of establishing rapport or a trusting relationship when conducting an evaluation (Witt, Elliot, Kramer, & Gresham, 1994). When a trusting and sincere relationship is established with the child, the examiner is better able to obtain optimal performance from the child in the testing situation. The following strategies will be he helpful in establishing rapport with the child (DEC, 2000):

1. The child should be familiar with the examiner and the setting.
2. The examiner should be aware of the child's interest and use this information to achieve a trusting relationship with the child before testing.
3. The examiner should be familiar with the child's cultural background or language or consult with a colleague who has this expertise.
4. The examiner should respond in a sensitive manner to the preschooler's concern or needs during testing.
5. The examiner should give appropriate approval and reinforcement to motivate and keep the child focused on the task.

## Summary

- Assessment is recommended because information gathered during the assessment process serves as the foundation for intervention for preschoolers with special needs.
- The ecological perspective is important in the assessment of preschool children because it is holistic and takes into consideration all aspects of the child and his or her environment.
- Stages of the assessment process include child-find, developmental screening, diagnosis, individual planning for program and intervention, performance monitoring, and program evaluation.
- Types of assessment measures include norm-based tests, curriculum-based or criterion-referenced tests, tests that are adapted for disabilities, process tests, and task analysis.
- Alternative methods of assessment include observation, checklists and rating scales, arena assessment, play-based assessment, assessment of multiple intelligences, assessment of emotional intelligence, dynamic assessment, authentic assessment, and family assessment.
- There are a number of important considerations in the assessment of preschool children. These include special issues in the assessment process, the significance of the family in the assessment process, nondiscriminatory assessments, and the importance of establishing rapport in the testing situation.

## *Key Terms*

alternative assessment
assessment
assessment of emotional intelligence
assessment of multiple intelligences
authentic assessment
criterion-referenced instruments
curriculum-referenced tests
developmental delay
developmental screening
dynamic assessment
ecological perspective
environmental risk

family assessment
judgment-based assessment
natural methods of assessment
nondiscriminatory assessment
norm-referenced instruments
performance assessment
play-based assessment
portfolio assessment
program evaluation
reliability
task analysis
validity

# 5

# *Environments for Learning*

## Chapter Outline _____

*Types of Settings*
  Home-Based Services
  Center-Based Services
  Combination Home- and
    Center-Based Services
*The Law and Settings for Learning*
*The Process of Integrating Young Children
with Special Needs with Typically
Functioning Children*
  Least Restrictive Environment
  Mainstreaming
  Inclusion
  Natural Environments

*Early Intervention Teams*
  Multidisciplinary Teams
  Interdisciplinary Teams
  Transdisciplinary Teams
*Service Coordination*
  Responsibilities of the Service Coordinator
  Family-Centered Service Coordination
*Interagency Collaboration*
  Procedures to Establish Interagency
    Coordination
  Guidelines for Facilitating Interagency
    Collaboration

This chapter explores learning environments—the settings in which young children with special needs receive services. In selecting a learning environment for a child, it is essential to consider the individual child's needs as well as the needs of the family. Family members are central to the early intervention team and need accurate and unbiased information so they can make informed choices about services for their child and themselves. This chapter also examines ways to coordinate the services provided by several professionals or agencies.

## *Early Childhood Snapshot*   THE ROLE OF THE SERVICE COORDINATOR

The *service coordinator* is a person who helps parents effectively coordinate the assistance of professionals and foster interagency collaboration. A parent of a child with special needs can be torn by the demands of the various professionals and agencies working with a child, without the help of a service coordinator.

Marion Walters is the mother of three children who have different special needs. She is striving to work with the many service providers and agencies, but she feels overwhelmed with the various professionals and agencies who are assisting her children. Each has different expectations and goals. The occupational therapist wants Mrs. Walters to work with her oldest child on methods of self-feeding. The speech therapist asked her to fol-low up on language development techniques for her middle youngster. The physical therapist asked her to use movement exercises for the baby, who is hypotonic. The psychologist requests that she use behavior management strategies to improve parent-child interactions with all three children.

With so many people and demands, Mrs. Walters is becoming very flustered, frustrated, and confused. She needs help to order, organize, and prioritize the overwhelming and conflicting directives from providers and agencies. What she needs is *one* person who can help organize and fulfill all these requirements through a unified plan. In short, Mrs. Walters needs the help of a service coordinator.

A number of issues are related to the selection of a learning environment: (1) the different types of settings for providing intervention for young children, (2) how the law influences the child's placement for services, (3) the integration of children with special needs with "typical" children, (4) the role of the service coordinator, (5) how various agencies coordinate their services, and (6) the types of early intervention teams.

# Types of Settings

Three settings are used to provide services to young children with disabilities: *home-based* settings, *center-based* settings, and a *combination* of home- and center-based settings. Each of these options has certain benefits.

## Home-Based Services

Home-based settings are used provide services to children in their own homes. The interventionist comes to the child's home and works individually with the child and the family. Most importantly, the interventionist works with the parents (or caregivers) to implement the activities and trains the parents to work with the child. Home-based services are considered more normalized because the *natural* environment for the child is the home. Visits by the early interventionist are scheduled weekly or biweekly as needed. Progress of the child is monitored by the family members and the professional.

Home-based settings offer a realistic option in rural areas where it is impractical for children to travel long distances to early childhood centers. A home-based approach may be more economical, since the costs of maintaining a center can be eliminated.

A possible disadvantage of the home setting is that it may place undue stress on parents as they become the child's primary teacher. Their teacher role can interfere with their parent role as a nurturers of the child. Another possible disadvantage is that related personnel and specialists may not be available to come to the home, so that services provided to the family may not be as comprehensive as at an early childhood center. Also, parents may not have any contact with other parents, as they would in a center-based program.

Benefits of home-based programs include:

- *Intensive and individualized programming can be provided in the home setting.* Children do not have to spend time waiting their turns to participate in activities (Noonan & McCormick, 1993).
- *Learning occurs in the child's natural environment.* The problem of generalizing skills from the early childhood center to the home is eliminated (Dunst, Hamby, Trivette, Raab, & Bruder, 2000).
- *The family is intensely involved in the intervention.* The interventionist can readily determine family priorities and jointly plan with family members.
- *Parent-child interactions are stronger.* More opportunities are available to work together than in a center-based program.
- *Parents develop a positive relationship with the early interventionist.* Parents are more likely to follow through on the interventionist's suggestions (Hanson & Lynch,

1995). To develop this positive relationship, the interventionist must acquire a sensitivity to the family's culture, values, and beliefs (Lynch & Hanson, 1998).

## Center-Based Services

In center-based programs, children are transported to preschool centers where professionals from many disciplines can provide a variety of services. Center-based programs may offer services such as physical and occupational therapy, speech and language instruction, psychological services, medical diagnosis, social work, and early childhood special education. Inclusive, center-based preschools are supported by the DEC (2000) and the National Association for the Education of Young Children (NAEYC) (Bredekamp & Copple, 1997) so that young children with disabilities are integrated with their typically functioning peers. Inclusive center-based settings have the following benefits:

- Children with special needs have the opportunity to play with children with and without disabilities and to make friends with them.
- Children have access to many appropriate toys that they may not have in their homes.
- Children with special needs have the opportunity to develop social skills as they interact with typically functioning peers (Bricker, 1998).
- The families of children with disabilities have the opportunity to make friends with families of children who do not have disabilities.
- Families of children with special needs can feel accepted and supported by the inclusion in normal community activities, such as parent groups and social outings at the preschool center (Dunst, Trivette, & Deal, 1994a, Dunst & Bruder, 1999).
- Preschool children without disabilities and their families learn to accept children with special needs (Richey & Wheeler, 2000).

## Combination Home- and Center-Based Services

Combined home- and center-based program have the advantages of both settings. The combined program has flexibility and can be individualized to meet the child's needs. The child can receive the full range of services in the center and the naturalistic environment of the home (Cook, Tessier, & Klein, 2000).

# The Law and Settings for Learning

The legislation of IDEA-1997, PL 99-457, and PL 102-119 affects the placement of young children with special needs.

### Services for Infants and Toddlers, Part C
- *The states may have programs for infants and toddlers with disabilities or who are at risk.*
These provisions are included in Part C of the law, which is voluntary or permissive

legislation. Under Part C, states can apply for federal grants to establish a statewide co-ordinated system of services to eligible infants, toddlers, and their families.

• *An individualized family services plan (IFSP) is required for each eligible infant/toddler and the family.*  The IFSP is family centered, in contrast to the IEP, which is more child focused.

• *Infants and toddlers are identified as eligible for services with the term developmental delay.*  The criteria for *developmental delay* are determined by each state.

• *Early intervention services must include a multidisciplinary assessment, service coordi-nation, and a written IFSP developed by a multidisciplinary team that includes the parents.*  Services that may be provided should be designed to meet the developmental needs of the child and the concerns of the family. These services are special education, vision, assistive technology, social work, audiology, early identification, family support, health, medical (for evaluation purposes only), psychological services, occupational and phys-ical therapy, transportation, speech and language therapy, and transition. Transition was added as a service to minimize disruptions in service or adjustment problems be-cause of changes in placements when a child reaches her or his third birthday.

• *The IFSP requires a statement of the natural settings in which early intervention ser-vices are delivered.*  Natural settings for infants and toddlers include the home, child-care centers, play groups, or any other settings for typical children of this age group.

*Natural settings for young children with special needs include a variety of environments.*

### Services for Preschoolers

- *Services are required for 3- through 5-year-old children.* Under IDEA-1997, all states must now provide *a free, appropriate public education (FAPE), including special education and related services for 3- through 5-year-old children with disabilities.* Related services include audiology, counseling services, early identification, medical services for diagnostic purposes, occupational and physical therapy, parent counseling and training, psychological services, recreation, school health services, speech and language therapy, social work services, and transportation (Brown & Rule, 1993).

- *Use either the IEP or IFSP for 3- through 5-year old children.* With the passage of PL 102-119 in 1991, the assessment team can use either an individualized education program (IEP) or an individualized family services program (IFSP) for eligible children.

- *The role of parents is strengthened.* The law acknowledges the important role of parents or guardians in making decisions about their child's services. Parents must sign permission for the placement, and they are entitled to a hearing before their child can be excluded, placed, or terminated from a special program. Assistance in the form of parent training also can be given to the parents if requested and thought necessary to help the child benefit from special education and related services.

## The Process of Integrating Young Children with Special Needs with Typically Functioning Children

Several terms are used to decide the process of integrating children with special needs with their typically functioning peers, such as the least restrictive environment, mainstreaming, and inclusion.

### Least Restrictive Environment

The *least restrictive environment (LRE)* specified in IDEA-1997 requires that eligible children be placed in the most normalized setting possible. The term *least restrictive* means that the child with special needs is to be educated with typically functioning children to the extent appropriate (Lerner, 2000)

Another provision in IDEA-1997 (PL 105-17) that affects the placement of eligible preschoolers is the *continuum of alternative placements* (see Figure 5.1). This provision assures that public schools provide various options for educational placements that meet the unique needs of preschoolers with disabilities. Placement options for preschool children include regular preschool classes, developmental kindergartens, resource rooms, special classes and schools, child-care settings, and other combinations of placements. However, the type of placement should not be confused with the amount of supports and services offered in a specific setting. Any regular preschool can be an appropriate if there are the necessary resources and services to meet the needs of the children (Davis, Kilgo, & Gamel-McCormick, 1998). Preschoolers with special needs do not have to be in a special setting with separate services in order to learn. Learning opportunities can be found in a variety of regular settings in which young

**FIGURE 5.1**    *Educational Environments for Preschoolers with Disabilities*

*Regular class* includes children who receive services in programs designed primarily for nondisabled children, provided the children with disabilities are in a separate room for less than 21 percent of the time receiving services. This may include, but is not limited to, Head Start centers, public or private preschool and child-care facilities, preschool classes offered to an age-eligible population by the public school system, kindergarten classes, and classes using co-teaching models (special education and general education staff coordinating activities in a general education setting).

*Resource room* includes children who receive services in programs designed primarily for nondisabled children, provided the children with disabilities are in a separate program for 21 to 60 percent of the time receiving services. This includes, but is not limited to, Head Start centers, public or private preschools or child-care facilities and kindergarten classes.

*Separate class* includes children who receive services in a separate program for 61 to 100 percent of the time receiving services. It does not include children who received education in public or private, separate, day or residential facilities.

*Separate school* includes children who are served in publicly or privately operated programs in which children receive care for 24 hours a day. This could include placement in public nursing home care facilities or private residential schools.

*Residential facility* includes children who are served in publicly or privately operated programs in which children receive care for 24 hours a day. This could include placement in public nursing home care facilities or public or private residential schools.

*Homebound/hospital* includes children who are served in either a home or hospital setting, including those receiving special education or related services in the home and provided by a professional or paraprofessional who visits the home on a regular basis (e.g., a child development worker or speech services provided in the child's home). It also includes children 3 to 5 years old in a hospital setting on an inpatient or outpatient basis. However, children receiving services in a group program that is housed at a hospital should be reported in the separate school category. For children served in both a home/hospital setting and in a school/community setting, report the child in the placement that comprises the larger percentage of time receiving services.

*Source:* U.S. Department of Education (2000).

children participate (Dunst, Hamby, Trivette, Raab, & Bruder, 2000). Therefore, in the implementation of the least restrictive environment, the team should consider the following (Cook, Tessier, & Klein, 2000; Peterson, 1987):

- Will the placement provide appropriate intervention through special services and individualized programs that will increase the child's chance of being successful in the LRE?
- Will the setting be culturally compatible with the values and beliefs of the family?
- Will the placement provide age-appropriate stimulation that is responsive to the child's education and caregiving needs?
- Will the LRE placement have a well-trained staff to provide appropriate intervention services?

The LRE requirement is now easier to implement than in the past because there are more integrated early childhood programs available. Most regular early childhood programs enroll at least one child with special needs (Miller, 1996; Sandall, 1993).

Options that can fulfill the LRE requirements for children with disabilities include:

- Part-or full-time participation in publicly funded programs such as Head Start. In Head Start, no eligible child can be denied admission because of the nature and severity of her or his disability (Peterson, Barber, & Ault, 1994).
- Integrated preschool programs in public school settings.
- Integrated public or private community preschool programs.
- Integrated child-care centers.
- Preschool special education classes in public schools in which integration in kindergartens is possible.
- Reverse integration in which typical preschoolers are placed in special classes for children who have special needs.

In the school year 1998–99, 53 percent of preschoolers were served in general education classes, 31 percent in resource rooms, 8 percent in separate classrooms, and 8 percent in other settings, including residential facilities and home/hospital programs (U.S. Department of Education, 2000).

## Mainstreaming

*Mainstreaming* is the practice of placing a child with disabilities into general education classes or normalized settings on a selected basis when the child can profit from this placement (Guralnick, 1994). In the case of young children, mainstream settings could include regular preschool classes, kindergartens, child-care facilities, Head Start, and community nursery schools. In early mainstreaming models, children with special needs were expected to compete with their typically functioning peers without specific interventions. Today, views on mainstreaming have changed. The child's program must be designed to meet the child's IEP or IFSP goals within the mainstream setting. The goals for each child are individualized, and successful mainstreaming requires varying types of intervention. There needs to be wholehearted commitment to the mainstream process on the part of teachers, administrators, and families (Salisbury, 1993; Salisbury & Vincent, 1990). Presently, the concept of mainstreaming is being replaced with the philosophy of inclusion in many early childhood settings (Richey & Wheeler, 2000).

## Inclusion

The philosophy of inclusion is more broad than that of mainstreaming, as *inclusion* refers to the concept that all children with disabilities have the right to be fully included in all the activities and routines of the regular early childhood classes (DEC, 2000). Under the inclusion policy, children with special needs are not removed from their classrooms to obtain necessary services and resources; these resources are provided in the regular classroom. Services include supportive staff, such as special educators, aides, speech and language therapists, occupational and physical therapists, school nurses, hearing and vision specialists, and technology specialists. Resources can include adaptive equipment, furniture, and computers (Miller, 1996). The policy of inclusion is supported by the Division for Early Childhood (DEC) of the Council for Exceptional

Children. The DEC advocates the continual development and dissemination of inclusive services, more training programs in inclusive and collaborative practices for service providers, and flexible fiscal and administrative procedures that support inclusion (DEC, 2000). Supporters of inclusion practices point to several advantages in placing young children with disabilities in inclusive settings (Diamond, Hestenes, & O'Connor, 1994; Wolery & Wilburs, 1994):

- Children with disabilities demonstrate higher levels of social play and more appropriate social interactions when integrated fully with their typically functioning peers than do children in self-contained special classes (Baker, Wong, & Walberg, 1995; Lamorey & Bricker, 1993).
- Inclusive classes appear to offer more opportunities for children to practice newly acquired skills with their peers (in comparison to youngsters in special education classes) (Demchak & Drinkwater, 1992; Diamond, Hestenes, & O'Connor, 1994).
- Children with special needs who are enrolled in inclusive settings make gains in language, cognitive, and motor development that are comparable to their peers in special education (Jones & Rapport, 1997).
- Children with disabilities display more advanced play skills when they are with typically functioning children. However, even in inclusive placements, young children with disabilities are more likely to engage in isolated play and chosen as desired playmates less frequently than are their classmates without disabilities (Odom & Brown, 1993).
- Children without disabilities also benefit from inclusive classes. Typically developing preschoolers make developmental gains that are at least equivalent to those of youngsters in nonintegrated programs. Moreover, families and professionals believe that inclusive classes encourage children to be more accepting of differences and disabilities in people (Miller, 1996; Peck, Carlson, & Helmstetter, 1992; Wolery & Wilbers, 1994).

## Natural Environments

It is important to realize that just physically placing young children with special needs with their typically functioning peers in inclusive settings is not enough (Bricker, 1995). In order for inclusion to be successful, appropriate services and supports need to be provided to meet the needs of each child. The degree of or amount of services needed may vary, but the goal is to ensure that every child is learning and developing optimally. Learning opportunities need to be identified in the everyday activities and routines of the inclusive settings. These settings are often referred to as *natural environments*—places in which children would participate in if they did not have disabilities, such as, child-care programs, homes, play groups, and regular preschool programs (Dunst, Hamby, Trivette, Raab, & Bruder, 2000). Following are suggestions to increase the effectiveness of placing young children with special needs into natural or inclusive settings:

1. The philosophy of natural environments must be valued by families of young children without disabilities and by community members (Dunst & Trivette, 1994; Howard, Williams, Port, & Lepper, 1997).

2. Children with disabilities must have opportunities to become full-time members of their peer groups (Dunst & Bruder, 1999).
3. More research is needed to find specific pedagogical practices that will increase the success of a variety of natural environments and inclusive placements (Rule, Losardo, Dinnebeil, Kaiser, & Rowland, 1998).

## Early Intervention Teams

Effective teamwork is essential for successful provision of early intervention services. There are three types of teams: multidisciplinary, interdisciplinary, and transdisciplinary.

### Multidisciplinary Teams

On the *multidisciplinary team*, the professionals provide isolated assessment and intervention services. This includes individual report writing, goals, and separate therapies for the child and the family. This type of teaming can lead to fragmented services for children and to confusing, conflicting reports to parents who are viewed as passive recipients of information about their child (Bruder & Bologna, 1993; McGonigil, Woodruff, & Roszmann-Millican, 1994).

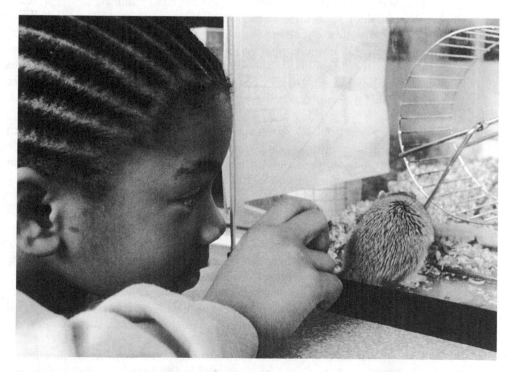

*Teachers should consider the child's needs and interests.*

## Interdisciplinary Teams

On an *interdisciplinary team*, each professional still assess and intervenes separately, but the team does meet at some point to discuss their results and jointly develop intervention plans. There is a formal commitment between the professionals and the family for sharing information about assessment and intervention. Even though the family members are considered members of the team, their input often is considered secondary to the information provided by the professionals. In addition, professional turf issues may present problems. Sometimes, interdisciplinary team members do not understand or respect the professional expertise of other members from different disciplines (Bailey, 1996).

## Transdisciplinary Teams

On the *transdisciplinary team*, the professionals and families share roles and purposely cross disciplines when they assess, plan, and intervene. Effective transdisciplinary teams rely on the collaboration of each team member. Each participant understands that his or her goals will not be achieved unless the other team members achieve their respective objectives. Transdisciplinary teams strive for a nonduplication service delivery system and the active involvement of the family (Bailey, 1996; Losardo & Notari-Sylverson, 2001).

Continuous communication among all team members, including the family, is present in transdiciplinary teams. All participants teach, learn, and work together to accomplish the goals of the child and the family. Team members need to be willing to share their knowledge with each other and be open to acquiring new skills (Cook, Tessier, & Klein, 2000). Decisions are made by team consensus. Although all team members share responsibility for the development of the service plan, it is usually carried out by one professional, who is appointed the primary service provider, and the family.

The transdisciplinary approach currently is considered the best practice because (1) it avoids duplication of services, (2) it views the whole child's development as integrated, and (3) it emphasizes the importance of the family as equal, contributing members of the team (Briggs, 1993; Miller, 1996; DEC, 2000).

The development of a transdisciplinary team typically requires that the participants go through a process called *role transition* that is composed of the following steps: role extension, roll expansion, role exchange, role release, and role support (Bailey, 1996; Pugach & Johnson,1995; Bricker & Widerstrom, 1996):

- In *role extension*, team members engage in activities to improve their own expertise and skills.
- In *role expansion*, the members begin to learn about the other disciplines. In this phase, the professionals exchange information about the terminology and basic procedures of each other's disciplines.
- In *role exchange*, the participants implement intervention in different specialties under direct supervision of the designated specialist. For example, the speech therapist implements some motor therapy under the supervision of the occupational therapist.
- In *role release*, the individual team members practice new techniques independently—that is, without continuous consultation and supervision. However, role release

should be interpreted as role replacement. Each participant's expertise is valued and necessary to the team.

- In *role support*, there are times when specific interventions are too technical for the primary service provider to implement. In these cases, the team member from the required discipline will work directly with the primary provider and the family to provide this support.

Integrated therapy occurs when transdisciplinary teams deliver related services directly in the preschool center. Currently, many early childhood special educators recommend the provision of integrated therapy in the natural routine and activities of the early childhood center (Davis, Kilgo, & McCormick, 1998; DEC, 2000). For example, at snacktime, the speech and language therapist can work with the child on his or her communication goals, such as verbalizing or signing a request for juice. The occupational therapist can promote self-help skills, such as pouring juice from a pitcher. The physical therapist may work on the proper positioning of the child while eating. In this way, the child is not pulled from the room for isolated therapy and can participate in the regular preschool routines. The teacher can implement the therapists' suggestions during the everyday activities of the early childhood center. These activities provide the child with many opportunities to practice and generalize new skills in natural settings where they will be needed.

# Service Coordination

The term *service coordinator* is used in IDEA-1997 and was introduced in earlier laws (PL 99-457 and PL 102-119). The responsibility of the service coordinator is to assist families of infants and toddlers in assessing early intervention and related services that are specified on the child's IFSP and to coordinate with other relevant agencies (Bruder & Bologna, 1993). The service coordinator may be a professional from the discipline most relevant to the needs of the family and child or any individual, including a family member, who is qualified to carry out the duties of the job. Although service coordination is not mandated for preschoolers (in Part B of IDEA), many preschool teachers, professionals, and parents provide service coordination function on an informal basis.

## Responsibilities of the Service Coordinator

For the families of young children with special needs, the many professionals, agencies, and assessment and intervention services can be confusing and bewildering. The purpose of service coordination is to help parents of young children with special needs organize and access these disparate services. Service coordination activities include the following functions for families (U.S. Department of Education, 2000):

- Coordinate the performance of evaluations and assessments.
- Facilitate and participate in the development, review, and evaluation of IFSPs.
- Help families identify available service providers.

- Coordinate and monitor the delivery of available services.
- Inform families of the availability of advocacy services.
- Coordinate with medical and health providers.
- Facilitate the development of a transition plan to preschool services, if appropriate.

Individuals with a variety of backgrounds may serve as the service coordinator for a family. The Division for Early Childhood (DEC) of the Council for Exceptional Children recommends that each family have the opportunity to select from the available service coordinators the person whose skills best match the needs and preferences of the family. The states have different lead agencies that are responsible for implementing the law, including the departments of education, developmental disabilities, public health, mental health, and social services. These agencies could provide the service coordinator. The service coordinator may be selected from the direct service providers working in the early intervention program. In some cases, a staff member, such as a social worker, can be assigned the role of full-time service coordinator for all the families served by the early intervention program. In other cases, the coordinator may come from another public service program or be contracted from a private agency. A local coordinating council could assign a coordinator based on family needs and inputs. Family members, to the extent they desire, may be trained to become service coordinators. Experienced parents could be trained to serve as coordinators for other families.

## Family-Centered Service Coordination

Service coordination needs to be family centered and based in local communities. Interagency cooperation is necessary in early intervention to provide services and avoid duplication. The services that are provided should be geographically accessible to families.

Family-centered service coordination requires that professionals respect the families as primary decision makers. The family should be considered partners, to the extent they wish, in planning, monitoring, and evaluating services. Families often know their children best and are most consistently involved with them (Dunst, 1999). The service coordinator should respect the family's culture, child-rearing practices, and its perceptions of the child's needs and disabilities. If cultural differences are not taken into account, the services proposed by the service coordinator may be considered inappropriate and resisted by the families (Lowenthal, 1996).

An *enabling model* of service coordination integrates family-centered and community-based philosophies. This model improves the family's capability to negotiate service systems and obtain needed resources. Effective service coordination creates ways for families to become competent, to identify their own needs, and to access resources (Dunst & Bruder, 1999; Dunst & Trivette, 1994).

The enabling model of service coordination builds on family strengths in obtaining resources by assistance and encouragement, rather than actually doing the job for them. It is based on the belief that doing for others, despite good motives, may create dependence and passivity in families. Promoting and enhancing family competence will further the role of families as agents of change. It is hoped that eventually families develop a sense of confidence and competence in dealing with the service network. Cooperative rather than dependent interactions with professionals are encouraged (Dunst & Bruder, 1999; Dunst, Trivette, Davis, & Cornwall, 1994).

The following are guidelines for effective service coordination with families (Howard, Williams, Port, & Lepper, 1997). The effective service coordinator should:

- Ensure that the needs of individual family members are not forgotten.
- Facilitate collaboration between professionals and families.
- Recognize that service collaboration can range from simple to complex functions.
- Be recognized by agencies as possessing the necessary authority to gather information, coordinate services, and be an advocate for the families.
- Emphasize parent empowerment and enablement.
- Assist families to access informal support systems, such as the extended family, friends, neighbors, church, and social organizations.
- Help families find the financial means to cover the costs of services.

## Interagency Collaboration

Many different agencies have been established to deal with the varied types of services needed by young children with special needs. The diverse agencies include community advocacy groups, nonprofit associations, state agencies, local government agencies, and private groups. Each agency has its own funding, administrative methods, eligibility requirements, and system of service delivery. Often, the result is that there are many parallel, independent programs that duplicate services and compete for clients and funding. Gaps in the service system occur because there are no systematic interagency procedures to assure the coordination of services.

The purpose of interagency collaboration is to coordinate the services of this array of independent separate agencies. Each agency provides a specific service or function. To expect any one agency to service all the needs of the family and child is unrealistic and may put too much of a burden on the agency. One agency rarely has the needed personnel or can afford to pay for such extensive services. However, if agencies collaborate, they can contribute a share of their expertise and resources and reduce their expenses.

In fact, interagency collaboration is required under the polices of PL 99-457 and Part C of IDEA-1997. State and local community agencies are to work together to meet the tremendous challenge of providing a comprehensive, coordinated system of services to infants and toddlers and their families. The legislation makes interagency collaboration not just a suggested best practice but a recommended procedure (*Federal Register*, 1989). Specifically, the regulations state:

> Since no one agency has the funding sources to provide all the necessary services, states may use their interagency agreements to clarify transition options and develop appropriate procedures and activities. With proper planning, the interagency agreements between the State Educational Agency and other agencies providing services to handicapped infants and toddlers should contain enough flexibility so that lapses in delivery of services will not occur. (p. 1644)

According to IDEA-1997, the following activities should be conducted by each state to further collaboration among agencies: (1) plan and implement an interagency program of early intervention services; (2) facilitate the coordination of payment for these services from federal, state, and local services; and (3) further the abilities of states to provide quality early intervention assistance to families of infants and toddlers with disabilities.

In serving young children with special needs, the best interests of the family and child are served by a *continuum of care* that requires coordination among disciplines and agencies. Individual services are not sufficiently comprehensive, and they lack a holistic perspective. The care of the entire family needs to be considered. Service providers from different agencies should work together to create the kind of service delivery essential to provide for the psychosocial, physical, motor, adaptive, language, and cognitive development of the young child with disabilities and the possible needs of the family. Services needed are so varied and comprehensive that they require the pooling of multiple resources that can be accomplished through interagency collaboration (Bruder & Bologna, 1993; Bricker & Widerstrom, 1996).

Benefits of interagency collaboration are that agencies can expand services through resource sharing, cope more effectively with funding limits, improve family accessibility to services, normalize service delivery through working with community preschool programs, and promote communitywide planning rather than depending on a patchwork of isolated program (Hanft, Burke, & Swenson-Miller, 1996).

## Procedures to Establish Interagency Collaboration

The steps in establishing interagency collaboration consist of planning, implementation, and evaluation.

*Planning.*     The first step, the planning process, is a significant one because it establishes a framework for all subsequent activities. A plan for collaboration should include the following topics (Harbin & McNulty, 1990).

1. *Definitions.* The target population should be defined. What children and families are eligible for services? What services can be provided?
2. *Policy statements.* These should include the goals for the intervention services. Is it the policy to provide an integrated service system that will better serve the needs of the participants? Should the policy include family support, services in community settings, or other services? The purposes for the intervention services should be explained in the policy statements.
3. *Policy objectives.* Goals need to be set to fulfill the purposes for the intervention services. These could include family-focused objectives; roles and responsibilities of the families and providers; placements of children in typical, preschool settings; and so forth. A single line of authority for the agencies should be delineated in case of problems and conflicts.
4. *Services.* The implementation of the policies and goals are discussed here. These can include procedures for implementing child-find or case finding, service co-

ordination, direct service provisions, coordination of activities at the state and local levels, a statewide directory of services for referral purposes, and coordinated transition services for the children and families.

***Implementation.*** Implementation of the interagency agreements is the second step in the process of interagency collaboration. This step cannot be rushed because it will take time for agencies to change their administrative structures and program activities to conform to interagency agreements. The impact of these agreements might be different for each agency. This can be a crucial stage because each agency will need to maintain services for its clients while working toward interagency networking. Changes that are made too quickly can be viewed by personnel as interfering with their abilities to deliver services to clients. A transition plan may be needed that addresses changes in staff roles and budgets. In-service training can be provided to assist the staff's adjustment. Regular meetings of the participants in the interagency network will facilitate the effective communication necessary to implement the plan. Strong leadership and teamwork will encourage the participants to continue their efforts in the implementation stage (Fowler, Haines, & Rosenkoetter, 1990; Harbin & McNulty, 1990).

***Evaluation.*** The last step is the evaluation of the interagency collaboration. This stage sometimes is not given sufficient focus because so much energy is being directed to the planning and implementation phases. However, evaluation is vital to keep the interagency network responsive to change. The following questions need to be answered in the continuous evaluation process: Are there any gaps in services? How can they be remedied? Should procedures be changed because they are not working effectively? The ultimate test for collaborative efforts is whether specific policies and practices will lead to services that will improve the functioning of young children and their families (Bruder & Bologna, 1993).

## Guidelines for Facilitating Interagency Collaboration

The following recommendations can help develop interagency collaboration (Hanson & Widerstrom, 1993; Peterson, 1991):

1. Sufficient *time* is required to develop interagency collaboration. Hasty policy development is an inappropriate strategy if the goal is to seek more coordinated services.
2. Sufficient *funding* for services is necessary. The financial responsibility of each agency involved in the collaborative process needs to be defined.
3. Federal and state agencies should coordinate their policies regarding eligibility, funding, and certification (Bruder & Bolgna, 1993).
4. Many local communities need more technical assistance in examining their resources to reach a cohesive system of services. The state and local interagency coordinating councils could provide this assistance.
5. Successful interagency collaboration requires strong leadership. Leaders can be found among agency administrators, state and local interagency councils, service providers, parents, and local communities. Leaders can help develop policy,

advocate for necessary legislation, facilitate group decision making, and provide the vision needed for the development of a coordinated system of services (Bruder & Bologna, 1993; Swan & Morgan, 1993).

6. Broad-based participation is required at the state and local levels for effective interagency collaboration. To overcome resistance to change, people affected must be involved in the change process (Kontos & File, 1993).

7. Service coordinators and families need to be aware of the services provided by diverse community agencies. The service coordinators and families must be seen by these agencies as processing the necessary authority to advocate for appropriate services.

8. Professional training is needed to assist early interventionists in gaining the knowledge and skills necessary to work on interagency teams (Straka & Bricker, 1996; Hanft, Burke, & Swenson-Miller, 1996). Skills in communication, problem solving, and negotiation are essential.

9. Families of young children with disabilities need to become significant members of interagency teams. The families are the consumers of interdisciplinary services and can evaluate the effectiveness of a coordinated system of services. Gaps or duplications in this system can be identified by the participating families (McCollum & Stayton, 1996).

## Summary

- There are a variety of environments for intervention or types of service delivery. Three settings for providing services to young children with special needs are the home, center, and combination settings.
- There are several major laws that affect the provision of services for young children with special needs. Perhaps the most important law is the Reauthorized Individuals with Disabilities Education Act of 1997 (PL 105-17). Earlier early childhood special education laws include PL 99-457 and PL 102-119.
- Especially important in the laws regarding services for young children with disabilities are Part B and Part C. Part B affects preschool children, ages 3 to 6. Part C affects infants and toddlers, birth to age 3, and their families. Part B of IDEA mandates services for eligible preschoolers. Many services, according to Part C, are permissive for infants, toddlers, and their families.
- There are several suggested environments for integrating young children with special needs with typically functioning children. An important consideration within the law is the continuum of alternative placements and the least restrictive environment. Models for integrating children include mainstreaming and inclusion. The inclusion model is recommended by many professionals in the fields of early childhood special and regular education.
- Effective teamwork is essential for successful intervention services. In early intervention, there are three types of teams: multidisciplinary, interdisciplinary, and transdisciplinary. The transdisciplinary team is the recommended choice of many

early childhood specialists because it avoids duplication of services and emphasizes the roles of the families as equal members of the team.

- Service coordination assists families of infants and toddlers with disabilities in accessing early intervention and related services. The service coordinator plays an important role in serving children with special needs and their families.
- Many different agencies often serve a child with disabilities. Interagency collaboration is required to provide appropriate services to families of young children with special needs.

## Key Terms

center-based services
continuum of alternative placements
home-based services
inclusion
integrated therapy
interagency collaboration
interdisciplinary team

least restrictive environment
mainstreaming
multidisciplinary team
natural settings
service coordination
transdisciplinary team

# 6

## *Curriculum Development*

## *Chapter Outline*

*Defining the Curriculum*
Early Intervention Curriculum for
Children with Special Needs
Guidelines for Developing
an Inclusive Curriculum
Evaluation of the Curriculum

*Curriculum Routines and Schedules*
Daily Schedule of Curriculum Activities
Learning Centers
The Naturalistic Philosophy
The Value of Cooperative Learning
in the Curriculum

*Types of Early Childhood Curricula*
The Developmental Curriculum
The Cognitive Curriculum
The Constructivist Curriculum: The Reggio
Emilia Approach

The Ecological/Functional Curriculum
The Behavioral Curriculum
The Psychosocial Curriculum

*The Developmentally Appropriate Practice
(DAP) Guidelines and Curriculum*

*The Role of Play in the Curriculum*
The Importance of Play
Play and Children with Special Needs

*Establishing the Physical Environment
for Learning*

*The IEP and the IFSP and the Curriculum*
Individualized Family Service
Plan (IFSP)
Individualized Education
Program (IEP)

This chapter reviews the philosophies, models, and practices for fashioning a curriculum for young children who are at risk or who have disabilities. A well-planned curriculum for young children with special needs stimulates learning experiences through a broad range of activities. Several curriculum models are used in the field of early childhood education in programs for typical children, and these curriculum approaches can be applied to young children with special needs. The major curriculum models are the developmental curriculum, the cognitive curriculum, the constructivist curriculum, the ecological/functional curriculum, the behavioral curriculum, and the psychosocial curriculum. The strengths and limitations of each of these curriculum approaches are explored in this chapter.

Also discussed is *developmentally appropriate practices* (DAP) and curriculum that stem from the recommendations from the field of early childhood education. This curriculum reflects a philosophy of using daily routines as the natural context for teaching skills. Attention focuses on the application of this philosophy to curriculum for children with special needs.

The chapter also reviews the curriculum of play and the value or play activities for learning for all children, and especially for children with special needs. Suggestions are given for how the physical environment can be arranged to foster learning. Finally, the curriculum implications of the individualized education program (IEP) and the individualized family service plan (IFSP) will be examined.

*Early Childhood Snapshot*    SELECTING AND MODIFYING A CURRICULUM
FOR AN INCLUSIVE PRESCHOOL CLASS

This example illustrates how a teacher in an inclusive preschool selects and implements a curriculum for the children with special needs in his class.

Mr. Edwards is the teacher in an inclusive preschool class in which most of the children are typical 3- and 4-year-olds. Several children in this class have disabilities and these children have either an IEP (individualized education program) or IFSP (individualized family service plan). Also, several children in this class are identified as environmentally at risk.

After studying several curriculum models, Mr. Edwards decided to employ a curriculum called activity-based intervention (Bricker & Cripe, 1992). He selected this curriculum model because it will be useful for his children with special needs. The curriculum model uses developmentally appropriate activities in natural settings to help children practice the functional skills and objectives on the IEPs or IFSPs of the children with disabilities.

This activity-based intervention curriculum model proved to be particularly useful for Jonah, a 4-year-old with developmental delays in fine and gross motor and expressive language skills. One of the sensory activities selected for the curriculum was blowing bubbles—an activity that turned out to be a motivating source of fun for all the preschoolers in the class.

In planning the activity-based intervention curriculum, the transdisciplinary team, which included Mr. Edwards and several related service staff members, planned ways to meet Jonah's IEP goals by modifying the developmentally appropriate activity of blowing bubbles. The occupational therapist on the team first modeled the activity and then gave guided assistance to Jonah when he had difficulty grasping the bubble wand. In this way, he could practice his fine motor skills. The physical therapist placed the container of soapy water on the floor instead of on a table so that Jonah and some of the other children with physical challenges could have easy access to it. The speech/language therapist helped Jonah practice the *b* sound when he blew a bubble. When Jonah said "buh," Mr. Edwards said, "Bubble. You blew bubbles." Here, Jonah's teacher used the natural language stimulation techniques of repetition and expansion to assist Jonah with his expressive language. The modifications to the developmentally appropriate activity in a natural setting helped Jonah practice the skills that were identified as needs on his IEP.

## Defining the Curriculum

A *curriculum* is a set of experiences that are designed to accomplish stated developmental or learning objectives (Hanson & Lynch, 1995). Three major tasks for developing curriculum are (1) establishing the content, or what is taught; (2) finding appropriate skills for each child; and (3) identifying methods for teaching the content and skills (Wolery & Fleming, 1993). The curriculum for early intervention programs for children with special needs should be based on a theory of learning, contain guidelines for implementation, and include plans for evaluation (Sandall, 1993). The curriculum also should provide for a child's holistic development through integrated learning experiences (Bricker, 1998).

## Early Intervention Curriculum for Children with Special Needs

The philosophy underlying the curriculum for young children who are at risk or who have disabilities involves the following components (Cook, Tessier, & Klein, 2000; Driscoll & Nagel, 2002):

1. *The content.* The content of the curriculum must have meaningful goals for the child, and the curriculum content should be culturally relevant. The content of the curriculum should foster the development of the child with special needs and encourage self-directed learning and positive relationships.
2. *The child's stage of development.* The curriculum design and the activities selected should be appropriate for the child's stages of development.
3. *Intervention strategies.* The philosophy underlying the curriculum should lead to the selection of methods that are effective in teaching children with special needs.
4. *Social relationships.* The curriculum should provide activities that nourish social relationships. The context for teaching skills should involve social interactions of the child with significant adults, such as caregivers and teachers, as well as with other children.

## Guidelines for Developing an Inclusive Curriculum

Young children with special needs are increasingly receiving services in integrated or inclusive settings. The following guidelines offer useful considerations in developing an appropriate curriculum for inclusive settings (Richarz, 1993; Richey & Wheeler, 2000):

- Young children, both those with and without disabilities, should share a common curriculum.
- Adaptions should be made so that the curriculum is appropriate for children with diverse learning styles and competencies. Instructional techniques should include both child- and teacher-directed activities.
- Experiences should stem from child initiations, as well as teacher-initiated activities.
- Play experiences should foster active engagement and interaction of all the children.
- An ecological approach should involve professionals and families in coordinating the curriculum to meet the needs of every child participant. Involving families helps to ensure the ecological validity of the curriculum.

## Evaluation of the Curriculum

Evaluation is a necessary part of the early intervention curriculum. High-quality programs regularly evaluate the effectiveness of their curricula. Evaluation results lead

*The curriculum should provide activities to nourish social relationships.*

to needed changes in the curriculum, and this process should result in more positive outcomes for children and their families. The following types of questions should be considered when evaluating an early intervention curriculum (Bricker, 1998; Richey & Wheeler, 2000):

- Do the curriculum activities reflect a theory and philosophy?
- Does the curriculum address the development of the whole child?
- Does the curriculum provide for specific goals for each child?
- Does the curriculum allow for learning in small and large groups and in one-to-one interactions?
- Does the curriculum accommodate a wide range of abilities and developmental levels?
- Does the curriculum include activities for children from diverse cultural and economic backgrounds?
- Does the curriculum promote adaptive skills and independence?
- Does the curriculum promote the generalization of skills across a range of natural settings?
- Does the curriculum stress the functionality or usefulness of the activities in young children?

## *Curriculum Routines and Schedules*

### *Daily Schedule of Curriculum Activities*

The curriculum consists of a series of activities, known as the *daily schedule*. Some preschool instructional programs are full-day programs; others are half-day programs. Figure 6.1 shows a sample daily schedule for both types of programs. Both provide for a variety of activities—motor, communication, cognitive, adaptive, and social.

### *Learning Centers*

Learning centers are places in the early childhood classroom where specific activities can be carried out. They might include a dramatic play area, a housekeeping area, a block corner, a manipulative materials center, an arts and crafts center, a language area, a computer

**FIGURE 6.1** *Sample Daily Schedule*

#### *Full-Day Preschool Program*

| | |
|---|---|
| 8:30– 9:00 | Arrival and free play |
| 9:00– 9:20 | Group/Theme presentation |
| 9:30–10:30 | Centers (e.g., art, blocks, music, dramatic play, manipulatives, computer) |
| 10:30–10:45 | Cleanup, transition to group |
| 10:45–11:00 | Group: Follow-up to theme—Language oriented |
| 11:00–11:30 | Outside/Movement |
| 11:30–11:45 | Wind-down group/Story |
| 11:45–12:00 | Transition to lunch |
| 12:00–12:30 | Lunch/Grooming |
| 12:30– 2:00 | Rest/Nap |
| 2:00– 2:15 | Grooming |
| 2:15– 2:45 | Centers/Free play |
| 2:45– 3:00 | Music group |
| 3:00– 3:15 | Dismissal |

#### *Half-Day Preschool Program*

| | |
|---|---|
| 8:15– 8:30 | Arrival/Health Check/Grooming |
| 8:30– 8:50 | Morning circle and planning time |
| 8:50– 9:45 | Work time/Centers |
| 9:45–10:10 | Cleanup and snack time |
| 10:10–10:30 | Small group/Individual work |
| 10:30–11:00 | Gross motor/Fine motor |
| 11:00–11:30 | Preparation for departure and outside time |
| 11:30 | Dismissal |

area, a science table, a music area, a sand and water table, a motor area, and more. Learning centers offer open-ended and child-directed activities that focus on the development of multiple skills (Davis, Kilgo, & Gamel-McCormick, 1998; Fox, Hanline, Vail, & Galant, 1994). Figure 6.2 is a diagram of a preschool classroom with learning centers.

For children with special needs, a learning center can also be used to practice target skills. In the inclusive class, learning centers allow children with disabilities to work alongside their typically functioning peers. Each center should offer the materials and resources necessary to activate learning by children with diverse abilities. For example, the block corner would have blocks of varying compositions, sizes, and shapes, along with accessory toys, such as trucks, cars, and miniature people, so that the children can construct imaginative and creative structures. To accommodate the learning centers for children with special needs, teachers must know the children's unique preferences so that the centers will be responsive to and appropriate for the varying needs and interests of the preschoolers. In addition, teachers must know how the different activities will help fulfill the individual goals and objectives for the children with disabilities.

## The Naturalistic Philosophy

The naturalistic perspective of the curriculum emphasizes that teaching should occur within the context of daily routines in natural environments, such as the home or preschool center. Methods of instruction should be responsive to the child's choice of activities, use natural cues, and be as least intrusive as possible. Techniques include incidental teaching, guided learning, and the use of novelty (Bricker, 1998; Noonan & McCormick, 1993). Incidental teaching involves using a prompt in a routine event. For example, when the child points to a toy to request a turn, the adult models the name of the toy to prompt the child to say the word. In guided learning, the child does the task as independently as possible with assistance given only if necessary. Novelty—for example, a new game—is used to focus the child's attention on the activity. Table 6.1 shows an example of a daily preschool half-day program of activities with accompanying objectives.

## The Value of Cooperative Learning in the Curriculum

Cooperative learning emphasizes the cooperation of young children in the learning process (Lowenthal, 2001). Cohen (1994) defines *cooperative learning* as "students working together in groups small enough so that each individual participates in a collective task that is clearly defined." Several features of cooperative learning are valuable for young children with and without special needs: (1) emphasis on success for each child, (2) recognition of each child's achievements, and (3) opportunities for modeling and practice of social skills (Johnson & Johnson, 1998). Cooperative learning builds self-esteem and fosters the acceptance of children with disabilities by their typically functioning peers.

In cooperative learning, the children work together. A goal is to make sure that each child is successful regardless of diverse developmental levels. Some examples of cooperative learning in a preschool class could be painting a group mural, dramatizing a familiar story, or working on a cooking project. Teachers must plan how to involve each child in the project and how to teach or model necessary social skills, such as solving conflicts or communicating effectively with other group members (Johnson & Johnson,

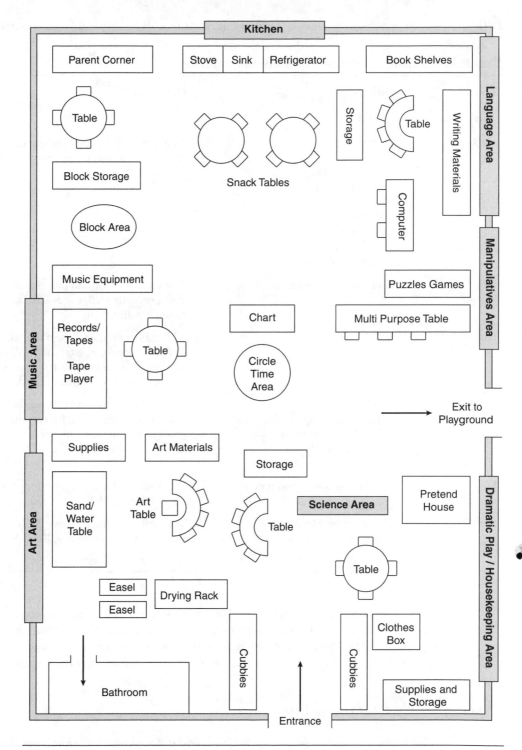

**FIGURE 6.2** *Diagram of a Preschool Classroom with Learning Centers*

*Source:* Adapted from *Developmentally Appropriate Curriculum* by Kostelnik/Soderman/Whiren, © 1999. Reprinted by permission of Pearson Education, Inc., Upper Saddle River, NJ.

**TABLE 6.1**    *Examples of Preschool Routines with Objectives*

| Time | Activity | Objectives |
|------|----------|------------|
| 9:00 | Arrival | |
| 9:00–9:30 | Free-play and choice of learning centers:<br>**1.** house play<br>**2.** manipulative<br>**3.** library corner<br>**4.** blocks<br>**5.** water table<br>**6.** arts and crafts<br>**7.** science table | The child will practice and use communication, socialization, fine motor, and cognitive skills. |
| 8:30–10.00 | Cleanup and toilet time | The child will use and practice adaptive skills, receptive language skills, including following directions. |
| 10:00–10:15 | Snack time | The child will practice and use adaptive skills, socialization, cognitive skills (one-to-one correspondence), fine motor skills, language, and communication skills. |
| 10:15–10:45 | Circle time:<br>**1.** Music (songs & finger play)<br>**2.** Movement games (musical chairs)<br>**3.** Show-and-tell | The child will use and practice language and communication skills, socialization, gross motor, and fine motor skills (grasping objects in show-and-tell). |
| 10:45–11:15 | Outdoor or motor room play | The child will use and practice gross motor skills, language skills, and socialization skills. |
| 11:15–11:30 | Dismissal (children put on wraps, collect belongings, and sing a "goodbye" song) | The child will use adaptive skills, language skills, and socialization skills. |

1997). Inclusive groups of not more than three or four children are recommended, because preschoolers tend to work better together in small clusters rather than in large ones (Harmin, 1994). The children progress from being very dependent on teacher guidance and help to becoming more independent and relying instead on peers for assistance.

## Types of Early Childhood Curricula

This section describes several early childhood curriculum models: the developmental curriculum, the cognitive curriculum, the constructivist curriculum, the ecological/functional curriculum, the behavioral curriculum, the psychosocial curriculum, and the developmentally appropriate curriculum. Each curriculum model is based on a different theory of learning, but each model has also incorporated new features based on current research and practical experiences with preschool children with special needs. Developmentally appropriate practice (DAP) guidelines recommended by the National Association for the Education of Young Children (NAEYC) also affect curriculum in early childhood. These guidelines are discussed later in this chapter. Table 6.2 summarizes these curriculum models.

**TABLE 6.2** *Curriculum Models for Early Intervention*

| Curriculum Model | Theory | Intervention |
| --- | --- | --- |
| Developmental Curriculum | Based on typical developmental sequence. Children will naturally develop these abilities in a rich environment. | A rich environment will provide opportunities for motor, adaptive, cognitive, social/emotional, and communication learning. |
| Cognitive Curriculum | Children develop thinking skills through direct experience and activities. | The learning environment should provide opportunities to develop thinking skills. |
| A Constructivist Curriculum: The Reggio Emilia Approach | Based on constructivist theory, children have the right to be active participants in their own learning. Teachers have the right to expand on this learning through teaching. Parents have the right to actively contribute to their children's development. | Focus on long-term relationships of the children with teachers, a responsive environment to support the child's active learning. |
| Ecological/ Functional Curriculum | Each of the child's environments (home, school, social) affects the child. | Intervention activities should be functional and provide a good match between school environment and the child. |
| Behavioral Curriculum | By managing the events in the environment, the child's behavior can be changed. | The teacher uses direct instruction and behavior management techniques such as shaping, prompting, and reinforcement. |
| Psychosocial Curriculum | Based on the theory that children's basic needs are relationship focused. | A supportive environment provides opportunities for development of relationships and opportunities to work through emotional issues. |
| Developmentally Appropriate Practice (DAP) Curriculum | Learning activities should be individual and age appropriate, real, concrete, and relevant to the children. Children learn through active engagement in their environments. | Uses play activities, child's interest, exploration, and active learning. |

## The Developmental Curriculum

The goal of the developmental model is to assist children with special needs in going through typical sequences of development. Early maturational studies conducted by Gessell and Amatruda (1947) documented typical developmental milestones of young children. These studies provide the foundation for the developmental model. The instructional content of the developmental curriculum emphasizes sequences in the areas of motor, adaptive, cognitive, social/emotional, and communication learning. In teaching young children or who are at risk or who have disabilities, the instructional strategies are similar to those used with typical youngsters.

## The Cognitive Curriculum

The work of Jean Piaget (1971) and concepts from the field of cognitive psychology provide the basis for the cognitive curriculum in early childhood education. The emphasis of the cognitive curriculum is the teaching of thinking. Piaget demonstrated that children's thinking is different from that of adults. He showed that children progress through a series of thinking stages that reflect increasing cognitive development as they advance toward adult thinking. Piaget's theory also emphasized that children need active engagement for learning—an idea that leads to the theory of constructive learning. *Constructive learning* means that children learn in an environment that encourages them to build their own ideas and concepts and to engage in problem solving (Mahoney & Wheatley, 1994).

The following major ideas are emphasized in the cognitive curriculum (Driscoll & Nagel, 2002; Kostelnik, Soderman, & Whiren, 1999):

- Activities should allow children to develop their own thinking.
- Activities should be appropriate for the child's stage of development.
- A child's concepts and learning develop through direct day-to-day experiences.
- Encouragement and reinforcement foster cognitive learning.

## The Constructivist Curriculum: The Reggio Emilia Approach

The Reggio Emilio approach to curriculum is based on constructivist theory. The approach was developed in the preprimary schools in Italy (Kostelnik, Soderman, & Whiren, 1999). This curriculum stresses that the goals of education should be to support the rights of the children, teachers, and parents. Children have the right to be active participants in constructing their own learning and understanding of the world. Teachers have the right to support this learning by deepening and expanding it through their teaching. Parents also have the right to contribute actively to their children's experiences of cognitive growth and development.

The educational principles of the Reggio Emilia approach focus on the image of every child, with or without disabilities, as having many strengths instead of just needs; on the importance of long-term relationships of the teachers with the children; on the value of the school environment to convey respect for the students; on the importance of long-term projects that depict the children's ideas; on the value of symbolic representations that act as languages for the students to communicate their ideas, such as in arts, crafts, dance, theater, and puppetry; and on the importance of the school in creating strong ties with the families and the community at large (Forman, 1996; Gandini, 1993). In the Reggio Emilia approach, the development of critical thinking in children also is encouraged within as supportive, nurturing environment.

## The Ecological/Functional Curriculum

The ecological/functional curriculum is intended to help young children learn the benefits of today's culturally and linguistically diverse society (Lynch & Hanson, 1998). This curriculum builds on the reality that young children must live and learn in many different environments, such as the home, school, neighborhood, and so on. Each of these environments has interactive effects on the child and the family.

The ecological/functional curriculum promotes family priorities by recognizing diversities in family cultures, languages, values, and ethnic backgrounds. The intervention activities that are selected for the curriculum should be functional and meaningful for the child—in the current setting as well as in a future setting. For meaningful learning to occur, there needs to be a good match between the environments and the child.

## The Behavioral Curriculum

The basis of the behavioral curriculum is the behavioral theory that a child's learning can be enhanced by changing and managing the events in the child's environment. From the behavioral view, the environment must be carefully structured, manipulated, and managed to foster effective learning. The specific objective of the behavioral model is to teach the child functional, age-appropriate, and useful skills.

One instructional method stemming from the behavioral model is called *direct instruction*, in which the objective is clearly delineated and the instruction is structured to meet that objective. Other strategies that stem from the behavioral model that are useful in early childhood settings are the procedures of *shaping, prompting*, and *reinforcing* (Umansky & Hooper, 1998).

The process of evaluating the child's acquisition of skills in the behavioral model requires frequent assessment and the collection of data. This allows teachers to know what the child's skill levels are and to make modifications in the program based on this evaluation of the child's progress (Sandall, 1993).

In the behavioral curriculum model, after the child's skill deficiencies are identified, the intervention consists of structured, teacher-directed instruction (Maag, 1999). The steps in the behavioral approach to instruction are:

1. The teacher first identifies a behavioral goal or a critical skill deficiency.
2. The teacher then conducts a task analysis of the skill to be taught by breaking the behavior into small, sequential steps.
3. The teacher directly teaches each necessary step until the child achieves the desired skill or behavior.
4. The teacher evaluates to ascertain whether the child has acquired the skill.

***The Naturalistic Approach to the Behavioral Curriculum.***   Currently, a more naturalistic approach to intervention is being incorporated within the behavioral curriculum model (Lerner, Lowenthal, & Egan, 1998; Rossetti, 1996). Instead of teaching a discrete skill in isolation, the skill is taught when needed in a naturally occurring activity. For example, in a structured behavioral curriculum, a child who lacks the skill of one-to-one correspondence might be taught to count blocks in an isolated therapy room. In the naturalistic curriculum approach, the teacher might ask the child to help prepare the table for snack time by counting the number of place settings needed and then placing one cracker at each place setting.

***Learning to Generalize Newly Learned Skills: The General Case Method.***   Another trend in the behavioral curriculum is to use methods that will help children generalize a newly learned skill to different situations and activities. Generalization may be difficult for some children because they do not transfer skills learned in isolated situations to other situations when needed (Bricker, 1998; DEC, 2000). A teaching strategy called the *general case method* is designed to help children learn to generalize. Two different general case strategies are recommended (Davis, Kilgo, & Gamel-McCormick, 1998; Umansky & Hooper, 1998):

1. Objectives for the child are generalized rather than specific. For example, the objective would be "The child will grasp small objects" instead of "The child will grasp little beads." Necessary modifications for the objective are listed.
2. The skills are taught using a variety of methods in many naturally occurring events. For example, the child learns to use the skill at home, at school, and in the community. The skills focus on functional behaviors across settings, materials, and people.

## The Psychosocial Curriculum

The psychosocial curriculum emphasizes the child's emotional and social development and growth. The curriculum was originally based on innate drive theories (Erikson, 1963), but the current approach focuses on modifications of Erikson's theories.

The major emphasis of the psychosocial approach today is that the teacher incorporates awareness of and attention to the preschoolers' emerging sense of autonomy and self-assertion into daily activities. In this sense, many regular classroom teachers and special education teachers can incorporate these constructs within other curriculum approaches. The psychosocial approach is also employed by agencies, schools, and centers that primarily serve children with emotional and social disabilities. The underlying tenets of this approach focus on relationship issues (Greenspan & Weider, 1998) and the ways in which these earliest relationships are manifested in later interactions.

## The Developmentally Appropriate Practice (DAP) Guidelines and Curriculum

*Developmentally appropriate practices* (*DAP*) are guidelines recommended for early childhood education programs by the National Association for the Education of Young

Children (NAEYC) (Bredekamp, 1987; Bredekamp & Copple, 1997; National Association for the Education of Young Children and National Association of Early Childhood Specialists in State Departments of Education, 1991). The DAP guidelines that were recommended by the NAEYC are shown in Figure 6.3.

The DAP curriculum is an integrated, holistic, approach to the education of young children. It is strongly influenced by the Piagetian constructivist theory. This perspective views the child's development as an outcome of both physiological growth and the child's interaction with the environment (Bredekamp & Copple, 1997). Developmentally appropriate practice emphasizes the importance of play and child-initiated, active learning. It also promotes an early childhood curriculum that is child centered and allows young children to make some choices and decisions about what is learned. In using the DAP model, interventionists need to strive for congruence between their instruction and what is individually appropriate for the child's developmental level of interests (Driscoll & Nagel, 2002). Developmentally appropriate programs reflect the natural learning abilities of children, assisting them to grow socially, emotionally, cognitively, and physically. Motivation is viewed as being intrinsic in children; that is, children have a natural desire to explore and learn from their environment (Mahoney & Neville-Smith, 1996). The DAP curriculum strongly recommends that children with disabilities be fully included in natural environments in which typical children participate, such as in the home, community settings, and preschools. Necessary services and supports are provided to meet their needs in these settings. Teachers need to foster the children's feelings of belonging and acceptance by their typically functioning peers (Bredekamp & Copple, 1997).

Two early childhood programs for young children with special needs that are compatible with developmentally appropriate practice are the High/Scope Model (Taulbee, 1988) and the Transactional Intervention Program (Mahoney & Powell, 1988).

The *High/Scope Model* (Schweinhart, Barnes, & Weikart, 1993) is a program intended for both typically functioning and at-risk young children. It uses an instructional approach that emphasizes toddlers' and preschoolers' strengths and their abilities to

**FIGURE 6.3** *Developmentally Appropriate Practice (DAP) Guidelines*

*Recommendations of the National Association for the Education of Young Children*

- Activities should be integrated across developmental domains.
- Children's interests and progress should be identified through teacher observation, examination of work portfolios, and (for school-aged children) student self-evaluation.
- Teachers should prepare the environment to facilitate the child's active exploration and interaction on physical, social, and cognitive levels.
- Learning activities and materials for very young children should be concrete, real, and relevant to their experience; the complexity, challenge, and abstraction of activities should increase as children understand the skills involved.

*Source:* Based on materials in S. Bredekamp and C. Copple, eds., *Developmentally Appropriate Practice in Early Childhood Programs*, Revised edition (Washington, DC: NAEYC, 1997). Copyright by the National Association for the Education of Young Children.

learn through exploration and discovery. The children are asked to plan, carry out, and evaluate their own activities. Active learning and creativity are encouraged. The interventionist is a facilitator who enhances the learning process by providing interest centers. These centers consist of a variety of stimulating materials and offer many different play opportunities. The High/Scope Model allows each child to work at activities that are developmentally appropriate and self-paced (Dunlap, 1997; Kostelnik, Soderman, & Whiren, 1999).

The *Transactional Intervention Program (TRIP)*, developed by Mahoney, Robinson, and Powell (1992), is another example of a program for children with special needs that uses developmentally appropriate practices. The focus of TRIP is on the interaction between infants, toddlers, and their caregivers. The goal of intervention is to increase the frequency of children's active and spontaneous participation by improving the quality of the caregivers' interaction with them.

Evaluations of TRIP show that positive developmental gains were made by very young children with disabilities. These gains were associated with caregivers being more responsive and imitative of children and less directive with them. Results also demonstrated that a responsive, child-oriented style of caregiving is an effective means of promoting children's development. A major implication of the research findings is that direct instruction does not appear to be necessary in order to further the development of young children with special needs (Mahoney, Robinson, & Powell, 1992).

***DAP and DEC Recommended Practices.***    The early childhood special education professional organization, the Division for Early Childhood within the Council for Exceptional Children (DEC), has incorporated many practices of DAP in the development of their recent curriculum guidelines (DEC, 2000). Several earlier criticisms of DAP have been addressed in this document, which demonstrates that the DAP philosophy of the field of early childhood education and the early childhood special education philosophy have gradually blended together in many ways (Carta, 1994; DEC, 2000; Umansky & Hooper, 1998).

The themes of the DEC-recommended practices that reflect early childhood special education are (Davis, Kilgo, & Gamel-McCormick, 1998; Odom, 1994):

- The right of all children to be included in natural settings
- The importance of individualization
- A deemphasis in the use of standardized assessment tests
- An integration of assessment and curriculum
- The values of child-initiated activities and a child-centered approach
- The use of active engagement to learn independent functioning
- The importance of personnel competence

The recommendations of both DAP and DEC are to identify relevant practices for all children and to understand when modifications of teaching methods are required for specific youngsters (DEC, 2000). With the current movement toward inclusion of children with special needs in natural settings, more youngsters with disabilities will be served with their typically functioning peers. Therefore, professionals in both early childhood education and early childhood special education need to work together to increase knowledge about appropriate interventions for all children (Kostelnik, So-derman, & Whiren, 1999).

***Implementing DAP and DEC Recommended Practices.***   Three curriculum pro-cedures serve to implement the DAP guidelines and the DEC recommended practices: activity-based intervention, learning centers, and a naturalistic perspective. Learning centers and the naturalistic perspective have been described previously in this chapter. *Activity-based intervention* is "a child directed, transactional approach that embodies in-struction on children's individual goals and objectives in routine, planned or child-initiated activities and uses locally occurring antecedents and consequences to develop functional and generalizable skills" (Bricker, 1998, p. 11).

To develop skills, activity-based intervention capitalizes on the child's play and routine or planned activities that children enjoy. Several goals on a child's IEP or IFSP can be addressed during play and in the normal routine of the day. For example, when the children are playing at the water table during free-play time at the preschool cen-ter, the child would practice fine motor skills (reaching, grasping, and releasing the water toys), social skills (sharing and taking turns), communication (modeling the more advanced language of peers and the expansion of language by the teacher), adaptive be-haviors (washing and drying the water toys), and cognitive skills (problem solving about how best to empty the water from the table during clean-up time).

The activity-based intervention approach has other advantages. It is useful for families as well as for professionals. It is adaptable to the different needs of babies and young children. It can be effective in diverse settings. It can also generalize functional skills into routine activities (Richey & Wheeler, 2000).

## *Early Childhood Snapshot*   ACTIVITY-BASED INSTRUCTION

This example illustrates how a teacher used activity-based instruction in a natural environment with a developmentally appropriate routine to meet a child's IEP goals in the cognitive, language, and fine motor areas. The adult follows the child's lead as to his or her interests, motivation, and choice of activities. The teacher plays with the toys or games selected by the youngster.

Benje was a 4-year-old preschooler who had developmental delays in cognitive, language, and fine motor skills and was placed in an inclusive pre-school classroom. The children in his class were having their snack time, and his teacher, Ms. Hoy, asked Benje to be the helper for the snack time ac-tivity. For this activity, Benje first handed each child in the group a cup and napkin. (This activity gave him practice in one-to-one correspondence for the cognitive skill of counting.) He also practiced reach-ing, grasping, and releasing objects. (These activi-ties gave him practice in fine motor skills.) When he encountered difficulties in these activities, Ms. Hoy used verbal and physical prompts to guide him so that he successfully accomplished these activities.

While the children were eating crackers and drinking juice, Ms. Hoy provided language practice. She talked about the snacks, using short, repetitive sentences and the self-talk technique of natural stimulation. She said, "My crackers are crunchy. Crunch, crunch go the crackers. I like to eat crackers." When Benje wanted more juice, he said, "More." Ms. Hoy responded quickly to his request, using a language expansion technique, by saying, "More? You want more? You want more juice? Well, here it is."

# The Role of Play in the Curriculum

> Play is the highest expression of human development in childhood, for it alone is the free expression of what is in a child's soul. (Froebel, 1896)

## The Importance of Play

The quotation by Frederich Froebel (1896), who pioneered the kindergarten movement, highlights the basic need of children to play and the essential role that play serves in the young child's development. Play is a natural and joyful activity for children. Through spontaneous and creative play activities, children acquire motor, language, cognitive, and social abilities. As children engage in play, they learn in a natural way about movement, colors, shapes, textures, forms, sizes, language, rules, and interacting with other people. The typical child learns through motor play about moving, jumping, and playing with balls, ropes, tricycles, wagons, and playground equipment. Language is learned through play with others, naming and rhyming games, poems, and nursery rhymes. Cognitive and thinking abilities are developed as the child uses crayons, plays counting games, matches shapes, plays with pots and pans, and categorizes and group items. Social skills are nurtured through playing with another child, playing house, and taking part in group activities.

The significance of play as a path for the child's development and learning is widely recognized by early childhood educators who strongly encourage that play activities be an essential part of the curriculum. There are many definitions of *play*, but within the various definitions, we find certain common concepts (Bricker, 1998; Linder, 1993; Umansky & Hooper, 1998):

- Play is spontaneous.
- Play actively involves the child.
- Play is intrinsically motivated.
- Play has a positive effect.
- Play is fun.
- Play occurs with people and with objects.
- Play promotes growth in many areas of development, including language, motor, adaptive, and social/emotional ones.

## Play and Children with Special Needs

The value of spontaneous play for child growth is well recognized today by early childhood educators. Most children usually need no instruction for playing. For children who have disabilities or who are at risk, however, play poses a challenge. They may fail to develop play activities by themselves in a spontaneous manner. The toys and settings used by typically functioning children may be unsuitable for children with special needs. They may need specially constructed and adapted toys, to be taught how to play, and to have special arrangements of play materials.

Children with special needs may encounter serious difficulties in play activities. Children who are at risk may lack experiences and the background needed for play.

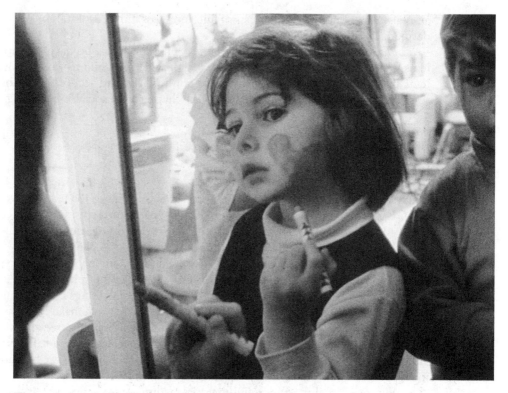

*The curriculum should offer opportunities for children to play.*

Children with developmental delays can have a restricted and less sophisticated repertoire of play skills compared to their "typical peers." Youngsters with physical challenges may engage more in solitary play and less in exploration. Children with autism
have difficulty with symbolic play. Children with hearing impairments engage more in
solitary play. Youngsters with visual impairments can be delayed in their toy exploration
and in their social play skills. Children with language delays may not have the speech
and language skills necessary to interact appropriately with their peers or to make their
needs known (Blasco, 2001; Linder, 1993).

Because play is a primary means for learning, it is essential to plan for the development of play skills for young children who are at risk or who have disabilities. The
curriculum should be planned to furnish appropriate opportunities for children with
special needs to play with their typically functioning peers. A play-based curriculum can
incorporate activity-based instruction as a way to teach instructional goals through play
(Bricker, 1998).

The environment of the early childhood class can be arranged into indoor and outdoor activity centers. These centers can motivate children to participate in construction
activities and symbolic and sensorimotor play. Construction activities include blocks,
sand and water play, painting and drawing, clay carpentry, and puzzles. Symbolic play
consists of opportunities for role playing, playing in the house corner, and playing with
miniature toys that are replicas of people or actual objects, such as families, trucks, and

animals. Sensorimotor play consists of fine and gross motor exploration (Kostelnik, Soderman, & Whiren, 1999).

*Play therapy* is a strategy for helping young children who have emotional problems. With this strategy, a play therapist encourages the child to work through problems by playing with real-life toys in the confidential and secure setting of the play session. Play therapy is further discussed in Chapter 9 on social/emotional problems.

## Establishing the Physical Environment for Learning

The design of the physical environment creates the setting for teaching young children. Exploration and interactions are encouraged when necessary modifications are made for children with special needs in inclusive setting (Bricker, 1998). Adequate space should be provided both in the classroom and on the playground.

Children with physical challenges may need ramps and enough space to maneuver their wheelchairs and walkers. Tables and chairs need to be sturdy to give support to youngsters who lose their balance easily. Nonskid floor coverings can prevent tripping. Toys can be adapted through the use of mechanical switches that make them easier to manipulate. For children with visual impairments, the room should be free of obstacles. The door should be fully open or shut. Sharp edges of tables need to be padded. Toys that have auditory or tactile components should be selected such as books that can be read by pressing a button to hear the story (Davis, Kilgo, & Gamel-McCormick, 1998).

Easy accessibility of toys and materials is important. Toys that are easy to take out of their storage spot and put back are more likely to be used. Bailey and Wolery (1992) suggest that large items, such as blocks and trucks, be placed on open shelves. Small items, such as beads and cubes, can be stored in containers. The children's artwork should be displayed at their eye level. This could vary for children who are in wheelchairs or who are not ambulatory. Work from all the children needs to be displayed and changed according to the current themes of the curriculum.

## The IEP and the IFSP and the Curriculum

Two types of written documents that are developed by a team and that guide curriculum planning for young children with disabilities are the individualized family service plan (IFSP) and the individualized education program (IEP). This section provides pertinent information about both the IFSP and the IEP. A sample of the IEP, shown in Figure 6.4, has the following sections:

- Background Information
- Team Members
- Section 1: Current Levels of Performance
- Section 2: Goals and Objectives
- Section 3: Special Education and Related Services

- Section 4: Participation with Typical Peers
- Section 5: Modification/Adaptation of Regular Education
- Section 6: Determination of Least Restrictive Environment
- Section 7: Procedural Safeguards

A sample IFSP is shown in Appendix D.

## Individualized Family Service Plan (IFSP)

The IFSP is used for infants and toddlers with disabilities, but may also be used for preschoolers. The focus of the ISFP is on intervention for the family as well as the child. In some ways, the IFSP and the IEP are similar, but there are important differences.

***Components of the IFSP.***    The components of the written IFSP must include the following:

1. A statement of the infant/toddler's present level of functioning in physical development (including vision, hearing, and health status), cognitive development, social/emotional development, communication, and adaptive development
2. A statement of the family's strengths, needs, concerns, and priorities relating to enhancing the child's development
3. A statement of the major outcomes expected for the child and the family (including time lines and evaluation criteria)
4. A statement of the specific early intervention services necessary to meet the unique needs of the child and the family
5. Projected dates for the initiation of services and their expected duration
6. The name of the service coordinator who will be responsible to implement the IFSP and to coordinate with appropriate agencies and people
7. A statement of the natural environments where the services will be provided
8. The steps that will be taken to ensure successful transition into the next program or services when the child reaches her or his third birthday

***Purposes of the IFSP.***    The IFSP is primarily different from the IEP in that it is intended for infants and toddlers and emphasizes the role of the family. It supports the natural caregiver roles of the family members. Therefore, the IFSP is family centered, which differs from the focus on the child in the IEP. The IFSP contains a voluntary statement of the family's strengths, needs, and concerns relating to the child's development. A service coordinator is provided to help the family implement the IFSP and coordinate the services. Another difference is that there needs to be a statement of the child's level of development on the IFSP. On the IEP, a statement of the child's present level of educational performance is required instead. In addition, transition services are required for infants and toddlers on the IFSP but not for preschoolers on the IEP. (For further information on the IFSP process, see Chapters 2, 5, and 8.) The following section concentrates on formulating outcome statements, which represents an initial step in designing an individualized curriculum for eligible infants and toddlers.

FIGURE 6.4 *Sample Individualized Education Program (IEP)*

## BACKGROUND INFORMATION

Student's Name: ___Rosa M.___                Date of Meeting: ___9-11-2001___

Age: ___4 years, 1 month___   Primary Disability: ___Developmental delay___

Parent(s)or Guardian(s): ___Ellen & Jack M.___

Address: _____   City, State, Zip: _____

School: ___Trailway___   Grade or Class: ___Early Childhood Class___

Child's Dominant Language: ___English___

## TEAM MEMBERS

Parent(s)or Guardian(s): ___Ellen & Jack M.___

District Representative: ___Janice Pearson, Principal___   Counselor: ___José Ortiz___

School Psychologist: ___Albert Kemp___   Occupational Therapist (OT): ___Lois Lanki___

Speech/Language Therapist: ___Sally Mott___   Special Education Early Childhood Teacher: ___Molly Leaver___

## SECTION 1: CURRENT LEVELS OF PERFORMANCE

*Adaptive Behavior* and *Interdependent Functioning.* (See Goal 1, Section 2.) Observations of occupational therapist, teacher, and parents. Rosa is not toilet trained, but she is making progress with structured toilet training programs at school and at home.

*Social-Emotional.* (See Goal 2, Section 2.) Reports and observations of teachers, counselor, parents, and psychologists. Rosa interacts with adults only. Makes no efforts to interact/play with peers/siblings. She exhibits fears when children play near her (shakes, cries at circle time, play time, and playground where children interact next to her).

## SECTION 2: GOALS AND OBJECTIVES

**Annual Goal 1:** ___Improve Adaptive Behavior/Independent Functioning___

**Short-Term Objectives:**

**1.** Rosa will pull down her pants independently at toilet.

Implementors: Teacher, occupational therapist at school, parents at home

Projected implementation/completion date: ___10-6-2001___

Instructional Method. Collaboration

| Monitored Schedule | Evaluation | Criteria for Mastery | Date of Review | Percent of Objective Met |
|---|---|---|---|---|
| ☐ Daily | ☐ Tests | ☐ 70–80% | ☐ 10-6-2001 | 20 |
| ☐ Weekly | ☐ Charting | ☐ 81–90% | ☐ 11-6-2001 | 35 |
| ☐ Monthly | ☐ Observations | ☐ 91–100% | ☐ 12-6-2001 | 50 |

**2.** Rosa will pull up her pants independently after toileting.

**Annual Goal 2.** Improve interactions with peers and siblings.

**Short-Term Objectives:**

**1.** Rosa will role a ball to a peer (at school) or sibling (at home) and take her turn and wait for the other's turn.

Projected implementation/completion date: ___10–6–2001___

<u>Instructional Method.</u> Collaboration

| Monitored Schedule | Evaluation | Criteria for Mastery | Date of Review | Percent of Objective Met |
|---|---|---|---|---|
| ☐ Daily | ☐ Tests | ☐ 70–80% | ☐ 10-6-2001 | 20 |
| ☐ Weekly | ☐ Charting | ☐ 81–90% | ☐ 11-6-2001 | 35 |
| ☐ Monthly | ☐ Observations | ☐ 100% | ☐ 12-6-2001 | 50 |

**2.** Rosa will catch a ball with physical and verbal prompts by teacher (at school) or occupational therapist or parent (at home).

Projected implementation/completion date: ___10-6-2001___

<u>Instructional Method.</u> Collaboration

| Monitored Schedule | Evaluation | Criteria for Mastery | Date of Review | Percent of Objective Met |
|---|---|---|---|---|
| ☐ Daily | ☐ Tests | ☐ 70–80% | ☐ 10-6-2001 | 20 |
| ☐ Weekly | ☐ Charting | ☐ 81–90% | ☐ 11-6-2001 | 35 |
| ☐ Monthly | ☐ Observations | ☐ 100% | ☐ 12-6-2001 | 50 |

## SECTION 3: SPECIAL EDUCATION AND RELATED SERVICES

| Professional | Type of Service | Time (minutes per week) |
|---|---|---|
| Social worker | Consultant | 20 minutes |
| Psychologist | Integrated service | 50 minutes |
| Occupational therapist | Integrated service | 40 minutes |
| Early childhood educator | Integrated service | 1620 minutes |

## SECTION 4: PARTICIPATION WITH TYPICALLY FUNCTIONING PEERS

**1.** Rosa will participate fully with peers in an inclusive class.

## SECTION 5: MODIFICATION/ADAPTATION OF REGULAR EDUCATION

(Specify if for <u>regular education class</u>, special education class, nonacademic, or extracurricular activities.)

**1.** Break task into small steps, Use task analysis
**2.** Encourage physical proximity with other children, as much as Rosa can tolerate.

## SECTION 6: DETERMINATION OF LEAST RESTRICTIVE ENVIRONMENT

**1.** Full-time instruction in regular class.
**2.** Small class size and child-teacher ratio needed to provide necessary social/emotional support.

## SECTION 7: PROCEDURAL SAFEGUARDS

☐ Copy of IEP guidelines given to parent(s)
☐ Copy of parents' rights given to parent(s)
☐ Parent involvement in IEP
☐ Parental agreement to IEP
☐ Parental disagreement to IEP
☐ Parent or guardian signature

*Formulating the IFSP Outcomes.*   Outcomes are family focused on the IFSP and should be written with the family's words, not the interventionist's. Outcomes are positive changes that the family and team members want to see for the child and family members (Davis, Kilgo, & Gamel-McCormick, 1998). Rosenkoetter and Squires (2000) suggest that these outcomes be written as "in order to" or "so that" statements that families can generate—for example: "Mrs. Davis will find a baby-sitter for Tommy in order to return to work." At this point in the IFSP process, there may be the greatest potential for conflict. Professionals and families could have different values and cultural beliefs about child rearing, disabilities, and medicine (Lynch & Hanson, 1998). Negotiation and compromise about expectations for the child can assist the interventionist and the family members to agree on the priorities for the family. However, the family focus of the IFSP means that the family is the primary decision maker. Therefore, if no consensus is reached, the family's priorities must take precedence over those of the professionals (Hanson & Lynch, 1995). A sample IFSP is shown in Appendix D.

### Individualized Education Program (IEP)

The IEP is a written document prepared by a team to guide services delivery. The team identifies annual goals and short-term objectives for children with disabilities, and the IEP therefore guides the curriculum. The IEP is for children ages 3 through 5.

*Components of the IEP.*   The components of the written IEP must include the following:

1. The child's present level of educational performance
2. Annual goals and short-term objectives or (benchmarks) in areas for which the child requires specially designed instruction
3. A statement of the specific educational services needed
4. The extent of regular class participation and justification in the least restrictive environment
5. The criteria, evaluation procedures, and schedules for determining (at least on an annual basis) whether the instructional objectives are being achieved

The IEP must be developed by a team that includes at least the parents (or guardians), the general education teacher, a special educator, and a representative of the school district, such as the principal. When the child is initially evaluated, there also should be a representative of the school at the IEP meeting.

*Formulating the IEP goals and Objectives or Benchmarks.*   The task of developing goals and objectives on the IEP is a joint responsibility of the parents, teachers, and other team members. Goals and objectives (or benchmarks—a term used in the 1997 IDEA) are included in the IEP document. They can be visualized as a road map. The goals are the final destinations and the short-term objectives are the routes one takes to get there. The goal should state the needed skills based on the assessment of the child. Goals are broad in scope and identify the skill areas for instruction. For example, a goal might be "Charlene will improve her expressive language skills." Short-term objectives or benchmarks are more descriptive and detailed. They are intended to target the intervention and to accelerate learning (Tenbrink, 1999). An objective needs to be functional and realistic and should improve the child's functioning (Bricker, 1998). Three components of short-term objectives are (1) a definition of the specific behavior observed in the skill area, (2) the conditions under which the behavior is to be preferred, and (3) the criteria for determining the adequacy of the behavior (Lerner, 2000). An example of a short-term objective for Charlene based on her present performance might be "Charlene will increase her production of two (three-word) phrases in spontaneous speech."

## Summary

- A curriculum is a set of experiences designed to master developmental or learning goals.
- A curriculum in inclusive settings may need to be adapted to meet the varied learning styles and competencies of children with special needs.
- There are several types of curriculum models that are used with young children with special needs. The developmental curriculum assists young children with special needs to progress through typical developmental sequences. The cognitive curriculum stresses that learning develops through direct experiences. The constructivist curriculum of the Reggio Emilia approach focuses on the right of children to be active participants in constructing their own learning. The ecological/functional curriculum emphasizes the goodness of fit between the environment and the learner. The behavioral curriculum focuses on teaching the child skills through direct instruction. The psychosocial curriculum approach focuses on emotional growth and relationship-based issues.
- The developmentally appropriate practice (DAP) guidelines and curriculum were proposed for early childhood programs by the National Association for the Education of Young Children (NAEYC). The DAP curriculum stresses the importance of play, child-initiated activities, and developmental appropriateness. The early childhood special education organization called the Division for Early Childhood (DEC) has also proposed recommended practices that take into consideration the DAP guidelines. The recommended practices are intended to blend the practices from early childhood education and early childhood special education in the curriculum.
- The activity of play performs a key role in the curriculum for young children with special needs. Early childhood curriculum in natural, inclusive settings highlights the value of play.
- The physical environment is another important element in early childhood programs. A naturalistic perspective can assist inclusion because it calls for instruction in the context of the daily routines of the children and in the organization of the physical environment for learning.
- Preschool children with disabilities must have either the individualized education program (IEP) or the Individualized Family Service Plan (IFSP). Infants and

toddlers with disabilities must have the IFSP. Both the IEP and IFSP have implications for the child's curriculum because they incorporate curriculum goals, objectives, and desired outcomes for each target child.

## Key Terms

activity-based intervention
behavioral curriculum
benchmarks
cognitive curriculum
DEC recommended practices
developmental curriculum
developmental appropriate practice (DAP)

direct instruction
ecological/functional curriculum
general case method
naturalistic approach
psychosocial approach
Reggio Emilia approach

# Motor Development and Medically Related Problems

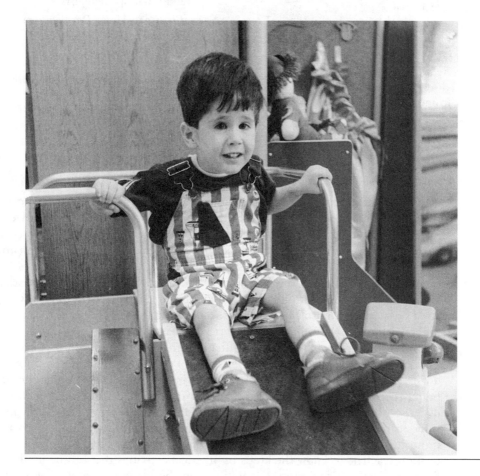

## Chapter Outline _____

*Normal Motor Growth and Development*
   Theories of Motor Development and Delays
   Sequence of Motor Development
   Milestones in Motor Development
   Recent Concepts about Motor Development

*Atypical Motor Development: Delays
and Disabilities*
   Effects of Motor Limitations
   Assessment of Motor Problems

*Characteristics and Types of Motor
and Physical Disabilities*
   Static Central Nervous System Anomalies
      or Insults
   Progressive Diseases
   Spinal Cord and Peripheral Nerve Injuries
   Structural Defects
   Other Types of Physical Impairments

*Medically Related Disabilities*
   Acquired Immune Deficiency
      Syndrome (AIDS)
   Prenatal Exposure to Crack/Cocaine

Fetal Alcohol Syndrome/Effect
Asthma

*Intervention Strategies for Children with Motor
Delays and Physical Disabilities*
   Functional Intervention Activities
   Positioning, Handling, and Feeding Children
      with Motor Disabilities
   Cautions for Working with Children Who
      Have Motor Disabilities
   Movement Education
   Activities for Motor Development
   Resources for Adaptive Equipment
   Specialized Services: Occupational Therapists
      and Physical Therapists

*Special Issues in Motor Development*
   Developmentally Appropriate
      Physical Education
   Inclusion
   Guidelines from the Americans with
      Disabilities Act
   National Organization for Rare Disorders

$Y$oung children naturally seek and enjoy opportunities to move, reach, and stretch as they grow and develop motor skills. Many children with special needs, however, have motoric developmental delays or exhibit physical impairments. Caring for a child with chronic developmental disabilities affects the whole family (Gabor & Farnham, 1996). Parents, teachers, and interventionists need to provide special opportunities and adaptations for these children to enhance their motor skills. The approach to working with children who have motor disabilities has shifted from providing direct services to the child by specialists in isolated settings to a more transdisciplinary approach in the natural environment (Washington, Schwartz, & Swinth, 1994).

This chapter looks at motor difficulties that young children with special needs may encounter and also at disabilities that are related to medical conditions. By understanding motor development as it occurs in typically developing children, we can better recognize the nature of atypical motor development. The chapter also explores different theories of motor development and disabilities as well as delays and deviations in motor development that range from mild developmental delays to severe motor disabilities. It is important for early interventionists and preschool special education teachers to know the kinds of practical activities that can be used with children. To facilitate inclusion, adaptations can be made in the environment, in the

## *Early Childhood Snapshot*  TAQUISHA: A CHILD WITH MOTOR PROBLEMS

The developmental history of a child who exhibits motor delays or motor disabilities may reveal specific incidents that help explain the child's current motor problems. In this example, we follow the birth history, diagnostic course, and intervention plan for Taquisha B.

Taquisha is now 3 years old. She has had an assessment, including a thorough developmental history. Taquisha was born prematurely at 28 weeks gestation. As the first child of Marvella and Thomas B., the history showed that like most parents of premature babies, her parents were totally unprepared for the premature birth. There was no apparent reason for the premature delivery. Taquisha's mother had received appropriate prenatal care during her pregnancy, taken prenatal vitamins, and followed a healthful diet. She stopped drinking alcohol and coffee, and she had never used illicit drugs or smoked.

At birth, Taquisha weighed 1,500 grams (3 lbs., 5 oz.). She experienced periods of apnea (not breathing) and bradycardia (rapid heartbeat), and suffered from Respiratory Distress Syndrome (RDS). The medical diagnosis showed that Taquisha had periventricular leukomalacia (PVL), which is an ischemic lesion of periventricular white matter in the brain that often results in later motor problems. Taquisha spent four weeks in the Neonatal Intensive Care Unit before she was discharged to her parents' care. Initially, Taquisha had seizures, but these have not recurred since the neonatal period.

The family's pediatrician reported that Taquisha's motor development at age 6 months was delayed. He noted fluctuating muscle tone and suspected that she might have cerebral palsy. As Taquisha grew into toddlerhood, it became evident that she did have cerebral palsy. At age 3, she is now enrolled part time in a special education setting. She also attends an inclusionary community preschool setting three afternoons a week.

Taquisha's cognitive functioning is currently about one year delayed. Her vision is corrected with glasses to 20/20, and she hears normally. Motor function is impaired, and she receives both occupational and physical therapy. Although Taquisha is friendly and pleasant, her social and emotional development is somewhat immature and delayed. Her current IEP goals emphasize several areas of motor development, including assistance in developing independence in self-help skills. Taquisha's receptive and expressive language are also mildly delayed, and she receives speech therapy twice weekly.

Both parents have played an active role in seeking diagnosis and intervention for their daughter. Prior to this evaluation, they had sought physical therapy for Taquisha and were very active in having her assessed in order to obtain additional services. Her parents are pleased with her placement in the educational programs and have managed well at home.

preschool curriculum, and with equipment in the preschool setting for children with motor problems.

# *Normal Motor Growth and Development*

Historically, the fields of psychology and education equated the development of motoric skills with cognitive development (Gesell, Ilg, & Ames, 1977). This practice was particularly unfortunate for children with motor disabilities, since they were often assumed to have mental retardation accompanying their specific motor deficits. More recently, developmentalists have focused on the relationship between motoric and cognitive development during the early childhood years.

## Theories of Motor Development and Delays

Several theories about motor development relate to the diagnosis and treatment of young children with special needs. Four of these motor theories will be explored: (1) the classic *developmental motor theory*, which began with the early developmental studies conducted by Arnold Gesell and his colleagues; (2) the *interactional view of development* generated by the developmental psychologist, Jean Piaget; (3) the *theory of sensory integration*, which is based in the field of occupational therapy, originating with the work of Jean Ayres; and (4) a special education perspective of *perceptual-motor learning*, popularized by Newell Kephart.

***Developmental Motor Theory: Gesell.***    Through extensive longitudinal studies of children, Gesell and his colleagues (Gesell & Amatruda, 1947) found that children's development follows a natural progression during preschool years. A typical community preschool operating with a curriculum that features a developmental emphasis reflects Gesell's philosophy. As a practical application of his theory, Gesell emphasized a "developmental school placement" in which "each child should be allowed to develop at his own rate and not be put under undue stress to satisfy the demands of a school system. . . . The growth of a child is slow but steady. We need to be willing to await its manifestations" (Gesell, Ilg, & Ames, 1977, p. x).

***Importance of Sensory-Motor Learning: Piaget.***    Piaget's (1952) theory of child development differs from that of Gesell. Piaget explained development as a series of hierarchical stages, qualitatively and quantitatively different, that show horizontal and vertical change over time as a result of a child's interaction with the environment.

Piaget concluded that active interaction with the environment is a primary learning mode for children. The child's progression from one stage to another is influenced by four major variables:

1. Maturation
2. Experiences with the physical environment
3. Influence of the social environment
4. The child's fluctuating state of equilibrium

For Piaget, the child first learns during the *sensorimotor period* and this stage provides the foundation for all later stages of learning and development. During the sensorimotor period, which lasts approximately from birth to 2 years of age, the child learns through movement and sensory experiences. Children engage in sensorimotor behaviors, such as touching and feeling objects, grabbing, releasing, throwing objects, putting objects in their mouths, creeping, crawling, walking, and running. During this period, the child's intelligence is not reflective; the child deals only with the most concrete aspects of the world.

The subsequent stages of Piaget's developmental hierarchy are *preoperational thought*, *concrete operations*, and *abstract thinking*, and they are discussed in other relevant sections of this book.

Practical manifestations of Piaget's theory in the motor realm include the concept that children are active and inquisitive participants in their intellectual development. In order to learn, they need to be able to make things happen—to act upon and interact physically with their environment.

***Sensory Integration: Jean Ayres.*** The theory of sensory integration offers another view of motor development and motor deviations. The concept of sensory integration was first proposed by occupational therapist, Jean Ayrés (1978, 1981). It continues to be a widely accepted practice today in the field of occupational therapy (Case-Smith 2000; Fisher, Murray, & Bundy, 1991; Sherman, 2000). However, some researchers find the results of studies using sensory integration to be unconvincing (Griffer, 1999; Mauer, 1999). Sensory integration functions are developed during the preschool years, with the most rapid maturation of intersensory function occurring before the age of 8. The acquisition of sensory integration functions is thought to build a foundation for later academic learning.

Sensory integration theory stipulates that the cause of developmental problems of certain young children is the child's inability to integrate the tactile system, the vestibular system, and the proprioceptive system. This lack of sensory integration leads to many developmental problems. The therapy focuses on intervening with special motor activities that are designed to improve the child's sensory-motor integration. Sensory integration therapy is used with young children to build sensory integration motor development at an early age (Sherman, 2000).

One of the problem areas for children with sensory integration disorders is called *tactile defensiveness.* This problem involves the child's inability to tolerate touch or even being touched by certain textures. Children who are tactilely defensive tend to avoid sensory stimulation from touch as much as possible. They find labels in the collars of shirts irritating, will protest if their socks have seams, and resist even a soft gentle touch. These children are less likely to resist a firmer touch or being rubbed with fabric that is rough, such as a terrycloth towel. Therapy includes touching and rubbing skin surfaces, using lotions, and brushing skin surfaces.

Another kind of sensory integration therapy that occupational therapists may use is vestibular stimulation. This therapy involves stimulation through a variety of exercises in planning body movements and balance, such as swinging and carefully controlled spinning exercises that avoid overstimulation of the vestibular system (Cohn, 2001). May-Benson (2000) finds that children with sensory-integration problems are also often impaired in the area of adaptive coping skills—those skills a child uses to meet personal needs and to adapt to the demands of the environment. These children present as more frustrated and anxious than their typically developing peers and have difficulty managing stressful situations and completing tasks.

***Perceptual-Motor Learning: Kephart.*** Newell Kephart (1963, 1971) was a special educator, a developmental psychologist, and a pioneer in the field of learning disabilities.

Kephart's theories stressed the importance of motor learning, emphasizing the necessity for a child to establish a stable perceptual-motor world as a foundation for more advanced learning. He believed that before children begin to learn to perform academic tasks, such as reading and writing, they first must have sufficient motor experiences to organize and orient themselves to the world around them.

Kephart viewed motor development as progressive changes in motor behavior and believed children learn to perform motor activities with a high degree of precision and accuracy. His treatment involved providing children with specific motor skills training so they learn to make motor generalizations.

## Sequence of Motor Development

Several major sequences of motor development are presented in Table 7.1 (O'Donnell, 1969). The patterns pertain to typically developing children who do not have motor disabilities and who have had environmental opportunities for movement and development. The principles of the sequences of motor development are useful in understanding typical growth and development and also in analyzing at what point a child's development may deviate from normal. There are several developmental checklists and assessment instruments that provide approximate time tables for motor development in the typically functioning child (see Appendix C).

## Milestones in Motor Development

*Developmental milestones* refers to specific accomplishments that children achieve as they mature and grow. Typically, children follow a normal developmental sequence as they learn motor skills. Motor performance and the quality of movement begin simply, and gradually become more complex as the child learns to integrate and combine simple motor movements into more complex motor patterns.

**TABLE 7.1**    *Sequences of Motor Development*

| *Pattern* | *Description* |
|---|---|
| Cephalocaudal | Head-to-foot progression |
| Proximo-distal | From spine and center of body out to the extremities |
| Mass to specific | Undifferentiated movements lead to more specific, directed movements |
| Gross motor to fine motor | Large-muscle to small-muscle progression |
| Maximum to minimum muscle involvement | Progression from whole body efforts to more efficient ones |
| Bilateral to unilateral | Progression from use of both sides of the body to one side—laterality |
| Orderly development | Rate may vary, but sequence and pattern are the same |

***Reflexes.*** The earliest movements of infants are reflexes that provide the foundation for the growth and development of the motoric system. These reflexes are characterized as rather rigid and fixed responses to the environment and to stimulation. There are two types of reflexes: primitive and postural (Bukatko & Daehler, 1992).

*Primitive reflexes* help infants survive and protect them during the first year of life. For example, when the infant's cheek is touched, the baby's reflex is to turn his or her head in the direction of the touch and open the mouth for sucking. After the child progresses to the level in which these primitive reflexes are no longer necessary for survival, the primitive reflexes usually disappear. In children who are developmentally delayed, however, these early primitive reflexes are often retained, hampering the child's mobility and motoric development.

*Postural reflexes* assist the child in maintaining an upright posture and orientation. The postural reflexes usually disappear or become incorporated as voluntary behaviors as the child develops. An example of a postural reflex is head control and the reflex of lifting the head while lying face down.

***Gross Motor Skills and Fine Motor Skills.*** Motor developmental milestones include accomplishments in gross motor skills and in fine motor activities. *Gross motor activities* include large motor skills, such as crawling or walking. *Fine motor activities* involve smaller movements, such as eye-hand coordination, using a spoon, or cutting with scissors. As the child develops, he or she gradually increases motor control. Key developmental motor milestones include learning to reach for and grasp objects, developing upright positioning skills, creeping and crawling, standing, and walking. Developmental motor milestones are listed in Appendix C.

***Plasticity of the Brain.*** The young child's developing brain shows the capacity for alternate regions of the brain to take on the specialized sensory, linguistic, and other functions managed by the cerebral cortex (Nelson, 2000). The plasticity of the brain serves as a buffer against damage or injury to the brain. For example, if a preschool child sustains an injury to the brain and loses skills originating from that location in the brain, other parts of the brain take over for the injured section (Bukatko & Daehler, 1992; Lennenberg, 1967). For a child with a brain injury, the healthy areas of the brain continue to develop in the motor areas until the age of about 7 or 8, while some minor changes will continue to take place through adolescence (Hanson & Harris, 1986). Appropriate early intervention for such a child can maximize the child's chances for improvement.

## Recent Concepts about Motor Development

Some researchers have noted limitations in the traditional view of motor development, suggesting that dynamic systems theory and motor programs theory should also be considered in analyzing motor development. Two theories for considering motor development are (1) the dynamic systems theory of motor development and (2) motor programs theory. Bailey and Wolery (1992) state that study and utilization of these two theories might add to our knowledge of the motoric system and how it develops.

The *dynamic systems theory of motor development* hypothesizes that the human organism functions as a system with several subsystems. Further, the subsystems interact with each other in continual transactions. The dynamic systems theory of motor development provides an explanation for a number of motor observations (Bailey & Wolery, 1992; Guiliani, 1991). Why does one developmental task progress while another regresses? Why does a small change in the system produce a large change in behavior? Why does a child move through periods of stability and instability? Why do some behaviors emerge unexpectedly and without prior observation?

*Motor programs theory* is another concept about motor development that views the central nervous system as a control center in which motor commands are stored. The motor programs theory suggests that motor tasks may be modified depending on feedback given to the system (Bailey & Wolery, 1992; Brooks, 1986).

# Atypical Motor Development: Delays and Disabilities

Before looking at atypical motor development, it is first necessary to examine the course of normal motor development and its implications for cognitive learning (Bigge, 1991). Human learning begins with motor learning. As young children move, they learn. As noted by Piaget (1952), movement is essential for effective interaction with the environment and becomes a primary learning channel for early learning. Young children need many opportunities for motor movement at home, at play, and within and outside of the school setting. Young children need to be engaged in activities that promote movement on a daily basis in preschool curriculum, and the child's motor activities should be integrated with other activities.

## Effects of Motor Limitations

For children with motor delays, limitations in movement can impede the development of perceptual skills and have an adverse impact on other kinds of learning and social skills development (Greenspan, 2001). Preschool children with motor problems are a heterogeneous group, with motor impairments ranging from very mild to extremely severe. A child with mild cerebral palsy may look very much like her or his peers but suffer from minor incoordination and perhaps might be diagnosed with a mild learning disability in elementary school. A child with severe motor impairments may be unable to walk or not be able to take care of personal needs, such as feeding oneself.

Physical impairments may be classified according to the severity of the impairment, the clinical type of impairment, and the parts of the body that are affected. For example, children with a *mild* motor impairment can walk unassisted, use their arms, and communicate well enough to make their needs and wants known. Children with a *moderate* impairment require some special help with locomotion and need more assistance than their peers with self-help and communication. Children with a *severe* impairment are usually not able to move from one place to another without being carried or the aid of a wheelchair (Denier, 1993).

*Human learning begins with motor learning.*

## Assessment of Motor Problems

The term *motor delay* might mean a maturational lag or a problem that may disappear in time. Many motor disabilities, however, are more severe and long lasting. Some motor problems that seem to be motor delays during the preschool period may develop into motor disabilities if they do not improve over time.

Assessment of a child's motor development includes an evaluation of both fine and gross motor skills and the way in which the child adapts to the environment (Greenspan, 1999, 2000a). One study conducted in Philadelphia (Klein & Stull, 2000) indicated that parents were found to be least accurate at detecting developmental delays in the fine and gross motor and adaptive areas. They were best able to detect speech/language problems and behavioral delays. Therefore, most referrals for assessments for motor delays will probably come from medical personnel.

Sometimes it is difficult to assess motor delays. When the presenting problem is severe and obvious, the diagnosis is usually made earlier. For example, the child with spina bifida may have many problems that are evident from birth (Mayes, 1999). In the case of cerebral palsy, the child is usually not diagnosed until 12 to 18 months of age. With some forms of muscular dystrophy, the child may have a normal early childhood course, but at about age 4 or 5, clumsiness may be noted, and the disability would first be diagnosed at that age (Hanson & Harris, 1986). The assessment of motor development is also discussed in Chapter 4, and specific instruments used in evaluating motor development are described in Chapter 4 and in Appendix A.

# Characteristics and Types of Motor and Physical Disabilities

Several factors influence the extent of the child's motor problem: the nature of the disability, the timing of the diagnosis, the severity of the disability, and the number and extent of the associated problems, if any (Hanson & Harris, 1986).

The nature of the disability can be classified as:

1. Static central nervous system (CNS) anomalies or insults
2. Progressive diseases
3. Spinal cord and peripheral nerve injuries
4. Structural defects
5. Other types of physical impairments

Next is a description of the various motor impairments that affect preschool children within this classification system.

## Static Central Nervous System Anomalies or Insults

In static CNS anomalies there has been some type of nonprogressive brain damage to the child. This could be due to genetic disorders, such as Down syndrome, or to birth injuries, infection, trauma, or lack of oxygen during the birth process or at any other time. The most common of the static CNS anomalies is cerebral palsy. Lin (2000) studied the ways in which families cope when their children have cerebral palsy. He found that joining associations such as United Cerebral Palsy helped parents with coping behaviors.

*Cerebral Palsy.*    This is not a single disorder, but several disorders of movement and posture that are due to a nonprogressive abnormality of the immature brain. The brain damage that causes cerebral palsy may also produce a number of other disorders, including mental retardation, seizures, visual and auditory deficits, and behavior problems. A child who suffers brain damage at birth because of a lack of oxygen may show signs of cerebral palsy during his or her first year of life (Batshaw & Perret, 1986).

In the school-age population, over 50 percent of children with physical disabilities have cerebral palsy. Approximately one out of every 200 children has some form of cerebral palsy (Hanson & Harris, 1986). Only 60 percent of all cases of cerebral palsy have an identifiable origin.

There are several known causes for cerebral palsy, including teratogens (any agent that causes a defect in the fetus, such as radiation, drugs, infections, and chronic illnesses), chromosomal abnormalities, intrauterine infections, and problems in fetal/placental functioning. In addition, complications of labor and delivery and neonatal complications—such as sepsis, asphyxia, and prematurity—may be causative factors. In early childhood, incidents such as meningitis, head injuries, and exposure to toxins may also be identified as a source of brain injury that causes later problems (Batshaw & Perret, 1986).

Clinical observation is used to assess and identify children with cerebral palsy. Although a physical examination is used in the diagnosis of cerebral palsy, there are no specific tests to identify this disorder. The neurological examination includes tests of muscle tone, strength, and various reflexes. The physician also observes carefully for unusual movements such as ataxia (poor coordination), chorea (jerky movements), athetosis (twisting and writhing movements) and others (Hanson & Harris, 1986). Cerebral palsy is divided into two types, *spastic* (also called pyramidal) and *nonspastic* (extrapyramidal). Children who present with low or high muscle tone may be suspected of having cerebral palsy.

***Muscle Tone Problems.*** Injury to the motor area of the brain generally results in some degree of abnormal muscle tone. *Tone* is a term used to describe tension within the muscle itself. To function normally, the muscles of the body must maintain a degree of tone (Bigge, 1991).

*Hypertonicity.* The child with hypertonia has too much muscle tone. Another name for hypertonicity is *spasticity*. Children with hypertonia are stiff and have limited ability to move. Their muscles feel hard in the areas that are affected. When one attempts to passively move the affected arm or leg, there is resistance to the passive movement. Motor milestones are frequently delayed in children with hypertonia. Because of increased muscle tone in their chests, breathing may be difficult due to decreased movement of the ribs. Also, when the facial and oral muscles are involved, articulation is often difficult (Hanson & Harris, 1986).

Hypertonicity tends to occur when there are abnormal or persistent primitive reflexes. A reflex is considered abnormal when it is obligatory to the extent the child is unable to overcome it. Primitive reflexes that occur normally very early in development may persist long after they should have been integrated. The therapist's job is not to treat the reflexes, but to develop the missing components of movement that will reduce reflex behavior and improve physical functioning.

*Hypotonicity.* Low muscle tone (hypotonicity) appears as floppiness in a young child (Bigge, 1991). It becomes difficult for the baby to lift his or her head and arms against gravity. The child with hypotonia has great difficulty assuming and maintaining positions against the force of gravity. Motor milestones are usually delayed because of the generalized low muscle tone.

One type of disability usually characterized by hypotonia is Down syndrome (Hanson & Harris, 1986). When pulled to a sitting position, a child with hypotonia shows headlag, which disappears by about 4 months of age in a typically developing child. When propped to sit, the child falls forward, has difficulty raising his or her head, and exhibits little stability in the trunk. Children who are hypotonic will use their widely spaced legs to sit in a "W" sitting position, sitting between rather than behind their legs. Interventionists should actively discourage this position.

Whenever hypotonia is apparent, the physical therapist works to improve the function of the trunk extensors and flexors with therapeutic exercise. Children with hypotonia usually have very lax ligaments, which results in excessive movement at the joints. (This is referred to by laypersons as being double jointed.) The child's muscles may feel soft and doughy (Hanson & Harris, 1986). Because of the low muscle tone in the chest and face muscles, breathing tends to be shallow, and these children have difficulty sustaining sounds when attempting to cry, babble, or talk. The low tone in the jaw and tongue muscles results in the jaw hanging open and the tongue hanging out because of the effect of gravity pulling the jaw and tongue down. This has implications both for speech production and feeding.

*Fluctuating Tone.*    Some children show variations in tone, ranging from hypotonia to hypertonia. Tone may change in different body parts depending on the child's position or the activity in which he or she is involved (Hanson & Harris, 1986). The most common type of motor disability in which fluctuating muscle tone occurs is athetoid cerebral palsy.

## Progressive Diseases

Progressive diseases of the brain, nerves, or muscles produce motor impairment that generally gets worse over time. Fortunately, these diseases are very rare, since they often result in death at a premature age. Muscular dystrophy is one of the progressive diseases of the brain, nerves, or the muscles that produces motor impairments that worsen with the passage of time (Hanson & Harris, 1986).

***Muscular Dystrophy.***    Muscular dystrophy constitutes a group of chronic, progressive disorders that affect the voluntary muscles. Bigge (1991) indicates that the disease is inherited and is usually not detected until the child is a toddler and begins to fall down frequently due to muscle weakness. There is gradual weakness and decline in muscle strength and health; however, intellectual functioning is not affected. Call and Ziter (1985) find that during the first year of life, some children with muscular dystrophy fail to gain weight and many present with a risk factor for failure to thrive.

This group of disorders comprises only a very small fraction of children with physical disabilities. Most of these diseases lead to a premature death. Duchenne muscular dystrophy is one example of a fatal progressive neurological disease. Children with Duchenne muscular dystrophy generally die in their early 20s.

## Spinal Cord and Peripheral Nerve Injuries

Spinal cord and peripheral nerve injuries are generally static like cerebral palsy, except for some rare tumors that continue to grow. The largest group of children in this category have spina bifida.

***Spina Bifida.***    This is a typical example of an injury to the central nervous system that is static. Spina bifida occurs in one of every 1,000 live births (Bailey & Wolery,

1992). The diagnosis of spina bifida is usually made at birth, since there is an external sac containing the meninges and spinal cord exposed on the child's back (Bigge, 1991). The exception to this diagnosis is spina bifida occulta, which is less severe, and is generally only identified by x-ray or the presence of a hair whorl at the base of the spinal column and may never be identified.

Spina bifida is a malformation of the spinal column with cystic swelling around the spine. Paralysis occurs below the lesion. Hydrocephalus is common; intelligence may be normal. Bowel and bladder control are often affected. The actual cause is unknown, but the condition develops as a result of the failure of closure of the neural tube (Batshaw & Perret, 1986).

*Folic Acid.* The use of folic acid in women of child-bearing age has been found to reduce the incidence of spina bifida and other neural tube defects (Oakley, 1998; Spina Bifida Association Website www.spaa.org, 2001). The key is having enough folic acid in the system before pregnancy, at least for one month before conception. As of January 1998, the Food and Drug Administration required food manufacturers to fortify enriched grain products with folic acid. In addition, medical doctors have advised women of child-bearing age to take 400 micrograms of folic acid daily—the amount found in a typical over-the-counter multivitamin pill.

## Structural Defects

Structural defects are just what they sound like. In all cases, something is missing— for example, a limb or some support structure for the nerves and muscles is not adequate. Some of these defects may be static, or they may be progressive and difficult to manage. Examples of diseases in this category are childhood arthritis and osteogenesis imperfecta.

*Arthrogryposis Multiplex Congenita.* This is a condition that is present at birth and is characterized by stiffness of the joints. There may be little to no movement in the child's joints. This is caused by thickened joint capsules, shortened muscles, and decreased muscle bulk. The legs turn out and the hips are prone to dislocation. It is important to remember that not only are the children's joints stiff but their bones are osteoporotic; that is, they break easily. Interventionists are advised to keep handling to a minimum and to move children very gently (Denier, 1993).

*Osteogenesis Imperfecta or "Brittle Bones."* This is a disease in which improperly formed bones break easily. Bigge (1991) describes the condition as generalized, involving other tissues such as the teeth, the skin, and the whites of the eyes. In the congenital type of osteogenesis imperfecta, fractures may be present at birth and children may die within the first few years of life. Early treatment and medication provide the potential to prevent deformities and improve clinical outcomes (Plotkin, Rauch, Bishop, Montpett, Ruck-Gibis, Travers, & Glorieux, 2000).

In the latent type, the condition first appears in childhood. The bones are fragile, and the limbs are thin and may be deformed. Treatment consists of protection from injury to the child's bones. Braces, surgery, and crutches may be required. In some instances, surgery is conducted in which the surgeon cuts the bone and threads it over a rod. Deafness sometimes accompanies this disorder.

This condition is sometimes misdiagnosed as child abuse because of frequent hospital visits for fractures early in the child's life. In all cases of osteogenesis imperfecta, it is important that the child be handled with extreme caution in the classroom and during physical activity so as not to fracture any bones.

## Other Types of Physical Impairments

There are other types of physical impairments that may be causative or associated with motor disabilities—namely, traumatic injuries and multiple disabilities.

***Trauma: Head and Spinal Cord Injury.***    Some physical disabilities may be caused by head and spinal cord injuries. This type of injury may occur from automobile or bicycle accidents, gunshot wounds, or physical abuse and other causes. Traumatic brain injury (TBI), an injury to the brain caused by being hit by something or shaken violently, results in changes in thinking and reasoning. These injuries can also cause deficits in hearing and vision (National Information Center for Children and Youth with Disabilities, 1999). The effects may be mild to severe. Memory may be affected and it may be difficult for these children to learn new information.

***Multiple Disabilities Including Seizures and Convulsive Disorders.***    Children with multiple disabilities may have other problems in addition to their physical disabilities, including visual, auditory, visual and auditory, and convulsive disorders (Bigge, 1991). Perceptual problems and severe to mild communication disorders may also occur in these children. Children with cerebral palsy or other motor disabilities may have additional associated problems because the brain has been damaged. Over half of the children with cerebral palsy have mental retardation and/or learning disabilities (Hanson & Harris, 1986). In addition, many of these children have seizure disorders. Communication problems are common. In some instances, children with cerebral palsy may be blind and/or deaf. They may also suffer from nutritional problems because of swallowing disorders and regurgitation of food.

***Seizures and Convulsive Disorders.***    Many children with physical disabilities also have seizures. A single episode of a seizure that does not recur does not require medication. Individuals with repeated seizures have epilepsy, also called a *seizure disorder.* About 50 percent of all the children with epilepsy have normal intelligence; however, there is a higher incidence of learning disabilities among the population of children with epilepsy (Batshaw & Perret, 1986).

A seizure, or a convulsion, starts in an area of the cortex containing nerve cells (neurons) that are more apt to discharge than normal cells. Seizures are "sudden, excessive, spontaneous, and abnormal discharges of neurons in the brain accompanied by alteration in motor function and/or sensory function, and/or consciousness" (Smith & Lukasson, 1995, p. 523). Three major types of seizure disorders are depicted in Table 7.2.

**TABLE 7.2** *Types of Seizure Disorders*

| Type of Seizure | Characteristics |
| --- | --- |
| Generalized absence or rolling of the eyes (Petit mal) | A blank stare, lasts only seconds. May also show rapid blinking. Often mistaken for daydreaming. |
| Generalized tonic-clonic (Grand mal) | A convulsion—bodily stiffness followed by jerking movements. Usually lasts a minute or two. Child may lose bladder control. |
| Complex partial (Psychomotor) | May start with blank stare, followed by chewing or repeated movements that seem out of place and mechanical. Child may seem dazed. Lasts one to two minutes. |

*Note:* Information from publications distributed by the Epilepsy Foundation of America.

***Medications Used to Control Seizures.*** Several medications are used to control seizure disorders. In some cases, the seizures will be controlled by the medication, but the child may exhibit drowsiness or incoordination as a side effect of the seizure medication. Interventionists need to know what side effects may occur from taking a particular anticonvulsant medication. This information may be obtained from the school nurse, the child's physician, the parents, or from the *Physicians' Desk Reference*, which is available in public and university libraries. Organizations such as the Epilepsy Foundation of America also provide information about anticonvulsant medications. Their phone number is (800) EFA-1000.

# Medically Related Disabilities

There are many medically related disabilities that affect motor functioning, pose additional serious risks to children, and may have long-term deleterious effects. Medically related disabilities pertain to certain diseases and/or the ingestion of teratogens on the part of the mother during pregnancy. Prenatal exposure to crack/cocaine and/or alcohol may have far-reaching effects on the unborn child and result in significant developmental delays that are manifested during the preschool years.

The conditions and diseases that are discussed in this section include children diagnosed as positive for the human immunodeficiency virus (HIV) or with acquired immune deficiency syndrome (AIDS), prenatal exposure to crack/cocaine, and Fetal Alcohol Syndrome (FAS).

## Acquired Immune Deficiency Syndrome (AIDS)

The human immunodeficiency virus (HIV), believed to be the cause of acquired immune deficiency syndrome (AIDS), ranks among the top 10 leading causes of death for children under age 4 in the United States (Layton & Davis-McFarland, 2000). In 1993, approximately 3,605 children under the age of 5 were reported to have AIDS (Centers for Disease Control, 1993). In 1997, there were an estimated 6,032 children under age 5 who were infected with the virus (www.ucsf.edu). This may represent only a percentage of those diagnosed, since many cases are not reported. Many children with HIV now live longer due to newer medications and treatment.

Teachers of preschool children are working with an increased number of children who are HIV-positive and/or have developed AIDS. These children have to cope with many obstacles, educational and medical, and fight for their survival. HIV infection appears to compromise language development (Davis-McFarland, 2000), and developmental delays occur in nearly 90 percent of children infected (Layton & Scott, 2000). Since the number of children who are infected with HIV is increasing, teachers should be aware of and implement specific precautions when working with all youngsters.

The term *universal precautions* is applied to serving individuals in both the medical and educational fields (Layton & Davis-McFarland, 2000). In order for these precautions to be *universal*, they must be applied when working with every child. Adopting universal precautions serves at least two functions. First, should a child be HIV-positive, his or her identity is protected and confidentiality is kept, since parents and administrators would know that *all* children were treated with universal precautions the child would not have to be identified. Second, since not all children who are HIV-positive have been diagnosed and may not show symptoms, a teacher or child-care worker might contract the virus from an apparently symptom-free child unless precautions are taken.

Bowe (1995) and Bruder (1995) caution that because the virus is transmitted through bodily fluids, all teachers should use latex gloves when diapering or handling a child's cuts or scrapes to avoid coming in contact with blood and other bodily fluids. In addition, teachers are encouraged to wash their hands frequently and wash surfaces and toys with bleach after play sessions.

## Prenatal Exposure to Crack/Cocaine

In the 1980s, the use of cocaine and particularly the crack form of cocaine escalated in the United States (Chapman & Elliott, 1995). Chasnoff (1989) finds that estimates of the numbers of affected infants vary and are most certainly underreported; however, it is estimated that 11 to 15 percent of babies born in the United States were exposed in utero to alcohol or illicit drugs.

As young children began to enter the school system diagnosed with disabilities that were the result of "prenatal exposure" to drugs, articles appeared in both the popular press and professional articles warning teachers and interventionists that the "crack-babies" were coming to the schools and that they should ready themselves for the onslaught of these children, who were like no other children to enter the school system (Myers, Olson, & Kaltenbach, 1992). The initial hysteria died down and left administrators and teachers with a group of children, some of whom exhibited severe involvement with multiple developmental delays (Griffith, 1988) and some who had little to no apparent delays or central nervous system involvement.

The issue for interventionists is that children who are prenatally exposed to drugs and suffer deleterious effects are still children and that we have had children with these types of symptomology before. Brain injury, seizures, short attention spans, and learning disabilities are not new conditions for special educators (Mayes, Granger, Bornstein, & Zuckerman, 1992). However, there are certain techniques and methods that have proved effective when working with these children. The controversy about the potential deleterious effects of prenatal exposure to cocaine continues in the research literature. Tronick and Begghly (1999) find that long-term global impairment may not be substantiated, but there is a cumulative risk for exposed children. Recent studies also indicate that the environment in which a child who has been prenatally exposed also affects his or her development. An inconsistent and chaotic environment affects children's abilities to form attachments, and may result in disrupted patterns of arousal and attachment, as well as difficulties in behavioral regulation (Greenberg, 2000; Mayes, 1999; interview with Chasnoff at www.reconsider.org, 2000).

Two websites that offer information about prenatal exposure to drugs and alcohol are the American Academy of Pediatrics at www.aap.org, and the Center for Substance Abuse Prevention at www.samhsa.gov.

Table 7.3 illustrates the potential effects of prenatal exposure to drugs. It highlights the areas in which children who are prenatally exposed to crack/cocaine may be affected.

## Fetal Alcohol Syndrome/Effect

Fetal alcohol syndrome (FAS) is an irreversible condition caused by consumption of alcohol by the mother during pregnancy, marked by a pattern of physical and mental birth defects (Smeriglio & Wilcox, 1999). This disorder was first identified in the 1970s (Jones, Smith, Ulleland, & Streissguth, 1973). Alcohol is a teratogen, which is an agent or factor that causes the production of physical defects in a developing embryo. Alcohol use during pregnancy can cause deficits in cognition and language, physical malformations, and behavior problems in affected children.

Alcohol has been implicated as a damaging chemical agent for unborn children. Substances, such as alcohol and drugs, cross the placental barrier. Fetal Alcohol Syndrome is caused by alcohol passing from the bloodstream of the mother through the placenta and into the bloodstream of the fetus (Trask & Kosofsky, 2000). Alcohol passes through the placenta in the same concentration as is present in the mother's body, but the ratio of alcohol to body weight is much higher for the fetus. The fetus has an underdeveloped liver and thus cannot metabolize alcohol. Therefore, the fetus must rely on diffusion to eliminate the alcohol, and this process cannot begin until the mother's blood alcohol level has decreased, so the fetus is exposed to high concentrations of alcohol over a long time.

Burgess and Streissguth (1992) state that fetal alcohol syndrome is now recognized as the leading known cause of mental retardation in the Western world. They report that one out of every 500 to 600 children in the United States is born with FAS, although this may be a conservative estimate. This condition has been observed across all socioeconomic and ethnic groups, although certain Native American tribes and less

**TABLE 7.3**    *Prenatal Substance Abuse Behavior, Learning and Developmental Indicators for Infants and Preschool Children*

| Motor and Neurological Development | Affective and Behavioral Development |
|---|---|
| Tremulousness | Mood swings, rapid shifts in mood |
| Poor visual attention and following | Irritable, impulsive behaviors |
| Staring spells, bizarre eye movements | Depressed affect, decreased laughter |
| Decreased awareness of body in space | Difficulty with transitions |
| Problems in fine motor dexterity | Constant limit testing |
| Clumsiness, gross motor incoordination | Difficulty with self-regulation |

| Social Attachment Development | Attention and Concentration |
|---|---|
| Decreased response to praise | Attention deficits |
| Decreased eye contact | Increased distractibility |
| Decreased use of gestures | Decreased accommodation in problem solving |
| Decreased stranger anxiety | Impulsivity |
| Indiscriminate attachment to new people | Gives up easily |
| Aggressiveness with peers | Decreased visual scanning of all stimuli |
| Decreased compliance with verbal direction | Decreased use of trial and error strategies |
| Decreased use of adults for solace, comfort, and recognition | Delay in satisfaction of task completion |

| Language Development | Play |
|---|---|
| Fewer spontaneous vocalizations | Decreased spontaneous play |
| Delayed acquisition of words | Increased aimless wandering |
| Decreased use of words to communicate wants and needs | Does not generalize acquired adaptive skills in play |
| Shows errors in picture/object identification | Cannot organize own play, appears perplexed and confused |
| Difficulty in "word finding" at preschool level | Easily overstimulated by people, movement, and noise |

*Source:* Adapted from U.S. Department of Education (1993).

advantaged socioeconomic groups show proportionately higher representations (Burd & Moffatt, 1994).

Fetal alcohol syndrome is associated with specific characteristics in affected children—including pre- and postnatal growth deficiency, facial malformations, and central nervous system deficits—that may result in mental retardation, hyperactivity, or motor problems. Children with FAS may be small for gestational age, have congenital heart defects, droopy eyelids, microcephaly, and joint abnormalities.

In order to qualify for a diagnosis of FAS, an individual must display symptoms in each of the following three areas (adapted from Aase, 1994):

1. Prenatal or postnatal growth retardation (height and/or weight)
2. Central nervous system involvement
3. Facial dysmorphology
   a. Microcephaly (unnatural smallness of the head)
   b. Microopthalmia (unnatural smallness of the eyes)
   c. Poorly developed philtrum (vertical ridges between nose and mouth), thin upper lip, and flattening of the maxillary area (underdevelopment of the mid-facial jaw bone region)

Children who demonstrate some, but not all, of these characteristics may be identified as having fetal alcohol effects (FAE).

As in other types of medically related disabilities, there is a continuum of effects obvious in children with FAS. Some of them show severe mental retardation, others exhibit mild learning disabilities. Children diagnosed with FAS or FAE typically perform poorly on measures of intelligence and achievement, exhibit difficulties in motor coordination, demonstrate behavioral difficulties such as short attention spans, and show physical abnormalities and growth retardation. Preschool children may exhibit one or more of the following (adapted from McCann, 1996):

| | |
|---|---|
| Short elf-like appearance | Seizures |
| Excessive and intrusive talk | Microcephaly |
| Language delays | Attentional deficits |
| Speech impairments | Emotional lability |
| Insatiable need for body contact | Poor peer relations |
| Hyperactivity | Poor judgment |
| Seem fearless, tend to wander | |

Because mothers who abuse alcohol and/or drugs and their children who have been drug exposed have difficulty coping with even moderate levels of frustration and tension, several levels of medical, family, and educational intervention are necessary to promote the child's health and development. However, there are few areas in which there are comprehensive, specialized services for mothers who are substance abusing and/or their children.

Often, mothers who abuse substances and drink alcohol are polydrug abusers (Tronick & Beeghly, 1999). That is, they may consume alcohol, smoke crack, smoke cigarettes, and take other harmful drugs during their pregnancy. The number of drug-exposed children is increasing rapidly and the medical complications of prenatal drug exposure appear be extensive and lasting. Zuckerman and Brown (1993) indicate that "as many as 20 to 30 million people in the United States abuse illicit drugs and 5 million are regular users" (p. 143).

In summary, early interventionists and teachers of preschool children will probably see an increase in the numbers of children who present with motoric, cognitive,

*It is important to provide intervention strategies that are functional and developmentally appropriate.*

and behavioral problems due to prenatal exposure to alcohol, crack/cocaine, and other drugs. Zuckerman (1990) put this issue in a larger perspective. He indicates that we should not be focused on FAS or crack/cocaine exposure, that it is essential to treat whole children and whole families in child-focused programs.

One positive aspect of these debilitating syndromes is that they are completely preventable. Prevention efforts have begun in high schools, colleges, hospitals, and throughout the medical services community.

## Asthma

Asthma is one of the most common diseases found in young children, affecting approximately 5 to 7 percent of all children in the United States (Lowenthal & Lowenthal, 1995; Simeonsson, Lorimer, Shelley, & Sturtz, 1995); however, it affects 10 percent of poor children (Miller, 2000). Many preschool children may be affected since one-third of the children who develop asthma do so prior to age 5. Symptoms of asthma include wheezing, shortness of breath, and coughing. Some cases of asthma are exercise induced; others result from allergic responses and other factors.

The incidence of asthma is rising in the United States (Bender, 1999), especially among poor, inner-city African American children (Simeonsson et al., 1995). Concerns regarding the child with asthma and school performance focus on several factors.

Medications that children may take for asthma can affect their attention span due to fatigue and loss of sleep. Absenteeism is another factor that affects learning and socialization. Lowenthal and Lowenthal (1995) find in their review of the literature that asthma accounts for more hospital admissions and absences from school than any other childhood disease. Some children with asthma have low energy and are unable to concentrate, focus well, and may generally feel poorly (Bender, 1999).

Early childhood specialists need to be aware that in order to manage a child with asthma, improved communication between parents, school personnel, and physicians is essential as is an understanding of parents' stress (Getch, Neuharth-Pritchet, 1999). In addition, an asthma management plan should be developed for each child at the time of the IFSP or IEP (Simeonsson et al., 1995).

## Intervention Strategies for Children with Motor Delays and Physical Disabilities

Piaget (1952) notes that the child's first learning experiences are motoric. This realization underscores the importance of movement for young children and allows them to explore and experience their world. There are several types of interventions for preschool children with motor problems. Interventions include four different forms, which are listed in Table 7.4 (Hanson & Harris, 1986).

### Functional Intervention Activities

When working with young children who have developmental disabilities, it is important to provide intervention strategies that are both functional and developmentally appropriate. Functional activities include those movements that would occur naturally in the environment. Use of functional movements enables the child to develop independence and self-sufficiency. Mahoney (1999) raises the issue of concern regarding establishment

**TABLE 7.4**   *Types of Intervention for Children with Motor Impairments*

| Type of Intervention | Description |
| --- | --- |
| Hands-on therapy | Occupational and physical therapy, education, speech and language therapy, recreational therapy |
| Assistive devices | Braces, splints, and adaptive equipment |
| Medication | Used to relax muscles, antibiotics for infections, and anticonvulsants for seizures |
| Surgery | To correct orthopedic abnormalities |

of an adult-centered view of functionality as opposed to a child-centered view. Developmentally appropriate activities are not too difficult for the child, nor are they too easy. The goals of intervention in the motoric area include (Hanson & Harris, 1986):

1. Helping the child to move as normally as possible
2. Teaching the child to use movement to initiate interactions with and to control aspects of the environment
3. Providing opportunities that allow the child to grow and gain independence

Horn (1991) argues for more collaboration among disciplines when working with children who have physical disabilities. She states that behavioral programming has been overlooked at times when implementing physical and occupational therapy. Multidisciplinary teams including special educators and psychologists should work with specific therapists to be the most helpful when planning intervention for young children with disabilities (Washington et al., 1994).

Children need to generalize the skills acquired in therapeutic situations to other milieux. Teachers and therapists should plan their interventions to incorporate several techniques; probe for simple generalizations across persons, settings, and training items; and observe performance in functional environments (Horn, 1991).

### Positioning, Handling, and Feeding Children with Motor Disabilities

For children with motor impairments, including cerebral palsy, appropriate handling and positioning will provide an important carryover of the goals sought in implementing the child's motor programs. Improper positioning and handling may maximize the child's muscle tone differences. Appropriate handling and positioning will provide an important carryover of the goals sought in carrying out the child's motor programs.

***Positioning.***    *Positioning* refers to placing the child in carefully selected positions in order to stabilize the body, normalize muscle tone, and prevent further deformity. When the child with motor disabilities needs to remain in a static position, the proper positioning is extremely important (Hanson & Harris, 1986). Consultation with occupational and physical therapists for proper positioning techniques is essential because there are certain cautions that need to be observed with each position. There are five basic positions that are generally appropriate for the child with motoric disabilities. Table 7.5 lists these positions.

Nancie Finnie (1975) has written a thorough reference for interventionists and parents who work with children with motor impairments, including cerebral palsy. Her text deals with the baby and child up to 5 years of age and is written clearly for parents and practitioners. She stresses the necessity for treatment to begin early because it is impossible to overemphasize the value of early treatment in combination with good handling, for the "earlier the treatment and the younger the child, the less the degree of probable abnormality" (p. 3).

**TABLE 7.5** *Positions for Children with Motor Impairments*

| Position | Description |
|---|---|
| Prone lying | Use of a bolster and/or wedge to prop child so that arms are free, and child can look around environment. |
| Side lying | Used to facilitate midline activities with hands. Arms are brought forward and gravity helps bring hands together. Keep head, trunk, and one or both hips flexed in this position. |
| Supported sitting | Adaptive seating to give the child the support in the trunk to free up the hands for functional activities, such as feeding or play. |
| Supported standing | Use of prone board or prone stander to allow child to "stand" upright and look at environment from this posture. Helps maintain the head upward against gravity and to use arms in the midline. |
| Supine | Lying on one's back. This position is used with children who are lower functioning and cannot be maintained well in other positions. |

For children who are able to move little, if any, on their own, changing the position at least once every 30 to 45 minutes is extremely important. Position changes will minimize the risks of developing redness or pressure sores over bony prominences (such as the elbow or ankle) and will give children an opportunity to view their environment from different vantage points.

***Handling.*** *Handling* is the process of carrying or moving a child from one position to another or from one place to another. Children with cerebral palsy are not only limited to movements that are stereotyped but they are also limited in their reactions and responses to being moved (Finnie, 1975). When anything is being done for the child, it is important that the child should not be passive and that he or she see what is being done and have someone talk about it while the handling and positioning are accomplished.

The goals of proper handling are to normalize muscle tone, prepare the child for movement, and facilitate movement (Cook, Tessier, & Klein, 1996). When handling and positioning, Hanson and Harris (1986) suggest the following guidelines:

1. Use key points of control.
2. Work toward symmetry—both sides of the body repositioned similarly so that one side looks like a mirror image of the other.
3. Work toward midline positioning. Many young children with motor problems are unable to get their hands together in midline of the body, and these skills are necessary for developing fine motor and self-help skills. Side-lying is helpful here.
4. Use only the minimal support needed when handling or positioning the child. For example, when carrying children who have developed adequate control of trunk muscles to sit independently on the floor, support should be given at the hips or lower trunk so that they will be actively using their upper trunk muscles

to hold themselves erect. This kind of support will not prevent them from using the muscle control they have developed so far.

*Key Points of Control.*    In planning activities to normalize tone, the occupational and physical therapist utilize the key points of control (Hanson & Harris, 1986). These key points of control involve handling the child at either the head, shoulders, trunk, or hips (Bobath & Bobath, 1972). The Bobaths devised a program for neurodevelopmental training (NDT), which is used throughout the world by occupational and physical therapists.

The key points of control are the more proximal parts of the body or those nearest the center of the body. When moving or positioning a child, it is important to concentrate on these key points.

*Feeding.*    Oral-motor activities are those involving the coordinated use of the muscles around the mouth, the tongue, and the jaw. Many young children with motor delay will also have delayed or abnormal oral-motor development. Delayed development in oral-motor control may lead to difficulties in feeding, drinking, talking, and breath control (Hanson & Harris, 1986).

Positioning is also critical in feeding the child with motor problems. If proper positioning techniques are not used during feeding, many children with abnormal muscle tone will have problems with gagging, choking, or swallowing (Cook et al., 1996). Bigge (1991) also advises that the following be considered in planning an effective feeding program: feeding techniques, feeding utensils, consistency of foods, consideration of normalizing oral hypersensitivity, cup-drinking techniques, social interactions, and diet.

For the preschool child who has some sitting balance, placement in a high chair or specially adapted chair is the preferred method for feeding. If the child is an infant or if the child has a severe motor impairment, the child may be propped with pillows against a support and seated in a supportive chair facing the parent (Hanson & Harris, 1986). Finnie (1975) stresses that adequate control of the whole child is essential while the child is being fed.

## Cautions for Working with Children Who Have Motor Disabilities

Prior to involving a child in any motor activity, the teacher should consult the student's medical record, therapists, or physician to determine if any specific activity should be avoided or encouraged. Specific conditions to watch for include heart disease, arthritis, hip dislocations, and brittle bones (Osteogenesis Imperfecta) when considering movement activities. In addition, medications may affect the child's tone and activity level.

One problem in particular, which occurs in about 14 to 18 percent of young children with Down syndrome, is *Atlanto-Axial Instability.* Children who exhibit this problem have an increased mobility of the first two neck bones due to laxity of the ligaments that hold these bones together (Peuschel, 1985). Children with Atlanto-Axial Instability who engage in very active play could suffer a serious cervical spine injury. Routine physical examinations on all children with Down syndrome for this problem is recommended.

## Movement Education

Many different activities can be used to encourage young children to participate in movement activities. Even the most severely involved child can participate when the interventionist is creative. For example, while visiting a local Chicago public school, we observed a kindergarten classroom in which three children were in wheelchairs. These children were turning and rolling and waving scarves in the air while music played, and the other children moved around the room. When the children in wheelchairs were asked what was going on, they responded, "Can't you tell, we're dancing!" Recently, Campbell (1999) has suggested using applied behavior analysis (ABA) to teach motor skills, motor control, and dynamic systems. Neurodevelopmental training (NDT) and ABA may be applied within the context of typically occurring activities and routines.

## Activities for Motor Development

The following list describes the kinds of motor activities that are appropriate for children who have motor delays and disabilities (adapted from Bailey & Wolery, 1992; Cook et al., 1999; Delgado & Combes, 1999; Finnie, 1975; Lerner, Mardell-Czudnowski, & Goldenberg, 1987; Miller, 1999; Wanzer, 1999):

1. *Sand and water tables.* The use of sand and water tables is helpful for fine motor and eye motor control.
2. *Music.* Music can be used to encourage preschool children to participate in movement activities; rhythm bands and adapted dancing will help involve children with motoric impairments. Songs can be used for fun and for transitions from one activity to another.
3. *Fine motor activities.* The use of puzzles, blocks, shape-sorting toys, clay, pegboards, form boards, crayons, fingerplay games, threading and stacking toys, nesting cups, and construction sets help with fine motor coordination.
4. *Opportunities for movement.* Abundant opportunities should be provided for movement, and children should be encouraged to move about the classroom. Various activities include those that take place on the floor as well as ones that require locomotion. Obstacle courses also provide motivation for movement.
5. *Motor activities and other skills.* Movement and training of specific movements may be embedded in training activities to reach other skills, such as language and social skills activities. For example, at snack time, children may set the table, count napkins and cookies, serve each other, and wipe the table and chairs at cleanup time.
6. *Naming body parts.* Teachers should name the parts of the child's body and describe clothes and their colors as they dress the child. For example, a teacher might say, "Help me push your foot into your shoe," or "Lean this way so that I can put your coat on you." This also enhances the child's self-concept and personalizes dressing time.
7. *Gross motor activities.* Activities such as crawling, hopping, sliding, running, throwing and catching balls, jumping, walking on tiptoes, and, for older children,

skipping should be encouraged. The use of balloons, blankets, and balls provide creative activities also.

8. *Snack time.* Snack time may be utilized for an expansion of motor activities. Pouring, cutting, folding, pushing chairs in and out, chewing, sucking on straws, and passing treats all enhance both motor and social skills.

9. *Dress up.* Putting on dress-up clothes, buttoning, zipping, attaching with Velcro, and putting on big shoes or hats all involve motor coordination.

10. *Rest and relaxation.* Children have a need for rest periodically, so vigorous activities should be alternated with more relaxing ones. There should be "quiet times" designated during the day.

## Resources for Adaptive Equipment

Adaptive equipment can help the young child with motor disabilities in positioning, mobility, eating, and other activities of daily living. Adaptive equipment can be very

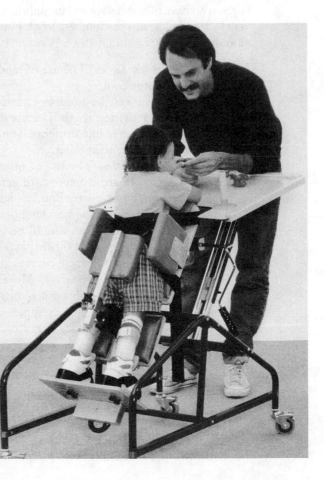

*Adaptive equipment can help the young child with motor disabilities.*

expensive, and the equipment needs to be changed frequently as the child grows. Hanson and Harris (1986) list several resources for parents. Some agencies maintain equipment-borrowing services and may assist parents with renting or borrowing equipment. Local agencies that serve children with disabilities—such as Easter Seals, Muscular Dystrophy Association, and United Cerebral Palsy—may also help parents.

Physicians and social workers may provide information about the purchase of equipment, and those families who qualify under Social Security, Medicaid, or Aid to Dependent Children may find assistance through these sources. Private insurance for medical and other health care may pay partial or full costs under major medical coverage (Hanson & Harris, 1986). Many parents can describe how a power wheelchair has improved their children's lives. Children who use power devices, such as power scooters or wheelchairs, generally become more involved with people and interested in objects (Tefft, Guerette, & Furumasu, 1999). For children with motoric delays, different types of assistive technology may also enhance their ability to communicate with others. Switches, optical pointers, and voice-controlled devices assist those children who have problems with the traditional mouse and keyboard (Duhaney & Duhaney, 2000).

## Specialized Services: Occupational and Physical Therapists

Children who have motor problems are often provided with specialized services from occupational therapists and physical therapists. More than 40 percent of all children enrolled in Part C programs nationally receive some form of physical or occupational therapy services (Campbell, 1999). Both specialists have training in working with motor problems and their work overlaps to some degree, but their fields of focus differ somewhat (see Table 7.6). The major goal of occupational therapy is to enhance a child's ability to interact competently and effectively in his or her environment (Rodger & Ziviani, 1999). Rodger and Ziviani suggest the use of play-based occupational therapy.

**TABLE 7.6**   *Areas of Specialization*

| *Occupational Therapist* | *Physical Therapist* |
| --- | --- |
| Delays in fine motor | Delays in gross motor |
| Visual-perceptual problems | Gait problems |
| Poor balance | Abnormal movement patterns |
| Delays in self-help skills | Abnormal muscle tone |
| Poor body awareness | Reduced righting and equilibrium reactions |
| Tremors and jerky movements | Orthopedic impairments |
| Problems functioning in the classroom | Problems in mobility and classroom functioning |

## Special Issues in Motor Development

### Developmentally Appropriate Physical Education

Physical education for students with disabilities is mandated under the Reauthorized Individuals with Disabilities Act (IDEA) of 1997 (PL 105-17) and considered a direct service. Sometimes adaptations are necessary when planning for students who have special needs. Adapted physical education is a subdiscipline of physical education with an emphasis on physical education for students with disabilities (Block, 1994). Adapted physical education programs have the same objectives as regular physical education programs, but adjustments are made in the regular offerings to meet the needs and abilities of students who have special needs (Cratty, 1988).

Developmentally appropriate physical education practices involve activities that are geared to a student's developmental status, previous movement experiences, fitness and skill level, body size, and age (Block, 1994). Developmentally appropriate practices suggest that programming and instruction should be different for preschool-aged children than for those of elementary school age. Younger children are afforded opportunities to promote the development of motor skills and movement competencies.

### Inclusion

Preschool children who have physical impairments are increasingly placed in regular classroom settings with typical preschool children. In order to make a smoother transition for these children, Knight and Wadsworth (1993) suggest the following guidelines for day-to-day, successful integration of students with physical disabilities:

1. *Parent involvement.* Teachers should obtain parental insights about the student's abilities and interests. Information from the parents about the student's medical history and emergency care plans should be included.
2. *Peer interaction.* Maximum socialization should be promoted to ensure a positive experience. It is helpful for the teacher to introduce any unfamiliar equipment to the class so that children may become familiar with it and ask questions; the child with physical disabilities should be involved to the fullest extent possible in activities; a consistent behavioral management program should be established.
3. *Environmental considerations.* Modifications to the classroom structure and routine should be made, as necessary. For instructional adaptations, input should be sought from professionals from a variety of disciplines; all involved persons should participate in development of the IEP or IFSP.

Craft (1994) describes inclusion for children in physical education classes as "the placement of a student with a disability, even a severe disability, into regular classes with typical peers in the neighborhood school, not as an occasional visitor, but as a member of the class" (p. 22). Creative and intuitive activities on the part of the physical education teacher can enhance participation in physical education classes by students with disabilities. Suggestions for including preschool children with disabilities in physical education classes are (McCall, 1994; Rizzo, Davis, & Toussaint, 1994):

1. Curricular changes are needed in the physical education program to increase the likelihood that inclusion will work.
2. Teachers may not always know the best way to perform a skill. They should involve the student in adaptation of various skills.
3. The use of an ecological task analysis (ETA) is an effective way for teachers to select and present the task goal, provide choices to the student, identify performer variables, and then give direct instruction.
4. The use of a relaxed approach to the completion of tasks will enhance social interaction and the child's natural sense of curiosity and exploration. Encourage preschoolers to demonstrate various ways to complete a task.

## Guidelines from the Americans with Disabilities Act

As of January 26, 1992, the Americans with Disabilities Act (ADA) requires public accommodations to provide goods and services to people with disabilities on an equal basis with the rest of the general public. The goal of the Americans with Disabilities Act is to afford every individual the opportunity to benefit from this country's businesses and services and to afford those businesses and services the opportunity to benefit from the patronage of all Americans. In writing from a Head Start perspective, Fink (1992) notes that although most individuals think of access as it applies to hotels, restaurants, theaters, and other places that serve the public, schools, agencies, and Head Start centers also must comply with this act.

Pratt (1999) makes suggestions for adaptive technology. Aller and Solano (2000) provide parents with responses to educational settings where funding excuses are presented. They indicate aspects of the law, eligibility, and insurance options.

Barriers to access must be removed wherever possible; however, since this act does not define exactly how much effort and expense are required, judgments are made on a case-by-case basis. A complete checklist for identifying accessibility problems in existing facilities may be found in the Americans with Disabilities Act and Head Start. Fink (1992) provides an open discussion with specific answers to questions raised about the ADA and how it relates to preschools and preschool facilities. Additional information can be obtained from:

Manual:   ARC/Texas (Association for Retarded Citizens), (512) 454-6694

Videotapes:   Eastern Washington University, (509) 359-6567

Answers to Specific Questions:   Department of Justice, Civil Rights Division, (202) 514-0301 (Voice), (202) 614-0381 (TDD)

## National Organization for Rare Disorders

Often, teachers and related services interventionists are confronted with a child who has a very rare disorder about which little is known. One organization that provides information to parents and professionals is the National Organization for Rare Disorders (NORD). This organization was created by a group of volunteer agencies, medical researchers, and individuals concerned about orphan diseases and orphan drugs. An *orphan disease* is one that affects fewer than 200,000 people, and an *orphan drug* is what the pharmaceutical companies describe as having little commercial value due to the small numbers of persons using the drug. Recent legislation has provided tax incentives for the development of orphan drugs. The objectives of NORD include:

- To act as a clearinghouse for information about rare disorders and to foster communication and sharing among families and researchers about these disorders
- To encourage and promote scientific research on rare disorders and to disseminate information about orphan drugs and diseases
- To focus the attention of government, industry, and the scientific community on the needs of people with rare disorders

The address for NORD is

NORD
P.O. Box 8923
New Fairfield, CT 06812 (203) 746-6518
www.rarediseases.org

Additional information about these types of diseases may be obtained from

March of Dimes Foundation
1275 Mamaroneck Avenue
White Plains, NY 10543 (914) 428-7100
www.modimes.org

## Summary

- It is essential for interventionists and teachers of young children with developmental delays or disabilities to understand normal motor growth and development. It is also important to be knowledgeable about atypical motor development, including motor disabilities and delays.
- Five categories of disabilities are (1) static CNS anomalies or insults, (2) progressive diseases, (3) spinal cord and peripheral nerve injuries, (4) structural defects, and (5) other types of motor impairments.
- Interventions for children with motor problems include working with occupational and physical therapists and the provision of services that are specified in the child's IEP or IFSP. Interventions for children with motor disabilities include specialized techniques for positioning, handling, and feeding. These activities are carried out with an emphasis on tasks that are functional and that generalize to other situations in the child's life.
- Teachers of young children with motor disabilities should know the cautions for working with children who have motor problems. For example, they should rec-

ognize the fragility of children with Atlanto-Axial Instability and Osteogenesis Imperfecta.

- Several key motor theories make significant contributions to this field—particularly, the theories of Gesell, Piaget, Ayres, and Kephart. A number of suggested motor activities for children with motor disabilities were suggested. Motor activities have potential applications for many interventions in classroom settings.
- Medically related disabilities may also affect motor and cognitive development. Among the disabilities discussed in this chapter are acquired immune deficiency syndrome (AIDS) and prenatal exposure to crack/cocaine. Fetal alcohol syndrome (FAS) and fetal alcohol effect (FAE) and implications of polydrug abuse on the part of pregnant women were also presented.
- Several special issues for motor development should be considered. Developmentally appropriate physical education is an important construct, with practical applications for inclusive settings. There are guidelines from the Americans with Disabilities Act for applications to preschool settings.

## Key Terms

adaptive equipment
AIDS
Americans with Disabilities Act
asthma
Atlanto-Axial Instability
cerebral palsy
fetal alcohol effect (FAE)
fetal alcohol syndrome (FAS)
folic acid
handling
hypertonicity
hypotonicity
muscular dystrophy

neurodevelopmental training (NDT)
Osteogenesis Imperfecta
polydrug abuse
positioning
postural reflexes
preoperational thought
primitive reflexes
proximo-distal reflexes
seizures
sensorimotor period
sensory integration
spina bifida
teratogen

# 8

## *Adaptive Behavior and Self-Help Skills*

## Chapter Outline _____

**Adaptive Behavior in Early Childhood**
   Defining Adaptive Behaviors
   Adaptive Behaviors in the Preschool
      Curriculum
   Role of the Family
**Principles of Adaptive Behaviors**
**Toileting Skills**
   Methods of Toilet Training
   Toilet Training at Night

**Eating Skills**
   Behavioral Techniques
   Gavage Feedings
**Dressing Skills**
   Sequence of Dressing Skills
   Suggestions for Teaching Dressing Skills
   Adaptations in Dressing Skills
**Grooming Skills**
   Grooming Equipment and Modifications

$M$any of the accomplishments of young children occur through attaining proficiency in adaptive behaviors. Adaptive behaviors in early childhood consist of age-appropriate skills that meet the demands of a youngster's natural environment—at home, in school, and in community settings. Numerous adaptive behaviors consist of socially acceptable skills that can be taught during early childhood. Adaptive behaviors include self-care skills, community self-sufficiency, personal/social responsibility, and social adjustment. When young children acquire these skills, they increase their independence and their ability to fit into natural, inclusive settings. For young children with special needs, intervention may be necessary for them to acquire adaptive behavior skills.

This chapter examines the nature of adaptive behavior in early childhood and discusses the principles of teaching adaptive behaviors. Early intervention methods for teaching the adaptive behaviors of toileting, dressing, and grooming skills are also discussed.

## Adaptive Behavior in Early Childhood

Adaptive behavior is not a single skill; rather, it consists of a composite of abilities that depend on a child's age and the cultural expectations of the family.

### Defining Adaptive Behaviors

Adaptive behaviors include self-care skills that are basic to independent functioning, such as eating, self-feeding, toileting, dressing, undressing, and grooming. The Task Force on Recommended Practices for the Division for Early Childhood of the Council for Exceptional Children provides the following definition of *adaptive behavior* in early childhood (DEC, 1993, p. 89):

> Adaptive behavior consists of changes in a child's behavior as a consequence of maturation, development, and learning to meet increasing demands of multiple environments. Independent functioning in these environments is the long-term goal. Instruction requires accommodating and adapting to support the specific strengths of individual children. Comprehensive intervention should address the following subdomains: self-care, community self-sufficiency, personal/social responsibility, and social adjustment.

## *Early Childhood Snapshot*    ERIKA LEARNING SELF-CARE SKILLS

Erika was a cheerful, 5-year-old child who exhibited severe developmental delays. Her individualized education plan (IEP) was developed by her family and the transdisciplinary team. A priority goal on her IEP was to have Erika toilet trained during the day. The transdisciplinary team felt that reaching this goal and learning this adaptive skill would improve Erika's adjustment in the inclusive setting of a regular kindergarten classroom, and it also would provide Erika with a measure of accomplishment and self-esteem. In addition, it would benefit her family economically because they would no longer have to purchase diapers.

The transdisciplinary team, which included her family, decided to try the rapid method of toilet training. The occupational therapist, Erika's teacher, and her parents worked together to implement the Rapid Method's procedures. The first step was to give Erika four cups of liquid during the day to increase her need to urinate and practice the method. Medical clearance was obtained to rule out any negative side effects from this procedure. The second step was to seat Erika on the toilet for 10 minutes. Then she was allowed 15 minutes off the toilet. In the next step, if she urinated in the toilet, she was reinforced with praise and edibles. Erika also was prompted to manage clothes appropriately and to flush the toilet. Completing these basic steps, as well as additional steps of the Rapid Method of toilet training, was effective. Erika was successfully toilet trained, and the goal on her IEP was achieved.

In addition to this general concept of adaptive behavior, there are several subskills of adaptive behavior (Horn, 1996). *Self-care* capabilities consist of skills needed for toileting, eating, dressing, and grooming. *Community self-sufficiency* refers to age- and culturally appropriate behavior of children, under adult supervision in community settings (e.g., stores, libraries, restaurants, etc.). Skills in the area of *personal/social responsibility* include independent play and cooperation with peers, appropriate interactions with adults and children, and responsible behaviors (e.g., looking both ways before crossing the street). The area of *social adjustment* refers to the abilities needed to adjust to new situations, regularity to task and its completion, and the amount of stimulation that is necessary for a child to make a response.

### *Adaptive Behaviors in the Preschool Curriculum*

Many children with special needs require intervention to learn adaptive behaviors. Teaching adaptive behaviors as part of the preschool curriculum is worthwhile for a number of reasons.

1. Many adaptive behaviors are needed for social acceptance in inclusive environments. For example, if children possess age-appropriate self-care skills and have the abilities to interact and play cooperatively with their peers, they are better able to fit into normal preschool settings.

2. Many adaptive behaviors are closely related to other developmental abilities. Interventions in the adaptive area also can benefit these other domains. For example, the self-care skill of eating appropriately at meal time requires fine motor ability (eating with a spoon, fork, and knife), social/communicative skills (taking turns during meal time conversations with others), and cognitive problem-solving strategies (deciding on appropriate helpings for food and drink).

3. Many of the target adaptive behaviors are acquired during early childhood and are part of the daily routines of young children. These behaviors are needed in many environments, such as home, school, community activities, and play.

4. Mastery of adaptive skills offers young children with special needs opportunities for accomplishment; they feel more competent, more successful, and more self-assured. For example, a common expression of preschoolers when they master an adaptive behavior task is a very pleased, "I did it!"

5. Independence in self-care skills contributes to a child's quality of life, self-esteem, and self-efficacy (Hatton, 1998).

### Role of the Family

Each family has its own preferences and expectations for teaching adaptive skills to children. For example, some families want their children to be independent as early as possible in their abilities to toilet, eat, or dress. Such family members take pride in their children's early accomplishments in the self-care areas. Other families, sometimes because of cultural traditions or personal preferences, enjoy doing these tasks for their youngsters, anticipating that the self-care skills will be acquired later.

Basic to the family systems approach (see Chapter 3) is a philosophy that the early interventionist should understand and respect the family's attitudes, values, and beliefs. The interventionist needs to recognize which adaptive skills are priorities for the family and considered to be culturally appropriate. Family members must be involved in the selection and instruction of these skills to the extent they desire. Listening to families about their priorities in adaptive behaviors for their children is an essential function for all transdisciplinary team members (Horn & Childre, 1996). Involvement of the family in planning and implementing intervention can help generalize the skills from the preschool center to the home and community.

## Principles of Adaptive Behaviors

All adaptive behaviors have certain commonalities that are useful to consider in planning (Bailey & Wolery, 1992; Bondurant-Utz, 2002; Farlow & Snell, 2000):

- *Adaptive skills are acquired gradually throughout the preschool years.* In learning how to dress, for example, the baby begins by cooperating with the caregiver by pushing his arm through the sleeve of the shirt. Later, as a toddler, he can take off the shirt, and as a preschooler, he can put it on. The interventionist will need to know the normal developmental sequence and prerequisite skills in order to teach young children with special needs in the adaptive skills.

- *Many adaptive skills consist of sequences called* chained responses. In chained responses, simple skills are linked together to perform more complex ones. The child needs to learn each step and sequence. For example, when toileting, she needs to recognize the need for toileting, go to the bathroom, remove the necessary clothes, toilet, wipe, put her clothes back on, flush the toilet, wash her hands, and go back to her activities. The interventionist needs to know the steps of the sequence in order to teach the youngster. Current research suggests that these chained responses be taught simultaneously rather than separately (Sewell, Collins, Hemmeter, & Shuster, 1998).

- *Adaptive skills are most effectively taught in natural situations when and where they are needed.* For example, instruction in play skills occurs when the child is ready to play with the other children. Toileting skills are taught when the youngster needs to go to the toilet, not at other times during the day. The early interventionist and other professionals, as well as the family, must work as a team to determine when to teach the skills at home, at school, and in the community. Adjustments can be made in the daily routines to allow more teaching trials. Eating skills, for instance, can be practiced during snack times as well as at meal times. Free play can occur more often so that the child can practice play skills.

- *Adaptive behaviors are often needed during daily routines and activities.* Adaptive behavior skills are useful not only during early childhood but also throughout the

*Adaptive skills are most effective when taught in natural situations.*

child's life. For example, appropriate peer interactions are necessary for children and adults. Adequate adjustment to new situations is important at all ages. Self-care routines occur on a regular basis throughout life.

• *Adaptive skills should be performed fluently and generalize to many other settings or situations.* For example, it is not only sufficient for children to learn how to wash themselves but they also must be able to do this with ease and whenever necessary. Practicing the skill in multiple environments will help generalize it.

## Toileting Skills

The balance of this chapter will focus on several of the self-care skills of adaptive behavior. Since many of the other adaptive behaviors are closely related to social/emotional, cognitive, motor, and communicative areas of development, interventions for those adaptive behaviors are described in the relevant chapters of this book.

Toileting is a major developmental milestone for any child but especially for one with special needs. For the typical child, bladder control usually develops between 24 to 36 months of age. However, the child with developmental delays may not achieve this control until about age 4 or later.

When the child with special needs is successfully toilet trained, many advantages are gained by the family. First, being toilet trained increases the independence of the child and furthers his or her acceptance in inclusive community placements. The child no longer has to wear diapers and therefore does not appear different from typically developing peers. Second, caregiving demands are reduced for the family when diapers do not have to be changed. Another important advantage is economic—the family saves money by not buying diapers. Toilet training can be reviewed by families as an important objective and be included on the child's IEP or IFSP.

To reach the goal of learning toileting skills, the following prerequisite skills are necessary (Farlow & Snell, 2000):

1. The child's urination and bowel movements are mostly regular with infrequent dribbling.
2. The child has the ability to release urine in large amounts.
3. The youngster is able to sit on the toilet.
4. The child should have one to two hours of dryness daily.
5. The youngster does not have an interfering medical condition, such as bladder infections, spina bifida, and so on. The child's physician should be consulted to rule out these conditions.
6. Normally, daytime control is achieved before nighttime control. It is appropriate to use diapers at night while the child is being toilet trained during the day.

### Methods of Toilet Training

Several methods for teaching toileting skills are described in this section: timed toileting, distributed practice, and the rapid method.

***Timed Toileting.***    While the child is learning the prerequisite skills, toilet training can be taught using the timed method. *Timed toileting* (or scheduled toileting) is a method in which the child is placed on the toilet for a few minutes at time when she or he would usually eliminate. If the child eliminates, positive reinforcement (verbal praise, edibles, toys, etc.) is given. If the attempt is not successful, the child is removed from the toilet without any consequences; when there is an accident, the youngster should be cleaned immediately (Farlow & Snell, 2000). An important part of timed toileting is record keeping. Data concerning the time the child was toileted and whether elimination occurred is recorded. Timed toileting helps the child understand why and when the toilet is used. This method, although frequently effective with typically developing children, has not been as effective with children who have disabilities (Noonan & McCormick, 1993).

***Distributed Practice.***    A method for toilet training called *distributed practice* is similar to timed toileting. This method is designed for children with mild disabilities. The distributed practice procedure relies heavily on positive reinforcement. Accidents are not punished and are responded to in a matter-of-fact way. This reduces the amount of negative interactions that can happen between the child and the caregiver if punishment is used. If accidents persist, different reinforcers are tried. If successful, the reinforcement is given after more and more lengthy intervals until it is no longer necessary. The procedure generally takes a few weeks to complete satisfactorily (Snell & Brown, 2000). The procedure for distributed practice has the follow steps:

1. Baseline data are collected on the child's pattern of elimination every half hour of the child's day for 14 consecutive days. If necessary, the charting of the data can be extended to 30 days (Baker & Brightman, 1997).
2. Each half hour, the caregiver checks on whether the child is wet or dry, where the elimination happened (in the toilet or in the pants), and how much food and liquid was consumed by the youngster during the time period.
3. The information is analyzed to determined elimination patterns. Training is initiated at the two most probable times during the day when the child will urinate.
4. Reinforcers are selected depending on the child's preferences. By interviewing the child and caregivers and by observation, the most powerful reinforcers can be chosen.
5. During the most probable times for elimination, the child is seated on the toilet after the caregiver says, "Let's go to the potty," or something similar. If the child eliminates, she or he is reinforced and removed from the toilet. If not successful, the child is removed from the toilet and then put back on for an additional five minutes. If then successful, reinforcement is given. If not, the child returns to her or his activities. The schedule should be followed consistently.
6. When success is achieved 75 percent of the time, training is extended to other periods of the day until the child is consistently dry.
7. The preschooler is taught at the same time how to communicate the need to toilet. The caregiver models the same words or signal each time toileting occurs and asks the child to repeat the message.

***Rapid Method.***   For children with moderate to severe disabilities, the *rapid method* has been used with some success (Baker & Brightman, 1997). The rapid method increases the intake of liquid so children will have to urinate more often. This process gives them numerous opportunities to practice and be reinforced. Many children will become independent in their toileting skills within a short time with this procedure. The training takes from four to eight hours each day for a period ranging from one to five days. It requires a ratio of one adult to one or two children and involves a lengthy commitment of time and effort. We should note that the rapid method has received some criticism because of its intrusiveness (Farlow & Snell, 2000; Snell & Brown, 2000). The procedure has the following steps:

1. The first step in the rapid method is to give children a great deal of liquid, as much as one to four cups for those weighing about 22 pounds and approximately four to seven cups for those weighing between 22 and 88 pounds. Medical clearance is needed before this method can be used, as a substantial increase in liquid can cause overhydration and result in symptoms such as nausea, vomiting, seizures, and coma.
2. Seat the child on the toilet for about 10 minutes. Then the child is allowed 15 minutes off the toilet. If the child urinates in the toilet, the amount of time off is gradually increased.
3. Reinforce the child with praise, edibles, and so on for staying dry on a regular basis. The child is prompted to perform the necessary activities for toileting, such as managing clothes and flushing the toilet. The prompts are removed when the child performs the activity independently.
4. This step is used when there are accidents. The caregiver first reprimands the child (e.g., "Don't wet your pants!"). Then overcorrection or positive reinforcement is used in which the youngster practices toileting, feels the wet pants several consecutive times, washes the wet pants, and wipes any urine off the floor.
5. The last step is the maintenance phase in which the child is regularly reinforced for staying dry.

This rapid method may result in temper tantrums and crying during step 4 (overcorrection) and should be used only if there is a need for speed training (Farlow & Snell, 2000).

## Toilet Training at Night

Nighttime training begins when children are successful about 75 percent of the time with daytime training (Snell, 1987). There are four methods used at night.

***Method 1.***   This method limits the child's intake of fluids about two hours before bedtime. Then the child is awakened a few minutes before his or her usual elimination time and is placed on the toilet for five minutes. Praise is given for successful urination. If the bed is wet, no comments are made. The accident is recorded on a chart, and the child is awakened earlier the next night. In the morning, the child is praised if she or he remained dry during the night. The wake-up periods are gradually delayed until the child remains dry all night.

***Method 2.***    The second method uses a signaling device, which is a pad under the bed-sheet. When the preschooler wets the bed, the alarm sounds. Then child is then awakened and practices going to the toilet. Praise is given for not wetting the bed during the night (Fredericks et al., 1975; Houts & Liebert, 1984). When signaling devices are used, the equipment needs to be monitored so that it is used safely.

***Method 3.***    This method is the rapid procedure developed by Azrin, Sneed, and Foxx (1973), which is similar to the daytime one. It involves the use of increased fluids, a signaling device on the bed, hourly checks to see if the child is dry, overcorrection or positive practice in case of accidents, and reinforcement for elimination in the toilet.

***Method 4.***    In this method the child takes the medication Tofranil for the nighttime toileting. Some children have an immature biological mechanism for concentrating the urine during the night and have more frequent urination. When they become more mature, the medication is reduced and then eliminated. Children should also avoid drinking fluids for several hours before they go to bed. This method has been effective with children who do not have disabilities.

# Eating Skills

For infants, toddlers, and preschoolers, eating skills include eating while being fed, eating independently, and drinking. A chart of typical development of eating skills is displayed in Table 8.1. Usually by the age of 3, children will be able to eat well with spoons and can use forks for spearing food. They are usually able to help themselves to portions of food. By age 4, preschoolers can independently use eating utensils. In teaching eating skills, it is important to remember that mealtimes are for socializing as well as for nutritional purposes. Pleasant mealtimes will help generalize and maintain eating skills (Orelove & Sobsey, 1996).

## Behavioral Techniques

Intervention for children with special needs in eating skills involves a team effort that includes the family. Other team members involved in this instruction could include occupational and physical therapists, speech and language clinicians, nutritionists, early interventionists, and medical personnel.

Of course, the intervention goals and methods will depend on the age of the child. For babies, the intervention could emphasize positive baby-caregiver interactions during feeding, the provision of appropriate types and textures of food, and the assessment of adequate oral-motor functioning space. With toddlers, the focus is on furthering independence in eating skills and on ensuring pleasant mealtime routines. With preschoolers, intervention concerns are related to the establishment of good eating habits and more independence in self-feeding.

Children with severe disabilities may have difficulty with being fed, eating independently, and drinking. Methods of intervention include therapeutic feeling, system-

**TABLE 8.1    *Typical Development of Eating Skills***

| Approximate Age | Skill |
| --- | --- |
| Birth to 4 months | Suck-swallow reflex refined |
| 4 to 6 months | Attempts to hold bottle |
| | Begins to eat pureed food |
| | Begins to drink from a cup |
| 7 to 9 months | Finger feeding begins |
| | Holds bottle or cup independently |
| 10 to 15 months | Bites soft food |
| | Self-feeding attempts |
| 15 months to 2 years | Chews food with different textures |
| | Self-feeding of finger foods |
| 2 years | Holds cup and drinks |
| | Uses spoon |
| 3 years | Uses fork |
| 4 years | Independence in use of spoon, knife, fork, dish, cup |
| 5 years | Makes sandwiches and simple meals |

atic instruction, positioning, techniques, and adaptive equipment (Bowe, 1995; Orelove & Sobsey, 1996).

***Therapeutic Feeding.***    *Therapeutic feeding* consists of rubbing or stroking to decrease hypersensitivity around the mouth and stretching to develop muscle tone in the oral-motor area (Copeland & Kimmel, 1989). Other techniques that can assist a young child with feeding are methods that will facilitate jaw control, lip closure, swallowing, and chewing. For further information, the reader can review research conducted by Magnusson and Justen (1981), Azrin and Armstrong (1973), and Umansky and Hooker (1998).

***Systematic Instruction.***    *Systematic instruction* includes a task analysis of the target skill, reinforcement, shaping, prompting, modeling, and response-cost procedures. In a task analysis, the interventionist breaks down the skill into a sequence of small steps. Snell and Brown (2000) give the following examples of a task analysis for eating with a spoon:

1. Pick up the spoon.
2. Move it to the bowl.
3. Scoop up food with the spoon.
4. Bring the spoon to the mouth.
5. Open the mouth.
6. Put in the food.
7. Move the spoon back to the bowl.
8. Chew and swallow.

The interventionist begins teaching on the initial step that the child has not mastered and continues with the sequence until the whole task has been achieved. The *reinforcement* part of systematic teaching rewards appropriate self-feeding behaviors with the powerful reinforcers of food and drink. *Shaping* is when the child is reinforced for his or her best approximation of the target behavior. *Prompting* is when extra cues, such as verbal or physical guidance, are provided to the child in training. *Modeling* is the demonstration of the appropriate behavior. The caregiver, interventionist, or another child could be models. *Response-cost* procedures penalize the child for inappropriate behavior. In teaching self-feeding skills, the response cost could consist of a time delay in which food or drink is withheld for a brief period while the child is taught to respond appropriately. Young children with disabilities may need multiple teaching sessions daily to learn new self-feeding skills. Instruction is given at natural eating times, including meals and snack times (Cook, Tessier, & Klein, 2000; Horn & Childre, 1996).

***Positioning Techniques.***    *Positioning techniques* are important for intervention for self-feeding because they emphasize proper support for the child. Unless the child is still being bottle or breast fed, the best position is usually to be as upright as possible (Snell & Brown, 2000). This position is essential for normal swallowing, for coordinating breathing and eating, and for preventing choking. The child's feet should be as secure as possible, either flat on the floor or with a support for stability. The shoulders and arms should move freely in order to encourage independent hand-to-mouth movements during self-feeding. The person feeding the child should be seated on a low chair with the face at eye level with the child. The food needs to be positioned below the child's face so as to encourage him or her to slightly bend or flex the neck while eating. This position makes it easier for the child to swallow (Copeland & Kimmel, 1989). The food and the person feeding the child should be directly in front of the child (Umansky & Hooker, 1998). The only exception to this is when the feeder, in order to provide adequate physical assistance, needs to be positioned behind or alongside youngster.

The position of the spoon or cup when it comes in contact with the child's mouth is important to prevent gagging. The bowl of the spoon needs to be inserted only partially in the mouth. If the entire bowl is inserted, it can cause gagging. It also makes it difficult to tip the spoon to transfer the food to the mouth. For most youngsters, food should be placed in the middle of the mouth on the tongue. When drinking, the rim of the glass is positioned on the child's lower lip to encourage a good lip seal. The timing of the food or liquid presentation is important. Eating and drinking have to be coordinated with breathing. This facilitates the feeding process and helps to ensure against choking (Orelove & Sobsey, 1996). If a child is having trouble coordinating eating with breathing, avoid foods that are easy to choke on, such as grapes, popcorn, peanuts, and bacon.

***Adaptive Equipment.***    Some *modified equipment and adaptations* can make self-feeding easier for children with special needs. The child should be able to drink from the cup without having to tip back his or her head. Many children with disabilities will gag when they tip their heads back to drink. By cutting away part of the rim of the cup, it can be tipped back without hitting the child's nose or making the head tip back. Short, squat cups that do not turn over easily and that can be held without problems are recommended initially (Campbell, 2000). Clear, plastic cups are best because they allow the feeder to see the fluid in the cup and in the child's mouth (Morris & Klein, 1987). If the child has a weak grasp, a cup with two handles is easier to hold.

Some children who tend to gag easily will do better when using modified spoons. Plastic or rubber-coated spoons are recommended more than metal ones, as the former transfer heat less quickly when feeding the child (Campbell, 2000). Nonmetal spoons also are preferred for children who bite down on utensils, since these spoons are softer and cause fewer injuries. Disposable plastic spoons are not recommended because they could break and leave splinters in the mouth. For easier eating, the spoon should fit the size of the child's mouth. Bowls and plates can be adapted by raising their sides. This modification makes it easier for the youngsters to fill their spoons with the food and lift the spoons to their mouths (Bailey & Wolery, 1992). Figure 8.1 displays some examples of adaptive equipment for eating. This equipment should be used only when necessary. The goal is for children to use normal eating utensils as soon as possible (Janney & Snell, 2000).

Spoon with an easy-to-grip handle

Cup with a spout to make drinking easier

A mat that adheres to the table to make it easier to use a bowl for eating

---

**FIGURE 8.1    *Utensils for Adaptive Eating Skills***
*Source:* Original drawings by Lee Cohn, with permission.

### Gavage Feedings

Even with the use of adaptive equipment and positioning techniques, some young children will not be able to obtain adequate nutrition by oral feedings. Because of their disabilities, they cannot suck or swallow. They may need tube or gavage feedings. Feeding tubes can be inserted through the nostrils, through the mouth, or through the stomach. A nasogastric tube is one that is inserted through the nose to the stomach. A gastrostomy tube is placed through the wall of the abdomen into the stomach. An oral gastric tube is placed in the mouth. Food and water are administered through the tubes (Campbell, 1995). Tube feedings should be given during regular meals and snack times.

The feeding problems that can develop from gavage feedings of young children include the loss of normal swallowing and sucking, which lessen because of lack of practice and stimulation; lack of stimulation to the mouth; and the inability to differentiate between different taste and food textures (Bazyk, 1990). Caregivers need special training on how to manage gavage feedings and the necessary equipment (Campbell, 1995). Children could develop diarrhea as a result of unclean equipment that is contaminated with bacteria. Appropriate care of the equipment should be discussed with the family, other team members, and health-care professionals (Orr, 1997). Generally, physicians will recommend the transfer to oral feedings as soon as the child is capable.

## Dressing Skills

Dressing skills not only are important for children to achieve independence but also to help them look physically attractive. Appropriate dressing skills can facilitate acceptance of children with disabilities by their typical peers in inclusive settings (Farlow & Snell, 2000).

### Sequence of Dressing Skills

In the normal sequence of developing dressing skills, children by 7 to 12 months of age will cooperate with their caregivers by holding out their arms or legs while they are being dressed. At about age 1, youngsters can pull off loose shirts and push down wet pants. At age 1½, they can take off their socks and shoes. By 2 years of age, they can pull their arms through the sleeves of the shirts and pull on their pants. At age 3, children usually learn to put on shoes, socks, and clothes that have front openings. Fastening and buttoning skills are learned between 3 to 4 years of age (Cook, Tessier, & Klein, 2000).

### Suggestions for Teaching Dressing Skills

Recommendations for teaching skills in dressing include the following (Bailey & Wolery, 1992; Orelove & Sobsey, 1996):

1. Teach dressing skills at natural times when they are necessary. This type of teaching will facilitate the generalization of the skills. Since occasions usually occur at

home and at the preschool or day-care center, families and early interventionists have many opportunities to teach dressing skills to children.

2. Teach the whole task sequence rather than isolating and practicing individual steps. For example, teach the whole process of zipping rather than just matching the two sides of the zipper. Recent research (Sewell, Collins, Hemmeter, & Shuster, 1998) indicates that the total task method results in more rapid learning.

3. Teach in a gradual sequence, proceeding from the easy tasks to the most difficult. For example, teach undressing before dressing because undressing is easier to learn.

4. Select loose-fitting and large-sized clothes. To make the task easier for children who have difficulty with dressing, use clothing that is at least one size too large for the child (Orelove & Sobsey, 1996).

5. Work toward partial dressing participation as a goal for some children. For children who may never achieve total independence in their dressing skills because of physical limitations, an appropriate objective can be for them to participate as much as possible.

6. Use peer demonstration and learning by observation to help children acquire dressing skills (Dowrick & Raeburn, 1995).

## *Adaptations in Dressing Skills*

Adaptation in positions and modifications in clothing can assist the child. In positioning children with motor impairments, Orelove and Sobsey (1996) advise not to dress

*Teach dressing skills at natural times.*

them in the supine (on their backs) position. Most children in this position tend to push their head and shoulders back and stiffen their legs and hips. Instead, dress such youngsters while they are sitting up. Supported sitting may be necessary. If they are unable to sit, dress them in the side-lying position, which makes it easier for them to bend their legs and feet.

Modifications of clothing are helpful to children with severe impairments. Clothing should be simple, with as few fasteners as possible. Shirts with large buttons should be selected. Pants with elastic waists are easier to put on than those with snaps and zippers. Short pants are simpler than long ones. Velcro fasteners are easier to manipulate than buttons or zippers (Campbell, 2000). Velcro also can be used on shoes instead of shoes laces. The preschooler's shoes can be color coded to help distinguish the right shoe from the left one. Clothing with reinforcements may be needed to reduce wear from braces. In using these modifications, caregivers are warned not to make the clothes appear too different from those of other children. To facilitate acceptance, children with disabilities need clothing similar to that of typically functioning peers (Sewell, Collins, Hemmeter, & Shuster, 1998).

## Grooming Skills

Grooming skills include bathing, washing, brushing teeth, and combing and brushing hair. The natural sequence of these skills for typical young children is the following (Bailey & Wolery, 1992): At about 2 years of age, toddlers will make attempts at performing some of these tasks. When they are 4 or 5 years old, they bathe and dry themselves with assistance and supervision. At about 4 years of age, they can wash and dry their hands and faces independently. Children typically begin brushing their teeth at age 3 but they don't do a good job until they are 4 or 5 years old. As babies, they allow caregivers to brush their hair. As toddlers, they pretend to do this task for themselves. However, they are not totally successful until age 4 or 5. By learning functional and appropriate grooming skills, children with special needs can decrease their dependence on caregivers and increase their acceptance by typical peers in inclusive settings.

Grooming skills generally are taught to children with special needs using a total task approach similar to teaching dressing skills. In this method, a task analysis outlines the steps. Then all the steps are taught each time the child practices the skill in the natural setting. For example, the following is a task analysis of the steps for washing hands (Noonan & McCormick, 1993):

1. Turn on the water.
2. Wet the hands.
3. Pick up the soap.
4. Lather the palms.
5. Replace the soap.
6. Lather the backs of the hands.
7. Rinse the hands.
8. Turn off the water.

9. Pick up the towel.
10. Dry the hands.
11. Hang the towel on the rack.

### Grooming Equipment and Modifications

Modifications can be made to simplify grooming tasks for young children with special needs. For example, for bathing, a variety of simple equipment can be used. A towel or rubber mat can be placed on the bottom of the tub to prevent skidding. A child with poor head control may need a folded towel to cradle the back of the head and keep it out of the water.

For the older child with unstable balance, a small plastic inner tube or tub seat can be used as a guard against slipping. The youngster should be placed in the tube or seat bottom first with his or her legs and arms over the sides. Then as the child gains more control, the tube can be placed around the waist and the chest. This position allows the arms to be free to splash and play in the water. Soap is easier to handle if it is placed in a bath mitt or on a string around the child's neck. Long-handled bath brushes are useful for scrubbing hard-to-reach body parts. For the caregiver, a small stool, placed by the side of the tub, is an essential piece of equipment. It allows the person to bathe the child without bending and straining the back.

For brushing teeth, a young child can practice brushing, but the actual cleaning should be done under adult supervision. Appropriate care of the teeth is especially important if children have any feeding difficulties, drooling, tongue thrust, or gum disease resulting from seizure medication. Careful and frequent cleaning of the teeth and gums can reduce infections and irritations that can lead to serious gum disease (Faine, 1994). Electric toothbrushes are useful for children with disabilities. Toothpaste is not essential, for it is the brushing of the teeth that stimulates the gums and cleans the teeth. However, pleasant-tasting toothpaste sometimes is a motivator for the child to practice brushing teeth. Regular attention to dental hygiene in early childhood will establish important lifelong routines for children with and with out disabilities.

## Summary

- The area of adaptive behavior is important for young children with and without disabilities because their acquisition of these behaviors can further their independence and self-esteem in natural environments.
- Acquiring adaptive skills is a major goal for young children with special needs.
- An important role of the family is determining appropriate adaptive skills for their children.
- There are several common principles concerning adaptive skills: (1) Adaptive skills are acquired gradually through early childhood. (2) They consist of a sequence of behaviors. (3) They are effectively taught when needed in natural routines. (4) Adaptive skills need to generalize easily and fluently to varying situations. Many adaptive behaviors are highly related to other developmental areas, such as

social/emotional, cognition, communication, and motor. Interventions for these areas are discussed in the appropriate chapters in this book.

- The adaptive skills described in this chapter include toileting, eating, dressing, and grooming.
- Toileting is a major developmental milestone for every child, for it signals independence, fewer caregiving demands, and economic benefits (families can stop buying diapers). Prerequisite skills for toileting include regular elimination patterns, dry periods, and the ability to sit on the toilet. Different methods of toileting are suggested for children with mild and those with moderate disabilities. Toilet training methods include timed toileting, distributed practice, the rapid method, and use of medication. Toilet training at night is begun when daytime training is successful.
- Eating skills emphasize methods of self-feeding for young children with special needs. Intervention for eating skills is a team effort. The team can include, in addition to the family, early interventionists, medical specialists, nutritionists, speech and language clinicians, and physical and occupational therapists. Knowledge of the sequence of normal eating skills development assists the team in planning interventions for children with disabilities. Methods of intervention consist of systematic instruction during natural routines, positioning, and the use of adaptive equipment.
- Dressing skills not only furthers the independence of children with special needs but also facilitates their acceptance by typically developing peers in inclusive placements, such as day care and preschool. Some useful suggestions for instruction include: (1) The whole task sequence should be followed in teaching rather than practicing each step in isolation. (2) The skills should be taught during normal routines when needed. (3) Loose-fitting clothing will make the task easier. (4) If a child cannot achieve complete independence, partial participation is the goal. Adaptations and modifications in clothing will simplify dressing skills.
- Grooming skills are important for children to learn. There are modifications for children with difficulties in grooming. Typically functioning peers in inclusive settings provide models for children with special needs to imitate in their performance of age-appropriate self-care skills.

## Key Terms

| | |
|---|---|
| adaptive behavior | prompting |
| adaptive equipment | rapid method of toilet training |
| chained responses | response cost |
| community self-sufficiency | self-care |
| distributed practice | shaping |
| gavage feeding | social adjustment |
| modeling | task analysis |
| personal/social responsibility | therapeutic feeding |
| positioning techniques | timed toileting |
| positive reinforcement | whole task sequence |

# 9

## *Social and Emotional Development*

*Chapter Outline* _____

*Defining Social and Emotional Problems*

*Theories of Social and Emotional Development in Young Children*
    Bonding and Attachment
    Erikson's Stages of Development
    Differences in Temperament
    The Role of Play in Social and
        Emotional Development

*Types of Social and Emotional Problems in Young Children*
    Attention Deficit Hyperactivity Disorder
    Pervasive Developmental Disorders and
        Autistic Disorder

    Aggressive Behavior
    Withdrawn Behavior
    Problems in Socialization

*Intervention Strategies for Young Children with Social and Emotional Difficulties*
    Humanistic Approach to Intervention
    Psychodynamic Approach to Intervention
    Behavioral Approach to Intervention
    Intervention Strategies for Helping
        Preschoolers with Social and
        Emotional Problems

As human beings, we have three fundamental social needs: (1) the need to feel autonomous—that our actions come from within ourselves and that we have the power to make things happen; (2) the need to have a sense of competency—to feel effective in what we do; and (3) the need to feel we are part of a social world (Deci & Ryan, 1990).

Young children are social beings with similar social needs. They interact socially with their parents, with other children, and with adults outside of the family. The types and quality of these social interactions have far-reaching effects on their development. Some children seem to be liked by everyone with whom they interact; whereas other children are ignored or avoided by others.

Young children view the world differently than adults. During the early childhood years, young children are primarily centered on themselves (egocentric), and they interpret the world entirely from their personal perspective. For example, 2-year-old Ellen was sitting in the sand, watching an ant crawling past her. Ellen interpreted the ant's movements from the perspective of her own body: The ant was first deliberately moving toward her and then as deliberately moving away from her (Kephart, 1971). Young children tend to assign personal meaning to a random event.

These traits of social and emotional development are often delightful to observe and may be appropriate for the child's developmental level. However, the process of working through these developmental tasks may cause preschool children to have conflicts with their parents and teachers. It is normal for young children go through brief periods of difficult times without perilous consequences. What distinguishes a normal developmental hurdle from a more serious problem is whether the behavior is appropriate for the child's age and the frequency and intensity of the behavior.

For some children with special needs, social development may not follow a stable and predictable course. During the preschool years, peer relationships are extremely important. However, being at risk or having disabilities often deprives children of the social experiences normally shared with peers. This lack of social experiences can lead to social and/or emotional problems (McConnell & Odom, 1999).

Children with severe emotional and social problems comprise a seriously underserved population in today's schools. Even so, the number of children identified as having emotional/behavioral problems during the preschool years is increasing. The prevalence rate for young children at risk for or with behavioral disorders is estimated at 10 to 15 percent of preschool children, and at 6 percent of those in Head Start (Conroy & Davis, 2000). Although the number of young children identified with behavioral disorders is still relatively small, they present a special challenge to the school and to teachers (Zabel, 1991). It is not known exactly how many of the young children who are receiving special services have social and or emotional difficulties. This is because many schools identify young children under a generic category, such as "developmental delay," although some districts still identify preschool children with emotional or behavioral problems within the special education diagnostic category of *emotional disturbance* (*ED*). Many children who have social and/or emotional problems are served in inclusive settings (IDEA, 1997). Greenspan (2000) provides a clear, informal system for identification of preschool children with emotional disorders. "If in two out of three main spheres of a child's life—home, school, and peer play—things appear to be going well, you can presume that the child is OK. On the other hand, if in two out of the three things are not going well because of a child's sadness, fear of aggressive behavior, he may indeed have a social/emotional disorder" (p. 23).

This chapter examines the social and emotional development of preschool children with special needs. The sections define social/emotional problems in young children, review theories of social and emotional development in young children, describe types of social and emotional problems, and provide intervention strategies for preschool children with social and emotional difficulties. Teachers need to be trained to utilize more effectively the existing mental health consultant resources to establish contextually relevant home and school-based interventions for children who evidence significant emotional and behavioral problems (Fantuzzo, Stoltzfus, & Lutz, 1999).

## Defining Social and Emotional Problems

A controversial issue in special education concerns the definition of emotional disturbance (ED) under the Individuals with Disabilities Education Act (IDEA) of 1997. The current definition of *emotional disturbance* is:

> A condition exhibiting one or more of the following characteristics displayed over a long time and to a marked degree that adversely affects a student's educational performance:
>
> a. An inability to learn that cannot be explained by intellectual, sensory, or other health factors
> b. An inability to build or maintain satisfactory interpersonal relationships with peers and teachers
> c. Inappropriate types of behavior or feelings under normal circumstances
> d. A general pervasive mood of unhappiness or depression
> e. A tendency to develop physical symptoms or fears associated with personal or school problems
>
> The term includes children who are schizophrenic but not children who are socially maladjusted, unless they are seriously emotionally disturbed.

*Early Childhood Snapshot*   DAVID: A CHILD WITH PERVASIVE
DEVELOPMENTAL DISORDER

David is a 3½-year-old child who has just been diagnosed with Pervasive Developmental Disorder
(PDD). His parents reported that there have been
problems with David since he was about a year
old. He would stiffen and resist cuddling, and he
stopped responding to the play initiatives of his
two older brothers (ages 6 and 8). After about the
age of 18 months, David seemed to prefer solitary
activities with repetition of simple acts. Although
his parents noticed these differences, they and
their pediatrician believed that David would "grow
out of it."

David continues to develop some language,
but he also shows delays in communication skills.
In addition, he is not interested in games or interacting with other preschool children. At times,
David flaps his hands and covers his eyes when he
is spoken to directly. At other times, he will communicate briefly with his parents or siblings.
David shows signs of tactile defensiveness and a
particular sensitivity to sound.

For the past four months, David has been
in a preschool setting. It was at his teacher's urg-
ing that his parents sought a full developmental
evaluation for him. An arena assessment revealed
delays in cognition, language development, and
social/emotional development. Strengths were
noted in fine and gross motor control.

His current preschool setting is willing to
continue to work with David and serve his needs,
but the teachers have expressed a need for additional help. An IEP was drawn up that provides
him with specific speech and language assistance
and a preschool special education teacher to work
with both David and the staff of his preschool
three times a week.

David's parents are very worried about his
future, and they seem to have many unspoken
concerns and issues. Because of these factors, a social worker will also meet with the preschool
teachers and with the parents on a regular basis.

One reason many professionals are critical of the federal definition of ED in the
federal law (IDEA) is that it excludes children who are socially maladjusted. Many
scholars and researchers recommend that the terminology *emotional or behavioral disorder* is a more descriptive and accurate way to describe these children (Hallahan &
Kauffman, 1994). IDEA stipulates that any child demonstrating serious emotional disturbance as early as the third birthday must receive the full range of appropriate assessment and intervention services (Fantuzzo et al., 1999).

## Theories of Social and Emotional Development in Young Children

Competencies in social and emotional abilities do not occur in a vacuum. The child's
social and emotional development is the result of many interactive experiences and mutual engagement between parent and child. With an active child and an active caregiver, social and emotional competencies emerge through mutual regulation and
reciprocity (Greenspan & Greenspan, 1985).

The child's earliest socialization occurs between the child and mother shortly
after birth. Later aspects of social and emotional growth materialize through relation-

ships that develop after the first early relationship between the infant and the initial caregiver. Through these broader relationships, the child begins to develop social skills or social competencies. Social skills allow children to develop positive relationships with others. An essential component of appropriate social behavior is effective communication (Walker, Schwarz, Nippold, Irvin, & Noell, 1994).

It is important to know about several different aspects of social/emotional development in preschool children. The following section discusses (1) the importance of bonding and attachment, (2) Erikson's developmental stages, (3) temperamental differences in children, and (4) the role of play in social/emotional development.

## Bonding and Attachment

The terms *bonding* and *attachment* refer to early relationships between the infant and mother. These early interactions are thought to form the basis of social and emotional development. Bonding and attachment have different meanings, although the research literature reveals overlapping and exchange between these two concepts.

***Bonding.*** *Bonding* is viewed as the mother's affectional tie to the infant. There is general acceptance that bonding is a critical component of the parent-infant relationship and that bonding occurs during the earliest interactions between a child and his or her mother.

Although the bonding model has received wide acceptance, there are some questions about it. The early research on maternal infant bonding focused on the necessity for mother and infant interactions at the time of birth. However, later studies show that simply having early contact is not a guarantee of healthy bonding. Svejda, Pannabecker, and Emde (1982) suggest that the bonding model should be reexamined because (1) many parents who do not have early contact with their babies still go on to develop loving relationships with their children, (2) there is no actual time-limited period for attachment, and (3) newer, current models emphasize the interactional and transactional aspects of development.

This newer information about bonding is especially important for parents of children who were admitted to neonatal intensive care units or transported to distant hospitals soon after birth. These parents may feel disappointed or guilty about their lack of *bonding time*. Svejda and colleagues (1982), however, emphasize the long-term aspects of developing attachment throughout the early childhood years, not just in the period immediately following birth.

***Attachment.*** *Attachment*, which is closely related to bonding, is defined as "an affectional tie that one person forms to another specific person or persons, binding them together in space and enduring over time" (Ainsworth, 1973, p. 1). The specific and exact consequences of attachment are not completely understood. Yet, the formation of a secure attachment is an important process within which both parent and child play an active and interactive role (Sameroff, 1987; Sameroff & Fiese, 1990).

One of the basic needs of an infant is for emotional nourishment. With such care, babies will flourish. The essence of quality caregiving lies in the emotional relationship that is forged between parents and their child (Honig, 1993).

The processes of attachment and separation, or engagement and disengagement, are inextricably related; they can be viewed as opposite sides of the same coin (Stern, 1977). During the first year, the focus is primarily on attachment; smiling, gazing, clinging, and cooing are the major activities. During the second year, separation begins to bloom for the child, as he or she develops the skills of mobility, walking away from others, and getting involved with objects. According to Stern (1977):

> The structure and function of engagement and disengagement are interlocked so that the developmental history of one must encompass the developmental history of the other, regardless of which phase of development the child is in. The beginnings of separation and individuation must be contemporaneous with the beginnings of attachment. (p. 128)

In both the home and school settings, if separation activities are accomplished too quickly, the child may become fearful and/or anxious. In some situations, the child may be so frightened that she or he cannot play or learn and therefore withdraws. In other cases of hurried separation, the child becomes so anxious that he or she becomes very active as a defense against anxiety or depression. In the preschool environment, the child should feel as if she or he is separating from mother rather than being left by mother.

The seminal work on current theories and approaches to attachment theory stem from Bowlby's trilogy of books on attachment (1969), separation (1973), and loss (1980). Bowlby's work on the various aspects of attachment spans several decades. In 1950, he was asked by the World Health Organization to advise on the mental health of homeless children. In the final report to this committee, he stated, "What is believed to be essential for mental health is that the infant and young child should experience a warm, intimate and continuous relationship with his mother (or permanent mother-substitute) in which both find satisfaction and enjoyment" (1969, p. xi).

Bowlby and colleagues also found that even when other circumstances were favorable, the child's responses of "protest, despair, and detachment that typically occur when a child over the age of six months is separated from his mother . . . suggested that the young child's hunger for his mother's love and presence is as great as his hunger for food, and that in consequence her absence inevitably generates a powerful sense of loss and anger" (Bowlby, 1969, p. xiii). The effect on the child of this type of separation may be either for the child to cling to the mother excessively or to reject the mother as a love object, temporarily or permanently.

Lieberman's (1993) book about the emotional life of the toddler (ages 12 months to 36 months) covers recent research on emotional development in this age group from a psychodynamic perspective. One of Lieberman's basic premises is that the key to understanding toddler behavior is the process of separation/individuation that occurs within the relationship with the mother or caregiver and that the relationship is partially determined by the toddler's individual personality and characteristics.

If the attachment process does not go well, there may be subsequent deleterious effects on the child's emotional and social development. Insecure attachment may foreshadow difficulties with impulse control and negative peer interactions in the period between 4 and 6 years of age (Hartup & Moore, 1990).

A structured process to measure attachment was developed by Mary Ainsworth, a researcher who worked with Bowlby (Bowlby, 1969). Ainsworth used this approach initially to study infants in Ganda. In her research, Ainsworth set up a series of separations and reunions between the mother and child. During two of these separations, a "stranger" comes into the room. The child's behavior during the two reunions with the mother gives the best indication of the nature of the infant-mother attachment (Ainsworth, 1992; Ainsworth, Blehar, Waters, & Wall, 1978). The child's reactions during the "strange situation" are classified within four groups (Group D is not included in Ainsworth's analysis as a separate group; see Main & Solomon, 1986):

| Group | Description |
|---|---|
| A | *Insecure-avoidant.* These children actively ignore the parent upon reunion, turn and move away. |
| B | *Secure.* These children manifest mild distress following separation and respond positively to reunion with the mother, seeking comfort. |
| C | *Ambivalent-resistant.* These children resist parent overtures during reunion and show simultaneous anger and clinging. |
| D | *Insecure-disorganized/disoriented.* These children show behavior that is unpredictable, alternately show secure and insecure behavior patterns upon reunion, or show a diverse array of disorganized sequences of behavior. |

***Bonding and Attachment: Problems and Methods of Intervention.*** For many reasons, some children and their parents experience difficulties in the processes of bonding and attachment. Some children who are born prematurely or have been prenatally exposed to drugs have difficulty establishing and sustaining a relationship with their parents. Parents themselves may have to cope with emotional or environmental difficulties that hamper the process.

Sometimes there is a severe lack of attachment that affects the child's entire emotional development. The *Diagnostic and Statistical Manual of Mental Disorders* (4th ed.) describes a condition known as Reactive Attachment Disorder (RAD) of infancy and early childhood, which is characterized by "markedly disturbed and developmentally inappropriate social relatedness in most contexts" (p. 116). This disorder appears before age 5 and cannot be due to developmental delay or pervasive developmental disorder (Zeanah, Boris, & Lieberman, 2000).

A condition known as *failure to thrive (FTT)* is diagnosed when the baby's weight falls below the third percentile on standardized norms. Sometimes FTT is the result of organic dysfunction (organic failure to thrive). This diagnosis is made when there is a clear biological basis for the disorder (Field & Sostek, 1983; Marcovitch, 1994). Sometimes, the child will show significantly below-age expectations in height and/or weight based on national growth norms in the absence of a physical basis for growth failure. This type of FTT is diagnosed as non-organic failure to thrive (NOFT) and may be due to a variety of factors, including emotional problems in the caregiver, difficulties in attachment, and/or lack of education about infant nutrition.

One system of intervention for parents and their infants who are difficult to reach is suggested by Bernstein (1989). He terms the intervention *sensory-affective interaction (SAI)*, which is based on the premise that a series of interchanges that promote a child's experience of joy, success, and mastery in a positive atmosphere optimizes parent-infant attachment. In SAI, the parent's primary role is to respond contingently to the child and expand on the child's activity—both increasing the child's motivation and contributing to making the child feel effective.

## Erikson's Stages of Development

A well-respected framework for understanding the child's emotional and social development is the model developed by Erik Erikson (1963). Erikson's conceptualization of emotional/social development was initially influenced by the work of Freud. Emphasizing the context of the individual's functioning in society, Erikson examined development over the entire lifespan.

The Erikson model has eight stages of development; each is characterized by a conflict that must be resolved. These types of intrapsychic conflicts are normal and occur throughout development. According to his theory, individuals can move on to a new stage without resolving the conflict of earlier stages, but the conflict encountered in later stages will not be resolved until the prior conflicts are worked through successfully.

In examining Erikson's stages of development, it is important to keep in mind that although they are presented as polarities, there is a continuum operating between each of the two opposing forces, and in their own development most individuals lie on a point *closer* to either one or the other end. For example, in the first stage, most people are either relatively trusting or mistrusting in their daily lives, rather than fully trusting or completely mistrusting at all times.

The eight stages of development and the approximate ages for each stage of Erikson's model are (Erikson, 1963):

| *Stage* | *Age* |
|---|---|
| **1.** Basic trust vs. basic mistrust | Birth to 1 year |
| **2.** Autonomy vs. shame and doubt | 2 to 3 years |
| **3.** Initiative vs. guilt | 3 to 5 years |
| **4.** Industry vs. inferiority | 6 years to puberty |
| **5.** Identity vs. role confusion | Adolescence (puberty to 18) |
| **6.** Intimacy vs. isolation | Young adulthood (18–30) |
| **7.** Generativity vs. stagnation | Adulthood (30–65) |
| **8.** Ego integrity vs. despair | Senescence (65–death) |

The first three stages are relevant to development during the preschool years and are therefore explored further. The *basic trust versus basic mistrust* conflict occurs from birth to age 1. Erikson (1963) wrote about this stage:

> The amount of trust derived from earliest infantile experience does not seem to depend on absolute quantities of food or demonstrations of love, but rather on the quality of the maternal relationship . . . [and on] sensitive care of the baby's individual needs and a firm sense of personal trustworthiness within the trusted framework of their culture's life style. (p. 249)

A positive resolution of this stage combines a sense of "being 'all right,' of being oneself, and of becoming what other people trust one will become" (Erikson, 1963,

p. 249). A child whose basic needs for care are met at this stage will develop a sense of trust, which lays a foundation for a later positive self-concept. In contrast, a child whose needs are not met during this first critical year will develop a sense of mistrust that may persist throughout life.

The *autonomy versus shame and doubt* conflict occurs at the time that a child's muscular maturation is developing around the issues of "holding on and letting go" (Erikson, 1963, p. 251) and "becomes decisive for the ratio of love and hate, cooperation and willfulness, freedom of self-expression and its suppression" (p. 254). Children who successfully move through this stage are able to assert themselves and behave autonomously. Those who have difficulty may feel shame in later life when being assertive and self-doubt when asserting independence.

*Initiative versus guilt* has been described as a stage in which there is a "new miracle of vigorous unfolding . . . [and the] child is in 'free possession' of a surplus of energy which permits him to forget failures quickly and to approach what seems desirable (even if it also seems uncertain and even dangerous) with undiminished and more accurate direction" (Erikson, 1963, p. 255). Further, Erikson describes this phase as one in which "He [the child] develops a sense of industry—i.e., he adjusts himself to the inorganic laws of the tool world. He can become an eager and absorbed unit of a productive situation . . . [and experiences the] pleasure of work completion by steady attention and persevering diligence" (p. 259). Children who negotiate this phase successfully bask in their creativity and curiosity, which leads to later positive attitudes toward study, relationships, and work. Conversely, if they are made to feel that they are *bad* for asking questions and trying new endeavors, they may feel guilty about their efforts.

Applications of Erikson's theories are useful when interacting with and teaching preschool children. The framework is relevant with both typically developing children and children who have special needs. Children who have special needs will eventually pass through the same stages as typical children but may negotiate these crises at a later age and with greater physical and sensory difficulty depending on the nature of their disability. In some cases, children who function at a very low cognitive level may not advance through higher-level stages.

## Differences in Temperament

All children are born with innate characteristics, a personality, and a way of relating to the world that Chess and Thomas (1986) call *temperament*. Temperament has major implications for the child's future social and emotional development. In formulating self-concept, the child's evaluation of himself or herself is based on how others respond to his or her behavior.

Allport (1937) defines *temperament* in the following manner:

> Temperament refers to the characteristic phenomena of an individual's emotional nature, including his susceptibility to emotional stimulation, his customary strength and speed of response, the quality of his prevailing mood, and all peculiarities of fluctuation and intensity in mood; these phenomena being regarded as dependent upon constitutional make-up, and therefore largely hereditary in nature. (p. 54)

Thomas and Chess's (1977) developmental theory of temperament resulted from their research in the New York Longitudinal Study. They conceptualized temperament as early-appearing behavioral style, and they postulated ways in which an infant's temperament can motivate parental behavior. The authors also discussed the notion of "goodness of fit" between an individual's temperament characteristics and the child-rearing environment. From the 10 dimensions of temperament (see Table 9.1), they characterized infants as "easy," "difficult," and "slow-to-warm-up."

Thomas, Chess, Birch, Hertzig, and Korn (1963) define *temperament* as the underlying style or pattern of a person's behavior that sets the stage for his or her reactions to the world. The 10 factors measured through their research in the New York Longitudinal Study are shown in Table 9.1.

Chess and Thomas's (1986) theory suggests that infants display different temperaments; parents respond differently to infants with different temperaments; and these different parental responses lead to different social developmental outcomes for the child. Chess and Thomas suggest ways for obtaining information on a child's temperament, provide parental guidelines, analyze the effects of temperament on school functioning, and discuss temperament issues with children who have special needs.

One adaptation from the New York Longitudinal Study yielded a shortened version of the characteristics for infants from the age of 4 months and young children. The Carey Infant Temperament Questionnaire (Carey, 1970) was developed from the results of this study.

**TABLE 9.1**   *Ten Factors of Temperament*

| Temperament Factor | Description |
|---|---|
| 1. Activity level | Degree of activity; passive or active |
| 2. Rhythmicity | Regularity of behavior patterns; sleeping, eating |
| 3. Approach/withdrawal | Socially displaying a pattern of outgoing behavior or withdrawn behavior |
| 4. Adaptability | Ability to adjust to changes in environment |
| 5. Threshold of responsiveness | Amount of stimulation necessary to evoke child's response |
| 6. Intensity of reactions | Level of response to environmental events; intense or calm |
| 7. Quality of mood | Child's general disposition |
| 8. Distractibility | Degree to which stimuli from the environment will divert child's attention |
| 9. Attention span | Ability to focus attention on what's happening |
| 10. Persistence | Child's ability to stick with a task despite obstacles |

*Source:* Chess and Thomas (1986), pp. 120–121. Reprinted by permission.

*Play is a very important activity for young children.*

## The Role of Play in Social and Emotional Development

Play is very important for young children in many areas of learning, but it is discussed here because it is primarily through play that children learn about the social function of their behavior. Hanline (1999) states that the importance of play on a child's development cannot be understated. Other aspects of play are discussed in Chapter 6.

Over the years, philosophers, psychologists, and educators have recognized the critical role of play in the child's development (Malone, 1999). In fact, play behavior in young children has been analyzed in several ways. A classic analysis of the levels of play developed by Parten (1932) is shown in Table 9.2. The Greek philosophers Plato and Aristotle analyzed the role of play in their writings. Freud analyzed play on several levels, among them the use of play in young children to obtain mastery over painful events. Piaget viewed play as the child's way of gaining mastery over her or his environment.

The National Association for the Education of Young Children (NAEYC) (1987) developed a position statement on play:

> Children's play is a primary vehicle for and indicator of their mental growth. Play enables children to progress along the developmental sequence from the sensorimotor intelligence of infancy to preoperational thought in the preschool years to the concrete operational thinking exhibited by primary children. In addition to its role in cognitive development, play also serves important functions in children's physical, emotional, and social development. (p. 3)

TABLE 9.2  *Stages of Play*

| Level of Play | Description |
| --- | --- |
| Solitary Independent Play | Child plays alone and independently, without reference to other children |
| Onlooker | Watches, talks with other children at play, observes but does not participate |
| Parallel Activity | Plays independently, among other children; plays "beside" rather than "with" |
| Associative Play | Plays with other children; converses, interacts; similar activity shared by all; each child acts as he/she wishes |
| Cooperative or Organized Supplementary Play | Plays in a group that is organized for purpose; division of labor; efforts of one child are supplemented by others |

*Source:* Parten (1932).

In a study conducted by Okimoto, Bundy, and Hanzlik (2000), results suggested that when the shared goal of parents and therapists is to enable children to express their inherent playfulness, intervention to improve parent-child interactions may be more potent than intervention directed at improving the child's developmental skills.

Also, the use of play has proven successful in medical situations. Jessee, Wilson, and Morgan (2000) find that play helps allay feelings of loss of autonomy and control as well as fear of separation from parents in medical settings. These authors further describe the mechanism of prelogical thinking in young children under the age of 6, and a child's view of causation of illness.

Three sequential developmental levels of play were developed by Hupp (1989):

**Level 1**  Child is beginning to interact with objects, uses same movement for every toy (e.g., knocking things over, batting at toys)

**Level 2**  Child interacts with objects in functional ways, matches type of play with type of toy (e.g., manipulates, takes things apart, attempts to put them back together)

**Level 3**  Child interacts with toys, combines activities that require precise coordination (e.g., stacks, puts toys together in proper orientation)

The strategies used in social pretend play by young children with and without mild disabilities were studied by Lieber, Beckman, and Strong (1993). They found that preschoolers with mild disabilities participated in pretend play, but they tended to use more direct and disruptive strategies to enter play. Suggestions were offered to expand the notion of what constitutes social interaction for young children with disabilities. Lieber and colleagues suggest that social behaviors may have been viewed too simplistically, such as teaching a child to greet a peer in order to initiate an interaction. There may be a need to teach children a more adaptive indirect response.

Another study on structured play sessions observed preschool children with mild mental retardation and children without mental retardation (Kopp, Baker, & Brown,

1992). Children with developmental delays showed more disruptive entry into play, more regressive behaviors, and less positive affect; however, the two groups did not differ on communication behaviors or negative affect.

Preschool special educators need to be aware of the value of free-play time for children who have special needs. Arthur, Bochner, and Butterfield (1999) emphasize the importance of play for the enhancement of peer interactions. "Overteaching" on the part of the teacher may result in less time for play as a spontaneous activity. Classroom space and the design of the room may affect the types of play in which children will engage. The arrangement of a play area has several requirements and should be planned thoughtfully.

Warren, Emde, and Sroufe (2000) state that analysis of children's play narratives could be used to predict later anxiety. They find that the expression of negative expectations in play narratives may be a risk factor or mechanism for later anxiety. Opportunities for play can also be tied to later academic achievement. According to Hanline (1999), a preschool curriculum for children with disabilities that is based on play may encourage development of emergent literacy skills. Lonigan, Bloomfield, and Anthony's (1999) research supports this theory. The authors find that high levels of inattention may place preschool children at risk for later academic problems.

There should be both small spaces and large open spaces for children to play. Places for clay, easels, storage, kitchen, puppets, dress-up, and block play should also be provided in the preschool classroom. Opportunities for both indoor and outdoor play are important for young children. Questions that may be considered when planning play times include: What rules arise around play issues? What about sharing? Is there a convenient place nearby for an observer?

# Types of Social and Emotional Problems in Young Children

This section discusses several of the major emotional and behavioral conditions that are exhibited by young children with special needs—specifically, attention deficit hyperactivity disorder, pervasive developmental disorders, aggressive behavior, withdrawn behavior, and problems in socialization.

## Attention Deficit Hyperactivity Disorder

*Attention deficit hyperactivity disorder* (ADHD) is defined as a chronic neurobiological condition characterized by developmentally inappropriate attention skills, impulsivity, and often hyperactivity (American Psychiatric Association, 1994). This condition is also referred to as *attention deficit disorder* (*ADD*) by the Department of Education (Lerner, Lowenthal, & Lerner, 1995).

There is a marked increase in the identification of ADHD in the "under-5s" (Green, 1996). It is estimated that ADHD exists in about 4 to 5 percent of the school population and often the problem is evident in the preschool years. Young children with ADHD are described as "busy" and into everything as soon as they walked. Parents describe their preschoolers as having low frustration tolerance and a lack of sense. They are also considered demanding, generally dissatisfied, and noisy, and have been observed

*Early Childhood Snapshot*   A PRESCHOOL CHILD WITH ATTENTION
DEFICIT DISORDERS

Dr. Christoper Green is a pediatrician with a practice in Australia who specializes in ADHD in children under 5 years of age. He reports that children between the ages of 3 and 5 are increasingly being diagnosed with attention deficit disorder (ADD) or attention deficit hyperactivity disorder (ADHD).

Dr. Green reported on a 3-year-old patient with ADHD. His parents described him as unusually busy, into everything as soon as he walked. He skipped the usual separation anxiety and bolted whenever and wherever he wanted without fear. His mother said he had an explosive passage through the *terrible twos*. By age 3, his parents described his low frustration tolerance, lack of sense, and very demanding and generally dissatisfied personality. He was noisy and launched unthinking attacks on other children. The mother was asked if her son's behavior was as difficult for everyone. "Yes," the defeated mother replied, "Even our Pit Bull Terrier guard dog is frightened of Jaime."

*Source:* Adapted from Green (1996).

to launch unthinking attacks on other children. Children with ADHD are continually "on the go" and exhibit excessive gross motor activity. Parents report that in supermarkets, these children become unmanageable. They run about and pull things off shelves. Aggression sometimes characterizes young children with ADHD. Some parents report sequestering themselves in their homes, fearing to invite friends over (Lerner, Lowenthal, & Lerner, 1995). Barkley (2000) indicates that young children with ADHD manifest a deficit in response inhibition.

The most recent definition of ADHD appears in the *Diagnostic and Statistical Manual of Mental Disorders* (*DSM-IV*):

> The essential feature of Attention-Deficit/Hyperactivity Disorder is a persistent pattern of inattention and/or hyperactivity-impulsivity that is more frequent and severe than is typically observed in individuals at a comparable level of development. (American Psychiatric Association, 1994, p. 78)

Three subtypes of ADHD are identified in the *DSM-IV*: (1) primarily inattentive, (2) primarily hyperactive-impulsive, and (3) combined types. The *DSM-IV* criteria for identifying the three subtypes of ADHD are shown in Figure 9.1. In addition, other criteria include the following:

- Some hyperactive-impulsive or inattentive symptoms that caused impairment were present before age 7.
- Some impairment from the symptoms is present in two or more settings (e.g., at school, work, or home).
- There must be clear evidence of clinically significant impairment in social, academic, or occupational functioning.
- The symptoms do not occur exclusively during the course of a Pervasive Developmental Disorder, Schizophrenia, or other psychotic disorder and are not bet-

**FIGURE 9.1** *Diagnostic Criteria for Attention Deficit Hyperactivity Disorder*

### ADHD—*Inattention subtype*

Six (or more) of the following symptoms of inattention have persisted for at least 6 months to a degree that is maladaptive and inconsistent with the child's developmental level:

**(a)** often fails to give close attention to details or makes careless mistakes in schoolwork, work, or other activities;

**(b)** often has difficulty sustaining attention in tasks or play activities;

**(c)** often does not seem to listen when spoken to directly;

**(d)** often does not follow through on instructions and fails to finish schoolwork, chores, or duties in the workplace (not due to oppositional behavior or failure to understand instructions);

**(e)** often has difficulty organizing tasks or activities;

**(f)** often avoids, dislikes or is reluctant to engage in tasks that require sustained mental effort (such as schoolwork or homework);

**(g)** often loses things necessary for tasks or activities (e.g., toys, school assignments, pencils, books, or tools);

**(h)** is often easily distracted by extraneous stimuli;

**(i)** is often forgetful in daily activities.

### ADHD—*Hyperactive-impulse subtype*

Six (or more) of the following symptoms of hyperactivity-impulsivity have persisted for at least 6 months to a degree that is maladaptive and inconsistent with developmental level:

### *Hyperactivity*

**(a)** often fidgets with hands or feet or squirms in seat;

**(b)** often leaves seat in classroom or in other situations in which remaining seated is expected;

**(c)** often runs about or climbs excessively in situations in which it is inappropriate. (In adolescents or adults, it may be limited to subjective feelings of restlessness);

**(d)** often has difficulty playing or engaging in leisure activities quietly;

**(e)** is often "on the go" or acts as if "driven by a motor";

**(f)** often talks excessively;

### *Impulsivity*

**(g)** often blurts out answers before questions have been completed;

**(h)** often has difficulty awaiting turn;

**(i)** often interrupts or intrudes on others (e.g., butts into conversations or games)

### ADHD: *Attention deficit hyperactivity disorder: Combined subtype*

This subtype should be used if six (or more) symptoms of inattention and six (or more) symptoms of hyperactivity-impulsivity have persisted for at least 6 months. Most children and adolescents with the disorder have the Combined Type. It is not known whether the same is true of adults with the disorder. Inattention may often still be a significant clinical feature in such cases.

*Source:* Reprinted with permission from the *Diagnostic and Statistical Manual of Mental Disorders, Fourth Edition, Text Revision* (Washington, DC: American Psychiatric Association, 2000), p. 80.

ter accounted for by another mental disorder (e.g., Mood Disorder, Anxiety Disorder, Dissociative Disorder, or a Personality Disorder).

The pattern of behavior associated with ADHD often begins at an early age (between 3 and 7 years of age) and continues throughout childhood and into adolescence

*ADHD is characterized by developmentally inappropriate attention skills, impulsivity, and hyperactivity.*

(Barkley, 2000). Most children with ADHD begin to show signs that are identified when they enter a structured situation, such as the school or preschool environment (Lerner et al., 1995). Establishing the diagnosis of ADHD in children younger than 4 or 5 years of age is difficult because it is hard to differentiate children with ADD from those with the normal ebullience of childhood. History and observation provide the primary basis for diagnosis (Audreus, 1999). For preschool children, then, it is particularly important to note the child's level of development when considering whether the child's behaviors are symptomatic of ADHD. A caution appears in *DSM-IV* about making the diagnosis of ADHD too readily in the preschool-age group:

> Toddlers and preschoolers with this disorder differ from normally active young children by being constantly on the go and into everything; they dart back and forth, are "out of the door before their coat is on," jump or climb on furniture, run through the house, and have difficulty participating in sedentary group activities in preschool classes (e.g., listening to a story). (American Psychiatric Association, 1994, p. 79)

Evidence is growing that ADHD has a biological basis. It is thought that the neurological dysfunction involves the electrochemical transmission of the nerve impulses from one cell to another across a synapse. Individuals with ADHD may have a reduced level of the necessary neurochemicals. Insufficient neurochemicals impair the child's ability to control functions such as attention and inhibition (Riccio, Hynd, Cohen, & Gonzalez, 1993). There is controversy regarding the use of stimulant medications with the preschool population. Stein, Efron, Schuman, Blum, and Glanzmann (in press) indicate that stimulant medications should be considered only in extreme cases in children under the age of 5 years, and only after environmental interventions have been implemented without success.

It is suggested that a multimodal approach be used in treatment; that is, several methods should be used simultaneously. These intervention methods for ADHD include medication, family counseling and education, behavior management, and special education. Andreus (1999) suggests the need for collaboration between home and school.

## Pervasive Developmental Disorders and Autistic Disorder

Children with *pervasive developmental disorders* (*PDDs*) are characterized by "severe deficits and pervasive impairment in multiple areas of development. These include impairment in reciprocal social interaction, impairment in communication, and the presence of stereotyped behavior, interests, and activities" (American Psychiatric Association, 1994, p. 38). Getz defines *pervasive developmental disorders* as

> severe disorders simultaneously affecting several domains of a child's development, including: social skills, language, attention, perception, reality testing, and motor activity. The disorders are pervasive, affect a child early in life, and are life-long. Children present with varying degrees of impairment, hence PDD is considered a spectrum disorder. The most severe expression of the disorder is autism. (1993, p. 1)

Three major areas are listed in *DSM-IV* (1994) under the diagnostic criteria for Autistic Disorder:

1. Qualitative impairment in reciprocal social interaction
2. Qualitative impairment in verbal and nonverbal communication
3. Markedly restricted repertoire of behavior, activities, and interests

*Etiology.*    Definitive causal factors of the pervasive developmental disorders are not known at this time. Two major etiological shifts have occurred since 1943 when Kanner first identified autism as a syndrome:

1. Since the initial group of children identified as autistic came from upper-middle-class homes, a strong "correlation" was forged between social standing and the occurrence of autism (American Psychiatric Association, 1994; Donnellan, 1985). Research studies over the years have contradicted this earlier assumption and revealed that autism is present in all socioeconomic strata.
2. Bettelheim's (1967) original hypothesis that the parents were causative factors in autism has not been born out in controlled studies.

Four features define autism: early onset; social dysfunction; communication dysfunction; and unusual behaviors, stereotypes, and resistance to change (Koenig, Rubin, Klin, & Volkmar, 2000).

***Fragile X Syndrome.*** *Fragile X syndrome* is an inherited genetic disorder caused by a change of mutation in the genetic information on the X chromosome (Hagerman, 2000). There are three major markers for the disorder: (1) a long face, (2) prominent or long ears, and (3) large testicles in males (macroorchidism). The disorder affects both males and females, but the disorder is seen more in males, and they often manifest more serious symptoms than females (Weber, 2000).

Characteristics of children with this disorder are that they have cognitive difficulties ranging from learning disabilities to mental retardation and they exhibit hand-flapping or biting behaviors, poor eye contact, and tantrums. The disorder is identified through a DNA analysis for Fragile X Mental Retardation 1 (FMR1) (Finucane & Cronister, 2000). Many children with autism test positive for Fragile X syndrome.

***Parents of Children with Autism and PDD.*** In the past, parents were blamed for their children's autistic tendencies and chastised for lack of complete compliance with treatment therapies (Bettelheim, 1967; Schopler, 1985). Today, when a child is diagnosed with autism, parents may question their ability to care for their child and are understandably confused when faced with the myriad of decisions required when they seek diagnosis and treatment for their child with PDD.

Counseling parents of children with PDD is a challenging task. It is very frustrating for the parent to constantly "give" to these children without receiving the normal warmth, love, and affection that typical children bestow on their parents.

***Characteristics of Children with Autism and PDD.*** Formal evaluations on children with autism or PDD usually yield low scores in cognition (below 70 IQ), low scores in both receptive and expressive language, occasional outstandingly high scores in fine motor control, weak to no social skills, and variations in adaptive behaviors (Mayes et al., 1993).

In a young child, *sensory deficits* (impairments in vision and hearing) may result in the child ignoring her or his surroundings and thus acting like a child with PDD. However, in children with sensory deficits, there is not a concomitant deficiency in the quality of their social interactions, and once the deficit is identified and intervention is established, the child develops a communication system.

When young children are diagnosed with *mental retardation*, they do not usually manifest the social withdrawal evidenced in children with PDD. Although 75 percent of children identified with PDD have cognitive deficits that place them within the mentally retarded range (IQs of less than 70), it is their apparent lack of interest in communication and social interactions that distinguish them from children with mental retardation without PDD (Donnellan, 1985).

***Treatment Strategies and Intervention.*** Treatment for young children with PDD usually consists of intervention conducted by one or more members of a multidisciplinary team, such as an early interventionist, a social worker, an occupational or physical therapist, or a psychologist. The intervention plan may consist of both medical and educational/counseling approaches. Two of the educational approaches are discussed here: Greenspan's (1992) Developmental, Individual-Difference, Relationship-Based (DIR) model, and Lovaas's Applied Behavioral Analysis (ABA) model (Engel, 2000).

The DIR model for providing intervention to children with autism was developed by Greenspan (1992). His basic construct is that affective interactions build social and emotional development, intelligence, and morality. Greenspan and Wieder (1999) describe a functional developmental approach to autism spectrum disorders. They indicate that the DIR model attempts to facilitate understanding of children and their families by identifying, systematizing, and integrating functional developmental capacities. These "include the child's (a) functional-emotional developmental level, (b) the child's individual differences in sensory reactivity, processing and motor planning, and (c) the child's relationships and interactions with caregivers, family members, and others" (p. 148).

Lovaas's ABA approach is described by Engel (2000). This approach emphasizes functional skills and includes the application of scientific principles to teach appropriate behaviors and reduce inappropriate behaviors. There is a sequential approach to manipulating measurable components of a behavior, with later emphasis on generalization of emerging skills. Smith, Groen, and Wynn (2000) find that a less intense use of the Lovaas ABA method (25 hours a week) results in intensive early intervention with powerful results across the PDD spectrum.

In certain early childhood settings, children with autism are successfully integrated and included with other children for part or all of the school day. Odom (1994) suggests that early interventionists needed to recognize the varying needs of different children and make individualized accommodations for each child.

***Pharmacological Intervention.*** Medications have been used with children with PDD with little uniform success. Sloman (1991) reviews the use of medications in children with PDDs and provides a thorough summary of pharmacological agents, their effects, and potential adverse side effects. Medications used include chlorpromazine, trifluoperazine, thioridazine, and haloperidol. Sloman states that medication does not cure PDD and is not often indicated. However, when medication is considered, it is important that parents are empowered to make choices once they understand the purpose, process, risks, side effects, and alternative treatments for these disorders.

***Educational Approaches.*** Behavior modification has been used successfully with many children with autism (Lovaas, 1987). However, in the very young child, Greenspan (1992) finds that the prognosis is improved when interventionists rely "less on mechanical, structured treatment approaches, and more on relationship, affect-cuing based approaches" (p. 3). The primary goal of the relationship approach is to enable children to form a "sense of their own personhood—sense of themselves as intentional, interactive individuals" (p. 5). Greenspan elaborates on this inner sense as the process of the child engaging, focusing, and concentrating on two-way interactions. He also includes the child's capacity to symbolize and differentiate her or his experiences in this process.

*Developmental therapy* is a comprehensive program for children with emotional disturbance, behavior disorders, or autism (Wood, Combs, Grunn, & Weller, 1986). The intervention program is based on five stages of development across four areas: behavior, communication, socialization, and (pre)academic skills. The preschool focus is on responding to the environment with pleasure and responding to the environment with success. It includes information for classroom teachers that helps them identify children who may have emotional difficulties.

### Living with PDD as a Child: Retrospective Adult Viewpoint.

Little is known about how young children with PDD actually feel or what they may experience. Many children who have these disorders are mute and/or mentally retarded. Adults who apparently have had milder forms of autism and who have written about their experiences report poignantly about how very isolating it is to have this disorder.

One adult who writes about having autism is Temple Grandin. She is now in her fifties and is a successful college professor and consultant to the livestock industry. By her own admission, she was "a partially autistic child." In 1984, Grandin wrote about what it was like for her to live with autism during her early childhood years:

> At the age of 2½ to 3 I had many of the standard autistic behaviors such as fixation on spinning objects, refusing to be touched or held, preferring to be alone, destructive behavior, temper tantrums, inability to speak, sensitivity to sudden noises, appearance of deafness, and intense interest in odors. . . . I remember being able to understand everything that people said to me, but I could not speak back. Screaming and flapping my hands was the only way I could reply. (pp. 144–145)

Grandin's desire for physical contact as a child was very threatening to her, and she would not allow her mother to hold her. It is fascinating to read that she actually craved contact while prohibiting it:

> My mother told me that when I was an infant she felt "snubbed" because I did not want to be cuddled at 3–4 months of age. . . . I was her first child and she did not know enough to just hold me anyway even if I did not like it. (p. 151)

Recently, Grandin (2000) wrote that she appreciated her mother's insistence on structure and clear rules, which she felt helped her establish boundaries. She also stressed how valuable mentors had been to her during school and in her career.

### Related Disorders.

In addition to Autistic Disorder and PDD, the American Psychiatric Association categorized three other disorders: Rett's Disorder, Childhood Disintegrative Disorder, and Asperger's Disorder.

*Rett's Disorder.*   Rett's syndrome is characterized by an apparently normal early development followed by deceleration of head growth between the ages of 5 months and 4 years. Powers (2000) indicates that during the early childhood years, children with Rett's syndrome begin to manifest degenerative aspects of the disorder: loss of fine motor skills, development of stereotypic hand movements, impaired receptive and expressive language skills, psychomotor retardation, social withdrawal, seizures, and respiratory dysfunction. The disorder has been identified exclusively in females at this time.

*Childhood Disintegrative Disorder.*    Also known as Heller syndrome, this disorder is exhibited by those children who develop an apparent autisticlike disorder after a prolonged period of normal development. Volkmar (1992) and Powers (2000) indicate that this "late onset autism" differs from autism in terms of the pattern of onset, clinical features, course, and prognosis.

*Asperger's Disorder.*    This disorder overlaps to a degree with autism, and it probably constitutes a milder variety of autism (Rutter & Schopler, 1992). According to Szatmari (1992), these children are higher functioning and differ from the majority of children with autism whose IQs are usually within the mental retardation range, lack communicative language, and have poor prognosis.

## Aggressive Behavior

*Aggression* is defined as hostile and attacking behavior directed toward the self, others, or the immediate physical environment. Aggression may also include verbal communication that is intended to harm or irritate someone else. Typical aggressive behaviors during the preschool period include hitting, kicking, biting, shoving, and name-calling or other verbal provocation.

There are many different theories about the causes of aggression. For example, aggression has been analyzed as a natural instinct, a learned response, a reaction to frustration, and a response to group pressure (Berns, 1993). Developmentally, children begin to show aggressive behavior when they first socialize with peers during the second year of life. Often, their first quarrels are over toys and ownership: "It's mine!" "No, it's mine!"

Children who exhibit aggressive behaviors typically have difficulty with peer relationships. They are more likely to be rejected by their peers and have smaller peer networks than children who are not aggressive (Bukatko & Daehler, 1992). Capara, Barbaranelli, Pastorelli, Bandura, and Zimbardo (2000) find that early aggressiveness adversely affects both peer relations and academic accomplishments.

Aggressive behaviors can be viewed as a child externalizing his or her emotional problems by acting out on others and the environment. There are other ways that children may cope with emotional stress—for example, they may *internalize* their problems, which results in withdrawal from the environment.

## Withdrawn Behavior

Some children pull back from other children and their environment and withdraw from social contact. These children often appear disinterested in activities, often linger at the perimeter of socialized group activities, and may look as though they are daydreaming or depressed. In some instances, withdrawn children are also troubled by fears and phobias. Luby (2000) finds that impairments in mood and affect may be suggestive of depression in young children. He suggests programs to enhance the child's ability to identify and label emotions that might result in improved coping skills.

Children who are withdrawn may also show symptoms of immaturity and anxiety, which might limit them in social interactions as well as compromise their preacademic and readiness work (Hallahan & Kauffman, 1994).

### Problems in Socialization

Most children learn to interact with others in socially acceptable ways. However, certain individuals do not easily pick up on social cues and often are unable to perceive the prevailing mood of others. A lack of social perception may be a variant of learning disabilities. Deficits in social skills can affect most aspects of a child's life and may include problems in social perception, a lack of judgment, problems with making friends, and a poor self-concept. Sometimes there are concurring factors in a child's development that affect socialization and development of peer relationships. When children are unable to communicate with other children or express their feelings, this may result in a decrease in socialization. Lonigan, Bloomfield, and Anthony (1999) state that in addition to potential academic problems, children with language problems may be at high risk for development of social, behavioral, and emotional disabilities, which further impede academic success and make special education services more likely.

Children with problems in socialization may need direct instruction in social skills (McConnell & Odom, 1999). For these children, social skills training is an important aspect of the curriculum so they learn how to behave in social groups and how to react to others. Several strategies can be employed to encourage socialization among young children.

Guralnick (1990) suggests that patterns for grouping children, differential teacher attention, prompting children, and the selection of specific materials and activities all play a part in helping children who have special needs interact with each other and with typical children. Umbreit (1996b) provides specific directions for an intervention package that reduced disruptive classroom behavior in a preschool child who was included in a regular preschool setting.

## Intervention Strategies for Young Children with Social and Emotional Difficulties

Approaches to intervention are based on different theories about social and emotional development. Three of those approaches are discussed here: humanistic, psychodynamic, and behavioral.

### Humanistic Approach to Intervention

A humanistic approach to intervention concentrates on providing an atmosphere of love and trust in teaching and learning. Children are encouraged to be open and communicative persons. The approach is very nonauthoritarian. It is concerned with the child's immediate experiences in the "here and now," rather than with past experiences.

## Psychodynamic Approach to Intervention

The psychodynamic view of social and emotional problems looks at the child's problems in terms of unconscious conflicts and motivations. This approach is based on constructs drawn from psychoanalysis and related theories such as those from Freud (1966), Erikson (1963), and Klein (1952). Psychodynamic theory suggests that development proceeds through a series of sequential stages and that disruption can occur during any one of the stages of development. Disruptions of development may come from either overly restrictive or overly indulgent nurturance, or a number of other factors in the parent-child relationship.

The psychodynamic view focuses on the emotional features of disturbance, which are considered to be the results of conflicts among various drives. Treatment is usually one or more of a variety of forms of individual psychotherapy, designed to uncover, explore, and resolve these inner conflicts.

*Play Therapy.*    Some psychodynamically oriented therapists use play therapy in working with young children who have emotional problems. In play therapy, children are given real-life toys, such as dolls, doll houses and furniture, toys for punching and acting out aggression, and art materials. During the time the child is with the therapist, she or he is encouraged to create various scenarios and act out feelings through play. The play therapist encourages the child to work through problems in the confidential and secure setting where play therapy sessions take place. The therapist observes the child's play carefully, reflecting and responding to the child's needs and feelings (Axline, 1947).

*Theraplay.*    Theraplay has its roots in interactional theories of development, attachment theory, and developmental psychology. It is a short-term treatment method modeled on the natural healthy parent-infant relationship (Jernberg & Booth, 1999). The theraplay therapist works intensively with the child, taking charge, enticing the child into the relationship, and providing nurturing touch in active, physical, interactive play. The treatment is geared to the child's emotional level and as the therapy develops, parents become more actively involved with their child's treatment.

## Behavioral Approach to Intervention

The behavioral approach is based on the field of behavioral psychology and Skinner's (1957) work on reinforcement theory. It focuses on providing children with highly structured learning environments and materials. Behavior modification is the application of behavioral psychology to managing a child's behavior. It includes the use of various forms of reinforcement and environmental management to change behavior.

Applied behavior analysis requires that a child's target behaviors are carefully observed as well as stimulus or antecedent events and subsequent consequences. The child's behavior must be carefully charted, graphed, and counted. Interventions are based on the use of reinforcements to increase desired behaviors or decrease undesired behaviors.

Behaviorists believe that all behavior is learned and can therefore be unlearned and relearned or taught and modified. Further, learned behaviors are controlled by their consequences and are frequently "situation specific," or exhibited only in particular situations.

**Functional Behavioral Assessment.**    The disciplinary provisions outlined in IDEA (1997) mandate the use of functional behavioral assessment (FBA) for students with severe emotional problems. Although the target group initially was older children, Conroy and Davis (2000) believe that this provision is legally and practically applicable to preschool children, as well. *Functional behavioral assessment* is defined as "the process of determining relations between specific variables in the environment and problem behavior" (p. 164). Components of FBA include (Conroy & Davis, 2000; Shriver, Anderson, & Proctor, 2000):

1. Defining the challenging behavior
2. Determining the environmental events and factors that contribute to the challenging behavior
3. Using direct observation to identify the antecedents and consequences that occur before and after the challenging behavior
4. Developing hypotheses regarding the function of the behavior and the contextual factors that contribute to the challenging behavior
5. Validating these hypotheses
6. Developing an efficient and effective intervention that matches the function of the behavior

**Reinforcement.**    *Reinforcers* are consequences that increase the likelihood that a behavior will occur in the future. Positive reinforcers are selected to increase the occurrence of appropriate behaviors. *Punishment* may be defined as any consequence that reduces the rate or strength of the behavior being punished. Punishment can include mild reprimands, temporary withdrawal of attention, or loss of privileges.

**Shaping.**    *Shaping* is the reinforcement of certain behaviors that lead to a desired outcome. It is the systematic immediate reinforcement of successive approximations of the desired behavior until the desired behavior is established. Shaping is primarily used to establish behaviors that have not been previously manifested in the individual's behavioral repertoire (Walker & Shea, 1988).

**Modeling.**    *Modeling* is the provision of an individual or group behavior after which a child is to pattern his or her behavior. The child imitates or copies the behavior of others and may then be positively reinforced for modeling himself or herself after others (Walker & Shea, 1988).

**Contingency Contracting.**    *Contingency contracting* is also know as the *Premack principle* (Premack, 1959). A behavior that has a high rate of occurrence can be used to increase a behavior with a low rate of occurrence. Often, this type of contract is referred to as "grandma's law." Grandma might have said, "First you eat your spinach, then you get dessert." In school-related matters, contingency contracting translates to "If you do *X*, then you get to do *Y*."

***Behavior Recording.***    One aspect of behavior modification is the use of stringent systems of recording behavior. This is essential because of the underlying principle that people use behavior modification to alter (increase or decrease) specific behaviors. Thus, it is crucial that the teacher keep an accurate count of behaviors before, during, and after the intervention. The following steps are used in conducting an intervention:

1. *Select the target behavior* to be increased or decreased.
2. *Collect and record baseline data.* (This is done before the intervention has been utilized.) It is used to determine the subsequent amount of change and the effectiveness of the intervention.
3. *Identify appropriate reinforcers.* Check with parents, teachers, or the child when appropriate; direct observation is useful in determining reinforcers.
4. *Implement the intervention using appropriate reinforcers.*
5. *Collect and record intervention data.* (Note that there is often an initial increase in "negative" behavior as the child tests the limits.)
6. *Monitor the change in behavior.* After the behavior is established in the child's repertoire, remove the reinforcer and observe and chart whether the behavior continues to increase or decrease.

There are several schedules of reinforcement that can be used to modify behavior. *Schedules of reinforcement* refer to the pattern with which the reinforcer is presented or not presented in response to the exhibition of the behavior.

***Time-Out.***    *Time-out* is the removal of a child from an apparently reinforcing setting to a presumably nonreinforcing setting for a specified and limited amount of time. This approach is used to increase target behavior. It may be that the child is isolated in a corner of the classroom for a few minutes or removed entirely from the classroom for a short period of time. Brevity is essential for time-outs, and it should be noted that not all children find isolation an unpleasant experience.

## Intervention Strategies for Helping Preschoolers with Social and Emotional Problems

This section provides additional suggestions for helping children with social, emotional, and behavioral development (Berns, 1993; Cook, Tessier, & Klein, 1999; Greenspan, 1999; Huettig & O'Connor, 1999):

1. *Environment.* Create a safe, secure, nurturing environment at school as well as in the home if possible.
2. *Sense of mastery.* Develop a sense of mastery around the child's natural strengths; focus on strengths rather than negative behaviors.

3. *Books.*  In addition to typical preschool books, read books such as *A Book of Hugs* by Ross and Rader, *Alexander and the Terrible, Horrible, No Good, Very Bad Day* by Viorst and Cruz, and *Oonga, Boonga* by Wishinsky and Thompson. Reading these books will stimulate discussion about feelings and encourage children to share their painful experiences.

4. *Play activities.*  Provide abundant opportunities for play. Teachers are encouraged to engage in play with the children at times, to imitate children and join the play as a co-player or to assume a pretend role with the child.

5. *Pretend play.*  Encourage pretend and make-believe play. Have other children or teachers model pretend and fantasy play with toys. Change predictable responses to stimulate verbal response from the child.

6. *Transition activities.*  Use transition activities between activities. Give children a 5-minute and 1-minute "warning" that there will be change. Use music to encourage children to return to the circle or sharing area and to pick up toys.

7. *Toys.*  Select specific toys for children with disabilities. They need to be ones with which they will experience success, and the child can experience cause and effect. Toys should also be developmentally appropriate and durable.

8. *Puppets.*  Puppets are therapeutic and fun for most children. Sometimes a withdrawn child will exhibit previously undisplayed language and emotion when hiding behind the puppet screen.

9. *Aggressive behaviors.*  Let children know that aggression is not sanctioned in the classroom or on the playground. Set standards and consequences and stick to them.

10. *Alternatives to solve problems.*  Give children alternative ways to solve problems. Teach them how to verbalize their feelings and how to listen to others.

11. *Rules.*  Formulate rules and discuss the rules with the child as well as the reasons for them.

12. *Cooperative spirit among the children.*  Foster helpfulness and be a positive role model. Help children in the classroom learn to help each other.

13. *Role playing.*  When children are involved in conflicts, try to have them verbalize each other's feelings. They need to understand that aggression hurts the other child and causes resentment.

## *Summary*

- Important theories of emotional and social development in young children include the theories of bonding and attachment, stages of development, temperament differences, and the role of play in social and emotional development.
- The child's natural temperament appears early in life, and it has interactive effects in relating to caregivers and teachers.
- The child's play has relevance to social and cognitive development. Young children who are at risk or who have disabilities need opportunities for play. Play activities must be planned for in the curriculum.
- Specific behavior syndromes that affect young children include attention deficit hyperactivity disorders, pervasive developmental disorders, and autism.

- Preschool children often display aggressive or withdrawn behaviors. Aggressive behaviors are externalized behaviors. Withdrawn behaviors are internalized behavioral symptoms.
- Problems in socialization often affect young children. These children lack social perception skills and often need direct intervention to learn how to act with others.
- Intervention approaches are based on several theories of social and emotional development. They include humanistic theories, psychodynamic theories, and behavioral development.

## Key Terms

ABA
Asperger's disorder
attachment
attention deficit disorder
autonomy vs. shame and doubt
behavioral theory
bonding
contingency contracting
DIR
emotional disturbance
failure to thrive (FTT)
Fragile X syndrome
functional behavioral assessment

humanistic theory
initiative vs. guilt
modeling
parallel play
pervasive developmental disorder
psychodynamic theory
reinforcement
Rett's disorder
shaping
temperament
time-out
trust vs. mistrust

# 10

## *Communication and Language Development*

## Chapter Outline

*Definitions of Communication, Speech, and Language*

*Stages of Language Development*
   Prelinguistic Behaviors
   Emergence of Words
   Combining Words into Sentences
   More Advanced Language

*Theories of Language Acquisition*
   Behavioral Theory
   Innatist Theory
   Cognitive-Interactionist Theory
   Social-Interactionist Theory
   Integration of Theories
      of Language Acquisition

*Linguistic Systems of Language*
   Phonology
   Morphology
   Semantics
   Syntax
   Pragmatics

*Language Difficulties Associated
with Specific Conditions*
   Lack of Stimulating Experiences

   Cultural and Linguistic Diversity and Second
      Language Acquisition
   Hearing Loss
   Visual Impairments
   Cognitive Delays
   Auditory Processing Dysfunctions
   Autism and Pervasive Developmental
      Disorders
   Emotional Disturbances
   Speech Disorders
   Motor Dysfunctions, Injuries,
      and Structural Abnormalities

*Intervention for Children
with Language Problems*
   Naturalistic Teaching
   Parents as Language Trainers
   Behavioral Techniques for Language
      Development
   Classroom Interventions
   Activity-Based Intervention
   Peer-Mediated Intervention
   Teaching Language Skills to Children
      with Severe Disabilities
   Intervention Activities

The learning of language is a remarkable accomplishment that occurs during the early childhood years. It is true that certain animals have remarkable communication systems, but only humans have attained the most highly developed system of communication—speech. Language fulfills several very human functions: It furnishes a means of communicating and socializing with others, it provides a vehicle of thought, and it enables the culture to be transmitted from generation to generation.

The child learns language in a social setting; an adult (usually a parent) plays a critical role as a coach, guide, and teacher. The following parent-child conversation illustrates the parent's role in guiding a young child's emerging language and ability to communicate needs. The example shows an exemplary parental response to the child's emerging language.

> ***Child:***   "Cookie."
>
> ***Parent:***   "Cookie? I want cookie. Well, here it is!"

*Early Childhood Snapshot*    EILEEN: A CHILD
WITH LANGUAGE DELAY

Eileen is a 4-year-old child in an early childhood program who was identified with a language delay. Eileen's speech consists of one- or two-word sentences. Eileen's parents, along with the transdisciplinary team at her preschool, are using an approach called *naturalistic language teaching* to encourage her to use longer sentences in talking. By using natural language development techniques, Eileen's parents and the transdisciplinary team members furnish models of more complex language for Eileen to refer to as she is ready to use them.

In applying this method of natural language development, when Eileen said "Go" while point-ing to the window, her father used the technique of *expansion* and asked her, "Go out now?" Eileen repeated the expanded phrase, saying "Go out now."

Eileen's teacher used the technique of *parallel talk* for the natural language development approach. In this technique, her teacher described what Eileen was doing as she was playing nearby. As Eileen played with her doll, putting the doll in the bed, her teacher said, "My dolly is sleepy. Put dolly to sleep. Put dolly to sleep."

The close communication between the parent and school led to the reinforcement of natural language development methods both at home and at school in daily routines and activities.

Difficulty in learning language is the most common and often the first problem recognized in young children who are at risk or who have disabilities. Whatever other difficulties the child may have, over 80 percent have communication/language delays. Moreover, an untreated language disorder can diminish the child's abilities in many areas of functioning. Language problems can lead to pervasive social, cognitive, and educational consequences that have repercussions on the child's future development (Goldstein & Strain, 1994). The ability to communicate with others is critical to life skills (Downing, 1999).

This chapter examines language delays and disorders in young children. The chapter (1) defines the terms *language, communication,* and *speech;* (2) compares theories of language acquisition; (3) discusses the approaches to intervention that each theory suggests; and (4) reviews the sequential stages of language development in young children. The chapter also describes the basic linguistic systems of language (phonology, morphology, syntax, semantics, and pragmatics) and relates these linguistic systems to language problems encountered by young children. In addition, the chapter examines difficulties in acquiring language and intervention strategies for language disorders.

## Definitions of Communication, Speech, and Language

The three terms—*communication, speech,* and *language*—are related, but each has a different meaning:

- *Communication* refers to the exchange of messages through an interaction between two people, usually a speaker and a listener. For this exchange to be called a communicative act, it must be meaningful to both participants (Rice, 1995).

*Communication refers to the exchange of messages through an interactive behavior of two people.*

- *Language* refers to the knowledge and use of a symbolic code or set of rules involving syntax or grammar that transmits meaning from one person to another. The most familiar code system is oral language, but there are other code systems, such as computer languages, Morse code, and sign language. Oral language is often divided into receptive oral language or expressive oral language. *Receptive oral language* refers to the ability to listen to and understand the language of others. For example, when Genise can follow a direction such as, "Give me the shoe," she is demonstrating skill in receptive language. *Expressive oral language* is the ability to use language and communicate meaning to others in words so that another person will understand. For example, when Jamie says, "I want more milk," he is using expressive language to communicate a desire. As children develop expressive language skills, they learn to combine and order words that represent objects, people, and events in their environment.
- *Speech* is the verbal tool for conveying oral language. It consists of the speaker using the oral mechanism to produce actual utterances. The use of speech depends on the child's abilities with oral-motor skills, coordination of breathing, sound production, use of the tongue, placement of the lips and teeth, and articulation of sounds.

## Stages of Language Development

Language development normally follows a sequence of developmental stages: (1) prelinguistic, (2) the emergence of words, (3) the combination of words into sentences,

*Language development normally follows a sequence of developmental stages.*

and (4) advanced language (Hoge & Parette, 1995; Owens, 1996). Table 10.1 provides examples of developmental speech, language, and communication behaviors from infancy through age 4.

### Prelinguistic Behaviors

Research shows that from the first day of life, infants participate nonverbally in the communicative processes (Kaiser, 1993). Babies use crying to express hunger or discomfort. They show the intensity of their uncomfortable state by varying the pitch and duration of their crying. During the first few months of life, many of the communications of infants are not intentional; that is, they are not performed for a particular purpose. However, parents often respond to their children's cooing, smiling, and gazing behaviors as if they were meaningful or intentional. These preverbal behaviors are called *prelocutionary*. By 9 to 10 months of age, babies typically begin to engage in purposeful nonverbal communication, which is called *illocutionary*. An example of such communication is when babies gaze at their caregivers and raise their arms in order to communicate the wish to be picked up.

Caregivers often use a simplified, modified type of language called *parentese* when talking to their babies and preschoolers. Characteristics of parentese language include the use of short, simple sentences, a raised and exaggerated pitch, repetition of vocabulary and sounds, and talk about the "here and now." These modifications of normal language help young children to understand the language of their caregivers (Ratner & Harris, 1994).

**TABLE 10.1**    *Examples of Developmental Communication, Speech/Language Behaviors: Birth through Age Four*

| Age Range | Communication, Speech, and Language Behaviors |
|---|---|
| 0–3months | Regards persons momentarily<br>Quiets to voice<br>Looks at speaker's eyes and mouth<br>Searches for sounds<br>Makes comfort sounds<br>Cries when uncomfortable or hungry |
| 3–6 months | Smiles, coos in response to voice and adult smiling<br>Quiets when hearing caregiver's voice<br>Shows anticipatory response when seeing bottle<br>Expresses displeasure and excitement through crying and/or vocalizing<br>Laughs<br>Shows awareness of strange persons<br>Vocalizes in response to speech |
| 6–9 months | Discriminates strangers from familiar people<br>Vocalizes pleasure, satisfaction, anger<br>Produces a variety of consonant sounds<br>Uses a loud voice to attract attention<br>Babbles to other people<br>Extends arms to be picked up |
| 8–12 months | Intentionally vocalizes to initiate interactions with people<br>Waves bye-bye<br>Repeats a behavior that others laugh at<br>Anticipates a familiar event from signs (e.g., when placed in a high chair anticipates eating)<br>Expresses anger when a toy is taken away<br>Ceases activity when told "no"<br>Can participate in familiar games (e.g., peek-a-boo) |
| 12–18 months | Indicates needs by gesturing and vocalizing<br>Shows/offers objects to initiate social interactions<br>Uses gestures such as pointing to direct adult attention<br>Uses a few words<br>Gestures and vocalizes to "request" desired objects and events<br>Says "no" meaningfully<br>Responds to own name<br>Responds to names of familiar objects when seen<br>Responds to simple verbal direction<br>By age 18 months, vocabulary increases to 10 to 15 words |
| 18–24 months | Responds to two-word requests<br>Uses words to request desired objects and events<br>May use jargon<br>Speech is 50 to 65% intelligible<br>Can point to 3 to 6 body parts<br>Uses at least 10 to 15 words by age 24 months<br>Two-word sentences by age 24 months |

*(continued)*

**TABLE 10.1** *Continued*

| Age Range | Communication, Speech, and Language Behaviors |
| --- | --- |
| 2–3 years | Talks about past and future activities<br>Identifies objects when told about their uses<br>Shows interest in other's conversation<br>Answers simple questions<br>Asks increasing numbers of questions that serve these functions:<br>  —calling attention to self and events in the environment<br>  —regulating the behaviors of others<br>  —obtaining desired objects<br>  —pointing to pictures of familiar objects and people when named<br>  —commenting about objects and ongoing events<br>Produces 3- to 5-word sentences<br>Has vocabulary of 100 to 200 words |
| 3–4 years | Refers more frequently to the activities of others<br>Understands simple time concepts (*Tomorrow* Grandma is coming)<br>Adapts to listener's level of understanding by changing tone of voice and sentence structure<br>Produces 3–word sentences<br>Speech mostly understandable by strangers but some articulation errors<br>Follows a sequence of 2 to 4 related directions<br>Refers to self by saying "me" or "I"<br>Adds "s" to form plurals<br>Adds "ed" to form past tense. |

*Sources:* Adapted from Goldstein, Kaczmarek, and English (2002); Hunt and Marshall (2002); Puckett and Black (2000); and Wetherby and Prizant (1998).

## Emergence of Words

Children typically begin to use single words at about 12 months of age. Early words approximate some of the natural sounds the child makes, such as "ma-ma" or "da-da." It is of interest to note that a word similar to mama or dada is found in many languages. For example, Polish babies say "ta-ta" for daddy. The Hebrew word "emah" sounds similar to momma. Early words are those that are effective in bringing about a change. For example, *milk*, *more*, *outside*, and *ball* are common early words. Actually, when the child says a single word, it represents a longer idea. These single words are often called *holophrases*. For example, when the child says "ball," he or she may mean "Play ball with me." Once the child learns that things have names, words typically come very fast and the child's vocabulary increases rapidly.

## Combining Words into Sentences

Around 2 years of age, children generally put two or three words together to make short phrases or sentences. They first use telegraphic speech in which unessential words are omitted, such as saying "Baby want truck" instead of "I want my truck." There are striking similarities in what children from different cultures around the world talk about in this stage. Their conversations are about everyday objects, people, and events (Paul, 1994). Grammatical morphemes such as plurals or present and past verb tenses are gradually added to their speech. By 3 years of age, the child typically produces simple sentences that are similar to the syntax in adult speech but may not always be in the correct grammatical form. For example, the youngster may say, "I want a crackers." However, even very young children make few mistakes in the word order they use. They appear to follow the rules of their native language without realizing it (Trawick-Smith, 2000).

## More Advanced Language

Around 4 to 5 years of age, language becomes more sophisticated and develops at a rapid pace. Preschoolers now use more advanced and intelligible sentences and use complex syntax. For example, they may say, "He's reading a book, and I want it next." Preschool children can stay on one topic when conversing with other children and familiar adults. They can take turns with their conversational partners and adjust their language according to the needs or status of their listeners. For example, when talking to a younger sibling, the child may say, "Give me your candy!" When talking to an adult, the youngster may change the structure and tone of the sentence by saying, "Please give me some candy." At this point in language development, the child is able to use speech to express feelings and share experiences with other people. Preschoolers have the ability to use words and sentences to influence other people (Owens, 1996).

# Theories of Language Acquisition

How children acquire language remains somewhat of a mystery, although there are several different theories about how children actually learn language. The theories of language acquisition stem from the behavioral, innatist, cognitive-interactionist, and social-interactionalist theories of learning.

## Behavioral Theory

One of the early explanations about how children learn language is based on *behavioral theory*. The influential behavioral psychologist, B. F. Skinner (1959), provided a behavioral explanation of language learning. The behavioral view contends that the child's environment plays a key role in language acquisition through the processes of imitation and reinforcement. As adults or older children present stimuli to the child, they focus on an object and say the word. The child responds by imitating the words spoken by the adults. The adult's dynamic reinforcement of the child's language imitations is a reward for saying the word. For example, when the child imitates "daddy" with "da-da," the adult reinforces this imitation with enthusiastic attention, smiles, and perhaps even clapping.

In terms of intervention, the behavioral theory of language learning emphasizes the need for modeling language so the child hears it and imitates it and for reinforcing the child's verbal behavior. Thus, to learn language, the child needs the active participation of an adult or older child to provide models and reinforcement (Linder, 1993). However, the behavioral theory of language acquisition has been criticized because of research indicating that children tend to generalize their learned responses to more natural settings (Duchan, 1997; Trawick-Smith, 2000).

## Innatist Theory

The *innatist theory* of language acquisition differs from the behavioral view. The innatist theory proposes that language learning is innate and natural for human beings; it is not simply dependent on imitation and reinforcements (Chomsky, 1976). Children are born with an innate language acquisition device (LAD) that allows them to learn language. The innatist explanation is that children intuitively use this innate acquisition device to process the language that they hear in their environment. The child's innate language mechanism allows the youngster to learn a set of language rules. These rules enable the child, as a speaker, to generate an infinite variety of novel sentences and, as a listener, to understand an infinite variety of sentences spoken by others (Reid, 2000).

In terms of intervention, the innatist theory suggests that since language is a natural human phenomenon, the child's language will develop and flourish if the child is given a stimulating language environment. However, for young children who are at risk or who have disabilities, additional time and specific, planned intervention is needed to internalize the language system. Another limitation of this theory of language acquisition for intervention purposes is its focus on the learning of syntax with a lack of attention to semantics and pragmatics (Nelson, 1998).

## Cognitive-Interactionist Theory

The *cognitive-interactionist theory* of language is based on Piaget's (1962) ideas about the stages of cognitive growth in children. This view emphasizes the relationships among environmental experiences, the development of thinking, and language. According to Piaget, the child acquires the cognitive prerequisites for language through actual environmental experiences, such as sensory-motor interaction with the environment. These "hands-on" environmental experiences serve to stimulate the development of symbolic behaviors that include language.

For an example of this theory, consider children at a preschool playing at the sand and water tables. If the preschoolers with special needs are near their peers without disabilities, they can hear language models, build their vocabulary, and practice pragmatic skills of taking turns being speakers and listeners. Language concepts such as *heavy* versus *light*, *full* versus *empty*, and *wet* versus *dry* can be better understood through the actual experiences of playing with buckets of sand and water. An example of a symbolic experience is when the children pretend that their buckets of water and sand are containers of drinks and food. This symbolic play of pretending that an object represents something else can build readiness for language as another symbolic system.

In terms of intervention, the congitive-interactionist view stresses the need to ascertain what the child already knows about language and to provide active experiences to build language. Also important in this view is the concept of *readiness*. Piaget proposes that certain kinds of readiness are needed before children can learn language. Teachers and parents can help develop and build these readiness skills by providing active environmental experiences. For instance, preschoolers with language delays can engage in dramatic play with typical peers in an inclusive classroom. In dramatic play, children play different roles, pretending to be family members, fire fighters, police officers, office workers, and so on. While playing their roles, the children with language delays are encouraged to communicate with their peers and use language to express themselves. Dramatic play offers many opportunities to build awareness of language as a symbolic system for communication. Some teachers have questioned whether this theory is sufficient in terms of intervention to meet the language learning needs of children with severe difficulties (Harris & Graham, 1996).

## Social-Interactionist Theory

The *social-interactional approach* to language learning is a contemporary theory of language acquisition that stresses the social role in language learning. Some of the main assumptions of this theory are that language develops because human beings are motivated to interact socially, and caregivers support their children's language development through their interactions with them (Bruner, 1990; Nelson, 1998). Interest in this theory can be traced to the work of Vygotsky (1978a), who believed that cognition and language develop through the child's interactions with others. Vygotsky described the child's potential level of development as the "zone of proximal development" (ZPD). In the ZPD, the children are able to demonstrate higher-level cognitive abilities while interacting with supportive adults.

The concept of *scaffolding* applies here, as the adult provides graduated cues to assist the child in acquiring more advanced language (Bruner, 1990). For example, a child may say "da" when she sees her father. The father could respond, "Daddy," thus modeling the next stage of language development in which one-word utterances follow vocalizations (Lucariello, 1994). Intervention, from this perspective, requires the caregiver to create a dialogue or conversation with the youngster. The adult then plays a mediating role, shaping learning opportunities and bringing them to the child's attention (Trawick-Smith, 2000). According to some researchers, a possible limitation of this theory for intervention may be its emphasis on pragmatics and lack of focus on other language skills (Kamhi, 1996; Nelson, 1994).

## Integration of Theories of Language Acquisition

All of these theories can be useful in meeting the needs of children with language disabilities and delays. These children have diverse needs, and some theoretical perspectives will be better for intervention purposes than others. Instead of trying to select the best theory to meet the needs of all children with language difficulties, it would be more useful to select those theoretical perspectives that will help the individual child (Duchan, 1995; Nelson, 1998).

# Linguistic Systems of Language

The field of linguistics is the scientific study of the language systems. The linguistic systems offer a useful framework for analyzing all languages as well as the language deviations in children with language disorders. There are several underlying linguistic systems of oral language: phonology, morphology, semantics, syntax, and pragmatics. Every language can be analyzed through these language systems, and each language has different rules for its systems. The linguistic system provides a framework for content, use, and form of language (Owens, 2001).

## Phonology

*Phonology* refers to the sound system of language and includes the rules for structuring and sequencing speech sounds into words. A *phoneme* is the smallest sound unit in language. For example, the spoken word *sit* has three phonemes or sounds: /s/, /i/, /t/. The difference between the spoken words *hat* and *mat* is the sound of the initial phoneme. It is essential that children learn the sound system (for phonemes) of language. They must also discover that rhythm and pitch changes can make a difference in language. Babies use many phonemic sounds in their babbling long before they can combine phonemes into meaningful words. Children who are unaware of the phonemes, or sound system of language, are likely to have difficulty in learning to read (Lerner, 2000).

## Morphology

*Morphology* refers to the meaning units in words and is the rule system for the internal structure of words. A *morpheme* is the smallest unit of meaning in a word. For example, *boys* has two morphemes or meaning units: *boy* and *plural*. The roots, prefixes, and suffixes in words are also morphemes. Words are built up from the morphemes or meaning units of the language system. When children learn the rules, or morphology, they understand and use plurals, possessives, and different verb tenses. Morpheme development is typically evident by about 18 months of age and continues until approximately 5 years of age (Owens, 1996). Young children with language disabilities may have difficulty in learning the morpheme system and need specific intervention.

## Semantics

*Semantics* refers to the vocabulary of language, its content, or the meaning of words. Semantic development continues throughout one's life as people continue to develop their vocabulary to learn about the world. Children with language disabilities often have very limited vocabularies.

In terms of intervention, children expand their vocabulary to talk about events and experiences and to communicate with others. Children with limited vocabularies will need direct experiences and planned intervention to learn meanings of words and to build their vocabularies, and acquire strategies for better word retrieval.

## Syntax

The *syntax* system refers to the sentence structure of the language. Different languages have different rules for stringing words together into sentences. Rules of syntax in a language specify which sentences are acceptable in that particular language and how to transform sentences into new sentences. For example, in English, a question has a different syntactical structure than a statement. The typical child is able to formulate sentences by age 3 and at about 4 years of age can form fairly complex sentences. Children with language disabilities often have great difficulty formulating sentences. When they talk, others may not understand what they are saying because their language sounds garbled. They may be able to say single words or short phrases but not a sentence. For example, they may say, "Candy want me" for "I want candy." In terms of intervention, children with syntax problems will need many experiences and intervention activities to understand and formulate sentences.

## Pragmatics

*Pragmatics* refers to the use of language in social situations and to the purpose, function, or use of language. Children demonstrate their knowledge of pragmatics when they take turns in conversations, adapt their language to the social context, repair breakdowns in conversations, and show that they take the listener's prior knowledge into account when communicating. Young children typically acquire some pragmatic skills before they say their first words. For example, babies demonstrate prelinguistic, pragmatic skills when they point to and reach for desired toys while they vocalize and gaze at their caregivers. Through these behaviors, babies communicate their needs to caregivers. Prelinguistic pragmatic skills normally develop around age 10 months and are important for later language acquisition. It is often in the area of pragmatics that children with language impairments differ most from children who are typically developing language. Currently, intervention techniques are beginning to place more emphasis on pragmatics or the function of language (Abbeduto & Short-Meyerson, 2002).

# Language Difficulties Associated with Specific Conditions

Problems in language in young children who are at risk or who have disabilities stem from a number of conditions. Often, the first sign of a disability is the child's difficulty in learning language. An assessment is needed to determine the nature and the cause of the language difficulty. A language problem can be related to a variety of conditions, such as lack of language stimulation, cultural and linguistic diversity, hearing loss, visual impairments, cognitive delays, auditory processing dysfunctions, autism, emotional disturbances, speech disorders, and motor dysfunctions, injuries, and structural abnormalities. Each of these conditions is discussed in this section.

## Lack of Stimulating Experiences

To acquire language skills, children need environments that provide intellectual and verbal stimulation. Youngsters need extensive language interaction and experiences, modeling of language, and an abundance of reciprocal give and take. The lack of stimulating experiences in the young child's life leads to depressed development of speech and language. Psychosocial factors also can negatively influence language development. These factors include poor parent-child attachment; lack of family support systems (social, financial, emotional); inappropriate caregiver expectations; insensitivity to a child's needs and capabilities; maternal caregivers who are under age 18; parental sensory and mental disabilities; child abuse, child neglect, or rejection; and inadequate language modeling (Donahue-Kilburg, 1992; Lowenthal, 2002).

## Cultural and Linguistic Diversity and Second Language Acquisition

The child's cultural or language background might initially interfere with language learning in English. Teachers should recognize the linguistic and cultural differences of children and implement appropriate educational strategies to help them make a successful transition to the use of English in school settings. In today's world, teachers encounter many children whose native language is not English. It is important to know if the development of these children in their native language is appropriate for their age. Some children use a dialectical variation of English or speak in a mixture of two languages. When youngsters from bilingual homes are acquiring two languages, they need to learn different sound systems, vocabularies, and syntax. Initially, they may substitute the language systems of their native language for those of the second (Trawick-Smith, 2000). Also, the rules for conversations or pragmatics may differ in the two languages, which can be confusing for the second language learners. In some cultures, parents are more responsive physically through touch or facial expression to their children than to their use of language. Children need to learn English in school, but their language and culture must be incorporated and respected in the school program (Lagrander & Reid, 2000).

It is important for early interventionists to recognize that children who are bilingual or those with dialectical variations have language *differences*, not language *disorders*. Children should not be classified as having language disorders if their native language is developing normally. To help the child in early childhood settings, support for new language acquisition can be given through classroom organization strategies, language development techniques, and close communication with their parents. Classroom organization strategies that assist second language learning children include routines and the provision of a safe place in the classroom. Consistent routines help the children understand what events are occurring and make them feel more comfortable and secure. Safe places, such as a quiet book corner or an art corner, enable these children to get breaks from the demands of trying to communicate in a new language (Tabors, 1998). Language can be simplified by teachers who talk about the present rather than the past or future, simply by just using the important words in sentences, and repeat the words combined with gestures and facial expressions to assist comprehension. In working with bilingual parents, it is important for teachers to develop awareness of the parents' culture, language, and customs. A cultural interpreter or a bilingual person from the same community can assist the teachers in interviewing the parents to find out their priorities for the children and how best to maintain their home languages while transitioning to English in the classroom (Tabors, 1997).

## Hearing Loss

Children who are deaf have great difficulty developing speech and language because they are unable to hear and imitate speech sounds and receive no auditory feedback as they attempt to speak. Children with more moderate degrees of hearing loss also encounter problems with learning speech and language. Even mild or intermittent hearing loss, such as the condition of otitis media (middle ear infections), can interfere with the child's ability to hear and pronounce some of the phonemes. Children with a hearing loss may experience language delays, show difficulty following directions, and exhibit difficulties in articulation.

The severity of the youngster's language difficulties depends on the age of the child when the hearing loss occurred and the degree of loss. Three major reasons for hearing impairments are genetic conditions, disease, and trauma. Genetic conditions cause 40 to 60 percent of deafness in children. Disease, such as bacterial infections and viruses, and trauma, such as blows to the head or birth complications, account for additional damage to the auditory system (Langley, 1996).

Some common behaviors of deaf children include the use of many gestures, visual vigilance or close attention to facial expressions and movements in the environment, heightened sensitivity to touch, and the use of nonmelodic speech or a monotonous tone of voice. Children who are born deaf will need special training to acquire speech skills. Language skills will be reduced unless the youngsters are provided early intervention and training. If appropriate for a child's needs, the consistent use of hearing aids can lessen the effect of deafness on language acquisition (Fahey, 2000a). Children who have been exposed to language before becoming deaf have a greater chance of developing more proficient speech and language because the initial exposure to language provides a foundation for acquiring better skills (Mayer, 1996).

## Visual Impairments

Language delays in young children can be caused by visual impairments. Although most children who are blind eventually develop normal language skills, some rather significant differences in their rates of acquisition develop before the age of 5 years (Silberman, 1996). Lack of adequate vision can affect concept and vocabulary development. A child who is visually impaired can reverse pronouns and refer to themselves as "you" and call another person "I" or "me" (Nelson, 1998). If children cannot see clearly, it is difficult for them to recognize people, objects, and events being discussed by other people. Because of their disabilities, their experiences are limited. There may be a lack of opportunities to learn the pragmatics of language through play and other natural interactions. Specialized assistance is often necessary to acquire language concepts.

### Cognitive Delays

Cognitive delays lead to language and speech difficulties for some preschool children. Children with developmental cognitive delays acquire language in much the same fashion as their typically developing peers but at a slower rate and with less complexity (Hunt & Marshall, 2002). Children with mild and moderate delays need language stimulation that is planned to match their developmental ages. Thus, the child who is 5 years old chronologically but 2 years old developmentally should be listened to and talked to at the 2-year age level. The greater the degree of developmental delay, the more severely the impact will be on a child's speech and language skills. In many children with severe delays, rule-governed, symbolic language and speech may not develop. These youngster will need *augmentative communication* systems, which are discussed later in this chapter.

### Auditory Processing Dysfunctions

Auditory processing dysfunctions can also cause language delays (Fahey, 2000a). Children with dysfunctions in auditory processing may have impaired rates of processing for rapidly changing acoustic information. They perceive sound but have difficulty interpreting what they hear. Terms used to describe this dysfunction include *language delay*, *developmental aphasia*, *congenital aphasia*, and *specific language impairment*.

### Autism and Pervasive Developmental Disorders

One of the most puzzling social-emotional disorders that affects language development is the condition of *autism* or *pervasive developmental disorders* (*PDDs*). (This condition was discussed in detail in Chapter 9). The core symptoms of autism include impairments in speech, language, and communication skills and in language-related social and cognitive abilities (Wetherby & Prizant, 1999). Some children with autism display the following characteristics in their speech and language: echolalia; pronoun reversals; repetition of the same sounds and words; dysprosody or unusual pitch, rhythm, and inflections of speech; and severe impairments in comprehension, especially of abstract concepts. The American Psychiatric Association's (1994) definition of *autism* includes three diagnostic criteria: (1) qualitative impairment in social interaction, (2) qualitative impairment in communication, and (3) restrictive repetitive and stereotyped patterns of behavior, interests, and activities. In addition to delayed language development, children with autism may actively avoid social contact with other people and lack nonverbal communicative skills, such as pointing, gesturing, and head nodding. They have difficulty establishing joint attention or the ability to direct another person's attention to an object or event (Wetherby & Prizant, 1999). A related deficit is the inability to communicate for social purposes. Instead, many children with autism communicate mostly for the purposes of protesting an action or regulating the behavior of other people to meet their needs.

Intervention for young children with autism must include family members as active participants. A carefully coordinated, interdisciplinary team approach is necessary in early intervention to meet the needs of children with autism and their families (Rossetti, 1996). Currently, there has been a movement away from the behavioral approach to intervention to a more social-pragmatic one. This approach stresses more child-centered and spontaneous communication and interactions (Wetherby & Prizant, 1999).

### Emotional Disturbances

Behavioral and emotional disturbances also can lead to language problems. Symptoms of emotional or behavioral disturbances that are evident during the early childhood years include severe temper tantrums, repetitive movements (whirling, hand flapping), ritualistic play (lining up objects), hyperactivity, the lack of symbolic play, and extreme reactions to sensory stimuli (Windsor, 1995). Some recent research suggests that language deficits can trigger emotional disturbances because when children have language deficits, they may be unable to express their feelings in socially appropriate ways (Wetherby, Prizant, & Hutchinson, 1998).

### Speech Disorders

Speech disorders include problems in three areas: articulation, voice, and fluency (Lerner, 2000). Each of these speech disorders is described in this section.

***Articulation Disorders.***  The most common articulation difficulties are caused by structural defects, neuromotor defects, or hearing impairments. The four types of articulation disorders are substitutions (using one sound for another), distortions (mispronouncing the sounds), omissions (leaving out sounds), and additions (putting in extra sounds). Articulation errors are considered by speech and language therapists as the least serious of the speech disorders and the most responsive to intervention. Many articulation errors are developmental and disappear as the child matures, usually by age 6 or 7. However, by the age of 3 years, most vowel sounds should be pronounced correctly, and the child should be able to articulate consonant-vowel combinations (Bernthal & Bankson, 1998).

***Voice Disorders.***  Voice disorders include pitch, intensity, and voice quality problems. Possible causes are physiological, such as growths in the larynx, and voice abuse, such as excessive screaming and hearing impairments. Voice disorders are somewhat rare at preschool age. Less than 1 percent of preschoolers are estimated to have these difficulties (McLean & Cripe, 1997).

***Fluency Problems.***    The most common fluency problem is stuttering. Early intervention is often beneficial for dysfluency (Williams, 1999). The age of onset of dysfluency problems such as stuttering is typically between 2 and 7 years, and approximately 1 percent of the total population is affected. Some speech and language therapists believe that calling attention to the normal dysfluencies in the speech of young children will only cause them to stutter more. The following strategies can be used by parents and teachers when children are beginning to stutter (Fahey, 2000b):

1. Allow sufficient time to talk with the child.
2. Slow down your rate of speech when talking to the child by adding pauses.
3. Avoid interruptions.
4. Focus on the content of the child's conversation rather than on the dysfluency.

### Motor Dysfunctions, Injuries, and Structural Abnormalities

Children with motor dysfunctions such as cerebral palsy (see Chapter 7) frequently have associated speech, language, and communication (Hunt & Marshall, 2002). The term *cerebral palsy* refers to a number of disorders of movement and coordination that are caused by nonprogressive abnormalities of the developing brain (Batshaw & Rose, 1997).

The brain damage associated with cerebral palsy can result in a lack of voluntary control of the speech muscles. Affected children have difficulty in speaking with normal speed, fluency, and timing. Often, difficulties in language development and communication co-occur with the speech disorders (Blasco, 2001). Children with cerebral palsy can be candidates for the augmentative communication systems described later in this chapter (Romski & Sevcik, 1996).

Language difficulties also can accompany *traumatic brain injuries* (*TBIs*) from accidents, sport injuries, and physical abuse, especially if the TBI affects the left hemisphere of the brain. Children with TBI in this hemisphere can have subtle but long-lasting problems with verbal learning, thinking, and integrating new information (Fahey, 2000a). Other speech and language problems are associated with cranofacial or structural abnormalities such as cleft palate. Teachers, medical personnel, and speech and language therapists need to work together as a team to implement appropriate interventions.

## Intervention for Children with Language Problems

A number of useful interventions can be used with young children with communication and language problems. Teachers and caregivers can use a variety of methods to teach language skills.

*Naturalistic teaching in language instruction occurs in informal settings.*

## Naturalistic Teaching

*Naturalistic teaching* is language instruction that occurs in informal settings such as in the home or classroom. This instruction takes place in daily routines and activities instead of in isolated therapy rooms. Other characteristics of naturalistic teaching are (1) the topics of conversation are child initiated and follow the child's interests and (2) the continuation of the child-initiated activity and the topic of interest are the natural reinforcements for communication.

Naturalistic interventions use a range of language facilitation strategies, such as modeling developmentally appropriate language, expanding the child's language by providing more elaborate models, balancing the length and frequency of the child and the adult taking turns in communicative exchanges, responding to the child's efforts to communicate, and incidental prompting to obtain more complex language (Yoder et al., 1995). Two examples of naturalistic language interventions are milieu teaching and responsive interactions.

***Milieu Teaching.*** *Milieu teaching* is a strategy in which adults, such as parents and teachers, deliberately arrange the environment with interesting materials to encourage a child's language and development (Kaiser, Hancock, & Hester, 1998). The adult follows the child's interest and teaches language by providing specific prompts, corrections, and reinforcements for the child's responses. The language training occurs in natural settings, routines, and activities. Three procedures are used in milieu training:

1. The first procedure is *mand-model* in which the adult attends to the youngster's choice of an activity or toy, requests or "mands" (demands) a response from the child about the activity, provides a model to imitate, and then gives the child the toy or material of interest.

2. The second procedure is the use of a *time delay* in which the adult looks at the preschooler expectantly or questioningly for 15 seconds. The delay gives the child time to respond before the adult provides a model of the appropriate language. The adult may repeat the model twice, each time waiting for the youngster to talk before giving her what she wants.

3. The third procedure is *incidental teaching*, which requires that the child initiate a topic of conversation and that the adult converse about the topic. The adult follows the child's lead and stays with the topic only as long as the preschooler is attentive. Taking turns is emphasized in these interactions. If the adult focuses on the same topic as the child, joint attention of both participants is assured. By talking in short, simple sentences and by repeating often, adults can stimulate the language development of the children during daily routines. This type of intervention is thought to generalize more efficiently than direct teaching of language because the language training resembles natural language interactions. Milieu teaching also has been demonstrated to be more effective than direct teaching for children in the early stages of language development (Nelson, 1998; Yoder et al., 1995).

***Responsive Interaction.***    *Responsive interaction* is another example of naturalistic language intervention. This intervention does not use prompts, as in milieu teaching. Instead, responsive interaction places emphasis on developing an interaction style that promotes balanced turn taking and communication between the adult and the child (Mahoney & Neveille-Smith, 1996). This intervention is based on the theory that children learn new language and will use their existing language more often when they hear appropriate language models in the interactions with responsive caregivers. Adults learn the basic principles of responsive interactions, such as following the child's lead, taking turns, matching and extending the child's topic of conversation, responding appropriately to the child's communicative attempts, and providing developmentally appropriate language models. Teaching strategies include the use of expansions, expatiations, parallel talk, and self-talk.

*Expansion.*    *Expansion* is useful for children who are talking but not in complete sentences. The adult listens to the child's words, tries to understand the whole idea that the child wants to communicate, and repeats the sentence in a more complete but simple form. The caregiver lets the youngster know he or she was understood and presents the child with a more complete language model (Lerner, Lowenthal, & Egan, 1998):

*Child:* "Go." (points to the door)

*Adult:* "Go out?"

*Child:* "Go out." (Shakes head to indicate yes)

*Adult:* "You want to go out now?"

*Child:* "Go."

*Adult:* "Go out now."

*Child:* "Go out now."

*Expatiation.* *Expatiation* is accomplished by first following the child's lead in conversation. The caregiver focuses on what the child says, not on the way it is said. The adult lets the child know he or she has listened and adds new information. The following illustrates expatiation:

*Child:* "Boy eats."

*Adult:* "Yes, he's eating crackers."

*Parallel Talk.* *Parallel talk* is the strategy of describing what the youngster is doing or seeing. For example, if a child is banging a block on the floor, the parent might say, "Hit the block. Hit the block on the floor. Bang, bang, bang. My block. Hit the block."

*Self-Talk.* When using the strategy of *self-talk*, adults talk about what they are doing, seeing, or feeling while the child listens nearby. For example, if a teacher is cutting paper, she or he might say "I have to cut the paper. Cut the paper. I need scissors. My scissors. Cut, cut, cut. Cut the paper." This technique of self-talk also gives the child an opportunity to hear more mature phrases, sentences, and vocabulary. Some simple rules need to be followed when using this method: Caregivers need to speak in simple, short phrases; describe their actions and thoughts; and not expect the children to imitate them directly. Self-talk and parallel talk allow children to hear models of more complex language and to realize that language is fun and useful (Lowenthal, 1995).

## *Other Activities for Natural Language Stimulation*

As part of natural language teaching, there also are a number of adult-initiated, informal activities that can stimulate conversations or verbal responses of young children (Bricker, 1998; Quill, 2000; Wetherby & Prizant, 1993). Some examples of these activities are:

1. Doing something funny, such as placing your shoe on your head and then waiting for the children to verbalize their surprise
2. Locking the door or blocking the way when the children are ready to go outside and then waiting for the children to protest
3. Placing interesting toys out of reach and then waiting for the child to request them

4. Interrupting a usual routine, such as not providing snacks at snack time, and then waiting for the children to request them.
5. Stopping or pausing in the middle of a game and then waiting for the child to protest
6. Giving a peer a turn in a fun game and then waiting for the target child to ask for a turn.

These activities are examples of what Wetherby and Prizant (1993) refer to as "communicative temptations," or teasers, that can be implemented as additional natural language stimulation techniques.

## Parents as Language Trainers

Parents can be trained, with the help of speech and language therapists, to assist their children with language delays by providing natural language stimulation during daily activities. The parents can use parallel talk, self-talk, expansions, and expatiations. In general, parents are trained to wait for their children to initiate activities, to follow their lead, and to comment on their interests by using simple but complete phrases and sentences. Parents are shown how to reach specific language goals by using nondirective conversations and child-responsive language (Hancock & Kaiser, 1996). Building a close working relationship with parents in the language intervention process will assist the children in generalizing the skills learned in the early childhood program to their homes and communities (Kaiser, Hemmeter, Ostrosky, Fischer, Yoder, & Keefer, 1996).

## Behavioral Techniques for Language Development

Formal techniques of language development incorporate behavioral strategies and direct teaching by speech and language therapists and teachers (Cole, 1995; Maag, 1999). These consist of prompting, shaping, specifying correct responses, and reinforcing these responses. *Prompting* is used when the child has difficulty imitating a target response. For example, the child is assisted by giving him or her the first sound of the target word or a physical prompt, such as pointing to the object to be named. *Shaping* is a technique in which the therapist accepts the child's approximation of the word or sentences and then reinforces (gives praise, favorite toys, activities, etc.) for closer and closer approximations of the target response. *Identifying correct responses* is a procedure in which only the correct verbal responses are reinforced.

One criticism of behavioral or direct teaching is that newly learned language skills can be difficult for a child to generalize to new situations. The teaching is usually done by the therapist in an isolated therapy room. The child may have difficulty applying the new skills to more natural settings, such as at home or in the preschool class (Rossetti, 1996). Another criticism of behavioral techniques is that they are so adult directed that the children are not actively engaged in the process of language acquisition (Warren & Yoder, 1994).

### Classroom Interventions

Classroom interventions that stress the function of child language in the preschool include (Brown & Conroy, 2002; Cook, Tessier, & Klein, 2000):

1. *Use language for peer interactions during play.* The teacher encourages the children to talk with each other while they play.
2. *Use language to get help.* The child wants to play with a toy but cannot reach it. The teacher gives the youngster the toy when she or he asks for it.
3. *Use language to tell about events.* The teacher asks the child to tell about an event that happened at home. The teacher encourages the other children to listen and respond. The child is then reinforced for his or her use of language.
4. *Use language to defend against peer aggression.* The teacher models with words how to prevent a peer's aggression. The child is told to say "Quit it" rather than physically hitting or shoving the peer.

All these strategies can be ways for teachers to stimulate the language development of children in the preschool class.

### Activity-Based Intervention

Activity-based intervention is an approach developed by Bricker (1998) that utilizes natural language instruction by the teacher. Bricker defines *activity-based intervention* as "a child-directed, transactional approach that embeds training on a child's individual goals and objectives in routine or planned activities and uses logically occurring antecedents and consequences to develop functional and generalizable skills" (p. 11). Child-directed transactions require the teacher to attend to the child's interest or activity. The adult joins the child and converses about the activity. Language stimulation is embedded in or carried out during the normal routines of the day. Specific language goals are addressed, such as learning how to request something. For example, during snack time, the children are encouraged to ask for more juice or crackers if they want them. The antecedents for this request would be the juice and crackers on the table. The consequence would be that after making the request, the children would get the juice or crackers. The goal of learning how to request something could then easily generalize to other daily activities (Bricker, 1996).

### Peer-Mediated Intervention

Peer-mediated intervention involves the training of normally functioning peers to help the preschoolers with language disabilities to communicate more during play. The peer trainers are taught communicative strategies, such as establishing eye contact, initiating play and conversation, prompting the child with special needs to request turns, repeating and expanding the target preschooler's language, describing the child's play, and requesting clarification of unclear statements (Nelson, 1998; Windsor, 1995). The preschool trainers may need to be reminded to continue using prompts when they play with the children with disabilities. The adults can monitor the children's play and suggest strategies for the peer trainers to try. Verbal prompts can easily be given by the adult when necessary. Peer intervention provides models for learning new social and communicative skills. It also can generalize easily from one setting to another—for example, from the classroom to the playground (Conroy & Brown, 2002).

## Teaching Language Skills to Children with Severe Disabilities

Many children with severe disabilities will not develop conventional oral language. Children who are deaf may need a system of total communication in which sign language or manual communication is taught along with oral language. Teaching both methods of communication is thought to facilitate language learning (Mirenda, 1999). Sign language consists of the following symbol systems: signed English, American Sign Language, and fingerspelling. Signed English is a system of signing that is similar in syntax to the English language. There is a sign for every word, and there is the same word order as in spoken or written English. Signed English has been taught to children with mental retardation, with autism, and children who are deaf.

American Sign Language (ASL) is the language of the majority of deaf children in the United States. ASL has its own syntax, semantics, and morphology. Another method of communication is fingerspelling, in which the words are spelled with the manual alphabet of 26 letters. These letters have a one-to-one correspondence with the traditional alphabet.

Some young children with multiple disabilities will not be able to acquire manual or verbal language, due to either cognitive or motor delays. For these children, an augmentative system should be developed (Beukelman & Mirenda, 1998). Augmentative devices can range from simple lap trays and story boards to electronic communication boards and computerized systems. Augmentative communicative systems are designed to meet the individual needs of a child and can be modified according to his or her development. The objective of the augmentative system is to make it possible for the child to interact with other people. Recent research indicates that augmentative language learning can be integrated in the children's daily routines and activities as opposed to using artificial training routines (Downing, 1999). Children with severe mental impairments and physical disabilities may benefit the most from augmentative communication.

## Intervention Activities

Early childhood educators should know the communication, speech, and language behaviors expected at developmental stages and the specific interventions to help children to acquire these skills. Table 10.2 provides some suggested interventions for fostering speech and language development for language skills expected at ages 1 through 6.

**TABLE 10.2  *Suggested Interventions at Various Stages to Help Young Children Acquire Speech and Language Skills***

| *Speech and Language . . .* | *Intervention Activities to Encourage Language* |
| --- | --- |
| ***By Age 1***<br>Recognizes name<br>Says 2 to 3 words besides "mama" and "dada"<br>Imitates familiar words<br>Understands simple directions<br>Recognizes words as symbols for objects: *car*—points to garage, *cat*—meows | Respond to the child's coos, gurgles, and babbling.<br>Talk to the child as you care for him or her throughout the day.<br>Read colorful books to the child every day.<br>Tell nursery rhymes and sing songs.<br>Teach the names of everyday items and familiar people.<br>Play simple games with the child such "peek-a-boo" and "pat-a-cake." |
| ***Between 1 and 2***<br>Understands "no"<br>Uses 10 to 20 words, including names<br>Combines two words, such as "Daddy bye-bye"<br>Waves good-bye and plays pat-a-cake<br>Makes the "sounds" of familiar animals<br>Gives a toy when asked<br>Uses words such as "more" to make wants known you.<br>Points to his toes, eyes, nose<br>Brings objects from another room when asked | Reward and encourage early efforts at saying new words.<br>Talk to your baby about everything you are doing when you are with him or her.<br>Talk simply, clearly, and slowly to your child.<br>Talk about new situations before you go, while you are there, and again when you are home.<br>Look at your child when he or she talks to you.<br>Describe what your child is doing, feeling, hearing.<br>Let your child listen to children's records and tapes.<br>Praise your child's efforts to communicate. |
| ***Between 2 and 3***<br>Identifies body parts<br>Carries on "conversations" with self and dolls<br>Asks, "what's that?" and "where's my . . . ?"<br>Uses 2-word negative phrases such as "No want"<br>Forms some plurals by adding "s" (*book, books*)<br>Has a 450-word vocabulary<br>Gives first name, holds up fingers to tell age<br>Combines nouns and verbs ("Mommy go")<br>Understands simple time concepts (*last night, tomorrow*)<br>Refers to self as "me" rather than by name | Repeat new words over and over.<br>Help your child listen and follow instructions by playing games, "Pick up the ball," "Touch Daddy's nose."<br>Take your child on trips and talk about what you see before, during, and after the trip.<br>Let your child tell you answers to simple questions.<br>Read books every day, perhaps as part of the bedtime routine.<br>Listen attentively as your child talks to you. Describe what you are doing, planning, and thinking. |

*(continued)*

**TABLE 10.2** *Continued*

| *Speech and Language . . .* | *Intervention Activities to Encourage Language* |
|---|---|
| **Between 2 and 3 (continued)** | |
| Tries to get adult attention: "Watch me." | Have the child deliver a simple message for you ("Mommy needs you, Daddy"). |
| Likes to hear same story repeated. | Carry on conversations with the child, preferably when the two of you have some quiet time together. |
| | Ask questions to get your child to think and talk. |
| | Show the child you understand what he or she says by answering, smiling, and nodding your head. |
| | Expand what the child says. If the child says, "More juice," you say, "Adam wants more juice." |
| **Between 3 and 4** | |
| Has sentence length of 4 to 5 words | Talk about how objects are the "same" or "different." |
| Has vocabulary of nearly 1000 words | Help your child to tell stories using books and pictures |
| Names at least one color | Let your child play with other children. |
| Understands *yesterday, summer, lunchtime, tonight, little-big* | Read longer stories to your child. |
| Begins to obey requests like, "Put the block under the chair." | Pay attention when your child is talking. |
| Knows his/her last name, name of street on which he/she lives, and several nursery rhymes. | Talk about places you have been or will be going. |
| **Between 4 and 5** | |
| Has sentence length of 4 to 5 words | Help your child sort objects and things (for example, things you eat, animals . . . ). |
| Uses past tense correctly | Teach your child how to use the telephone. |
| Has a vocabulary of nearly 1,500 words | Let your child help you plan activities such as what you will make for Thanksgiving dinner. |
| Points to colors: red, blue, yellow, and green | Continue talking with your child about his or her interests. |
| Identifies triangles, circles, and squares | Read longer stories to your child. |
| Understands *in the morning, next, noontime* | Let your child tell and make up stories for you. |
| Speaks of imaginary conditions such as "I hope" | Show your pleasure when your child comes to talk with you. |
| Asks many questions, "Who?" and "Why?" | |
| **Between 5 and 6** | |
| Has a sentence length of 5 to 6 words | Praise your child when she or he talks about her or his feelings, thoughts, hopes, and fears. |
| Has a vocabulary of around 2,000 words | Comment on what you did or how you think your child feels. |
| Defines objects by use (for example, You eat with a fork) and can tell what objects are made of | |

**TABLE 10.2    *Continued***

| *Speech and Language . . .* | *Intervention Activities to Encourage Language* |
| --- | --- |
| ***Between 5 and 6 (continued)*** | |
| Knows spatial relations like *on top*, *behind*, *far*, and *near* | Sing songs, make rhymes with your child. |
| | Continue to read longer stories. |
| Knows his/her address | Talk with your child as you would an adult. |
| Identifies a penny, nickel, and dime | Look at family photos and talk to him or her about your family history. |
| Knows common opposites like *big-little* | |
| Understands *same* and *different* | Listen to your child when he or she talks to you. |
| Counts 10 objects | |
| Asks questions for information | |
| Distinguishes left and right hand in himself/herself | |
| Uses all types of sentences and clauses. For example: "Let's go to the store after we eat." | |

*Source:* Adapted with permission from LDA (Learning Disabilities Association of American, Pittsburg, PA).

## Summary

- Language delays and difficulties can have a negative impact on the social, cognitive, and educational development of children.
- The act of *communication* is defined as a meaningful exchange of messages between a speaker and the listener. *Language* refers to the knowledge and use of a symbolic code or set of rules involving syntax or grammar that transmits meaning from one person to another. *Speech* is the verbal tool for conveying oral language.
- Children go through predictable sequential stages of language learning. The stages of language development are prelinguistic, the emergence of words, the combination of words into sentences, and more advanced language.
- There are several theories about how language is acquired, including the behavioral theory, the innatist theory, the cognitive-interactionist theory, and the social-interactional theory. The social-interactional is the most contemporary of these theories. All of the theories can be integrated for intervention purposes.
- The linguistic systems of language are phonology, morphology, syntax, semantics, and pragmatics. Pragmatics is currently an area of emphasis in the linguistic systems.
- Language problems associated with specific conditions include lack of stimulating experiences, hearing loss, cultural-linguistic diversity, visual impairments, cognitive delays, processing dysfunctions, autism, emotional disturbances, speech disorders, motor dysfunctions, injuries, and structural abnormalities.
- Current intervention strategies for language disorders include naturalistic approaches such as milieu teaching and responsive interactions.

- Classroom interventions can incorporate naturalistic language teaching in daily routines and activities.
- Augmentative communication methods in natural settings are helpful for children with severe disabilities.
- Guidelines in language training are given for training teachers and parents and peers.

## Key Terms

| | |
|---|---|
| augmentative communication | phonology |
| communication | pragmatics |
| language | prelinguistic |
| milieu teaching | semantics |
| morphology | speech |
| naturalistic teaching | syntax |

# 11

## Cognitive Development

## Chapter Outline _____

***What Are Cognitive Skills?***

***Theories of Cognitive Development***
   Piaget's Theories of Cognitive Development
   Vygotsky's Theories of Cognitive Development
   Constructive Learning Theory
   A Cognitively Oriented Curriculum
      for Young Children at Risk:
      The High/Scope Project
   Activity-Based Approach for Young Children
      with Disabilities

***Intervention Strategies for Teaching***
***Cognitive Skills***
   Benefits of Early Intervention
      on Cognitive Development

   Characteristics of Cognitive Activities
   Promoting Cognitive Learning
      in the Curriculum
   Suggestions for Early Intervention Activities
      to Foster Cognitive Development

***Early Literacy***
   Importance of Early Literacy
   Precursors to Reading and Writing
   Phonological Awareness
   Assessing Phonological Awareness

***Using Computer Technology***

***Tips for Teachers: Strategies for Building Early***
***Literacy Skills***

*Cognitive abilities* are clusters of mental skills that enable the child to know, be aware, think, conceptualize, use abstractions, reason, think critically, solve problems, and be creative. The young child's evolution of thinking and reasoning evolves from the infant's first reflexes to the development of complex problem-solving strategies. Piaget (1954) considers the development of cognition as the child's construction of reality. Early childhood educators should recognize that the process of thinking is involved in

### *Early Childhood Snapshot*    BONNIE: A CHILD WITH COGNITIVE DIFFICULTIES

The theories of Piaget emphasize the need to match the child's cognitive development with the demands of the school curriculum. A mismatch can create serious difficulties.

    Bonnie, age 5, was diagnosed with a mild delay in cognitive development. Her placement was in an inclusive kindergarten. This kindergarten class was introduced to a formal reading program, but Bonnie had much difficulty coping with this curriculum. She could not remember the sight works, she was unable to understand the phonics instructions, and she could not do the reading worksheets.

    Although Bonnie had initially looked forward to being in kindergarten, her frustration with the demands of the curriculum began to take its toll. She began to complain of not feeling well and often did not go to school. When she did go to school, she would cry because she could not preform the work. Finally, Bonnie developed a school phobia, refusing to go to school at all.

    The problem was a mismatch between the school curriculum in the inclusive kindergarten class. There was insufficient support to meet Bonnie's needs.

all forms of learning—motor, perceptual, language, and social learning. Children use cognitive abilities in every area of the curriculum.

Children who are at risk or who have disabilities may experience difficulties with certain cognitive skills. Some children have difficulty in the perception of objects—recognizing, differentiating, or comparing objects in their environment. Some children encounter memory problems in recalling or remembering what they have seen or heard. Poor cognitive skills can interfere with the acquisition of communication skills, in the process of learning, using, or understanding language. Other children have difficulty in other areas of cognition, such as forming concepts, making judgments, thinking through a sequence of events, or problem solving.

This chapter reviews the nature of cognition, explores several theories of cognitive development in young children, and examines intervention strategies for improving cognitive abilities. Cognitive implications of early literacy experiences and ways of fostering early literacy in the lives of young children are also examined. Finally, the chapter discusses the use of computers by children.

## What Are Cognitive Skills?

*Cognitive skills* are the many mental abilities related to thinking and learning. Cognitive functions are needed for knowledge and recognition, development of concepts, organization of ideas, remembering, problem solving, labeling and naming, understanding cause-and-effect relationships, drawing inferences, developing rules and generalizations, and making judgments and evaluations. *Cognition* occurs in all areas of learning. Preschool children need cognitive skills for learning in every phase of the early childhood curriculum—adaptive and self-help abilities, motor skills, language and communication, perceptual recognition, early literacy and preacademic activities, social relationships, and problem-solving operations.

Cognitive abilities develop during all of an individual's life, beginning with infancy and early childhood. There are many manifestations of the child's developing cognitive abilities. For example, when the infant recognizes the nipple or mother's face, this is evidence of a developing perceptual skill and a growing ability "to know." Other evidence of the development of ongoing skills in young children can be readily observed, such as the young child playing at putting pots and pans inside each other; the child realizing that pushing a button or bell results in a ringing noise or buzz; a 15-month-old trying to feed a cup of milk to a child in a picture; or the youngster who looks for the horse in back of the television set as the horse on the screen rides off and disappears into the sunset. The learning of language is so closely related to the development of cognitive skills that we cannot separate language learning from cognitive development. Four-year-old Dean talks about the "two girls with same face" in his preschool class. This language shows he has developed the concept of *twins* even though he does not know the word to express this concept. For the infant and toddler stage, motor development is an integral part of cognitive learning. The infant will plan motor actions to grasp an object or move to a target. The toddler learns to imitate movements and sounds and plays games such as peek-a-boo.

To illustrate the baby's growing cognitive abilities, we can observe Aaron's developing cognitive skills over a period of time through his reaction to a common object—a set of keys. As a newborn, he responds to the auditory stimulus of the keys, turning his head when the keys are rattled. At a few months of age, the moving keys attract Aaron's attention and he stares at them and then visually tracks the keys as they are slowly moved. A few months later, he reaches for the keys and later hits them to make them move. Still later, Aaron holds the keys and then explores them by putting the keys in his mouth. As he learns to release objects from his grasp, he enjoys dropping the keys from his high chair and, a little later, throwing the keys on the floor. Aaron's first movements in crawling and his steps in walking are to obtain the set of keys. At 16 months, he tries to insert the key in a keyhole, imitating what he has observed others do. By this stage, the concept of *keys* has been formed and the word is added to his vocabulary, first understanding it when others say it (receptive language) and later actually saying the word himself (expressive language). Thus, a common object such as a set of keys can be used to stimulate a variety of cognitive functions over a period of time—auditory perception, visual perception, memory, motor skills, cause and effect, concepts, relationships, and labeling. It is important that parents and other caregivers be aware of and offer such opportunities to stimulate learning and cognitive development.

## Theories of Cognitive Development

Several theories and applications contribute to our knowledge of cognitive development in young children. Many of these theories provide the basis of general early childhood programs.

### Piaget's Theories of Cognitive Development

Since the 1960s, the field of early childhood education has been strongly influenced by Piaget's ideas about cognitive development in children (Piaget, 1952, 1954, 1962). Piaget recognized that the thinking of children is different from that of adults, that it develops sequentially through a series of stages, and that cognitive development depends on a child's actual concrete experiences.

Piaget's theories about cognitive development have many applications for intervention programs for young children with special needs. For children who are environmentally at risk, Piaget's views on cognitive development was applied in a well-known High/Scope curriculum. This program, which first began in 1969, was designed for children from families with low income who were considered at risk environmentally. The follow-up longitudinal research of the children who were initially enrolled in this program has continued over many years. The research shows consistent benefits for the children in the program (Schweinhart, Barnes, & Weikart, 1993).

**Piaget and the Cognitive Curriculum.**    The foundation for the cognitive curriculum is based on Piaget's theories of cognitive development in young children. Piaget (1952, 1954, 1962) emphasized the sequential development of thinking that young children gradually acquire through concrete experiences. The cognitive curriculum emphasizes activities that develop cognitive abilities, such as perception, discrimination, memory, concept formation, problem solving, and decision making.

***Piaget's Stages of Cognitive Growth.***    Jean Piaget devoted his life to studying how children develop cognitive abilities. One of Piaget's important insights about children is that they do not think like adults but pass through distinct stages of development that are characterized by particular types of thinking.

A key feature of the Piagetian theory is the concept of sequential stages of cognitive development. Each child progresses through each of these stages in a common sequential manner. Age levels are attached to each stage, but these are only approximations of the age at which each stage is reached. Some children master a particular stage earlier than others. Certain cognitive behaviors are manifested at each stage, and the teacher can determine the child's stage of development by examining the tasks that a child is able to perform consistently.

- *Sensorimotor period: Birth to age 2.*  The child learns through sense and movement and by interacting with the physical environment. By moving, touching, hitting, biting, and so on, and by physically manipulating objects, the child learns about the properties of space, time, location, permanence, and causality. (The sensorimotor period was discussed in greater detail in Chapter 7.)
- *Preconceptual thought period: Ages 2 to 4.*  Expressive language begins during this period and the child makes rapid progress in learning the names of objects and using speech to communicate ideas. During this period, the child masters an increasingly larger set of concepts. Learning is accomplished through imitation, symbolic play, drawings, mental images, and verbal evocation of events. The child's thinking is egocentric and dominated largely by the world of his or her own perceptions. (This period was discussed in Chapter 10.)
- *Intuitive thought period: Ages 4 to 7.*  This stage is an extension of the preconceptual thought period. It is characterized by the mastery of more complex forms of language. In addition, laws of physics and chemistry—such as conservation of number, mass, and the like—are brought under control.
- *Concrete operations period: Ages 7 to 11.*  The child develops the ability to think through relationships, to perceive consequences of acts, and to group entities in a logical fashion. Children are now better able to systematize and organize their thoughts. These thoughts, however, are still shaped in large measure by previous experiences, and they are dependent on concrete objects that the children have manipulated or understand through the senses. Children can now deal with aspects of logic, including classes, number relationships, and reversibility.
- *Formal operations period: Ages 11 to 15.*  This period reflects a major transition in the thinking processes. At this stage, instead of observations directing thought, thought now directs observations. The individual now has the capacity to work with abstractions, theories, and logical relationships without having to refer to the concrete. The formal operations period provides a generalized orientation toward problem-solving activity.

*How Cognitive Structures Develop (Schemata).*    Another important dimension of Piaget's theories of cognitive development is the idea that children learn through action. From the moment of birth, the child is the active interpreter of the environment. In effect, he or she builds what Piaget calls an internal *schemata*, or an inner construct of the world. This schemata becomes the basis for further thought. The concepts of *assimilation* and *accommodation* are central to Piaget's theory of cognitive development.

*Assimilation* is the process by which children take into their models of thinking the awareness of aspects of the environment. Through the process of assimilation, children build a knowledge base by adding new information gained through experience. Young children often do this during their play activities. That is, children incorporate new experiences into their already existing schemata, or cognitive structures.

In *accommodation*, children revise their internal schemata to fit their observations when confronted with something they cannot understand. Through the process of accommodation, children integrate new information by reorganizing their current cognitive structure. The child focuses on the new features of the situation and changes the internal schemata or cognitive structure accordingly.

In other words, the child adapts to the environment and structures knowledge in two complementary ways—assimilation and accommodation. Take the example of a young child picking up a ball. The process of assimilation of a grasping technique already mastered will help the child in picking up the ball. The child also will accommodate to the new features of this ball by modifying her or his cognitive structure (for example, the ball rolls and bounces). In accommodating, there is an expansion of the existing internal cognitive structure. Cognitive development results from a succession of these expansions in the internal cognitive structures. Cognitive development is cumulative and interactional.

## Vygotsky's Theories of Cognitive Development

The theories of a Russian psychologist, Lev Vygotsky (1978a), contribute significant ideas about cognitive development in children that have application for early childhood programs. Vygotsky recognized that children learn within a social context and that the role of the significant adult (parent, teacher, or other person) is a critical element in guiding the learning. The adult serves as a mediator, assisting in making the environmental events meaningful to the child. For example, Anne is playing with a box of assorted buttons with her grandmother, and Anne decides to sort the buttons by color—red, green, blue, and so on. There are several buttons that do not have a color but are shiny and diamondlike. Anne does not know how to sort these buttons. Her grandmother and Anne discuss the characteristics of these buttons and Anne suggests they are all "sparkly." So Anne creates a new classification called "Sparkly" and puts these buttons together. The adult serves as a mediator in this social situation, but the child solves the problem and makes the decisions. The process of child learning through gradual adult guidance is referred to as *scaffolding*.

The role of social aspects of learning was also evident when 10-year-old Maria tried to teach her 7-month-old brother, Joseph, the game of patty-cake. Joseph did not attempt to play patty-cake again with his parents. But when Maria would walk into the room, Joseph smiled and displayed his patty-cake actions. Maria, of course, was thrilled.

Another important component of Vygotsky's theories is known as the *zone of proximal development (ZPD)*. This theory notes that a range of difficulty levels exist for any task. The lower end is a level that is very easy for the child, and the upper end is a level beyond the child's capacity. The ZPD refers to the midpoint and is the appropriate level for learning. This theory can be thought of as the Goldilocks theory. Find the level that is not too easy and not too hard, but just right. The ZPD level provides a challenge but can be accomplished with the assistance of the adult in the environment. For example, Jake is learning to use a spoon to eat. He can pick up pieces of food with hand and put them in his mouth, but he cannot yet use the spoon to pick up the food. His mother helps by guiding Jake to pick up a piece of food, put it in the spoon, and then eat it from the spoon. This would be the ZPD level for Jake. The role of the adult is to guide learning by finding the appropriate level for the child.

### Constructive Learning Theory

Another cognitive theory is the constructivist view of children's thinking, which underscores the importance of active learning and encouraging children to construct their own solutions to problems (Resnick & Klopfer, 1989). Constructive learning is based on the view that children actively construct their own solutions to problems. For example, in number learning, each child actively builds his or her own mental structures of numbers. Research shows that young children construct early number ideas as they develop meanings in mathematics. For example, children in all cultures count on their fingers to find solutions to number problems. Even though the emphasis in the school may be on memorizing number facts, children initially rely on their own methods of counting to compute sums. They naturally invent and rely on their own arithmetic procedures when the methods allow them to cope with their environments in a meaningful manner (Resnick & Klopfer, 1989).

One implication of the constructive learning view is that young children should be encouraged to develop and use invented mathematics for solving problems. These experiences will help them build mental structures. It is not enough to have teachers tell and show them how to do it. Constructive instruction requires that children become actively involved in their learning and figure out their own solutions to problems.

### A Cognitively Oriented Curriculum for Young Children at Risk: The High/Scope Project

The High/Scope Project was begun in 1962 in Ypsilanti, Michigan. It is a longitudinal experiment designed to reveal the effects of early intervention on children who are economically disadvantaged. These youngsters lived in poverty and were considered to be environmentally at risk. The framework underlying this project represents a *transactional approach* to the relationship between heredity and environment, between the individual and his or her field of operation. Based on the theories of Piaget, one area of application is the development of cognitive ability. The High/Scope Project compares an experimental group that received a daily preschool program with weekly home visits, and a control group that received no intervention program.

The longitudinal research followed the lives of the children who were in the High/Scope program through adulthood and clearly shows that the intervention strategies contributed to their cognitive ability. The research showed lasting effects of early intervention for participants identified as environmentally at risk. The research also showed that a stimulating preschool environment enhances the cognitive ability of children (Schweinhart, Barnes, & Weikart, 1993; Schweinhart & Weikart, 1980). The High/Scope program has been evaluated extensively and found effective with children from economically disadvantaged homes. The model has been widely disseminated throughout the nation.

## Activity-Based Approach for Young Children with Disabilities

An activity-based curriculum for young children who have special needs was developed by Bricker and Cripe (1992) and Bricker (1995). The curriculum of the activity-based approach builds on the consistent use of daily activities, events, and interactions. This approach also supports inclusion goals in which children with disabilities are integrated with children who do not have disabilities. Two critical qualities of the activity-based curriculum are (1) it is based on a naturalistic environment that encourages participating in meaningful activities of interest and relevance to children and (2) it includes activities that promote interactions between children (Bricker, 1995; Bricker & Cripe, 1992).

The activity-based curriculum uses meaningful activities that occur regularly (e.g., outdoor play time, washing up for snack). The activity could be child initiated, such as asking for a certain book to be read or initiating a game of peek-a-boo. The activity could also be staff planned but still use authentic activities for children, such as taking a walk or washing baby dolls. Activity-based approaches easily promote children's genuine participation in program activities because the teacher can vary the activities for each participating child (Bricker & Cripe, 1992). For example, using the activity of pretend food preparation, children can initiate a variety of activities appropriate for the cognitive, linguistic, and motoric developmental level. The teacher should seek naturalistic environments for the activities. For example, when it snowed in Austin, Texas, a very rare event in that part of the country, the children were very excited about the snow when they came to school in the morning. Their early childhood teacher took advantage of this fortuitous opportunity by cancelling her planned activity and allowing the children to play outside in the snow. In northern Minnesota, snow would not be such a motivating event and the teacher would not be as likely to conduct the activity-based curriculum outside in the snow.

In the activity-based curriculum, the teacher encourages activities that promote interaction between children with disabilities and without disabilities. Adults must encourage those interactions that promote the integration. Activities that promote natural and satisfying interactions among children will ensure that the child with disabilities feels a part of the larger group. For children without disabilities, the interactions will help develop healthy attitudes and include children with disabilities in their activities.

# Intervention Strategies for Teaching Cognitive Skills

The early childhood years are crucial for all children, but for the child who has special needs, these years are especially critical. Many of the intervention strategies that are used in early childhood programs with special needs promote cognitive learning.

## Benefits of Early Intervention on Cognitive Development

Early intervention activities enhance the cognitive development of young children (Lerner, 2003; Peck, Odom, & Bricker, 1993; Barnett, 1995). Overall, the cumulative early intervention research shows:

- Early childhood intervention with children who are at risk or who have disabilities leads to improvement in many areas of functioning, including cognitive development.
- The positive effects of early intervention last over time. The benefits of early intervention are still evident when the children reach adulthood.
- Providing early intervention is a cost-effective undertaking for society. Children who receive early intervention become productive citizens. They become tax *payers* instead of tax *receivers*.

## Characteristics of Cognitive Activities

Activities should be planned with the child's developmental stage of cognitive growth in mind. Often, opportunities for teaching thinking activities are unplanned and can be incidental. For example, Sarah, age 3, had inadvertently opened her piggy bank and spilled out the coins. She and her mother devised a sorting game that they played together. First, Sarah compared the coins and noted that some were silver and some were copper. Then her mother got two small bowls, and Sarah compared each coin, decided whether it was a copper or silver color, and then placed the silver coins in one bowl and the copper coins in another bowl. Through this game, she used the cognitive skills of classifying and sorting.

Activities that emphasize the teaching of thinking are built on the following assumptions:

1. *The activities are to enhance the child's cognitive development, not to take away the individual freedom that is a condition of healthy psychological growth.* Both the teacher and the child initiate activities. The teacher plans and prepares the activities for the child, but at the same time the child has the freedom to participate or not participate and has individuality of style and timing in responding to the task.
2. *The activities are developmentally appropriate to challenge the child's thinking but not too difficult to invite failure.* The teacher's task is to know the general type of activities that are appropriate for the child's cognitive stage. The activities must be difficult enough to challenge the child's thinking. However, if they are too difficult, they could lead to failure and a psychologically unhealthy use of low-level thinking.

3. *The child is involved in and focuses his or her attention on the activity and not on the teacher as the source of knowledge.* It is the child who initiates intellectual growth. The teacher can only provide the occasional prompt, facilitate, and encourage.

4. *Activities are performed by each individual child with a group of peers with whom she or he relates socially and cooperatively.* A small group of children provides an effective atmosphere for cognitive learning. Children learn from imitation and are encouraged by the successful activities of others.

5. *Teachers provide the model of a thinking person for the child.* The teacher must be free from rigid regulations and take the initiative within the general structure. The teacher can influence a child's developing intelligence by providing occasions and opportunities and by serving as a model of a thinking person to imitate.

## *Promoting Cognitive Learning in the Curriculum*

A common body of preschool activities that promote cognitive learning are used in the preschool programs, regardless of the theoretical basis of that curriculum. The activities usually include experiences with colors, shapes, numbers, letters, parts of a whole, the function and use of objects, and language/communication. The child learns to make comparisons, classify, categorize objects, build vocabulary, reason, and make judgments (Bailey & Walery 1992; Barnett, 1995).

In planning these activities, early childhood educators and early interventionists should keep in mind the developmentally appropriate practice (DAP) guidelines: Activ-

*Children learn through action.*

ities should be conducted in a naturalistic environment, they should promote interactions between children, they should involve children with disabilities and typical children, they should involve the activity-based curriculum, they should encourage exploration, they should be child oriented, and they should be based on the interests of the child. To the extent possible, given the child's individual needs, early interventionists should take care that activities not be conducted in isolation, they should not rely on a formal structure, and they should not be adult directed (Bricker, 1995; Bricker & Cripe, 1992).

The following activities can be used to promote cognitive learning for young children with special needs:

1. *Promote active learning.*  Find opportunities for children to engage in activities such as the following: Explore the environment using all the senses. Discover relationships among objects, people, and events through direct experiences. Manipulate, transform, and combine materials to discover new ways to use materials. Choose materials and activities for meaningful purposes. Acquire skills for using tools and equipment. Use the large muscles in play activities.

2. *Encourage language opportunities.*  Create opportunities to engage children in communication with others and develop language through activities such as the following: Talk with other children or adults about personally meaningful experiences. Describe objects, events, and their relations. Express feelings in words. Have the child's own words written down and read back to the child. Have fun with language by listening to stories and playing word games.

3. *Provide experiences for children to learn about objects and symbols.*  Help preschoolers with special needs learn about objects and symbols through experiences such as the following: Recognize objects by sound, touch, taste, and smell. Imitate actions and sounds. Relate models, photographs, and pictures to real places and things. Role play. Make models, drawings, and paintings. Observe that spoken words can be written down and read back.

4. *Help children learn to classify objects.*  Find opportunities for young children to group objects such as the following: Describe attributes of things, organize, sort, and classify objects. Notice and describe how things are the same and different (sorting and matching). Use and describe objects in different ways. Talk about the characteristics that something does *not* possess or the class it does *not* belong to. Hold more than one attribute in mind at a time. Distinguish between "some" and "all."
   - Group objects on the basis of function. For example, put together all of the things that a person can drink.
   - Group objects on the basis of common attributes. For example, put together all of the red objects or all of the round objects.
   - Group objects on the basis of categories. For example, put together all of the furniture or fruit.

5. *Provide experiences with order and sequences (seriation).*  Seek opportunities in the classroom to help children learn about order and sequence through activities such as the following: Make comparisons. Arrange several things in order and describe their relationships.
   - Ordinal size: big, bigger, biggest; small, smaller, smallest, short, shorter, shortest
   - Ordinal positions: first, last middle, third

- Ordinal patterning: copying a sequence, as in a string of beads
- Time sequences: arranging pictures that tell a story in the correct time sequence

6. *Provide experiences with number and quantity.* Assist young children in learning about number, quantity, and early mathematical concepts through activities such as the following: Compare amounts of objects. Arrange two sets of objects in one-to-one correspondence.

7. *Provide experiences with spatial relationships.* Help youngsters see objects in relation to space through activities such as the following: Fit things together and take them apart. Rearrange and reshape objects. Observe and describe things from different spatial viewpoints. Experience and describe the relative positions, directions, and the distances of things. Experience and represent one's body. Learn to locate things in the classroom, school, and neighborhood. Interpret representations of spatial relationships in drawings, pictures, and photographs. Distinguish and describe shapes.
   - Body awareness and body concepts: naming and identifying parts of the body, moving parts of the body
   - Position: developing concepts such as *on, off, into, over, under, next to,* and *on top of.*
   - Direction: developing concepts such as *up, down, forward,* and *backward*
   - Distance: developing concepts such as *near, far, close to,* and *far from*

8. *Help children learn about time.* Create opportunities for children to learn about time through activities such as the following: Stop and start an action on a signal. Experience and describe different rates of speed. Experience and compare time intervals. Observe seasonal changes. Observe that clocks and calendars are used to mark the passage of time. Anticipate future events verbally and make appropriate preparations. Plan and complete what one has planned. Describe and represent past events. Use conventional time units in talking about past and future events. Note, describe, and represent order of events.
   - Beginning and end time intervals: *now, start, stop,* and *end*
   - Ordering of events: planning and evaluating concepts, such as *first, last, next,* and *again*
   - Different time lengths: *A short time, a long time,* and *a longer time*

## Suggestions for Early Intervention Activities to Foster Cognitive Development

***Teaching Concepts.***   In acquiring a concept, the child uses the thinking process of grouping assorted things according to common properties. The concept is the idea resulting from this process. For example, from many concrete experiences with different kinds of "chairs" (kitchen chair, rocking chair, high chair, living room chair), the child builds the idea or concept of *chair.* Although concepts may deal with concrete things, concepts are in themselves abstractions of an idea. For example, the concept of *roundness* develops from many concrete experiences with round objects—plates, balls, oranges, and Frisbees, for example. These objects are concrete—they can be touched, seen, and so on. The idea of *round,* however, exists only in the mind. The brain creates it. It is an abstraction, not a reality.

The concepts of the shape *round* or the color *red* are easier than more complex concepts, such as *weather* and *time*. Still more difficult are concepts such as *sharing*, *fairness*, and *taking turns*. As the concept gets further away from a basis of concrete experience, it becomes more difficult. Thus, the curriculum must give the child many concrete opportunities to develop and strengthen concepts. The child with special needs may have much more difficulty than the typically functioning child in developing concepts needed for further learning. If the child has a physical or sensory disability, he or she may not have the opportunity to have the primary concrete experience. For example, the child who is blind would have difficulty developing the concept of *color*, such as *red*. Since young children with special needs often have difficulty in recalling concepts, they need more direct experience with the elements of the concept.

To teach the *concept of the color red*, associate the red with an object the child is familiar with, such as catsup. If the new object is the color of catsup, it is red. Show the child a bottle of catsup. Group together objects and drawings that are red. Start with two objects (later three objects) of various colors. Ask, "Is this red?" Later on, after other colors have been taught, ask the child to identify the color when three colors are presented at one time. Have the child select the object that matches the color.

With young children with special needs, it is particularly important to move from awareness and recognition to expression. Therefore, it is useful to use "show me" activities. For example, give the child a green object and a red object. Ask the child to identify the red one. Then later, once the child has demonstrated recognition, ask the child, "What color is this?"

***Teaching Spatial Relationships.***    Spatial relationships, such as *on*, *in*, *between*, *under*, *in front of*, and *next to*, are often difficult for children with special needs to understand. Use a cardboard box and an object to help the child. Place the object (such as a block) *in* the box and say, "The block is *in* the box." The child is then asked to place the object *in* the box. The teacher places the object in the box and asks, "Where is the block?"

Similar activities are used to teach other spatial relationships. An obstacle course is another activity that can be used to facilitate the use of spatial relationships. First, each step is taught separately and sequentially; later, directions can be mixed. After the action, the teacher should verbalize the concept.

***Teaching Numbers.***    Number concepts, such as *more*, *less*, *first*, and *last* are important and should be included in the curriculum. To teach *one more*, have the child build a tower, then add one more block to it, then one more, and so on. Using a pasting activity, ask the child to paste on one more flower. At snack time, ask the child to take one more cracker. During a working period, ask the child to add one more bead to a chain. In other words, provide many opportunities to have a direct experience with the cognitive skill being taught. Routine activities, as well as free play, can provide opportunities for cognitive learning through incidental teaching.

***Teaching Classification Skills.***    Classification involves the grouping or sorting of objects according to some rule or principle. Children can be grouped into boys and girls, those wearing red and those wearing blue, or brown, blue, or hazel eyes. Classification can be difficult for children who confuse the physical object with the class to which it belongs. They may also have difficulty with the language of classification and with the fact that an object can belong to two or more classes. For example, one child could not see that a plate could be called "round" since it was a plate. When children were asked if the moon could be called "cow," they said no because it does not give milk. Children with special needs require many experiences in sorting and classifying. Other suggestions for classification include:

1. *Matching games.* Have several pairs of matching objects. Place one object of a pair in front of the child. Ask the child to "find one like this."
2. *Sorting games.* Have two containers and several objects. Ask the child to put the red items in one container and the blue items in the other. Do the same thing with shapes and textures. Later, ask the child to sort objects without the container—on a piece of paper or simply on two sides of a table. Then have the child sort a group of objects using his or her sorting principles.
3. *Classifying games.* Make nine geometrical cutouts: three triangles, three circles, three squares, one each of blue, yellow, and red. Have children sort them. At first, they will classify by color; later, they will sort by shape. The principle taught is that the way one classifies is arbitrary. Other objects that can be used for sorting are buttons, silverware, pictures, and toys.

***Teaching Sequencing.***    This cognitive skill involves recognizing the sequential order of things. The item is correctly placed when it takes into account the neighboring items and the sequence or pattern that the items form within the whole. There can be sequences in auditory activities, visual activities, and movement activities. There also is a sequence to daily events in the classroom. Some suggestions are as follows:

1. *Bead stringing.* One type of sequential activity is copying a bead pattern using different shapes or colors of beads. Initially, the child might best succeed by directly initiating a sequence strung on a wire that he or she can copy. Bead patterns can be placed on a transparency to use this activity with a group of children.
2. *Auditory pattern games.* A series of rhythm patterns can be made by clapping, tapping, or using a drum. The child copies the auditory pattern.
3. *Story sequence.* The child repeats a story by highlighting the sequence of events in the story. Three or four pictures that illustrate the sequence can be used, and the child places these in appropriate order (top to bottom or left to right) and then relates the story. Cartoons or comic strips can be cut apart and used for this purpose. Children need to be taught the relationship from one picture frame to the next. Flannel board cutouts also are useful in helping the child order the events of the story.
4. *Arranging.* The child is given several objects and asked to arrange them in a sequence. For example, four circles or sticks can be arranged from biggest to smallest or longest to shortest.

***Guessing or Discovery Games.***    Logical thinking involves reasoning and predicting. Some games help the child experience this process. Riddles are an activity children enjoy: "I am thinking of an object that is white, long, breaks easily, and leaves its mark on a chalkboard." When telling or reading a story, ask the child to guess what will happen next. Then check out the event to see if the child was correct. Use an ordered series with a pattern and have the child tell which one comes next.

***Creative Thinking.***   Divergent thinking focuses on open-ended lessons in which the child is encouraged to expand the thinking process into areas beyond those determined by the teacher. In divergent thinking activities, there is no right or wrong answer. For example, the teacher might ask a child, "Tell me all the ways you can use water." Play and dramatics can encourage this type of activity. This is an important part of the cognitive curriculum and should not be neglected.

***Toy Library.***   A toy library of games and play ideas and materials can bolster resources. This resource gives teachers, aides, parents, grandparents, and others who work with the child the opportunity to borrow materials and games for use with the child. Two organizations that lend toys and educational materials for young children are:

- U.S. Toy Library Association, 5940 W. Touhy, Chicago, IL 60648
- National Lekotek Center, 2100 Ridge Avenue, Evanston, IL 60204. Phone: (847) 328-0001

# Early Literacy

The foundations of literacy begin at birth. Long before children encounter formal school instruction in reading and writing, they should be involved with literacy experiences. Teachers who instruct young children should be aware of the importance of literacy development in the early years. Parents and early childhood teachers can support early literacy development in young children in many ways. The close relationship between early childhood education and reading research is recognized by the National Association of Educators of Young Children and the International Reading Association (McCardle, Cooper, Houle, Karp, & Paul-Brown, 2001; Dickinson & McCabe, 2001; Newman & Dickinson, 2001). However, significant numbers of children who enter school with insufficient preparation for learning to read will require instructional interventions that are simply beyond the capacity of the regular classroom teacher. National data show that 38 percent of the school children in the United States read below a basic level in fourth grade (National Center for Educational Statistics, 1999; Foorman & Torgesen, 2001).

## Importance of Early Literacy

*Early literacy* refers to the child's early entrance into the comprehensive world of words, language, books, poetry, and stories. Many young children begin to learn about writing and reading long before they start elementary school. Their early literacy activities may look quite different from more mature conventional forms of writing and reading. Children develop literacy through simultaneous and abundant experiences with oral language and experiences with books, stories, reading, and writing. One of the best

Early literacy *refers to children's early entrance into the world of words, language, books, poetry, and stories.*

beginning activities for developing literacy in young children is to read to them. Parents, grandparents, and teachers may overlook this essential stage in their haste to encourage early reading.

Literacy development begins in young children with activities using symbols, as children play, talk, fantasize, scribble, draw, and pretend to read and write. Between the ages of 1 and 5, children learn to use symbols to create and communicate meaning. They use symbols they invent for themselves and symbols they get from the environment and their culture. The use of symbols may be child drawings, gestures, marks on paper, or objects modeled in clay. These symbols make it possible to represent experiences, feelings, and ideas. When children use symbols, they are able to use one thing (such as a word) to represent an object. They can go beyond the immediate here and now and create imaginary worlds. That is what they do when they talk about story books and plots, make up stories, engage in pretend play, draw images on paper—and later when they read books and write stories. As children begin to experiment with writing and reading, they often do so in playful ways. They may find they can use these new symbolic modes in some of the same ways they used earlier in symbolic forms. Talking, drawing, and playing serve as "bridges" to literacy, as children discover that writing and reading offer them new and interesting resources for constructing and communicating meaning. Figure 11.1 provides an example of an early literacy experience with a drawing of a 5-year-old after she saw the movie, *101 Dalmatians*.

**FIGURE 11.1**   *A Child's Drawing of a Movie Experience*

## Precursors to Reading and Writing

It is essential to surround young children with a literacy environment, including print, the concept of what a word is, the sounds of language (or phonological awareness), and building experiences with stories and books. Early literacy emphasizes the use of authentic materials and provides many opportunities for expressive literacy, including talking and writing.

A number of factors are associated with literacy and reading problems in preschool children. These include oral language problems, lack of phonological awareness, rapid naming skills, knowledge of the alphabet, visual-motor abilities, auditory processing abilities, and motor skills.

*Early Writing.*   Educators who promote early literacy encourage early writing (see Figure 11.2). Some suggest that writing may be easier than and actually develops before reading. The early childhood curriculum often exposes children to activities of writing journals, drawing pictures, and labeling long before formal reading is introduced. Writing is a more self-involving task than reading because its meaning originates from within the writer and is known to the writer in advance. In contrast, reading requires the reader to be able to interpret someone else's ideas and use of language, which is a more difficult task for the beginner (Richek, Jennings, Caldwell, & Lerner, 2002).

**FIGURE 11.2**   *Examples of Early Literacy: Reading and Writing*

| *Early Reading* | *Early Writing* |
| --- | --- |
| This paragraph demonstrates an example of early literacy in reading. Mom read a story to Jennifer, age 2. The book was *Johnny Lion's Book* by Edith Thracher Hurd—a story about a young lion who dreams of going hunting in the woods. About an hour later, Jennifer, who had been playing outside, called to her father, "I read a book, Daddy." She had picked two big leaves, which she now held one lying flat on the palm of each hand. She and her father sat down on the steps, side by side, and Jennifer starting *reading* her *book*. "And a big bear went into the woods and she chased a big lion and she caught a big lion." Her father asked what the bear did then, and Jennifer answered, "Then the big bear went home to her mommy." | The following sentences show the sequential development of writing skills as Rachel wrote a series of letters to her grandmother. At age 2½, she made a series of wavy lines on a piece of paper and told her mother it was a thank-you note for a gift. At age 3, Rachel made letterlike marks on a piece of lined paper and told her mother it said, "Dear Grandma and Grandpa. Thank you for the lots of presents. Love, Rachel." At age 4½, Rachel made neat rows of letters and letterlike shapes (in no apparent order). She told her Mother that she had to write a thank-you note to Grandma. Then Rachel asked, "How do you spell, 'Dear Grandma I love my presents' "? |

*Source:* Adapted from J. B. McLane & G. D. McNamee. (1991). The Beginnings of Literacy, *Zero to Three, 12* (1), 1–8. Reprinted with permission.

To promote writing, children are encouraged to use "invented spelling," which is the beginning writer's attempt to write words by attending to their sound units and associating letters with them in a systematic, although unconventional way. Examples of invented spellings used by young children are *ez* for *easy,* or *1000ilnd* for *thousand island.* Children who are encouraged to use invented spelling and to compose anything they want in whatever way they can are much more willing to write (Richek et al., 2002).

***Early Reading.***   To promote early literacy, young children with special needs have to be exposed to an abundant and rich literature environment. Unfortunately, children with special needs tend to have significantly less supportive and less stimulating literacy environments at home than other children.

*Reading Stories.*   From an early age, children should hear stories, tell stories, and write journals and stories. Story reading is a particularly useful strategy for building oral language experiences. The following activities can help children with special needs build thinking skills, acquire language, figure out grammar, and learn the structure of stories (Richek et al., 2002):

- Read stories frequently (at least once each day) to small groups of five to seven children.
- Use strategies that help the children focus on the meaning while you read to maximize the children's understanding.
- Involve all the children in the story by asking questions appropriate to their developmental language level.

- Select predictable books (ones that have a pattern, refrain, or sequence) to read aloud, encouraging children to repeat the predictable elements. Examples of stories and books with predicable refrains are in Figure 11.3.
- Select well-illustrated books (ones with many illustrations closely tied to the text) to read aloud.
- Ask the children thought-provoking questions about the story.
- Read and reread favorite stories and let the children listen to them on tapes or records while following along in the book.
- Provide related follow-up activities using a variety of formats and manipulative materials

*Learning to Read/Reading to Learn.* Reading is one of the most essential skills taught in school. For children who learn to read, reading becomes the gateway to all other knowledge and a source of joy. If children do not learn to read efficiently, the path is blocked to every subject they encounter. Yet 15 to 20 percent of all children have difficulty learning to read during their critical first three years in school. Research shows that children who do not learn to read by third grade never catch up with their peers. However, early intervention procedures are effective in helping potential reading failures become successful readers (National Assessment of Educational Progress [NAEP], 1996).

Several principles for learning to read are compatible with the philosophy of early literacy and early childhood education. Based on current research, the following principles are recommended by the National Assessment of Educational Progress (1996) in their "Learn to Read/Read to Learn" document:

- *Create appreciation of the written word.* Long before children are able to engage in reading themselves, they must feel that reading is something they would like to do. They must develop an appreciation of the pleasures of written language and of the many ways language is useful.
- *Develop awareness of the written word.* Children need to develop a basic sense of what print looks like and how it works. They must learn how to handle a book,

---

**FIGURE 11.3** *Predictable Stories and Books*

---

Predictable stories and books have refrains or patterns that are repeated over and over. Children soon learn these refrains and say them along with the story reader. For example, in the story, *The Three Billy Goats Gruff*, the troll repeats, "Who is that trip trapping over my bridge?" Other good predictable books are:

*The Little Red Hen* by Paul Guildone. (Houghton Mifflin)

*Brown Bear, Brown Bear* by B. Martin. (Holt, Rinehart and Winston)

*Goodnight Moon* by M. W. Brown. (Harper and Row)

*Cat on the Mat* by B. Wildsmith. (Oxford Press)

*Have You Seen My Crocodile?* and *Pardon, Said the Giraffe* by C. West. (Harper and Row)

*The Very Hungry Caterpillar* by E. Carle. (Puffin)

*Where the Wild Things Are* by G. M. Sendak. (Harper and Row)

---

*Source:* Lee Cohn, with permission.

which way to turn the pages, and that printed words—not the pictures—tell the story when one reads. Children should learn that words are all around them—in newspapers, at the mall, on billboards, in signs, and on labels—and that written words have many different and valuable purposes.

- *Learn the alphabet.* Comfortable and early familiarity with letters is critical for learning to read. Children should learn the names of letters and to recognize and form their corresponding shapes.
- *Understand the relation of letters and words.* Children need to learn that printed words are made up of ordered strings of letters and read left to right. They should be helped to understand that when the combination or order of letters is changed, the word that is spelled also changes.
- *Understand that language is made of words, syllables, and phonemes.* The ability to think about words as a sequence of phonemes (sounds) is essential to learning how to read English, which is a language based on the alphabet. Children need to understand that sentences are made up of strings of words. They should become comfortable in hearing rhymes and creating rhymes. They should be led to play with the sounds of language until they can pull words apart into syllables and pull syllables into individual phonemes. (A phoneme is the smallest unit of sound. For example, the word *cat* has three individual sounds or phonemes.)
- *Learn letter sounds.* Given a comfortable familiarity with letters and an awareness of the sounds of phonemes, children are ready to learn about letter-sound correspondence. The most important goal at these early stages is to help children understand that the logic of the alphabetic writing system is built on these correspondences.
- *Sound out new words.* As children learn specific letter-sound correspondences, they should be challenged to use this knowledge to sound out new words in reading and writing. Making a habit of sounding out unfamiliar words contributes strongly to reading growth, not just for beginners but for all readers. Children

need to understand that sounding out new words can actually be a strategy for helping them unlock pronunciations of words they have never seen before, and can make what they are reading understandable.

- *Identify words in print accurately and easily.* The ability to read with fluency and comprehension depends on recognizing most words almost instantly and effortlessly. Once the framework for a new word or spelling has been laid through sounding and blending, the key to recognizing it quickly and easily is practice. The most useful practice is reading and rereading meaningful text made up of words the child has been taught to sound out. For beginners, such reading helps most if it is relatively easy. As a rule of thumb, no more than 1 in 20 words should cause trouble.

- *Know spelling patterns.* As children become reasonably capable of sounding out words in reading and spelling, it is important that they notice the similarities in their spellings. Awareness of spelling patterns that recur across words hastens progress in reading and writing.

- *Learn to read reflectively.* Although the ability to sound out words is essential for learning to read, it is not enough. Written language is not just speech written down. Instead, the written text brings new vocabulary, new language patterns, new thoughts, and new modes of thinking. To enjoy and profit from reading, children must also learn to take the time to reflect on these aspects of text.

There are many activities that early childhood teachers can use with all children to build a foundation for reading. For children with special needs, these activities are especially essential. By understanding the precursors of literacy and reading, teachers can build a solid foundation for the children to learn and succeed in school (see Figure 11.4).

## Phonological Awareness

One of the most significant findings of the recent reading research is the importance of phonological awareness in literacy development (Foorman & Torgesen, 2001; Lerner, 2003). *Phonological awareness* (or *phonemic awareness*) refers to the child's ability to focus on and manipulate the sounds (or phonemes) of language in spoken words. *Phonemes* are abstract units of language, the smallest units constituting spoken language. Learning to reflect about the phoneme sounds of language is more difficult than learning to understand and use language. Many children who have difficulty in learning to read are not sensitive to the phoneme sounds of language and words (Foorman & Torgesen, 2001; Lerner, 2003). Following is an illustration of the number of phonemes in several common words:

| Word | Number of Phonemes |
|------|--------------------|
| *oh* | 1 phoneme |
| *go* | 2 phonemes |
| *check* | 3 phonemes |
| *stop* | 4 phonemes |

Successful beginning readers must be aware of phoneme sounds within words to appreciate that the words *cat* and *hat* differ in a single phoneme sound. Children with poor phonological abilities are unable to tap out the number of sounds within a word

FIGURE 11.4    *Activities to Promote Early Literacy*

- *Engage children in oral language activities.*  Provide children with many opportunities to talk and to use oral language.
- *Surround young children with a literacy environment.*  Supply and read many books, stories, and poems, and then discuss them.
- *Use words and sound games.*  Play games to help children become aware that spoken words are constructed from sounds. Teach rhyming games, nursery rhymes, and poetry.
- *Build alphabetic knowledge.*  Help children recognize alphabet letters and encourage them to write these letters.
- *Make children aware of letter-sound correspondence.*  Help children begin to see the relationship between sounds and letters.
- *Help children build a beginning reading vocabulary.*  Plan activities to alert children to their first sight words. For example, complete a collection of their favorite words or logos.

such as *mop.* If a child is unable to reflect about the sound elements of language and to perceive the sounds within words, the alphabet system will remain a mystery. As children become aware of the phonological system, they gain entry into the alphabetic system. Written English is an alphabetic system with written letters of the alphabet representing speech sounds.

The *National Reading Panel* is a research group that was established by the National Institute of Child Health and Human Development to assess the status of research-based knowledge on the effectiveness of teaching children to read. After an exhaustive search of over 100,000 research-based studies, the National Reading Panel (2000) concluded that phonological awareness in instruction is needed by most young children to enter into the world of literacy. For at-risk learners and young children with disabilities, phonological awareness instruction is essential. This instruction is most effective in kindergarten and first grade. Table 11.1 provides examples of several phonological awareness tasks that teachers can use in instruction. (Lerner, 2003). The tasks are listed from easiest to hardest.

***Activities to Help Children Develop Phonological Awareness.***    The following activities are designed to help young children hear the sounds in words. The activities help children develop phonological awareness.

- *Finding things: Initial phonemes.*  Use real objects or pictures of objects. Say the name of the object and ask the children which picture or objects begins with the same sound. For example, ask, "What is the beginning sound of *milk, moon, man,* and *money*?"
- *Clapping names.*  Ask the children to clap out syllables in names and words. For example, clap "Jenn-i-fer" (3 claps), or "Zip-pi-ty-doo-dah").
- *Take away a sound.*  Have the children say their names or a word with the initial sound. For example, say, "___enjamin" Children in the group must identify the whole word.

**TABLE 11.1**  *Phoneme Awareness Tasks*

| Task | Activity |
| --- | --- |
| Phoneme segmentation | How many phonemes in *ship?* |
| Phoneme isolation | Tell me the first sound in *paste.* |
| Phoneme blending | What word is *s/k/u/l?* |
| Phoneme identity | Tell me the sound that is the same in *bike, boy, bell.* |
| Phoneme categorization | Which word does not belong: *bus, bun, run* |
| Rhyming | Did you see a fly kissing a _____ (tie)? |
| Phoneme deletion | Say *smile* without the /s/. |

- *Troll talk: Blending games.* The troll talks funny, saying the sounds of words separately. The children must guess the word by blending the sounds. For example, the troll says the phonemes "ch-ee-z", "p-e-n," "f-u-n," or "What is your "n-a-m? The children blend the sounds and identify the word or answer the questions.
- *Rhyming games.* Say a phrase and have the children think of a rhyming word. For example, "Did you ever see a fly kissing a ____?" The children might say "tie." "Did you ever see a hook kissing a ___?" The children might say "book."
- *Segmenting sounds.* To help children recognize the speech sounds in words, put a picture representing a short word on a card. Draw a rectangle underneath the picture and divide it into the number of phonemes in the word. Have the child say the word slowly, putting a counter (e.g., a penny, a plastic disc, a small cardboard circle, etc.) in each square as the sound is articulated.

**Research Findings about Phonological Awareness.**   A number of conclusions about the benefits of teaching phonological awareness and early literacy skills to young children have been made through extensive research (Foorman & Torgesen, 2001):

1. The number of children who encounter reading failure is reduced significantly through instruction with phonological awareness and phonemic information.
2. Children who are at risk for reading failure require explicit, comprehensive, and intensive instruction.
3. The kind of systematic and supportive intervention needed by children who are at risk for reading failure is most successful when children are in small groups of three or four children.
4. Children must learn the alphabetic principle and learn the sounds of language.

## Assessing Phonological Awareness

An informal test to assess a child's ability in phonological awareness is shown in Figure 11.5. The teacher first gives the practice items. Children are to tell which word does not belong in each practice item. Children with problems in phonological awareness will not be able to answer these questions.

FIGURE 11.5 *Phonological Awareness Test*

*Practice Items*

1. ball *nose* boat baby
2. hand head house *clock*
3. *fan* cat comb carrot

*Test:*

1. bicycle bell *ear* balloon
2. fish feather fort *pig*
3. nest *shoe* knee net
4. *bed* tree train truck
5. table toe tire *arm*
6. wagon *duck* whistle wheel
7. *frog* saw sock sun
8. flag flower *crown* fly
9. dig *rope* desk doll
10. key cow *tail* kite

*Source:* "Phoneme Awareness and Future Reading Ability" by V. Mann. *Journal of Learning Disabilities, 26* (4) (1993): 269. Reprinted by permission.

## *Using Computer Technology*

For young children with special needs, the computer offers many opportunities to explore, play, and learn. The experiences become an integral part of their overall development. The computer bestows a unique magic on children who have special needs by empowering them with a sense of independence and control. It can creatively present colors, distinguish differences such as *larger* and *smaller*, illustrate concepts such as *above* and *below*, and help with shape and letter recognition, counting, matching, and sequencing. The value of the computer may be greater for exceptional youngsters than for others in the population. It is widely acknowledged that computers enable ordinary people to do extraordinary things. But for the child who has special needs, a computer does even more. It enables extraordinary people to do ordinary things.

Computers can help young children develop independence, self-help skills, motor control, visual and auditory concepts, language skills, cognitive skills, and other precursor skills. With the computer, young children with special needs are able to control their environment and to make decisions. Even social skills can be encouraged through cooperative computer activities. Computer activities can help families and teachers meet IEP and IFSP goals.

Adaptive peripherals are particularly useful with young children. Speech synthesizers allow the computers to "talk" to the child. Switches can be plugged into the computer, allowing the child to use the computer without the keyboard. Alternative keyboards such as *Muppet Learning Keys, Power Pad,* and *Intellikeys* are especially useful with young children. With the *Touch Window,* the child can directly touch the screen to control the computer. Most important, young children with disabilities like using the computer. It is an enjoyable, motivating way of learning.

Table 11.2 offers some recommended software for preschool children with special needs (Forgan, 1996). The software programs are divided into the categories of (1) early learning, (2) exploration, (3) communication, (4) beginning users, (5) early literacy, and (6) keyboarding skills.

**TABLE 11.2**  *Computer Software for Young Children with Special Needs*

| Program Name | Publisher | Program Name | Publisher |
|---|---|---|---|
| **Early Learning** | | **Beginning Users (continued)** | |
| Putt-Putt Joins the Parade | Humongous | Katie's Farm | Lawrence |
| Putt-Putt Goes to the Moon | Humongous | | Productions |
| The Tree House | Broderbund | McGee | Lawrence |
| Millie's Math House | Edmark | | Productions |
| Trudy's Time and Play House | Edmark | Mickey's Colors and Shapes | Disney Software |
| Berenstein Bears Get | Broderbund | New Cause and Effects | Colorado Easter |
| in a Fight | | | Seal Society |
| Face Maker Golden Edition | Queue | Noises | Colorado Easter |
| | | | Seal Society |
| **Exploration** | | Old MacDonald II | UCLA |
| Just Grandma and Me | Living Books | | Intervention |
| The Playroom | Broderbund | | Program |
| Little Monster at School | Broderbund | Peek-a-Book on | Judy Lynn |
| Sammy's Science House | Edmark | Fundamental Concepts | Software |
| Thinking Things Collections I | Edmark | This Is the Way We Wash | UCLA |
| In Grandma's Attic | Soft Key | Our Face | Intervention |
| | | | Software |
| **Communication** | | Where's Puff? | UCLA |
| Exploring First Words | Laureate | | Intervention |
| Exploring First Words II | Laureate | | Software |
| Let's Go to the Moon | Laureate | | |
| | | **Early Literacy** | |
| **Beginning Users** | | New Kid on the Block | Living Books |
| Adventures of Quinn | Edmark | Harry and the Haunted House | Living Books |
| Cause/Effects | Judy Lynn | Dr. Seuss's ABC CD | Broderbund |
| | Software | Sesame Street Letters | EA*Kids |
| Children's Switch Progressions | J. J. Cooper | Kid Works 2 | Davidson |
| Clowns | Colorado Easter | Bailey's Book House | Edmark |
| | Seal Society | K. C. & Clyde | Don Johnson |
| Creative Chorus | Laureate | | |
| Dino-Maze | Academic | **Keyboarding Skills** | |
| Skillbuilders | | Kids Keys | Davidson |
| Early and Advanced | R. J. Cooper | Kids on Keys | Queue |
| Switch Games | | Stickybear Typing | Optimum |
| Early Concepts Skillbuilders | Edmark | | Resources |
| Fundamental Concepts | Judy Lynn | Mavis Beacon Teaches Typing | Mindspace |
| | Software | Dinosoft Typing Tutor | Maverick |

# Tips for Teachers: Strategies for Building Early Literacy Skills

This section offers some strategies for building early literacy skills in young children with special needs. These strategies are adapted from National Assessment of Educational Progress (1996).

### Create Appreciation of the Written Word

1. Share stories with children and invite them to explore a story's magic.
2. Share informational texts and invite children to wonder about the new ideas presented.
3. Take every opportunity to point out the ways in which reading is essential to the communications of everyday life (e.g., on labels, instructions, and signs).

### Develop Awareness of Printed Language and the Writing System

1. Make sure that children know how books are organized. Teach them the basics about books—that they are read from left to right and top to bottom, that print may be accompanied by pictures or graphics, that the pages are numbered, and that the purpose of reading is to gain meaning from the text and understand ideas that the words convey.
2. Read to children from books with easy-to-read large print. Use stories that have predictable words in the text.
3. Use "big books" to help children notice and learn to recognize words that occur frequently, such as *a, the, is, was,* and *you.*
4. Label objects in your classroom.

### Teach the Alphabet

1. A strong predictor of the ease with which a child learns to read is his or her familiarity with letters of the alphabet. This familiarity is a critical building block for learning to read.
2. It is important to go beyond knowing the names of letters. Children must also develop a sense of the purpose of letters.
3. Help children notice the letters in the print that surrounds them. Point out the letters in the words that you share with them everyday.
4. Engage children in activities that will help them learn to recognize letters visually.
5. Help children learn to form the letters. Encourage first attempts at writing by encouraging them to embellish their work with names and words.

### Help Children Develop Phonological Awareness

1. *Phonological awareness* refers to recognition of the sounds of language, the sounds of parts of words, of syllables, as well as the small speech sounds.
2. In listening and speaking, adults pay attention to the meaning of language rather than to sounds. To learn to read, however, children must be taught to pay attention to the sounds, or phonology of language. This is necessary for them to un-

derstand how speech is represented by print. Many children need special help in learning to develop phonological awareness.

3. Model and demonstrate how to break short sentences into individual words. For example, use the sentence, "Frogs eat bugs," and demonstrate with chips, cards, or other manipulatives how the sentence is made up of three words and how the order of the words matters. Using manipulatives to make sentences, play with each word and put it in order.

4. Help children develop awareness of the sounds of individual words by having them clap out syllables and listen for and generate rhymes.

5. Children should be comfortable in playing games with words, syllables, and rhymes.

### Develop Phonological Awareness

1. *Phonological awareness* refers to an understanding that words and syllables are comprised of a sequence of elementary speech sounds. This understanding is essential for learning to read an alphabetic language, such as English. The majority of children who have difficulty in learning to read fail to grasp the notion of the sounds within words.

2. In teaching phonological awareness, the focus of all activities should be on the sounds of words, not on letters or spellings.

3. Use strategies that make phonemes prominent in children's attention and perception. For example, model specific sounds, such as /s/ in the word *sat* and ask children to produce each sound in isolation and in many different words until they are comfortable with the sound and understand its nature.

4. Begin with simple words and simple challenges (e.g., listen for the initial /s/ in *sat*, *set*, *sip*, and *sad* . . . or for long /e/ in *me*, *see*, and *bee*).

5. Teach students to blend phonemes into words. Begin by identifying just one phoneme, (e.g., /s/-at), working gradually toward blending all the phonemes in the word (e.g., /s/-/a/-/t/).

6. Teach children to identify the separate phonemes within words (e.g., "What is the first sound of *soup*? What is the last sound of *kiss*?") Beginning phonemes are easier to identify than final phonemes.

7. Once children are comfortable listening for individual phonemes, teach them to break up words into component sounds (e.g., /m/-/oo/-/s/ = moose).

8. Create a sequence of segmenting and blending activities to help children develop an understanding of the relationship between sounds in words.

9. Provide children with more support when first teaching a task. For example, model a sound or strategy for making the sound. Then have the children use the strategy to produce the sound. Model and practice several examples. Prompt the children to use the strategy using guided practice and gradually add more examples. As the children master these skills, provide less teacher-directed instruction and more practice and challenge.

10. Make teaching phonological awareness a top priority. Opportunities to engage in phonological awareness activities should be plentiful, frequent, brief, and fun.

11. Phonological awareness is essential for learning to read, but it is not enough by itself. It must be coupled with instruction and practice in learning the relationship between letters and sounds.

### Teach the Relationship of Sounds and Letters

1. Children should learn the letters of the alphabet and discriminate each letter from the other because each stands for one or more of the sounds that occur in spoken words.
2. When presenting each letter, model its corresponding sound and have children produce the sound themselves. Many children need teaching that is explicit and unambiguous.

### Teach Children How to Sound Out Words

1. After children have mastered a few letter-sound correspondences, teach them to decode words or sound them out. Begin with small familiar words. Teach the children to sound out the letters, left to right, and blend them together, searching for the word in memory.
2. Model sounding out the word, blending the sounds together and saying the word. The ability to sound out new words allows children to identify and learn new words on their own.
3. Give children stories containing words that reflect the letter-sound patterns that have been taught and encourage them to sound out words whenever they are uncertain.
4. Help children learn spelling conventions, such as the use of the final *e* to mark long vowels, by comparing and contrasting lots of examples.

### Teach Children to Spell Words

1. Teach children to spell words by sounding their letters one by one. Model the sounding and spelling process for children as they spell.
2. Begin with short words children can sound out because these words follow regular spelling conventions (e.g., *cap*, *bat*, and *sit* instead of *cape*, *bait*, or *sight*).
3. Begin with simple words that do not contain consonant blends (e.g., *ham* and *pan* instead of *slam* and *plan*).
4. Encourage children to use spelling knowledge and strategies regularly in their own writing.
5. Introduce spelling conventions systematically. Begin with words that exemplify the most frequent and basic conventions and provide support and practice to help children generalize from these words to others. The goal is to help them see the spelling conventions in the words.
6. Use words in which letter-sound correspondences represent the most common sounds (e.g., *get* instead of *gem*).
7. Develop a sequence and schedule of opportunities that allow children to apply and develop facility with sounds and words at their own pace. Specify what skills to assess and when to assess them so that you will know when to move on. Take into account each child's background knowledge and pace in moving from sounding out to blending words to reading connected text.

### Help Children Develop Fluent, Reflective Reading

1. Help children learn to read fluently by requiring them to read new stories and reread old stories every day.

2.  Help children extend their experience with the words, language, and ideas in books by interactively reading harder texts with them and to them every day.
3.  Relate information in books of interest to children, such as holidays, pets, siblings, and games. Engage children in discussion of the topics.
4.  In both stories and informational texts, encourage wondering. For example, "I wonder what Pooh will do now?" "How do you think the father feels?" or "I wonder what frogs do in the winter? Do you think that's a problem? Why?"
5.  Model comprehension strategies and provide students with guided assistance.
6.  Point out how titles and headings tell what a book is about.
7.  Help children identify the main ideas presented in the text, as well as the supporting detail. Graphics help to reveal main ideas, and the relationship between text and graphics helps children understand what they are reading.
8.  Point out unfamiliar words and explore their meaning. Revisit these words frequently and encourage students to use them in their conversations.
9.  Show children how to analyze contextual cues to figure out the meaning of an unfamiliar word. Research shows that most vocabulary growth comes from learning new words in reading.

## Summary

- Cognitive abilities are clusters of mental skills that enable the child to know, be aware of, think, conceptualize, use abstractions, reason, think critically, solve problems, and be creative.
- Thinking and cognition are an integral part of all aspects of human learning. They occur in all areas of learning, and preschool children need cognitive skills for learning in every phase of the early childhood curriculum—adaptive and self-help abilities, motor skills, language and communication, perceptual recognition, early literacy, social relationships, and problem-solving operations.
- There are several theories of cognitive development that apply to young children and children with special needs.
- The ideas of Piaget provide a foundation for thinking about cognitive development in young children. Piaget's theories are also influential in the development of curriculum for early childhood programs and for programs for young children with special needs.
- Vygotsky's notions of the social realm of cognitive development and his ideas about the *zone of proximal development (ZPD)* and *scaffolding* have added much to early childhood programs.
- Constructive learning is based on the view that children actively construct their own solutions to problems and that this natural behavior should be encouraged.
- The High/Scope Perry Preschool Project, which was designed for environmentally at-risk children, provides many activities for a cognitively oriented curriculum for young children at risk.
- The activity-based approach for young children with special needs developed by Bricker offers a curriculum that uses meaningful activities that occur regularly and naturally.

- Intervention strategies are useful for teaching cognitive skills.
- Common activities in early childhood programs emphasize the learning of concepts, spatial relationships, classifying, sequencing, playing, and creative thinking.
- Early literacy begins long before children encounter formal school instruction in reading and writing. Children learn about symbols, books and stories, writing, and imaginary worlds.
- Early literacy promotes a variety of early literacy activities: early writing and experiences with stories.
- Many young children have difficulty in reading because they are not aware of the sounds in language. These children need to develop phonological awareness if they are to be successful in learning to read.

## *Key Terms*

accommodation
activity-based curriculum
assimilation
cognition
cognitive skills
computer technology
concrete operations
constructive learning
early literacy

formal operations
High/Scope Project
intuitive thought
phonological awareness
Piaget's stages of cognitive development
preconceptual thought
sensorimotor stage
zone of proximal development (ZPD)

# 12

## *Transition*

## Chapter Outline _____

*Overview of Transition for Young Children
with Special Needs*
    Defining Transition
    The Law and Transition
    People Involved in Transitions
    Research on Transitions for Preschool Children

*Factors Affecting Transitions*
    Support for Parents
    Time Frames
    Transportation
    Interagency Coordination
    Communication Issues
    Testing and Placement Issues
    Multicultural Considerations

*Planning for Transitions*
    Needs Assessment
    The Role of the Transition Coordinator

*Stages in a Coordinated Transition Plan*
    Stage 1. Initial Planning: Families
       and Service Providers
    Stage 2. The IEP or IFSP: Preparation,
       Planning, and Implementation
    Stage 3. Introduction to the
       New Program
    Stage 4. Evaluation of the Transition
    Research on Transitions: The STEPS Model

A transition marks a time of change in life. Any change may be stressful, but changes in school or intervention programs may bring worrisome problems for children and families. Moving from one educational service delivery system to another can trigger feelings of uncertainty and fear of traumatic adjustments in one's life (Bronfenbrenner, 1977; Hanson, 1999; Spiegel-McGill, Reed, Konig, & McGowan, 1990).

For young children with special needs and their families, the transition from one program to another can be particularly trying and a major source of stress and upheaval for both the child and the parents (Rous, Hemmeter, & Schuster, 1999). Some parents have already experienced a dramatic transition when they brought their infant home from the hospital's neonatal intensive care unit (Kolberg, Gustafson, & Ekblad, 1999; Young, 1993). Interventionists and teachers who serve young children and their families are also subject to strong feelings during transitions. It is at this time that the child leaves the closely knit program, and interventionists worry about how the toddler will fare in a larger setting.

This chapter emphasizes two major themes concerning transition:

1. The transition process affects everyone—the child who is making the transition to a new program, as well as others involved with the child (the family, service providers, and other support personnel from the agency or school).
2. The way in which the family manages transition, even the first transition for a child, will impact other key transitions made during the child's school years and over the child's lifespan.

*Early Childhood Snapshot*  THE TRANSITION FOR MELINDA
AND HER FAMILY

Melinda Z. is 2½ years old and her family lives in a small rural town in northern Wisconsin. Melinda is the fourth child of Linda and Harry Z. She has spina bifida, and she has had several surgeries to install and replace shunts to drain excess fluid from her brain and has had four surgeries to correct orthopedic problems. Each surgery and medical procedure required a three-hour drive and overnight stays at the hospital in the nearest city that was equipped to perform pediatric neurosurgical and orthopedic procedures.

Melinda's father is a farmer, and her mother is the farm business manager as well as a homemaker. The older siblings are 9, 12, and 13 years old and are in good health. Melinda is in the birth-to-3 early childhood program. For the past two years, she has received early intervention services at home on a weekly basis from an early childhood interventionist, Carol, who is a certified physical therapist. Carol is a member of a transdisciplinary team that includes an occupational therapist, a speech therapist, an early childhood special educator, and a social worker. Melinda's mother and Carol have built a very close relationship during the past two years, and Mrs. Z. is very pleased with the services and satisfied with this arrangement. Melinda has made positive progress, and the home intervention arrangement allows Mrs. Z. to continue her work at the family farm with little interruption.

In six months, Melinda will have her third birthday and will no longer be eligible for the birth-to-3 services. About six weeks ago, Melinda's home interventionist and physical therapist began discussing the upcoming transition with Melinda's mother. Mrs. Z. responded to this conversation about the upcoming new service plan with some resistance, dissatisfaction, and even anger.

Carol discussed her concerns about Mrs. Z.'s response with the transdisciplinary team. In the collaboration process, the transdisciplinary team provided Carol with several excellent suggestions on how to involve Mrs. Z. in the transition procedure, prepare Mrs Z. for the change, and employ methods for introducing Melinda and her mother to the new preschool environment. After conferring with her colleagues on the transition team, Carol invited Mrs. Z. meet with her and the team for one session without Melinda, in order to plan for the coming transition.

After listening to Mrs. Z. express her concerns at the meeting, Carol had a better idea of why she was resistant to the change. Mrs. Z. was worried about transportation because it would be a 45-minute bus ride for Melinda each way every day. Mrs. Z. was also worried about whether the new facility would provide a healthful snack for her daughter. Most of all, she felt abandoned by Carol, who had been the interventionist for Melinda for almost three years. Mrs. Z. expressed these worries: "How will I know what to do once you stop coming? I am afraid Melinda will lose the gains we have made over the past two years. I will have no one to talk to about my worries and fears for Melinda."

After Carol heard the issues that were concerning Mrs. Z., she was able to carefully outline realistic choices. Together, they constructed a time line so that Mrs. Z. could plan the best way to help her daughter with the transition. Carol made arrangments for Mrs. Z. to visit the new site without Melinda so that they could talk openly about her concerns. At the new site, Mrs. Z. met the bus driver, the classroom aide, and the new teacher. She was also given a videotape of children in the classroom to take home to Melinda. Carol was encouraged to connect Mrs. Z. with a "mentor parent" who has a 4-year-old child in the new program. Arrangements were also made for Melinda to visit the new program and meet her new teachers.

Carol has agreed with Mrs. Z. that she would like her to call Carol on a regular basis during the first few months after Melinda's transition. Once the transition plan was made, Mrs. Z. felt more confident and secure about her daughter's upcoming transition to the preschool early intervention program.

# Overview of Transition for Young Children
# with Special Needs

This section discusses several transition issues: definition of transition, how the law affects transition, people involved in the transition procedure, and research on transition for preschool children.

## Defining Transition

*Transition* is the process of moving or changing a child from one service component or delivery system to another (Hanson, 1999). Ideally, the transition should be a smooth passage or an evolution rather than a sudden and unsettling relocation into a new program. An expansion of the concept of transition includes changes that occur within a specific program. Such changes occur when a child moves to a new class, starts with a new teacher or begins service with a another service provider, or changes schedules and routines (Bailey & Wolery, 1992; Center for Innovations in Special Education, 1999).

***Transition for Young Children with Disabilities.***   As noted earlier, the funding patterns for early childhood special education services support two separate and distinct programs: one for children from birth to 3 years of age (the infant/toddler programs) and another for children from ages 3 to 6 (the preschool program) (Raver, 1991). An aim of the law (Reauthorized IDEA and PL 102-119) is to create a "seamless delivery system" with easy and smooth transitions for children from birth to 6 years of age (Harbin, McWilliam & Gallagher, 2000). However, at the present time, this goal has not yet been achieved. Usually, children who are identified as having disabilities during the first three years of life must move into a different type or program when they reach age 3. The transition activities defined under Part C of the Reauthorized IDEA focus on infants and toddlers and do not address children entering the preschool intervention system for the first time at age 3 (Rosenkoetter, 1992).

Young children who have been in birth-to-3 programs must make the transition to a preschool program when they reach age 3. This transition often causes anxiety for the parents. Some of the stress is because these 3-year-old children are often separated from their parents for the first time in their lives and transported on buses to the preschool program. Parents of children who do not have disabilities typically do not face this problem because their children do not experience this type of separation—being sent on a bus to a public or private kindergarten setting—until their child is 5 years old (Spiegel-McGill et al., 1990).

The next significant transition for young children who have special needs occurs at about age 6, as the child moves into either a mainstreamed kindergarten environment or a special education program in the elementary school. This transition is also fraught with potential problems for families and service providers.

The concept of *transitioning* refers to more than one element of service. It refers to the passage of the child and family from one set of service circumstances to another

(Healy, Keese, & Smith, 1987). From a broad perspective, transition should be viewed as a passage or evolution, the first in a series of moves that sets the stage for future transitions (Lazzari & Kilgo, 1989). We anticipate that in the near future the types of transition planning procedures now required for 3-year-olds will influence transition practices for children at age 6.

**Transition for Young Children at Risk.**    Children who are considered at risk also need transition planning. Some young children who are considered at risk are identified under Part C of the law and therefore are served under the federal regulations of Part C. Other young children who are at risk are not identified as having disabilities and are served through other kinds of programs for children at risk. The Head Start program serves 3- and 4-year-old children from families with low income. At the completion of a Head Start program, the child is likely to be placed in the public school kindergarten program, with little transition planning or articulation between the two services. Transition planning would benefit young children who are in other preschool programs for children at risk.

## The Law and Transition

The need for transition services during the preschool years is recognized in the law under Part C of Reauthorized Individuals with Disabilities Education Act of 1997 (PL 105-17) and in the earlier PL 99-457 and PL 102-119. La Paro, Pinata & Cox (2000) find that children with special needs require particular attention when making transitions above and beyond those of typical children.

Public Laws 105-17 and 99-457 require that an individualized family service plan (IFSP) be developed for infants and toddlers and that the IFSP must include a transition plan. The law requires that for children in the infants and toddlers program a conference be held to discuss the transition 90 days before the child reaches age 3 and becomes eligible for the preschool program. Parents have an integral part in this planning, so they become "long-term, independent, informed advocates for their children" (Speigel-McGill et al., 1990, p. 66).

All states must develop a transition policy for the transition that occurs at age 3. In addition, according to both Part B (for children ages 3 to 6) and Part C (for children from birth to age 3), agencies must provide documentation about transition procedures in order to continue receiving federal funding (La Paro et al., 2000). The transition plan for children when they reach age 3 must include the steps to be taken to support the transition of the child. Upon reaching age 3, parents need to be informed about and given transition assistance for (Rosenkoetter, 1992):

- Preschool services under Part B, to the extent that those services are considered appropriate, or
- Other appropriate services for children who are not eligible for preschool programs under Part B

The law requires that the following steps be taken to support the transition process:

1. *Discuss all facets of the transition and intervention with parents.* This includes discussions with, and training of, parents regarding future placements and other matters related to the child's transition.
2. *Prepare the child for the transition.* This includes procedures to prepare the child for changes in service delivery, including steps to help the child adjust to, and function in, a new setting.
3. *Communicate with the receiving school.* With parental consent, the transmission of information about the child is sent to the local educational agency to ensure continuity of services, including evaluation and assessment information and copies of IFSPs that have been developed for the child.

Interagency agreements should be made for planning the transition and the agreements should flexible. Interagency agreements are especially important when the (Part C) lead agency for infant and toddler services differs from the (Part B) lead agency for preschool services. For example, in a particular state the Part C lead agency might be the Department of Mental Health and the Part B agency the Department of Education. To ensure that there are no gaps in services for a child during transition, these different agencies must work together and coordinate their efforts (PL 105-17, 1997).

In addition to the transition of infants and toddlers at age 3, when the child moves from a birth-to-3 setting to the preschool program, transition planning is also essential for a smooth transition for the 5- to 6-year-old child who is leaving a preschool program and embarking on an elementary school career. The law allows for flexibility in the development of transition plans. It is up to the districts, individual service providers, and parents to determine what transition plans would work best on an individual basis. Although a transition plan is mandated for children moving from Part C (infant–toddler) to Part B (preschool), specific plans are not required for children transitioning from Part B programs into general kindergartens or first grade (La Paro et al., 2000). Early interventionists need training for planning transitions, and this need is recognized in the law. The Comprehensive System of Personnel Development (CSPD) in each state may include training provisions for personnel who coordinate transition services for infants and toddlers with disabilities between early intervention programs and preschool programs (Rosenkoetter, 1992).

## People Involved in Transitions

A number of different people are necessarily involved in the transition procedures: families, service providers, children, and administrators. The roles and responsibilities of each participant are described in this section.

*Families.*    The families of children who have disabilities or who are at risk feel comfortable over time with people and services at a particular setting. Moving their child from this familiar and comfortable setting, where their child is doing well and rapport has been established with the staff, to a new unknown setting can be very threatening.

Parents may have developed strong attachments to service providers (Vaughn, Reiss, Rothlein & Hughes, 1999). The law recognizes that the coming transition for their child creates feelings of stress and anxiety for families and that parents are often unprepared for all that a transition encompasses. Therefore, the law requires that families be included in transition planning (PL 105-17, 1997; PL 102-119, 1991).

Some families are able to identify and express their concerns, whereas others may not be fully cognizant of their concerns, or they may be unwilling to share their fears with service providers (Haines, Rosenkoettter, & Fowler, 1991). When families are served in the birth-to-3 setting, there are often expectations that the child may emerge from the program "cured" of the disability or ready for the community preschool like any other youngster. Sometimes it is these unspoken expectations that cause parents so much stress. With an increased emphasis on serving the child in a natural setting, in many cases the child will make a transition from a special education program to attend a regular preschool class, but there is still the likelihood that additional special services will be required. In any case, the child making the transition must make an adjustment to the new more inclusive setting from the more sheltered birth-to-3 environment.

In the birth-to-3 setting, the interventionist often meets with the parents and child together, without other children or parents present. Under this arrangement, the parents receive attention and support from the interventionist while the child's specific needs are met. At the end of the child's time in the birth-to-3 setting, parents are aware that their role will change, but they are often confused as to the role they will play in the new setting. The shift in delivery systems may be a challenging process for families (Hanson, 1999).

In a research survey conducted with over 200 parents of children in birth-to-3 programs, Egan (1989) found that parents had many personal, and sometimes unspoken, expectations for the new program. For example, in some cases, parents assumed they would accompany the child to the new setting on the bus; some parents hoped the birth-to-3 setting might make an exception for their child, permitting their child to stay in the original program past age 3. Many parents worried about their child taking a school bus at such a young age. A frequent comment was that parents did not see their child as being as "handicapped" as the children in the potential new setting. Many parents worried that the new teacher would not understand the family as well as the former interventionist, and parents were frequently concerned that their child would suffer from separation anxiety in the new setting.

However, the transition process is not always rocky. In many cases, the parents look forward to the new setting. For example, one mother who participated in a transition workshop said that she was relieved that her 3-year-old daughter would be transported to school on a daily basis and that she would no longer have to attend sessions with her child. She said, "The day that bus picked up Samantha I jumped for joy! It was finally my turn to go shopping or to an exercise class, to do something for **me**!" Some parents express delight that their child has reached a state of independence and would attend school with other children, thus enhancing the possibilities for socialization.

***Service Providers.*** Service providers in the birth-to-3 programs often have legitimate concerns about planning transitions with families. Many feel they can do more and want to provide more training in planning and conducting transitions with parents (Hanson, 1999). Service providers usually develop strong feelings about children in their programs, and they can have their own problems coping with these feelings about the child's transition (Egan, 1989). Service providers need preservice and in-service training about the transition process. The training can include discussions about planning the transition and ways to prepare the child for the new environment.

Because service providers tend to develop such strong relationships with the family and child in the birth-to-3 program, they often feel sorrowful about losing children and families from their programs. Sometimes they are fearful that the new setting will not be as suitable for the child as the one in which they provided service to the family. Separation from the families and children they have been working with for a long time causes distress for some service providers. They become comfortable in the role of nurturing the parents and helping them help their children. Unwittingly, at times this attachment may be deleterious to the process of transition for the families they serve. If the families sense the discomfort of the service providers, the families may be reluctant to change to the new setting.

When conducting in-service workshops on transition, the authors find that service providers readily acknowledge their own emotions when given the opportunity to express them. Once they examine their own feelings, they report that they are better able to support and help the parents in the transition.

*It is important to arrange a classroom visit to promote successful experiences in the transition process.*

***Children.***   The transition process, of course, affects the child. In their concern for the parents' adjustment to the transition and to the new setting, it is important that service providers not neglect the child's needs during the process. Children may have fears and fantasies about the new setting that need to be explored and discussed. In the case of children who are preverbal, these concerns will be manifested in pictorial, concrete, behavioral, and practical ways. It is helpful if the child is able to visit the new site and meet with the new service providers and teachers before the transition actually takes place. One rural district compensated for the distance problem by exchanging videotapes between the former and new settings, showing tapes of the classrooms, children, and teachers to children and families who will make the transition.

*Teaching Children Survival Skills for Transition.*   In addition to the emotional aspects of transition for the child, in most cases there will be different classroom demands placed on preschoolers as they enter the new program. It is crucial for children to develop the survival skills they will need in the new setting. Paramount among these skills is effective communication of one's needs by the child (Hanson, 1999). A curriculum for teaching survival skills needed for participating in activities in kindergarten and first-grade settings was developed by Rule, Fiechtl, and Innocenti (1990). Through extensive observations of mainstreamed settings, they found that to be successfully mainstreamed into kindergarten and first grade, children must possess the following behaviors:

1. Work independently
2. Participate in groups
3. Follow varied directions
4. Use varied materials

Through prompting and praising, children were taught to learn these four behaviors. Participation in a survival skills curriculum was successful in teaching young children who have special needs to learn the behaviors needed in kindergarten and first grade. Haines (1992) also found that it is important to arrange specific instruction to promote successful experiences for children with special needs in regular kindergarten classrooms. Vaughn and colleagues (1999) state that kindergarten teachers need to make specific adaptations for children with special needs.

***Administrators.***   The role of administrators in the transition process is critical. At the state level, early childhood administrators are to establish the guidelines to promote a smooth transition under the law. The administrators from the local education agency are also pivotal in determining the process of transition in their district or agency. Administrators must make sure that the transition complies with federal regulations. These regulations include convening a conference, with the approval of the family, at least 90 days before the child is eligible for the preschool program under Part B in accordance with state law (PL 105-17, 1997). In addition, administrators are responsible for allocating the amount of time service providers need for transition planning and coordination with each other and with families.

### Research on Transitions for Preschool Children

The research that has been conducted on preschool transitions shows that active participation in the transition process on the part of families reduces parental stress (Fowler, Chandler, Johnson, & Stella, 1988; Hamblin-Wilson & Thurman, 1990). Parent participation in the transition planning is required in the law. Service providers must begin planning the child's transition with the family. There are several ways for including parents in the transition plan.

One research study found that a group discussion on transition was particularly helpful for parents. This study measured the result of a series of six transition meetings held for families of children who were making transitions. The family meetings consisted of discussions on topics such as the effects of transitions, options in placements, communication skills, and legal and educational rights for families. As a result of attending these discussion meetings, parents reported that the training prepared them for their child's transition, taught them what to expect and how to communicate at meetings, and showed them how to be a life-long advocate for their child (Spiegel-McGill et al., 1990).

Another study found that asking about family transition concerns was helpful. This study focused on 91 families to find their major concerns about transition issues. Concerns centered on a lack of information about school district services, anxiety about working with an unfamiliar agency, and uncertainty as to whether the child would receive appropriate services. When parents were better prepared, they tended to feel most satisfied (Hamblin-Wilson & Thurman, 1990). Rous, Hemmeter, and Schuster (1999) investigated the impact of the Sequenced Transition to Education in the Public Schools (STEPS) model. They found that utilization of this model increased the number of formalized policies and procedures related to transitions.

Additional information on preschool transitions for children who have special needs may be obtained from the National Early Childhood Technical Assistance Development System (NECTAS) in Chapel Hill, North Carolina. This center provides references and summaries of federally funded preschool transition research projects. The contact person for NECTAS is Joicey Hurth, (919) 962-2001.

Hanson (1999), citing Shotts, Rosenkoetter, Struefers, and Rosenkoetter, found that successful transition promote "(a) placement decisions that meet individual needs, (b) uninterrupted services, (c) non-confrontational and effective models of advocacy that families can emulate throughout their children's lives, (d) avoidance of duplication in assessment and goal planning, and (e) reduced stress for children, families and service providers" (p. 2).

## Factors Affecting Transitions

Many different factors affect the transition process. Parents report that they need to find extra sources of support and assistance during transitions. The establishment of a time frame for the transition is necessary for both parents and service providers. Issues such as transportation arrangements, interagency coordination, communication, and the implementation of the IEP are crucial in planning the transition. Multicultural factors may also affect the entire transition process.

## Support for Parents

During transitions, families often express a need for additional support. Schools and agencies can assist parents in developing a network of persons to whom they may turn for support in times of stress during the transition process. By working with families to identify potential sources of support, service providers empower parents to learn how to access and utilize support in subsequent stressful situations as their child moves through the school system.

To help families access sources of support, it is useful to compile a list of potential helpers (or help agents). Discuss these help sources with the parents so that they can select persons who can assist them during the transition (Egan, 1989). Although the specific "help agents" in each district will vary, the suggestions provided in Figure 12.1 can serve as a basic core to be modified and expanded in individual instances.

In keeping with the concept of empowering parents as agents of change in the transition process, it is essential that the parents make the final decision about which helpers they would like to consult. Since parents will have diverse perceptions about the helpfulness of the different help agents, each family will find different persons to be suitable.

## Time Frames

The schedule of events leading up to and through the child's transition into a new program is an important consideration. The sequence of events and the timing of the transition activities are consequential for both families and service providers. Typically, since parents often have no prior experience with the educational system, they are unable to anticipate or prepare for meetings and IFSP or IEP conferences. Parents should be given sufficient advance notification to get ready for these meetings (Lazzari & Kilgo, 1989). Service providers also need an established time line in order to organize and coordinate transition activities.

Without well-developed time lines, transition activities may occur in a hurried manner just before the child's departure from the program. Transitions that are rushed and pressured limit the amount of participation by the child's parents and prove frustrating to the service providers as well (Haines, Rosenkoetter, & Fowler, 1991).

**FIGURE 12.1**   *Potential Help Agents for Families During the Transition Process*

| | |
|---|---|
| 1. Teacher from old program | 11. Occupational therapist |
| 2. Teacher from new program | 12. Administrator |
| 3. Parent mentor | 13. Friends |
| 4. Speech therapist | 14. Counselor |
| 5. Classroom aide | 15. Social worker |
| 6. Family members | 16. Psychologist |
| 7. Bus driver | 17. Medical doctor |
| 8. Physical therapist | 18. Other parents |
| 9. Service coordinator | 19. Nurse |
| 10. Transition coordinator | 20. Clergy members |

Ideally, parents and service providers should establish the transition time line at the start of the child's last year in the program. This usually provides a period of about nine months in advance of the transition. Planning the transition this far in advance allows the parents to participate fully in the transition activities and ensures that necessary paperwork and documents will be completed in a timely fashion.

Service providers should develop a master list of transition activities by recording all of the transition activities, placing them in a sequential order, and establishing chronologically a date for each to be accomplished. This master list may then be used on an individual basis with each family. Once dates for initiation of each activity have been established, parents should be given a copy of the time line schedule for future reference.

## Transportation

*Transportation* refers to the means of getting the child to the new placement and is one of the primary concerns for parents as their 3-year-old child makes a transition. Parents have legitimate concerns about bus transportation. They worry about their child's overall safety, the qualifications of the bus driver, and the length of time the child spends on the bus. When a family must use public transportation to the new setting, there may be a need for schedule changes for the entire family and alterations in child care arrangements (Haines, Rosenkoetter, & Fowler, 1991).

## Interagency Coordination

For a successful transition, it is essential that good communication links be established between the sending and receiving agencies and schools. Walter and Petr (2000) suggest that interagency collaborations need to have family-centered values as the core of these collaborations. The need for coordination is heightened when the sending agency is different from the receiving agency. The agencies may have different policies or expectations regarding the child's change of placement. Fowler, Haines, and Rosenkoetter (1990) stress that it is crucial for states to develop interagency agreements in order to clarify transition options and develop appropriate procedures in order to comply with federal regulations. Walter and Petr (2000) report that interagency collaboration helps turn "fragmented human services into a system that addresses the multiple needs of children and families in a more comprehensive way" (p. 494).

A smooth transition process requires local interagency coordination. Effective coordination leads to better communication with parents and personnel from both programs. The *Early Childhood Interagency Transition Model* (Gallagher, Maddox, & Edgar, 1984) presents the following clear guidelines for successful transitions:

- Records should be transferred from the sending to receiving agency.
- Transition events should be carefully timed.
- All participants should have completed awareness of the new program.
- Parents should be involved at all levels of the decision-making processes.
- Communication between agencies should continue after the transition has occurred.

## Communication Issues

Adequate systems of communication are needed by families and service providers during the planning stages for the transition as well as throughout the entire transition process. All persons involved in the transition must communicate to develop a common understanding. Successful transitions are more likely to occur when all of the individuals involved in the transition communicate effectively with one another. It is essential that families and service providers establish communication and rapport, but it is just as important for service providers from the sending and receiving agencies to communicate with each other about the child making the transition. If they do not communicate effectively, the responsibility for transferring the information between the two programs falls on the family at a time when they are least able to manage it.

When the family speaks a different language from the service providers, it is necessary to use knowledgeable interpreters. The interpreters should be well trained and able to make conceptual translations of idiomatic usage, not just literal translations (Anderson & Fenichel, 1989).

It is also helpful for families to learn communication skills in order to facilitate their participation in IFSPs and IEPs as well as in the transition process. A designated transition coordinator serves to establish and organize communication among all persons involved in the transition.

## Testing and Placement Issues

**Testing Information.**　Children often receive diagnostic testing at the time of the transition. It is important that service providers talk to families in advance of the assessment. The following topics should be addressed: definitions of tests, types of tests, evaluation in the natural environment, scores and what they mean, and the use of tests for making placement decisions and in developing IFSPs and IEPs (Innocenti, Rule, & Fiechtl, 1987).

Parents want to know about the new placement setting. Interviews with parents show that most are unaware of what the new placement will be like. Parents want specific information about the following five issues (Hanline, 1988):

| | |
|---|---|
| **1.** Location | Where will the child receive services: home, school, or center? Which school or center? |
| **2.** Type of service delivery | Service providers and classroom aides; individual or group instruction; special therapies? |
| **3.** Length of day | Morning, afternoon, or all day; lunch plans; number of days of attendance per week? |
| **4.** Role of parents in the new program | How much involvement; parent groups? |
| **5.** Contact person in the new setting | Whom can they call with questions? |

Families should also be informed that early intervention services are to be provided in natural environments whenever appropriate, including settings such as the home and community facilities where children without disabilities participate.

***Legal Rights.***    Service providers should help inform parents about the child's and family's legal rights. Parents should understand that they have the right to accept or reject any early intervention service without jeopardizing other services. Finally, it is important to restate that although IEPs are usually used with preschool children after age 3, IFSPs can be used with children ages 3 to 5 years (inclusive) if the state, local education agency, and parents agree (Rosenkoetter, 1992).

## Multicultural Considerations

When the family making the transition is from a culture other than the dominant one in the agency or district, there may be additional concerns that need to be addressed in transition planning:

1. In communicating with parents who do not speak English, it is essential that translators be procured who are trained and knowledgeable. Appropriate translators are needed for all meetings and conversations with parents who speak another language.
2. When working with families from culturally diverse backgrounds, it is important not to stereotype individuals from any culture and to always work with families on an individual basis. Follow the family's clues as to their comfort levels with the dominant language and culture.
3. In planning a transition with African American, Asian American, Hispanic American, and Native American families, consider factors that may facilitate the transition process. Take into account cultural differences because they will affect both the establishment of time tables for transitions and the planning process (McDermott, 2001).

The following are important considerations in working with culturally diverse families (Anderson & Fenichel, 1989):

1. The extended family is extremely significant in some cultures. For example, among some Asian American families, when an important choice is to be made, the oldest member of the family may be the decision maker for the entire family.
2. Service providers should be aware that families from some cultures take a long time to develop trust with the service provider.
3. In some cultures, the families are more "present oriented" than the more "future-oriented" school system. They are not concerned about "next year."

# Planning for Transitions

## Needs Assessment

Before a district or agency begins to plan and establish an overall transition system for families, the district should conduct a needs assessment to determine the transition practices that currently exist in the district. This needs assessment should be conducted early, before implementation of a new transition system. The information obtained from the needs assessment will set the stage for families, service providers, and administrators to work as partners in developing an effective transition plan for the agency or district.

When conducting a needs assessment, one method for evaluating the program's current transition activities is to hold workshops for parents and service providers (Egan, 1989). Goals for these workshops include (1) identifying the concerns of families, administrators, and service providers about preschool traditions; (2) providing an open forum for discussion of these issues; and (3) planning an organized system of transition based on federal regulations and the identified needs of the agency or district.

## The Role of the Transition Coordinator

Parents who are in the process of making a transition need a primary contact person with whom they can communicate about the transition. Service providers in the sending and receiving agencies also need a specific person they can contact when they require information about a particular child. The role of a *transition coordinator* serves this function. The transition coordinator acts as a nexus for communication and information to all parties involved in the child's transition. The transition coordinator is also responsible for developing the transition timeline, notifying participants of transition activities, and ensuring that the proposed activities take place on schedule.

Under Part C of the Reauthorized IDEA and of PL 99-457, the service coordinator assumes the responsibilities for the role of transition coordinator when the child is 3 years old. For the transition that occurs at age 6, this role may be filled by a number of individuals. Figure 12.2 illustrates the transition coordinator's position and role in the transition.

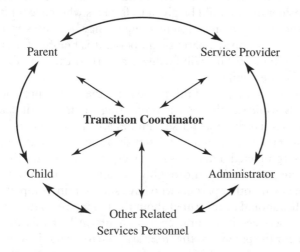

**FIGURE 12.2**   *Role of the Transition Coordinator*

# Stages in a Coordinated Transition Plan

To develop a coordinated transition plan, service providers from agencies and schools need to collaborate with the families they serve and with each other. The following four-stage plan is based on relevant literature and an adaptation from materials from several sources (Center for Innovative in Special Education, 1999; Egan, 1989; Haines Rosenkoetter, & Fowler, 1991; Innocenti, Rule, & Fiechtl, 1987; Kolberg, Gustafson, & Ekblad, 1999; Lazzari & Kilgo, 1989; Little, 1999). A multistage approach consists of sequential stages that involve families and service providers working together from the outset. This approach helps families recognize the importance of systematic planning for their children's future needs. It also provides opportunities for families to become more active participants in the transition process, at this time and for future transitions, as their child matures.

## Stage 1. Initial Planning: Families and Service Providers

During the first stage, service providers and families begin their initial discussions about the child's upcoming transition in accordance with the agency's or district's policy. Generally, this phase takes place about nine months ahead of the transition. Starting this process early enables parents and service providers to begin dialogues about the child's move to another program and encourages family participation in planning from the very beginning. This is the time when the entire concept of *transition* is introduced to the family and when service providers and families together draw up a time line for the transition process. At this time, the transition coordinator is also identified and assumes responsibility for coordinating transition and follow-up activities.

Parents are encouraged and assisted, if necessary, to put together a transition notebook in which they may keep the child's records and their own IFSP and IEP goals for their child. Extra consideration should be given to families who have limited reading or writing abilities; special communication techniques may be necessary for them. If the agency or district has developed a parent handbook, it is helpful if it is given to the parents in a three-ring binder. This will facilitate a start to the organization and record-keeping process for the families.

One important and sensitive aspect of this phase is for the service provider to provide support for the family while simultaneously promoting the family's independence and decision-making abilities. During this phase, families are also encouraged to select those persons who will assist them with their child's transition and are put in contact with mentor families who have completed transitions if they express a desire for that contact.

The family's legal rights should be thoroughly explained to the families. It may be helpful for them to meet with other parents who have successfully completed a transition. At this time, families should be informed about the federal regulations and preference for transitions to services in natural environments. All of this information should be written clearly for the parents so that they are able to review it later and keep it for reference for future transitions. This period of proactive planning will result in a better transition for the child and family.

## Stage 2. The IEP or IFSP: Preparation, Planning, and Implementation

During the second stage, families and service providers begin to actively plan for the child's assessment and subsequent IFSP or IEP conference. This generally occurs about six months ahead of the planned transition. At this time, families and service providers should refer to the transition time line and review it to make sure that all of the events have occurred on schedule and in sequence.

Service providers need to identify each family's preferences for participating in decisions about the new setting for their child. These decisions and information should be in writing so that parents may refer to them later, and they should be kept for reference in the transition notebook. Families need time to process the information they glean from these discussions, and they may wish to visit the potential sites whenever practical. It may be difficult to identify these sites this early in the process, but it is helpful to families if they are able to make some preliminary visits at this time.

## Stage 3. Introduction to the New Program

In the third stage, families are introduced to the new program and encouraged to share information about their child with the new service providers. Information such as the child's favorite activities, difficulties with daily routines, and rewards and discipline that have worked best with the child at home should be included. Families of children who are medically fragile should be especially encouraged to share their concerns with the new service providers and to demonstrate techniques they have found to be successful with their child.

Another very significant item for discussion is transportation. School or agency policy and the concerns families have need to be expressed and examined. This is another opportunity when families of children who are receiving services from the new setting may be invited to speak to the incoming families. It is useful for service providers to identify and discuss the similarities and differences between the two programs with families who are making a transition.

Whenever possible, it is helpful if the service providers from the new setting make a home visit or at least establish a brief individual conference with the family before the child enters the program. This procedure enables families to voice their concerns and priorities and to evaluate their own resources regarding transition, including sharing of this information with the service providers.

## Stage 4. Evaluation of the Transition

During this stage, families and service providers evaluate the effectiveness of the transition. The information gathered from these evaluations provides useful feedback for both the sending and receiving agencies and schools as well as for individual service providers. Taking the time to ask families to identify their satisfactions and concerns has another benefit in that the service providers are able to anticipate and identify concerns the families may have with the new site early in the program before they become frustrated by any potential problems.

The evaluation may be drawn up from the items and events scheduled on the transition time line and should include questions about the family's satisfaction or dissatisfaction with the timing of the transition, communication procedures, assessment process, program options, communication, and the child's adjustment to the new setting. Since children who have special needs and their families will continually undergo transitions throughout their lifetimes, it is essential that the service providers involved in the earliest preschool transitions help families to acquire the skills they need to manage a successful transition. It is also essential for families to be given a template for transitions that they may use in future transitions (Hanline, 1991).

### Research on Transitions: The STEPS Model

The Sequenced Transition to Education in the Public Schools (STEPS) model has been used extensively in early childhood transitions, since its development through a Handicapped Children's Early Education Program (HCEEP) model demonstration grant. Rous, Hemmeter, and Schuster (1999) find that utilization of the model over a one-year period of time results in positive changes in transition practices. The model includes four basic components (1) establishing an administrative structure, (2) outlining staff involvement and training, (3) developing family involvement options, and (4) addressing child preparation and follow-up (Rous et al., 1999). As a result of implementation of this approach to transition, all sites involved in the study increased their formalized plans and policies for transition.

## Summary

- Transition is the process of moving or changing a child from one service setting or delivery system to another. Preschool children who have special needs may make two transitions: one at age 3 and another at age 5 or 6.
- Transitions may be stressful for families, service providers, and children. Research shows that planning transitions and encouraging open communication among all parties involved increases the likelihood of a positive transition experience.
- Factors that affect the transition process include support for parents, time frames for the provision of services, transportation arrangements, interagency coordination, communication, the implementation of the IEP, and multicultural considerations.
- There is a need for an overall transition plan in the district or agency serving young children with special needs. The transition plan should include a needs assessment to determine what transition practices currently exist and the designation of a transition coordinator as a primary contact person.
- There are four stages in implementing a transition plan: (1) initial planning: families and service providers; (2) the IEP or IFSP: preparation, planning, and implementation; (3) introduction to the new program; and (4) evaluation of the transition.
- Developing a planned, systematic transition process involves coordination among sending and receiving service providers, children, and their families. Careful planning and open communication ensures a smooth transition for each child.

## *Key Terms*

evaluation of transitions
help agents for transitions
interagency coordination
multicultural factors in transitions
needs assessment
receiving school

seamless delivery system
survival skills
time frames
transition
transition coordinator

# Appendix A

# *Tests and Assessment Instruments*

## *Selected Instruments for Assessment and Evaluation*

This appendix contains a selected, alphabetized list of evaluation instruments and tests. The list is not exhaustive but provides brief descriptions of measures that are useful for assessing preschoolers with special needs and for voluntary identification of their families' resources, concerns, and strengths. The test descriptions are not designed to be evaluative. The names of the publishers are listed after the names of the tests. The addresses of the publishers are in Appendix B. Technical information about test standards and adequacies can be located in sources such as *The Standards for Educational and Psychological Tests* (American Psychological Association, 1995) and in *Assessment* (Salvia & Ysseldyke, 2000).

*Assessment, Evaluation, and Programming System.* Paul H. Brookes. A criterion-referenced instrument that assesses the fine and gross motor, adaptive, cognitive, social-communication, and social areas of development. Birth to 3 years.

*Battelle Developmental Inventory.* Riverside. A standardized test of multidomains including the cognitive, communication, motor, personal-social, and adaptive areas. Birth to 8 years.

*Bayley Scales of Infant Development.* The Psychological Corporation. Standardized test that provides scores from three scales: mental, motor, and behavior ratings. Ages 1 to 42 months.

*Brachen Basic Concepts Scale.* The Psychological Corporation. A screening test of concepts acquired in preschool, kindergarten, and primary grades. Ages preschool through primary.

*Branson Language Screening Test–2.* Western Psychological Services. A standardized screening test of vocabulary, grammar, visual and auditory perception, semantics morphology syntax, and pragmatics. Ages 3 to 8 years.

*Brigance Diagnostic Inventory of Early Development–Revised.* Curriculum Associates. A criterion-referenced inventory that assesses the following developmental areas: pre-ambulatory motor, gross motor, fine motor, self-help, prespeech, language, general knowledge and comprehension, social-emotional, and readiness. Birth to 7 years.

*Brunicks–Osoretsky Test of Motor Proficiency.* American Guidance Service. A normed test of fine and gross motor skills. Ages 4 to 16 years.

*Carolina Curriculum for Preschoolers with Special Needs.* Paul H. Brookes. A criterion-referenced instrument that assesses cognitive, communicative, social adaptive, fine motor, and gross motor areas of development. Ages 2 to 5 years.

*Child Behavior Checklist.* University of Vermont. A checklist of behavioral competencies, hyperactivity, and other behavioral problems of children. Parent checklists for ages 2 to 3 and for ages 4 to 18 years. Teacher's Report Form, ages 5 to 18 years.

*Clinical Evaluation of Language Fundamentals.* Psychological Corporation. An instrument that measures expressive and receptive language skills. Ages 3 to 6 years.

*Collier-Azusa Scales.* University of Texas. A test designed for use with children who are deaf-blind and who have severe disabilities. Five developmental areas are assessed: motor, perception, daily living skills, cognitive-communication-language, and social development. Birth to 5 years.

*Denver Developmental Screening Test–Revised.* Denver Developmental Material. A screening test of the following areas of development; personal-social, fine motor, adaptive, language, and gross motor. Birth to 6 years.

*Detroit Tests of Learning Aptitude–Primary: 2.* Pro-Ed. A normed cognitive test of overall mental functioning. Composites are provided that measure areas of mental processing. Ages 3 to 9 years.

*Developmental Indicators for the Assessment of Learning–Revised.* American Guidance Service. A preschool screening test of three developmental areas: motor, conceptual, and language. Some input also is provided about the social-emotional and physical areas. Ages 2 to 6 years.

*Developmental Test of Visual-Motor Integration.* Western Psychological Corporation. A visual-motor test of the child's abilities in copying designs. Ages 4 to 18 years.

*Early Childhood Environment Rating Scale.* Teachers College Press. An ecologically based instrument that was designed to evaluate preschool settings. The items are categorized in the following areas: personal care routines, furnishings, language-reasoning activities, fine and gross motor experiences, creative experiences, social development, and adult needs. Ages infancy and preschool.

*Early Language Milestone Screening Scale.* Modern Education Corporation. A screening test of communication that includes the auditory expressive, auditory receptive, and visual language areas. Birth to 3 years.

*Early Learning Accomplishment Profile.* Chapel Hill. Training-Outreach Project. A curriculum-based instrument that tracks a child's performance in developmental areas.

*Early Screening Inventory–Second Edition.* Teachers College Press. A screening test composed of three main sections: visual-motor adaptive, language cognition, and gross motor-body awareness. Ages 4 to 11.

*Expressive One Word Picture Vocabulary Test–Revised.* Western Psychological Services. A normative test of one word expressive vocabulary. Ages 2 to 12.

*Family Needs Scale.* Brookline Books. A rating scale for parents that has the following categories: food, shelter, vocation, child care, transportation, and communication. Parents are asked to rate their needs on a scale that ranges from "almost never a need" to "almost always a need." The scale is voluntary for the families.

*Family Functioning Style Scale.* Brookline Books. A rating scale of the qualities of strong families organized into three areas: family-identity, information-sharing, and coping-resource measures. Family members are asked to voluntarily respond to the items in these areas.

*Family Needs Survey.* University of North Carolina. An instrument that surveys family needs in the following areas: information, family and social supports, finance, explanation to others, child care, professional support, and community services. The survey is voluntary for the family.

*Family Resource Scale.* Brookline. An instrument that identifies a family's needs for social support and resources.

*Family Support Scale.* Brookline Books. A scale in which the family voluntarily rates their sources of support as to their amount of assistance to them.

*Gesell Developmental Scales–Revised.* Harper and Row. A criterion-referenced instrument that provides a developmental diagnosis in the areas of fine and gross motor, communication, personal-social, and adaptive behavior. Ages 4 weeks to 6 years.

*Goldman-Fristoe Test of Articulation.* American Guidance Service. A criterion-referenced test of articulation and stimulability for the correct production of speech sounds. Ages 2 to 16+.

*HELP for Special Preschoolers.* Vort Corporation. A criterion-referenced instrument that assesses the areas of self-help, motor, communication, social, and learning/cognition. Ages 3 to 6.

*Home Observation for the Measurement of the Environment–Early Childhood Edition.* University of Arkansas at Little Rock. An ecologically based instrument that assesses the quality and quantity of the physical environment of the home and the social, emotional, and cognitive supports given to preschool children in their homes. Ages 3 to 6 years.

*How Can We Help?* Child Development Resources. A survey of needs in which families voluntarily respond to questions about their needs/concerns in the following areas: information, child care, community service, medical and dental care, talking about our child, and planning for the future.

*Kaufman Assessment Battery for Children.* American Guidance Service. A standardized test of intelligence and achievement. Ages 2 to 12.

*Learning Accomplishment Profile.* Kaplan School Supply. A criterion-referenced test of five domains: cognitive, gross motor, language/cognitive, and self-help. Ages 6 months to 6 years.

*Leiter International Performance Scale.* Stoelting. A nonverbal normative test of intelligence. Ages 2 to 12 years.

*McCarthy Scales of Children's Abilities.* Psychological Corporation. A standardized test that provides a general cognitive index and profiles of the following abilities: verbal, nonverbal, number aptitude, motor coordination, and short-term memory. Ages 2 years, 6 months to 8 years, 6 months.

*Miller Assessment for Preschoolers.* Psychological Corporation. A screening instrument for developmental delays. Ages 2 to 9 years.

*Motor-Free Test of Visual Proficiency.* Pro-Ed. A test of visual perception without a motor component. Ages 4 to 8 years.

*Parenting Stress Index.* Pediatric Psychology Press. A screening and diagnostic instrument that measures the amount of stress in parent-child interactions. Child and parent characteristics are identified. Ages 3 to 10 years.

*Parent Needs Scale.* Guilford Press. An instrument containing 26 statements about possible needs of families of children with disabilities. The parents are asked to respond to the items to determine their needs. The survey is voluntary.

*Peabody Developmental Motor Scales.* Riverside. A normative and curriculum-based measure of fine and gross motor skills, including eye-hand coordination, finger dexterity, reflexes, locomotion, and balance. Birth to 83 months.

*Peabody Picture Vocabulary Test.* American Guidance Service. A normative test of receptive one-word vocabulary. Ages 2 to adult.

*Perkins-Binet Intelligence Scale.* Perkins School for the blind. A normative test of intelligence for children who are blind or visually impaired. Ages 3 to 18 years.

*Play Assessment Scale. Journal of Psychoeducational Assessment, 2,* 107–118. Play assessment of the cognitive, communication, and social skills of children with multiple disabilities. Ages 3 months to 3 years.

*Portfolio assessment.* A form of authentic assessment that involves evaluating progress through a collection of a child's work over time. At preschool age, the work can be documented in a portfolio through the use of a child's drawings, anecdotal records, photography, videos, and audio recordings.

*Pragmatics Screening Test.* Prentice-Hall. A test of pragmatics, including topic maintenance, formulation of speech acts, narration, revision of misunderstood directives, politeness, and the establishment of a referent for the listener. Ages 3 years, 5 months to 8 years, 5 months.

*Preschool Language Scale–3.* Psychological Corporation. A normative test of auditory comprehension, articulation, grammatical form and use, and basic concepts. Birth to 6 years.

*Preschool Learning Assessment Device.* Guilford. A test that uses a dynamic approach to assessment in the form of a test and retest model. The child is given a learning task to perform, and the assessor evaluates the preschooler's cognitive modifiabilty or the ability to improve performance through adult assistance. Preschool.

*Pyramid Scales.* Pro-Ed. A criterion-referenced test of adaptive behavior that includes the following subdomains: sensory skills, gross motor, eating, fine motor, toileting, dressing, social interaction, washing and grooming, language, recreation and leisure, domestic skills, reading, vocational, time, money, and number skills. The test is useful for individuals with severe disabilities. Ages childhood through adult.

*Receptive One-Word Vocabulary Test–Revised.* Academic Therapy Publications. A normative test of one-word receptive vocabulary. Available in English and Spanish. Ages 2–12.

*Receptive-Expressive Emergent Language Scale–2.* Western Psychological Services. A standardized test of prelinguistic skills of receptive and expressive communication. The information is obtained through parent report. Ages 1 to 3 years.

*Reynell-Zinkin Developmental Scales for Young Visually Handicapped Children.* Nfer-Nelson. A normative test of cognition and linguistic development for use with children who are blind or partially sighted. Birth to 5 years.

*Scales of Independent Behavior.* Riverside. A normative measure of independence and adaptive behavior in motor, social, communicative, personal living, and community living skills. Birth to adult.

*Sequenced Inventory of Communication Development–Revised.* Western Psychological Services. A standardized test of communication categorized into the following areas: sound discrimination and awareness, comprehension, motor, vocal, and verbal expressions. Ages 4 months to 4 years.

*Social Skills Rating System.* American Guidance Service. A rating scale that is ecologically based and provides information about the preschooler's social interactions with peers and adults. Preschool to adult.

*Stanford-Binet Intelligence Scale, Fourth Edition.* Riverside. Standardized test of general intelligence that yields mental age and intelligence quotient scores. Ages 2 to adult.

*System to Plan Early Childhood Services.* American Guidance Service. A judgment-based instrument comprised of three components: developmental, team, and program specifications. Information is gathered from several sources, instruments, and settings for the purpose of appraising developmental status, identification, prescription, program and progress evaluation. Preschool.

*Test of Early Language Development–2.* Pro-Ed. A normed test of expressive and receptive language including syntax, morphology, and semantics. Ages 2 to 8 years.

*Test of Early Social-Emotional Development.* Pro-Ed. A normative test of social-emotional development that has four components: a student rating scale, a teacher rating scale, a parent rating scale, and a sociogram. Ages 3 to 8 years.

*Test of Language Development-Primary–2.* Pro-Ed. A standardized test of grammatical understanding, receptive and expressive vocabulary, and expressive grammar. Ages 3 to 9 years.

*The Autism Screening Instrument for Educational Planning–2.* Pro-Ed. A screening test for autism that is a curriculum-compatible scale for diagnosis, placement, and program planning. Infants and preschoolers.

*The Columbia Mental Maturity Scale.* Psychological Corporation. A normative test of mental processing for children with language and motor deficits. Ages 3 years, 6 months to 10 years.

*The Hiskey-Nebraska Test of Learning Aptitude.* Author. A normative test for the assessment of children who are deaf or hearing-impaired. Ages 3 to 17 years.

*The Observation of Behavior in Socially and Ecologically Relevant and Valid Environments.* Plenum Press. An instrument that provides an observational method of assessment based on Piagetian theory. The test is a process-oriented instrument that is useful in estimating the abilities of children with multiple/severe disabilities. No specific ages are given.

*Transdisciplinary Play-Based Assessment–Revised.* Paul H. Brookes. A play-based arena assessment of the cognitive, communication, language, sensory-motor, and social-emotional areas of development. Ages 6 months to 6 years.

*Uniform Performance Assessment System.* Merrill/Prentice-Hall. A curriculum-referenced instrument for use with individuals whose developmental levels are below the age of 6 years. Areas assessed are pre-academic, communication, self-help, social, and gross motor. Adaptions are made for individuals with disabilities.

*Vineland Adaptive Behavior Scales.* American Guidance Service. A standardized measure of adaptive behavior in four areas: communication, daily living, socialization, and motor development. Birth to 19 years.

*Wechsler Preschool and Primary Test of Intelligence–Revised.* Psychological Corporation. A standardized test of intelligence that yields verbal, performance, and full-scale scores. Ages 4 to 6 years.

*Woodcock-Johnson Psychoeducational Battery III.* Riverside. A standardized test battery that has two sections: cognitive and achievement. Ages 2 to 90+ years.

# Appendix B

## Selected List of Test Publishers

The test publishers in this list are selected ones that commonly publish early childhood tests and instruments. The publishers are not necessarily endorsed by the authors.

*Academic Therapy Publications*
20 Commercial Boulevard
Novato, CA 94949-6191

*Allyn and Bacon*
75 Arlington Street
Boston, MA 02116

*American Guidance Service*
Publisher's Building
Circle Pines, MN 55014

*Charles E. Merrill Publishing Co.*
1300 Alum Creek Drive
Columbus, OH 43216

*Childcraft Education Corporation*
20 Kilmer Road
P.O. Box 3081
Edison, NJ 14052

*Clinical Psychology Publishing*
4 Conant Square
Brandon, VT 05733

*Curriculum Associates Inc.*
5 Esquire Road
North Billerica, MA 01862-2589

*Houghton Mifflin Co.*
1 Beacon Street
Boston, MA 02108

*Jastak Assessment Systems*
15 Ashley Place—Suite A
Wilmington, DE 19804-1314

*Kaplan School Supply Corporation*
P.O. Box 609
Lewisville, NC 27023-0609

*LinguSystems, Inc.*
716 17th Street
Moline, IL 61265

*Merrill/Prentice-Hall*
1 Lake Street
Upper Saddle River, NJ 07458

*Modern Curriculum Press*
13900 Prospect Road
Cleveland, OH 44136

*Modern Education Corporation*
P.O. Box 721
Tulsa, OK 74101

*Paul H. Brookes Publishing Co.*
P.O. Box 10624
Baltimore, MD 21285-0624

*Pro-Ed*
8700 Shoal Creek Boulevard
Austin, TX 78735

*Psychological Corporation*
555 Academic Court
San Antonio, TX 78204

*Riverside Publishing Co.*
425 Spring Lake Drive
Itasca, IL 60143-2079

*Slosson Educational Publications, Inc.*
P.O. Box 280
East Aurora, NY 14052

*Teachers College Press*
P.O. Box 1540
Hagerstown, MD 21740

*University of Michigan Press*
P.O. Box 1104
Ann Arbor, MI 48106

*University of Washington Press*
P.O. Box 85569
Seattle, WA 98105

*Vort Corporation*
P.O. Box 60132
Palo Alto, CA 94306

*Western Psychological Association*
12031 Wilshire Boulevard
Los Angeles, CA 90025

# Developmental Milestones:
# Infancy to Age Six

## Ages 0 to 3 Months

*Gross Motor Skills*
Turns head to both sides while on back.
Holds head up 90 degrees while on stomach.
Extends both legs.
Rolls from side to back.

*Fine Motor Skills*
Regards colorful objects briefly.
Follows with eyes downward.
Clenches fists.
Swipes at objects.

*Understanding of Language*
Searches with eyes for sound.
Responds to speech by looking at speaker.
Listens to voice for 30 seconds.

*Spoken Language*
Cries when hungry or uncomfortable.
Makes sucking sounds.

*Cognitive Skills*
Quiets when picked up.
Inspects own hands.
Reacts to disappearance of slowly moving object.

*Adaptive Skills*
Opens and closes mouth in response to food stimulus.
Naps frequently.
Sleeps 14+ hours per day.

*Social Skills*
Establishes eye contact.
Enjoys physical contact and tactile stimulation
Smiles.

## Ages 3 to 6 Months

*Gross Motor Skills*
Rolls from stomach to back.
Sits with slight support.
Holds head steady while sitting supported.

*Fine Motor Skills*
Holds hands unfisted.
Reaches for and grasps objects.
Shakes rattle.
Follows object with eyes without moving head.

*Understanding of Language*
Quiets to caregiver's voice.
Searches for and localizes sound.
Differentiates and responds differently to "friendly" and "angry" voices.

*Sources:* Batshaw (2001), Foruno et al. (1988), and Shelov and Hannemann (1998).

*Spoken Language*
Responds to sound stimulation by vocalizing.
Laughs, squeals, and coos.
Produces different sounds for
    different needs.

*Cognitive Skills*
Uses hands and mouth for sensory
    exploration of objects.
Plays with own hands and feet.
Initiates repetition of newly
    learned activity.
Searches for hidden object.

*Adaptive Skills*
Brings hand to mouth.
Places both hands on bottle.
Naps 2 to 3 times a day.

*Social Skills*
Discriminates strangers.
Enjoys social play.
Belly laughs.

## Ages 6 to 9 Months

*Gross Motor Skills*
Rolls back to stomach.
Sits without support.
Crawls.

*Fine Motor Skills*
Transfers objects from one hand
    to the other.
Manipulates toys actively.
Attempts to grasp small objects

*Understanding of Language*
Looks for family members when named.
Looks at pictures when named.
Responds to simple requests with gestures
    (e.g., bye-bye, up).

*Spoken Language*
Repeats some vowel and consonant sounds
    (babbles) when alone or when spoken to.
Says "mama" or "dada" unspecifically.
Shouts for attention.

*Cognitive Skills*
Responds to and imitates facial expressions
    of others.
Plays 2 to 3 minutes with single toy.
Plays peek-a-boo.

*Adaptive Skills*
Holds own bottle.
Mouths and gums solid foods.
Feeds self cracker.

*Social Skills*
Responds differently to strangers than
    to familiar people.
Smiles at mirror image.
Distinguishes self as separate from mother.

## Ages 9 to 12 Months

*Gross Motor Skills*
Stands with support.
Twists to pick up objects while seated.
Walks with both hands held.

*Fine Motor Skills*
Picks up objects with thumb and one finger
    (pincer grasp).
Places objects into container.
Removes objects from container.

*Understanding of Language*
Imitates gestures.
Stops ongoing action when told "no"
    (when negative is accompanied
    by appropriate gesture and tone).
Recognizes familiar words.

*Spoken Language*
Produces consonant sounds in babbling.
Babbles with inflection similar to adult speech.
Communicates meaning through imitation.

*Cognitive Skills*
Responds to simple verbal directions (e.g.,
    raises arms when someone says, "Come," and
    turns head when asked, "Where is daddy?").
Takes ring stack apart.
Moves rhythmically to music.

*Adaptive Skills*
Finger feeds self.
Holds out arms and legs while being dressed.
Holds cup with two hands, drinks
    with assistance.
Naps once or twice a day.

*Social Skills*
Copies simple actions of others.
Plays Pat-a-Cake.
Extends toy to show others.

## Ages 12 to 18 Months

*Gross Motor Skills*
Stoops and recovers.
Walks alone.
Throws ball forward.
Pulls toy, pushes toy.

*Fine Motor Skills*
Builds tower of three small blocks.
Places five pegs in pegboard.
Scribbles.
Turns pages of book.

*Understanding of Language*
Follows request to bring familiar object
    from another room.
Identifies two objects from group
    of familiar objects.
Identifies one or two body parts.
Enjoys explanation of pictures in book.

*Spoken Language*
Says first meaningful word.
Uses single words plus a gesture to ask
    for objects.
Uses "my" or "mine" to indicate possession.
Uses "no" meaningfully.
Has vocabulary of 10 to 15 words.

*Cognitive Skills*
Imitates actions and words of adults.
Recognizes several people outside of
    immediate family members.
Responds to words or commands with appro-
    priate action (e.g., "Stop that," "Get down").

Understands and responds to simple, familiar
    directions (e.g., "Give me the cup," "Show
    me your doll," "Get your shoes").

*Adaptive Skills*
Holds and drinks from cup with some spilling.
Chews food.
Removes socks and hat.
Sleeps at night 10 to 12 hours.
Naps once a day.

*Social Skills*
Recognizes self in mirror.
Plays ball cooperatively.
Imitates adult behavior in play.
Shows toy preferences.

## Ages 18 to 24 Months

*Gross Motor Skills*
Walks backward.
Seats self in child's chair.
Walks up and down stairs (hand held).
Runs fairly well.

*Fine Motor Skills*
Throws small ball.
Builds tower of six small blocks.
Turns knobs.
Imitates horizontal and vertical strokes.
Puts interlock beads together.

*Understanding of Language*
Follows series of two simple but related
    directions.
Identifies up to six body parts.
Understands personal pronouns.
Understands some action verbs and adjectives.

*Spoken Language*
Uses two-word sentences.
Names three pictures.
Refers to self by name.
Has vocabulary of about 50 words for
    important people, common objects, and
    the existence, nonexistence, and recurrence
    of objects and events (e.g., "more" and
    "all gone").

*Cognitive Skills*
Knows where things belong.
Matches sounds to pictures of animals.
Is able to match two similar objects
Looks at storybook pictures with adults,
    naming or pointing to familiar objects on
    request (e.g., "What is that?" "Where is
    the baby?").

*Adaptive Skills*
Unzips large zipper.
Removes shoes when laces undone.
Helps with simple household tasks.
Sits on potty chair.

*Social Skills*
Recognizes self in photograph.
Plays by self.
Displays a wide variety of emotions.
Attempts to comfort others in distress.

## Ages 24 to 30 Months

*Gross Motor Skills*
Catches large ball.
Kicks ball forward.
Walks up stairs and down stairs alone, both
    feet on step.
Jumps in place, two feet together.
Jumps a short distance.

*Fine Motor Skills*
Holds crayon with thumb and finger, not fist.
Folds paper.
Strings three large beads.
Snips with scissors.

*Understanding of Language*
Points to pictures of common objects when
    they are named.
Points to pictures involving action words.
Understands concept of one.
Understands two-step directions.

*Spoken Language*
Joins vocabulary words together to make two-
    and three-word sentences.
Shows frustration when not understood.
Sings parts of songs.

*Cognitive Skills*
Matches and uses associated objects
    meaningfully (e.g., given a cup, saucer,
    and bead, puts cup and saucer together).
Selects and looks at picture books, names
    pictured objects, and identifies several
    objects within one picture.
Demonstrates awareness of routine.
Recognizes familiar adult in photograph.

*Adaptive Skills*
Uses spoon with little spilling.
Washes and dries hands with assistance.
Pulls up pants with assistance.
Unbuttons large buttons.

*Social Skills*
Plays near other children.
Defends own possessions.
Becomes aware of gender differences.
Symbolically uses objects in play.

## Ages 30 to 36 Months

*Gross Motor Skills*
Stands on one foot.
Walks up stairs, alternating feet.
Walks on tiptoes.
Climbs on jungle gym.

*Fine Motor Skills*
Snips with scissors, follows line.
Imitates circular, vertical and horizontal strokes.
Rolls, pounds, squeezes, and pulls clay.
Paints with some wrist action; makes dots,
    lines, circular strokes.

*Understanding of Language*
Understands all common verbs and common
    adjectives.
Understands the concept of two.
Understands three-step directions.
Enjoys simple storybooks and requests
    them again.

*Spoken Language*
Joins words together to make three- and four-
    word sentences.
Speech is intelligible 80 percent of the time.

Gives first and last name.
Asks what and where questions.

*Cognitive Skills*
Identifies objects with their use.
Completes a three- to four-piece puzzle.
Stacks rings on peg in order of size.
Identifies several colors.

*Adaptive Skills*
Dresses self with assistance.
Uses fork and napkin.
Buttons large buttons.
Verbalizes need to use toilet.
May eliminate naps.

*Social Skills*
Separates easily from caregiver in familiar
    environment.
Participates in simple group activity
    (e.g., sings, claps, dances).
Experiences difficulty with transitions.
Begins to obey simple rules.
Knows gender identity.

## Ages 36 to 48 Months

*Gross Motor Skills*
Hops on one foot.
Pedals tricycle.
Catches a bounced ball.
Walks in a straight line.
Moves forward and backward with agility.

*Fine Motor Skills*
Draws circles and squares.
Draws a person with two to four body parts.
Drives nails and pegs.
Manipulates clay materials (e.g., rolls balls,
    snakes, cookies).

*Understanding of Language*
Understands concepts of same and different.
Understand size comparatives, (e.g., *big*
    and *bigger*).
Begins to understand sentences involving
    time concepts (e.g., "We are going to the
    zoo tomorrow").
Understands when told, "Let's pretend."

*Spoken Language*
Speaks in sentences of four to six words.
Tells about past experiences.
Has mastered some basic rules of grammar
    (uses *s* on nouns to indicate plural, uses *ed*
    on verbs to indicate past tense).
Can sing a song or repeat a nursery
    rhyme.
Speaks clearly enough for strangers to
    understand.

*Cognitive Skills*
Understands the concept of counting; counts
    to 3.
Correctly names some colors.
Knows own age.
Asks questions for information: *why* and *how*
    questions requiring simple answers.

*Adaptive Skills*
Pours well from small pitcher.
Spreads soft butter with knife.
Uses toilet independently.
Washes hands unassisted.

*Social Skills*
Joins in play with other children, begins
    to interact.
Shares toys, takes turns with assistance.
Engages in fantasy play.
Begins to negotiate solutions
    for conflicts.

## Ages 48 to 60 months

*Gross Motor Skills*
Does somersaults.
Swings.
Jumps from height.
Stands on one foot for 10 seconds
    or longer.

*Fine Motor Skills*
Copies triangle and other geometric
    patterns.
Copies a few capital letters.
Draws a primitive picture of a face.
Cuts on line continuously.

*Understanding of Language*
Enjoys jokes.
Follows three unrelated commands
  in proper order.
Understands sequencing of events when told
  (e.g., "First we have to go to the store, then
  we can make the cake, and tomorrow we
  will eat it").

*Spoken Language*
Recalls part of story.
Uses future tense.
Speaks in sentences of more than five words.
Vocabulary of about 2,000 words.
Talks about causality by using *because* and *so*.

*Cognitive Skills*
Knows own address.
Identifies nickel, dime, and penny.
Correctly identifies and names four
  to six colors.
Expands time concepts (can talk about
  *yesterday*, *last week* [a long time ago],
  *today*, *tomorrow*).

*Adaptive Skills*
Uses a table knife to cut easy food (e.g., a
  hamburger patty).
Dresses and undresses without assistance.
Laces shoes.

*Social Skills*
Plays and interacts with other children.
Plays "dress-up."
Seeks praise.
Wants to please friends.
More likely to agree to rules.

## Ages 60 to 72 months

*Gross Motor Development*
Skips.
Jumps rope.
Dances.
Rides bicycle with training wheels.

*Fine Motor Skills*
Copies triangle.
Prints name.
Colors within the lines.
Has handedness well established (i.e., child is
  left- or right-handed).

*Understanding of Language*
Understands approximately 13,000 words.
Uses pronouns correctly.
Understands opposites.
Understands size differences.

*Spoken Language*
Takes appropriate turns in conversation.
Speaks fluently.
Still learning such things as subject-verb
  agreement and some irregular past-
  tense verbs.
Communicates well with family, friends,
  or strangers.

*Cognitive Skills*
Knows birthday.
Names some letters and numerals.
Sorts objects by a single characteristic (e.g.,
  by color shape or size—if the difference
  is obvious).
Begins to relate clock time to daily schedule.
Attention span increases noticeably.

*Adaptive Skills*
Brushes teeth unassisted.
Ties bow.
Crosses street safely.

*Social Skills*
Chooses own friends.
Plays simple table games.
Plays competitive games.
Engages in cooperative play with other
  children involving group decisions, role
  assignments, fair play.

# Appendix D

## *Individualized Family Service Plan*

*Source:* Illinois State Board of Education, Springfield.

**CONFIDENTIAL DOCUMENT**

**CONFIDENTIAL DOCUMENT**                                                    Page 1

Child's Name: _____                    Who provided Information? _____                    Date: _____

## SECTION I: ENROLLMENT

**\*Child's Name:** _____                    **\*Date of Birth:** _____

**\*Gender: Male ☐  Female ☐**        **\*Child's Nickname:** _____        **\*Race:** _____

**\*Social Security Number:** ___-__-____        **\*Insurance Type(√) ☐ Private Insurance ☐ Medicaid ☐ Medicare ☐ Champus ☐ None ☐ DSCC ☐ Other**

**\*Child's Primary Language/Mode of Communication:** _____        Resident School Unit: _____

**\*Initial Referral Date:** _____        **\*LIC/LSA #:** _____        **\*Does the child have a medical diagnosis? (circle)  Y  N**

**\*Initial Referral Source:** _____        If yes, please list:

**\*IDEA Part H/B Eligibility:** _____        Primary Diagnosis: _____

Secondary/Other: _____

Name of Child's Primary Care Physician: _____        **Telephone Number (  )** _____

**\*Parent/Guardian/Surrogate Parent Information:  (circle one)**        (√) ☐ Surrogate Parent Requested        ☐ Participating

Name _____        Relationship to Child _____

Address _____        County _____

Town/City _____ State _____ ZIP _____        Primary Language/Mode of Communication _____

Telephone Day (  ) _____ Night (  ) _____        Best time to call _____

**\*Other Parent/Foster Parent/Caregiver Information:  (circle one)**

Name _____        Relationship to Child _____

Address _____        County _____

Town/City _____ State _____ ZIP _____        Primary Language/Mode of Communication _____

Telephone Day (  ) _____ Night (  ) _____        Best time to call _____

**\*Parent/Guardian/Surrogate Parent Information:  (circle one)**

Name _____        Relationship to Child _____

Address _____        County _____

Town/City _____ State _____ ZIP _____        Primary Language/Mode of Communication _____

Telephone Day (  ) _____ Night (  ) _____        Best time to call _____

**\*Service Coordinator Information:**

Name _____        Telephone _____

Agency Name _____

Address _____ Town/City _____ State _____ ZIP _____

CONFIDENTIAL DOCUMENT     *INDIVIDUALIZED FAMILY SERVICE PLAN*     **CONFIDENTIAL DOCUMENT**

Child's Name:     Who provided Information?     Date:     Page 2-A

### *SECTION II-A: FAMILY CONSIDERATIONS FOR THE IFSP*     This section is optional with informed, parental consent.

1. Please describe how you see your child (strengths, any concerns or needs).

2. Describe what you believe the strengths of your family are in meeting your child's needs.

3. What would be helpful for your child and family in the months or year ahead?

4. Please CHECK any of the following that you or other family members feel are important concerns or areas about which you would like more information and/or assistance?

**FOR YOUR CHILD**

- [ ] getting around
- [ ] communicating
- [ ] learning
- [ ] feeding, nutrition
- [ ] having fun with other children
- [ ] challenging behaviors or emotions
- [ ] equipment or supplies
- [ ] health or dental care
- [ ] pain or discomfort
- [ ] vision or hearing
- [ ] other _____

**FOR YOUR FAMILY**

- [ ] meeting other families whose child has similar needs/ support group
- [ ] finding or working with doctors or other specialists
- [ ] coordinating your child's medical care
- [ ] finding out more about how different services work or how they could work better for you
- [ ] planning or expectations for the future
- [ ] information about other available resources
- [ ] transportation
- [ ] child care
- [ ] finding or working with people who can help you in the home or care for your child so that you can have a break

- [ ] housing, clothing, jobs, food, telephone
- [ ] family training
- [ ] brothers, sister, friends, relatives and others
- [ ] information about the disability or diagnosis
- [ ] money to help with the extra costs of your child's special needs
- [ ] help with insurance/SSI/Medicaid
- [ ] recreation
- [ ] other _____

NOTES:

5. What else do you think would be helpful for others to know about your child and family?

6. Are there other concerns you would like to discuss?

**OUR FAMILY CHOSE TO COMPLETE THIS PAGE.**    [ ] YES    [ ] NO

CONFIDENTIAL DOCUMENT
Child's Name:

INDIVIDUALIZED FAMILY SERVICE PLAN
Who provided Information?

Date:

CONFIDENTIAL DOCUMENT
Page 2-B

SECTION II-B: ALL ABOUT OUR FAMILY

This section is optional with informed, parental consent.

WHO IS OUR FAMILY . . .

WHAT WE DO . . .

ABOUT OUR NEIGHBORHOOD, OUR COMMUNITY . . .

PEOPLE WHO ARE IMPORTANT TO OUR FAMILY ARE . . . RELATIVES, NEIGHBORS, FRIENDS, OTHERS . . .

THINGS WE LIKE TO DO AS A FAMILY . . .

OUR FAMILY CHOSE TO COMPLETE THIS PAGE.  ☐ YES    ☐ NO

Child's Name: _____

Who provided Information? _____

Date: _____

## SECTION II-C: ALL ABOUT MY CHILD

This section is optional with informed, parental consent.

| Activities or things | Prioritize Importance/ Time Frame | People my child is with in my home (names, ages, amount of time) |
|---|---|---|
| my child  I'd like my child | | |
| likes to do  to do | | |
| ☐ ☐ take a bath/play in water | ___ | |
| ☐ ☐ hold/play with toys | ___ | |
| ☐ ☐ watch/listen to tv | ___ | at day care/child care |
| ☐ ☐ play outside | ___ | |
| ☐ ☐ go to relative's/friend's house | ___ | |
| ☐ ☐ eat | ___ | |
| ☐ ☐ get and give hugs | ___ | with friends |
| ☐ ☐ play with Dad | ___ | |
| ☐ ☐ play with Mom | ___ | |
| ☐ ☐ listen to music | ___ | |
| ☐ ☐ ride in the car | ___ | |
| ☐ ☐ take naps | ___ | with neighbors, relatives |
| ☐ ☐ go to community center | ___ | |
| ☐ ☐ go to church/religious activities | ___ | |
| ☐ ☐ play with brother/sister(s) | ___ | |
| ☐ ☐ enjoy other children | ___ | in preschool |
| ☐ ☐ eat out | ___ | |
| ☐ ☐ go to a playground | ___ | |
| ☐ ☐ take a walk | ___ | |
| ☐ ☐ "roughhouse" | ___ | in other places |
| ☐ ☐ go grocery shopping | ___ | |
| ☐ ☐ other _____ | ___ | |

Comments/Priorities:

**OUR FAMILY CHOSE TO COMPLETE THIS PAGE.** ☐ YES ☐ NO

CONFIDENTIAL DOCUMENT

INDIVIDUALIZED FAMILY SERVICE PLAN

CONFIDENTIAL DOCUMENT

Page 3

Child's Name:

Date:

## SECTION III: SUMMARY OF CHILD'S PRESENT LEVELS OF PERFORMANCE

To be completed by the IFSP Team, drawing from description of the child, additional evaluations, assessments and/or observations, for each category. Includes needs and functioning in daily, routine settings and activities. Address all areas listed. This section is based on professionally acceptable, objective criteria including family report.

Statement of child's present level of physical development, including vision, hearing and health status:

CHILD'S STRENGTHS AND NEEDS

Present levels of performance in the following areas of development: communication (speech and language), cognition (thinking and reasoning), social/emotional, motor skills, and adaptive skills (such as dressing and eating).

Other information that is relevant to the development of this IFSP, including birth history, child's health history, medical diagnosis, child's nutritional status, etc.

### SECTION IV: NATURAL SETTINGS/ENVIRONMENT

The primary setting for young children is within the context of the family, their home, their culture, lifestyle and daily activities, routines and obligations. To the extent appropriate, services must be provided in the types of settings in which young children without disabilities, and their families, would participate. Section IV is intended to reflect a discussion of "what could be" for the child and family in terms of natural settings for EI services; not to reflect merely what is currently available.

| | |
|---|---|
| Check (✓) all sites to be considered as OPTIONS for early intervention services in your community.<br><br>Discussed    Selected<br><br>☐   ☐   **Child's Home**<br>☐   ☐   **Other Family Location**<br>☐   ☐   **Family Day/Child Care**<br><br>       **Community-Based Programs**<br>☐   ☐   Child Care Program<br>☐   ☐   HeadStart<br>☐   ☐   Infant/Toddler Play Group<br>☐   ☐   Preschool Program<br>☐   ☐   Early Childhood Program<br>☐   ☐   Early Intervention Classroom/Center<br>☐   ☐   Hospital<br>☐   ☐   Other _____ | Explain why sites selected are appropriate and reflect the most natural setting; and reasons why other sites were considered and rejected. Develop Outcome Statements to identify desired sites and measures that would be taken to implement services in the most natural setting. THIS SECTION SHOULD BE COMPLETED AFTER THE INDIVIDUAL OUTCOMES ARE DEVELOPED TO ENSURE THAT NATURAL SETTINGS CONSIDERATIONS HAVE BEEN UTILIZED.<br><br><br><br><br><br>Describe opportunities to interact with other children not receiving EI services and how interactions will be encouraged. |
| Indicate and describe below any changes necessary to permit this child to function more easily and successfully in the most natural setting (e.g., adaptations in rooms or environment, transportation, materials, equipment, technology, techniques or methods, curriculum, staff training, etc.) | |
| Describe accommodations to be used in ALL sites to promote successful participation. | Describe additional accommodations which are needed at certain sites only; indicate at which sites they are needed and why. |

CONFIDENTIAL DOCUMENT

INDIVIDUALIZED FAMILY SERVICE PLAN

CONFIDENTIAL DOCUMENT

Child's Name: _____

Date: _____

Page 5

### SECTION V: MAJOR OUTCOMES

Write only one Outcome for each page. Use 5-A, 5-B and so forth to identify each page individually. Each outcome will have several strategies, activities and/or services designed specifically to accomplish the Outcome.

WHAT DO WE WANT TO SEE HAPPEN? (Major outcome to be achieved; Annual Goal Statement for Part B preschool services)

WHAT DO WE SEE NOW? (Current status to include child and/or family resources, needs, priorities and concerns)

WHAT ARE SOME OF THE SPECIFIC THINGS THAT NEED TO CHANGE? (Reflects criteria used to evaluate outcome/mastery)

| THINGS WE WILL DO TO ACCOMPLISH THESE CHANGES (Strategies, Activities and Services) | Source of Support/ Resource | Location | Family's Evaluation | |
|---|---|---|---|---|
| | | | Date | Rating |
| | | | | |
| | | | | |

**Family's Evaluation:**

1. Situation changed; no longer needed.
2. Situation unchanged, still a need, strategy or project.
3. Implementation begun, outcome partially attained or accomplished.
4. Outcome completely accomplished or attained to family's satisfaction.

*SECTION VI: TRANSITION PLANNING CHECKLIST*     Use to identify transition activities into, within and from the Part H system.

| Transition Plan Provisions | Date Started | | Responsible Person(s)/Comments | Progress Notes/Dates Done |
|---|---|---|---|---|
| | From | To | | |
| Explore community program options for child. | | | | |
| Explore community program options for family members. | | | | |
| Discuss parental rights and responsibilities (i.e., procedural safeguards) under Part B. | | | | |
| Make available parent linkages related to transition. | | | | |
| Identify and implement steps to assist family members in evaluating available and eligible programs and services. | | | | |
| Send specific information to local education agency, with informed, written parental consent (referral to Part B system for eligibility determination/information for planning purposes). | | | | |
| Send specified information to other community programs upon parent request (with informed, written parental consent). | | | | |
| Identify and implement steps to help child and family prepare for transition. | | | | |
| Notify key medical care providers (with informed, parental consent) of the transition for activities and needs of the child and family members. | | | | |
| Other _____ | | | | |
| | | | | |
| | | | | |

## INDIVIDUALIZED FAMILY SERVICE PLAN

Child's Name:     Date:

### *SECTION VII: EARLY INTERVENTION SERVICES

| Column A Mo/Day/Yr Start Date | B Duration # Months or End Date | C Auth. Type | D Early Intervention Service Type | Related Outcome(s) (Page 5) | E Fund Source | F Provider Name | G Method | H Location (site) | I Frequency # of Times | Auth, Day, Wk, Mo, Qrt, Yr | Intensity Minutes/per Session |
|---|---|---|---|---|---|---|---|---|---|---|---|
| | | | Service Coordination | | | | | | | | |
| | | | | | | | | | | | |
| | | | | | | | | | | | |
| | | | | | | | | | | | |
| | | | | | | | | | | | |
| | | | | | | | | | | | |
| | | AT | Assistive Technology Equipment/Supplies | | | | J P/R/X | K HCPCS Code | L Description of Item(s) | M Qty | N Price |
| | | | | | | | | | | | |
| | | | | | | | | | | | |

Column C - Authorization Type:   AT: Assistive Technology-Equipment/Supplies

     DS: Direct Child Service

     E/A: Evaluation/Assessment

Column D - Early Intervention Service Options Include:

| | | |
|---|---|---|
| Assistive Technology | Occupational Therapy | Speech/Language Therapy |
| Audiology | Physical Therapy | Special Instruction |
| Medical Services* | Psychological | (Developmental Therapy) |
| (Diagnostic Purposes Only) | Service Coordination* | Transportation |
| Nursing/Health | Social Work | Vision |
| Nutrition | | |

*At no cost to the family if required to determine Part H eligibility, or to develop IFSP Outcomes

Column G - Method: Individual (I) or Group (G)

Column H - Location: Indicate Location Code and On Site (ON) or Off Site (OFF)

1. Home       5. Early Intervention Class/Program
2. Family Day Care       6. Hospital (Inpatient)
3. Regular nursery school/day care center       7. Residential Facility
4. Outpatient service facility       8. Other Setting

Column I - Frequency: Indicate Auth., daily, weekly, monthly, quarterly or yearly

     Intensity: Time in 15 Minute increments of One Session

Column J - Purchase (P), Rent (R), Repair (X)

Column K - HCPCS = Health Care Financing Administration Common Procedure Coding System

**\*THIS INFORMATION IS TRANSMITTED TO THE CENTRAL BILLING OFFICE (CBO)**

## SECTION VIII: OTHER SERVICES

To the extent appropriate, the IFSP must include a) medical and other services that the child needs but that are not required Part H services, b) the funding sources to be used to pay for those services and c) the steps that will be taken to secure these services and responsible person(s). This requirement does not apply to routine medical services unless a child needs those services and the services are not otherwise available or being provided. These services are not required Part H services and are included in the IFSP in order to reflect the comprehensive array of services and activities including, but not limited to, Part H services. Examples of other services include Respite Care, Well Child Care, Dental Care, Referral to WIC Services, Child Care Services, and so forth.

| OTHER SERVICE TYPE | PROVIDER INFORMATION | Person(s) Responsible Next Steps | FUNDING SOURCE | Mo/Day/Yr Start Date |
|---|---|---|---|---|
| | Name:<br>Address: | | | |
| | Name:<br>Address: | | | |
| | Name:<br>Address: | | | |
| | Name:<br>Address: | | | |
| | Name:<br>Address: | | | |

## SECTION IX: IFSP IMPLEMENTATION AND DISTRIBUTION AUTHORIZATION

The contents of this IFSP have been fully explained to me and, pursuant to Section 303.342(e): Parental Consent to Implement Early Intervention Services; I give my informed written consent to implement the services agreed to and described in this document.

_____
Parent/Legal Guardian/Surrogate Parent Signature

_____
(Other) Parent Signature

Date _____

Date _____

With informed, written parental consent, copies of this completed IFSP will be distributed to the following individuals: (✓ CHECK AS AUTHORIZED)

☐ Parents

☐ _____

☐ _____

☐ _____

_____
Parent/Legal Guardian/Surrogate Parent Signature

_____
Parent/Legal Guardian/Surrogate Parent Signature

### SECTION X: IFSP PLANNING TEAM

IFSP Meeting Participants: The following individuals participated in the development of this IFSP.

| NAME | TITLE/ROLE | AGENCY | SIGNATURE |
|------|-----------|--------|-----------|
|  |  | Family Member:<br>Telephone: |  |
|  |  | Family Member:<br>Telephone: |  |
|  |  |  |  |
|  |  |  |  |
|  |  |  |  |
|  |  |  |  |
|  |  |  |  |
|  |  |  |  |

IFSP Input: In addition to IFSP Meeting Participants, this plan was developed with information provided by the following person(s):

| NAME | TITLE/ROLE | AGENCY |
|------|-----------|--------|
|  |  | Name:<br>Telephone: |
|  |  | Name:<br>Telephone: |
|  |  | Name:<br>Telephone: |
|  |  | Name:<br>Telephone: |
|  |  | Name:<br>Telephone: |
|  |  | Name:<br>Telephone: |
|  |  | Name:<br>Telephone: |

INDIVIDUALIZED FAMILY SERVICE PLAN

Child's Name: _____

Date: _____

## SECTION XI: PROGRESS SUMMARY/MODIFICATIONS/REVISIONS TO OUTCOMES IN THE IFSP

As individual reviews are conducted, a single page should be developed for each Outcome. Number these 10-A, 10-B, and so forth.

| OUTCOME/PAGE NUMBER | PROGRESS SUMMARY | MODIFICATIONS/REVISIONS |
|---|---|---|
| | | |

Review Cycle: (✓ Check)  ☐ Quarterly  ☐ 6 Months  Other _____

SUMMARY COMMENTS:

_____
Parent/Legal Guardian/Surrogate Parent Signature

_____
Parent/Legal Guardian/Surrogate Parent Signature

_____
Service Coordinator Signature

_____
Service Provider Signature

_____
Other Signature: Type:

_____
Service Provider Signature

# Glossary

**accommodation**   A term used by Piaget to describe the process though which children build a knowledge base by adding new information gained through experience. The child incorporates new experiences into her or his already existing schemata or cognitive structures.

**activity-based curriculum**   The activity-based curriculum builds on the consistent use of daily activities, events, and interactions. It is based on a naturalistic environment that encourages participating in meaningful activities of interest and relevance to children, and it includes activities that promote interactions between children.

**activity-based intervention**   An intervention approach that stresses instruction for a child's individual goals in routine, planned, or child-initiated activities.

**adaptive behavior**   Skills needed to meet the demands of the environment and changes in a child's behavior as a result of maturation, development, and learning to meet the demands of many environments.

**adaptive coping skills**   Those skills a child uses to meet personal needs and to adapt to the demands of the environment.

**adaptive devices**   Equipment that enables individuals with disabilities to compensate for their disabilities. Examples are powered mobility equipment, augmentative communication, and adapted computers.

**adaptive equipment**   Equipment that can help the young child with motor disabilities in positioning, mobility, eating, and other activities of daily living.

**AIDS**   Acquired immune deficiency syndrome. Disease believed to be the result of infection of the HIV virus. AIDS inhibits the body's immune system's ability to fight disease.

**Americans with Disabilities Act (ADA)**   Legislation passed in 1992 that requires public accommodations to provide goods and services to people with disabilities on an equal basis with the rest of the general public.

**apnea**   Brief spells of not breathing.

**applied behavior analysis (ABA)**   Use of scientific behavioral principles to teach appropriate behaviors and reduce inappropriate behaviors.

**Asperger's disorder**   A disorder that overlaps with autism to some degree and is considered a mild form of autism.

**assessment**   The process of collecting information about a child for the purpose of making critical decisions concerning the youngster.

**assessment of emotional intelligence**   Systematic observation of the components of emotional intelligence based on a concept developed by Daniel Goleman. Some of the components are self-awareness, management of emotions, empathy, and conflict resolution.

**assessment of multiple intelligences**   Systematic observation of multiple intelligences based on a theory by Howard Gardner.

**assimilation**   A term used by Piaget to describe the process in which children integrate new information by reorganizing their current cognitive structures. The child focuses on the new features of the situation and changes the internal schemata or cognitive structure, accordingly.

**assistive technology**   Computer technology that includes devices to help children with disabilities.

**Atlanto-axial instability**   A problem sometimes seen in children with Down syndrome in which they exhibit increased mobility of the first two neck bones due to laxity of the ligaments that hold these bones together.

**attachment**   An affectional tie that one person forms to another specific person or persons binding them together and enduring over time.

**Attention deficit disorder (ADD)**   A disorder in which the essential feature is a persistent pattern of inattention and/or hyperactivity-impulsivity that is more frequent and severe than is typically observed in individuals at a comparable level of development.

**augmentative communication system**   A system of communication without speech whose purpose is to make it possible for one person to interact with another.

**authentic assessment**   Observations of skills performed in real-life situations.

**autonomy vs. shame and doubt**   The second of Erikson's stages of development, which revolves around issues of holding on and letting go, basically the conflict between freedom of self-expression and suppression of the child's self-assertion.

**behavioral curriculum**   Curriculum that is based on behavior theory that emphasizes changing, modifying, and managing the events in childrens' environments to further their learning.

**behavioral theory**   A theory of learning based on the ideas of B. F. Skinner, who is considered the father of behavioral psychology. Major tenets of behavioral theory include an analysis of behavior, its stimulus and consequences, systems of reinforcement, and direct instruction of skills.

**benchmarks**   Another term used in the 1997 authorization of IDEA for objectives on the IEP.

**biological risk**   Children who have conditions that are related to medical conditions, illness, or trauma, sometimes related to low birth weight, and who have a high probability for future disabilities.

**bonding**   The mother's or primary caregiver's affectional tie to the infant.

**bradycardia**   Slow heartbeat.

**case manager**   A service coordinator. The person under Part C of the law who coordinates services for the family, and for other specialists as they provide intervention for the child and family.

**case method instruction**   Instruction in which the students are asked to solve realistic family issues.

**center-based services**   A centralized location for services for young children with disabilities in which comprehensive services from many specialists are available.

**cephalocaudal development**   Sequence of motor development that refers to the progression of motor skills from the head to feet.

**cerebral palsy**   An illness characterized by several disorders of movement and posture that are due to a nonprogressive abnormality of the immature brain.

**chained responses of adaptive behaviors**   The linking of simple skills to perform more complex skills.

**children at risk**   The at-risk population of young children that has three subgroups: (1) environmental risk, (2) biological risk, and (3) established risk.

**children with disabilities**   Children with identified disabilities—such as physical, behavioral, cognitive, language, or learning disabilities—that require early intervention and special support strategies.

**cognition**   Refers to the "act of knowing." Cognitive abilities are clusters of mental skills that enable the child to know, be aware, think, conceptualize, use abstractions, reason, think critically, solve problems, and be creative.

**cognitive curriculum**   Curriculum, based on Piaget's theory, that emphasizes strategies that teach thinking and the need for children to learn through direct experiences.

**cognitive emphasis curriculum**   A program with activities that emphasize the child's thinking or cognitive development. Based on Piagetian philosophy.

**cognitive skills**   The mental abilities related to thinking and learning. Cognitive skills include knowing and recognition, the development of concepts, organization of ideas, remembering, problem solving, labeling and naming, understanding cause-and-effect relationships, drawing inferences, developing rules and generalizations, and making judgments and evaluations.

**cognitive theory**   A theory about the way children develop cognitive or thinking abilities. Cognitive skills include memory, discrimination, problem solving, concept formation, verbal learning, and comprehension skills.

**collaboration**   The process of working, respecting, and cooperating with others to achieve objectives.

**communication**   The exchange of messages through an interaction between a speaker and a listener. This interaction needs to be meaningful for both participants.

**community resources**   Agencies and organizations within the community that can be used by children with disabilities and their parents.

**community self-sufficiency**   A component of adaptive behavior that refers to age and culturally appropriate behaviors of children under adult supervision in community settings.

**computer technology** Using computers to help young children develop independence, self-help skills, visual and auditory concepts, language skills, and cognitive skills.

**concrete operations** A Piagetian term that refers to the stage of thinking at ages 7 to 11 years. During this period, the child's thoughts are still shaped by previous experiences, and they are dependent on concrete objects that the children have manipulated or understood through the senses.

**contingency contracting** Also known as the Premack principle. At its essence, this type of contract states; "If you do *X*, then you get to do *Y.*"

**continuum of alternative placements** A component of an IEP that assures that public schools provide an array of educational placements that meet the needs of children with disabilities.

**criterion-referenced instrument** A test that measures the skills the child has or has not mastered.

**cultural and linguistic diversity** Various cultural and language home environments in today's multicultural society that influence the growth and development of the child and the nature of intervention.

**culturally diverse families** Families in which the predominant culture and/or language is different from the mainstream. Sometimes referred to as culturally and linguistically diverse families.

**curriculum** A set of activities designed to achieve specific objectives in learning.

**curriculum-referenced test** A type of criterion-referenced test in which the curricular goals are the criteria for identifying objectives and measuring progress.

**custody issues** The questions involving which person or persons will serve as the child's legal guardian. In families in which there has been a divorce, one or both parents may serve as the child's guardian when making decisions about the child's welfare. Terminology varies depending on the state, but terms such as *joint legal custody, joint physical custody*, and *shared custody* may be used to define the parent's relationship to the child.

**DEC recommended practices** The practices recommended by the Division of Early Childhood, Council of Exceptional Children, for early intervention and early childhood special education for young children with special needs.

**developmental curriculum** Curriculum that assists children with special needs to go through the typical stages of development.

**developmental delay** A slowness in the growth of physical, behavioral, cognitive, language, or learning skills. The law permits schools to identify preschool children with disabilities under a general label, such as "developmental delay."

**developmental individual difference, relationship-based model (DIR)** A program that builds social and emotional development, intelligence, and morality for children with delays in social-emotional development. The program utilizes functional developmental capacities.

**developmental screening** A brief evaluation of a child's development. The purpose of the evaluation is to identify the child who needs further testing and to distinguish this child from typically functioning children.

**developmental theory** A theory that reflects a maturation view of child development. *Key* to this theory is the natural growth sequence of the young child. Under favorable, open circumstances, the child's own inner drive and need to learn will naturally emerge and develop.

**developmentally appropriate practice (DAP)** Guidelines set forth by the National Association for the Education of Young Children (NAEYC) for early childhood curriculum. The guidelines emphasize exploratory play, a child-initiated curriculum, a naturalistic setting, and child problem solving.

**direct instruction** A method of instruction in which the objectives are clearly specified and the instruction is structured to meet those objectives.

**directed teaching curriculum** A program with activities that emphasize the behavioral model of learning. Activities are teacher directed and planned.

**distributed practice** A method of toilet training in which elimination patterns are analyzed for the purpose of training the child. Reinforcement is given for success.

**dynamic assessment** An ecological approach to assessment that evaluates the child's ability to learn in a teaching situation.

**Early Head Start** A Head Start type of program for children younger than 3 years of age.

**early intervention** The provision of essential services and instruction during the critical early infancy, toddler, and preschool years.

**early literacy**   The child's early entrance into the comprehensive world of words, language, books, poetry, and stories.

**ecological/functional curriculum**   A curriculum that stresses meaningful learning and considers the environments in which children live and learn.

**ecological perspective**   Holistic assessment that uses information from the natural environments of the children being assessed and their performances in the developmental areas.

**educational environments**   The educational setting in which children are placed for instruction.

**empowering families**   Encouraging and enabling families to take an active role in decisions affecting their child's welfare. They have an important role in decision making and their competencies are valued.

**enabling families**   The help-giver creates opportunities for competencies to be acquired or displayed by families, which leads to their empowerment.

**environmental risk**   Conditions in an environment that may inhibit the normal growth and development of a child. Children from families with low income in which the parent is unable to perform essential parenting functions consistently may experience environmental risk.

**established risk**   Congenital or genetic disorders, which result in delays in cognition, physical/motor, speech and language, psychosocial, or adaptive skills.

**ethical dilemmas**   Situations that arise in which there are questions about not only what the law requires in a given situation but what is the right thing to do under certain circumstances.

**evaluation of transitions**   The phase during which families and service providers evaluate the effectiveness of the transition.

**failure to thrive (FTT)**   Failure to thrive is diagnosed when the baby's weight falls below the third percentile on standardized norms. FTT may be the result of organic dysfunction or other factors that relate to attachment and feeding issues.

**family assessment**   Voluntary evaluation of a family's strengths, resources, priorities, and concerns.

**family partnerships**   A partnership between the family and the early interventionist.

**family systems**   The family system consists of the child, the parent(s), caregivers, siblings, and extended family members, such as grandparents, neighbors, relatives, friends, and others who are closely involved in the child's life. These relationships are interdependent; that is, what happens to one member of the family system has an effect on other members of the family system.

**family systems theory**   An application of systems theory that states that what affects one part of a family system affects all of the other parts.

**fetal alcohol effect (FAE)**   Children who exhibit some, but not all, of the characteristics of fetal alcohol syndrome (FAS).

**fetal alcohol syndrome (FAS)**   An irreversible condition caused by consumption of alcohol by the mother during pregnancy, marked by a pattern of physical and mental birth defects.

**folic acid**   One of the B-vitamins which, when taken prior to and during pregnancy, has been found to reduce the incidence of spina bifida and other neural tube defects.

**formal operations**   Piagetian term describing a stage of development for children from ages 11 to 15. It reflects a major transition in the thinking processes. The child now has the capacity to work with abstractions, theories, and logical relationships without having to refer to the concrete. The formal operations period provides a generalized orientation toward problem-solving activity.

**Fragile X Syndrome**   A genetic disorder caused by a change of mutation on the X chromosome, resulting in cognitive and social emotional disorders in children.

**full inclusion**   A policy of placing all children with disabilities into normal or regular classes with their typical peers.

**functional behavioral assessment**   An approach to behavior modification that determines the relationship between specific variables in the environment and problem behaviors. This type of assessment is now mandated under IDEA-1997.

**gavage feeding**   Tube feedings for children whose disabilities prevent oral feeding.

**general case method**   A teaching strategy designed to help children generalize skills.

**handling**   A term referring to the process of carrying or moving a child from one position to another or from one place to another.

**Head Start**   Head Start began in the 1960s, targeting children from families with low income in which children had limited access to traditional early childhood services. Head Start legislation requires that children with identified disabilities comprise 10 percent of its enrollment. Head Start is recognized as an effective early childhood movement.

**help agents for transitions** Sources of support who can assist families during transition.

**High/Scope Project** A project begun in 1962 designed to reveal the effects of early intervention on children who are economically disadvantaged. The project is based on the cognitive curriculum of Piaget. The longitudinal study traces the impact of the project into adulthood.

**home-based services** Services for young children with disabilities performed in the child's home. Parents take on much of the responsibility of the intervention.

**humanistic theory** A humanistic approach to intervention that concentrates on providing an atmosphere of love and trust in teaching and learning, with an emphasis on open communication and the child's immediate experiences.

**hypertonicity** A condition in which the individual has too much muscle tone. Also known as spasticity.

**hypotonicity** A condition in which the individual has low muscle tone.

**inclusion** The placement of children with disabilities in general education placements with children without disabilities.

**inclusive settings** Settings that integrate young children with special needs and their typical peers.

**individualized education plan (IEP)** A written plan that contains individualized assessment procedures, services, and placements for eligible students with disabilities.

**individualized family service plan (IFSP)** A written plan that provides early intervention services for an eligible infant or toddler and is family centered. The IFSP can be substituted for an IEP for preschoolers (ages 3 to 5) with state permission.

**Individuals with Disabilities Education Act (IDEA) of 1997** Public Law 105-17.

**infants and toddlers** Part C of the Reauthorization of the Individuals with Disabilities Education Act of 1997 describes young children from birth through age 2 as infants and toddlers.

**informal family support programs** Those sources of support that exist apart from professional, therapeutic, or educational interventions. Examples include social organizations, religious organizations, and others.

**initiative vs. guilt** The third stage in Erikson's stages of development, which emphasizes the conflict between a child's curiosity and creativity and the potential for guilt when a child is made to feel *bad* for asking questions and trying new endeavors.

**integrated teacher training** Collaboration in programming among a variety of disciplines related to early childhood regular and special education training.

**integrated therapies** Therapy provided within the inclusive setting.

**integration** Settings in which children with disabilities are served with children who do not have disabilities.

**interagency collaboration** Agencies and professionals working together to provide appropriate services to families of children with special needs.

**interagency coordination** The process whereby sending and receiving agencies communicate information to facilitate a transition.

**interdisciplinary team** A team in which each professional assesses and intervenes separately, but the team does meet at some point to discuss and jointly develop interventions.

**interpreters** Personnel on the team who speak the language of the families and are able to explain what goes on in the school.

**intuitive thought** A Piagetian stage covering ages 4 to 7 years. It is characterized by the mastery of more complex forms of language. In addition, laws of physics and chemistry—such as conservation of number, mass, and the like—are brought under control.

**judgment-based assessment** The use of clinical judgments from multiple sources to collect assessment information about children.

**language** The knowledge and use of a symbolic code or set of rules involving syntax or grammar that communicates meaning between one person and another.

**lead agency** The agency appointed by the governor of each state to be the head agency for Part C (children from birth to age 3 who have disabilities). The lead agency coordinates activities with the other agencies in the state serving this age group.

**least restrictive environment** The initials LRE are often used to refer to the policy in IDEA to plan for the appropriate extent for children with disabilities to be with typical children.

**linguistic and cultural diversity**   See Cultural and linguistic diversity.

**mainstreaming**   A practice of placing children with disabilities into regular classes on a selected basis when the children can benefit from these placements.

**maltreated children**   Those children under age 18 who have been physically, mentally, or sexually abused or neglected by those adults responsible for the child's welfare.

**mediation**   A process that is offered without cost to the parents for resolving disagreements for parents about school issues.

**milieu teaching**   A strategy in which adults arrange the environment with interesting materials to encourage a child's language development.

**modeling**   A demonstration of the appropriate behavior. The child is supposed to pattern her or his behavior after the model.

**morphology**   The meaning units in words.

**multicultural factors in transition**   Concerns that must be addressed in transition planning when the family making the transition is from a culture other than the dominant one in the agency.

**multidisciplinary team**   A team in which the professionals provide isolated assessment and intervention services that are often fragmented and confusing to families.

**natural environments**   Placements—such as child care, homes, and preschools—that use play and other developmentally appropriate activities as learning opportunities.

**natural methods of assessment**   A method of assessment that uses information from the child's environment.

**natural setting**   Placements in normal settings, such as a regular classroom with typical children who do not have disabilities.

**naturalistic approach**   An instructional approach that emphasizes teaching within the context of a daily routine.

**naturalistic teaching**   Language instruction that occurs in natural settings.

**needs assessment**   An assessment that is conducted by the district to determine the transition practices that currently exist in the district.

**neurodevelopmental training (NDT)**   A program used by occupational and physical therapists that concentrates on manipulating and handling the child at either head, shoulders, trunk, or hips.

**nondiscriminatory assessment**   An assessment that does not discriminate against children from diverse cultural and linguistic backgrounds.

**normalization**   A principle that children with disabilities, even severe disabilities, should live at home with their families to provide the child with a normalized life experience. Historically, many young children with disabilities were placed in institutions soon after birth and isolated from society.

**norm-referenced instruments**   Tests that compare a child's performance to an appropriate referent group of children.

**Public Law 99-457**   The Early Childhood Amendments passed in 1986. This law amends Public Law 94-142.

**parallel play**   A type of play that occurs when a child plays among other children but does not interact with them and plays independently.

**Part B**   The part of the law that pertains to preschoolers with disabilities, ages 3 to 6.

**Part C**   The part of the law that pertains to the regulations for infants and toddlers with disabilities, from birth to age 3.

**performance assessment**   Information derived from observation of a child.

**personal-social responsibility**   A component of adaptive behavior in early childhood that focuses on both independent play and cooperation with peers, appropriate interactions with adults and children, and responsible behaviors.

**pervasive developmental disorder (PDD)**   A disorder in which children show severe deficits and pervasive impairment in multiple areas of development, such as difficulty with social interactions, communication, and stereotypic behaviors; however, these impairments are not severe enough to warrant a diagnosis of autism.

**phonological awareness**   The child's ability to focus on and manipulate the sounds of language in spoken words.

**phonology**   The sound system of language and rules for sequencing and structuring speech sounds into words.

**Piaget's stages of cognitive development**   In Piagetian theory, the series of sequential stages of cognitive development through which children progress. Each child progresses through each of these stages in a common sequential manner. While age levels are attached to each stage, these are only approximations of the age at which each stage is reached.

**play-based assessment** An assessment through observation of a child at play. Information can be obtained about the child's development and patterns of interaction with others.

**polydrug abuse** Abuse of several substances such as alcohol, tobacco, and cocaine or other drugs at the same time.

**portfolio assessment** A type of authentic assessment in which the assessor looks at a collection of a student's work arranged into a portfolio.

**positioning** Placing a child in carefully selected positions in order to stabilize the body, normalize muscle tone, and prevent further deformity.

**positioning techniques** Interventions that emphasize proper supports and position for a child with disabilities.

**positive reinforcement** The rewarding of appropriate behaviors to increase the chances that the behavior will occur again in similar situations.

**postural reflexes** Those reflexes that assist the child to maintain an upright posture and orientation.

**pragmatics** The use, purpose, and function of language.

**prelinguistic** The nonverbal participation in communication by infants.

**preoperational thought** The second stage of Piaget's theory of child development that occurs from 2 to 7 years. During this stage, thinking becomes representational and internalized.

**preschool special category** An option that states can use to avoid labeling a preschool child with a specific disability.

**preschoolers** In the 1997 Individuals with Disabilities Education Act, preschoolers are children ages 3 through 5.

**primitive reflexes** Those reflexes that help the infant survive and protect the infant during the first year of life.

**program evaluation** A systematic, objective evaluation for determining the effectiveness of interventions and the program itself.

**prompting** The provision of extra cues, such as verbal or physical guidance, to assist the child in acquiring skills.

**proximo-distal** A sequence of motor development that refers to development from the spine and center of the body to the extremities.

**psychodynamic theory** This theory looks at children's development in terms of unconscious drives, conflicts, and motivations. Two prominent theorists in this area are Freud and Erikson.

**psychosocial approach** An approach to teaching that emphasizes the psychological and social development of a child.

**rapid method** A toilet training method, used mostly for children with moderate to severe disabilities, that increases the intake of liquid so that the children need to urinate more often. The rapid method involves a lengthy commitment of time and effort for the trainer but in some cases can result in children achieving independence in toileting within a short time.

**Reactive attachment disorder of infancy and early childhood** A severe lack of attachment that affects the child's entire emotional development.

**receiving school** The new placement facility or service that results from transition—the child's new setting.

**respite care** The use of an organized service to provide temporary relief from the caregiving responsibilities associated with parenting a child with a disability.

**reinforcement** A behavior management strategy. A reinforcer is an event that follows a behavior and has the effect of controlling that behavior. Reinforcers are consequences that increase the likelihood that a behavior will occur in the future.

**reliability** The consistency of the test or instrument.

**Reggio Emilia approach** A type of curriculum based on constructivist theory.

**response cost** Procedures that penalize the child for inappropriate behavior.

**Rett's disorder** This syndrome has been reported in females and develops in the young child after a period of apparently normal development in the early childhood years. The disorder is accompanied by loss of fine motor skills, language skills, and social skills, combined with a tendency toward seizures and respiratory disorders.

**screening** A stage of the assessment process in which children are given a cursory examination to detect children who *may* have problems.

**seamless delivery system** Early intervention that is provided without disruption for children from birth to age 6.

**seizures** Sudden and abnormal discharges of neurons in the brain accompanied by changes in motor, sensory function, or consciousness. A common name is convulsion.

**self-care**   A component of adaptive behavior that consists of skills needed for behaviors such as toileting, eating, dressing, and grooming.

**semantics**   The vocabulary of language.

**sensorimotor stage**   According to Piaget, the sensorimotor period occurs from birth to 2 years of age. During this stage, the child learns through sense and movement and by interacting with the physical environment. By moving, touching, hitting, biting, and so on, and by physically manipulating objects, the child learns about the properties of space, time, location, permanence, and causality.

**sensory integration**   A theory used by occupational therapists that emphasizes the relationship between the neurological processes and human behavior.

**serious emotional disturbance**   One of the categories under IDEA that consists of a condition displayed over a long time and to a marked degree and demonstrating problems in socialization, interpersonal relationships, and other areas.

**service coordination**   A service provided in the IFSP to families of infants and toddlers that assists the families to access early intervention and related services. The responsibilities of a service coordinator is to assist the family in accessing these services and to coordinate with other agencies.

**shaping**   One of the approaches used in behavior modification that reinforces certain behaviors leading to successive approximations toward establishment of a specific behavior.

**social adjustment**   Abilities needed for adjustment to new situations and for regularity of behavior patterns.

**social learning theory**   A theory that recognizes that the social context in which learning occurs significantly influences the learning process. The social interactions between the child and others (parent, teacher, caregiver, other family members) are a needed ingredient in learning.

**speech**   The verbal mechanism for conveying oral language.

**stages of acceptance**   The stages of acceptance parents may experience in coming to terms with their child's disabilities. These stages are similar to those manifested by people who are grieving and include shock, disbelief, denial, anger, bargaining, depression, and acceptance.

**strange situation**   An evaluation of a child's attachment to his or her mother developed by Ainsworth that uses a series of specific separations and reunions with both the mother and a stranger.

**support groups**   Groups of parents and family members that are formed for the purpose of offering emotional and informational resources and support for families. The groups may be facilitated by families themselves or by professionals.

**survival skills**   Skills that children need to possess in order to adapt more easily to a new setting. Skills include working independently, group participation, following directions, and learning to use varied material.

**suspected abuse**   Physical or sexual abuse as well as neglect that professionals may suspect is happening and are mandated to report. Professionals are provided with immunity for such reports, even if the investigation proves that the suspicions were false.

**syntax**   The sentence structure of language.

**systematic instruction**   Instruction that includes a task analysis of the target skill. Also the use of procedures such as shaping, prompting, modeling, and response cost to assist the child in acquiring the skill.

**systems analysis**   A theory based on the idea that whatever happens to one part of a system affects all of the other parts.

**task analysis**   A process used in intervention that sequences the steps needed to reach an objective.

**temperament**   Certain innate characteristics, personality traits, and a way of relating to the world; an underlying style or pattern of a person's behavior that sets the stage for her or his reactions to the world.

**teratogen**   An agent or factor, such as alcohol, that causes the production of physical or mental defects in a developing embryo.

**therapeutic feeding**   A feeding intervention that consists of rubbing or stroking to decrease hypersensitivity around the mouth and stretching to develop oral-motor tone.

**theraplay**   An intensive, short-term treatment based on interactions modeled by the theraplay interventionist, which is modeled on naturally occurring healthy parent-child relationship activities.

**time frames**   The schedule of events, or "calendar," leading up to and through the child's transition into a new program.

**time out** The removal of a child from an apparently reinforcing setting to a presumably nonreinforcing setting for a specified and limited amount of time. It is used to decrease specific target behaviors.

**timed toileting** A method of toilet training in which the child is placed on a toilet at times he or she would usually eliminate.

**transdisciplinary team** A team in which the professionals and families share roles and purposely cross disciplines during assessment, planning, and intervention. This type of team avoids duplication of services.

**transition** Involves transferring or moving the child from one type of organized program to another. Going to a new placement can be a traumatic experience for the young child and should be carefully planned, coordinated, and monitored. Transition for young children with disabilities occurs for infants and toddlers at age three and for preschoolers at age six.

**transition coordinator** The primary contact person whom parents and service providers can contact during transition for specific information regarding a particular child.

**traumatic brain injury (TBI)** Injury to the brain caused by trauma, either by a forceful blow to the head, an accident, or being shaken violently.

**trust vs. mistrust** The first of Erikson's stages of development, the primary focus of which is whether the child's basic needs are met in a sensitive, predictable, and caring way.

**validity** The degree to which an instrument measures what it was designed to actually measure.

**whole-task sequence** The teaching of all the steps in a task analysis each time the child practices a target skill.

**zone of proximal development (ZPD)** Associated with the theories of Vygotsky. There is a range of difficulty levels for a task that the child is engaged in. The lower end is a level that is very easy for the child and the upper end is a level beyond the student's capacity. The ZPD refers to the midpoint and is the appropriate level for learning. This level provides a challenge but can be accomplished with the assistance of the adult in the environment.

# References

Aase, J. M. (1994). Clincial recognition of FAS: Difficulties of detection and diagnosis. *Alcohol Health and Research World, 18,* 5–9.

Abbeduto, L., & Short-Meyerson, K. (2002). Linguistic influences on social interaction. In H. Goldstein, L. A. Kaczmarek, & K. M. English (Eds.), *Promoting social communication* (pp. 27–54). Baltimore: Paul H. Brookes.

Abbott, C. F., & Gold, S. (1991). Conferring with parents when you're concerned that their child needs special services. *Young Children, 46* (4), 10–14.

Ainsworth, M. D. S. (1973). The development of infant-mother attachment. In B. M. Caldwell & H. Ricciutti (Eds.), *Review of child development research* (pp. 1–94). Chicago: The University of Chicago Press.

Ainsworth, M. D. S. (1992). Early caregiving and later patterns of attachment. In M. H. Klaus & M. O. Robertson (Eds.), *Birth, interaction and attachment.* Skillman, NJ: Johnson & Johnson.

Ainsworth, M. D. S., Blehar, M., Waters, E., & Wall, S. (1978). *Patterns of attachment: A psychological study of the Strange Situation.* Hillsdale, NJ: Erlbaum.

Allen, L., & Majidi-Ahi, S. (1989). Black American children. In J. Taylor Gibbus & L. Huang-Naheme (Eds.), *Children of color: Psychological interventions with minority youth* (pp. 148–178). San Francisco: Jossey-Bass.

Aller, S. K., & Solano, T. (2000). Tech for TOTS: Assistive technology for infants and young children, part 2. *Exceptional Parent, 30* (7), 64–67.

Allport, G. W. (1937). *Personality: A psychological interpretation.* New York: Holt.

American Academy of Pediatrics. (2001). Committee of Children with Disabilities. Developmental surveillance and screening of infants and young children. *American Academy of Pediatrics, 108* (1), 192–196.

American Psychiatric Association. (1994). *Diagnostic and statistical manual of mental disorders* (4th ed.). Washington, DC: Author.

American Psychological Association. (1995). *The standards for educational and psychological tests.* Washington, DC: Author.

Americans with Disabilities Act and Head Start: Practical strategies for developing compliance plans. (1992). *Quarterly Resource, 7* (1), 17–28.

Anderson, P. P., & Fenichel, E. S. (1989). *Serving culturally diverse families of infants and toddlers with disabilities.* Washington, DC: National Center for Clinical Infant Programs.

Andrews, K. B. (1999). ADHD: Implications for early childhood education. *Early Childhood Education Journal, 27* (2), 115–117.

Arcia, E., & Gallagher, J. J. (1994). Policy implications of differential status among Latino subgroups. *Infant Toddler Intervention, 4,* 65–73.

Arter, J. A., & Spandel, V. (1991). *Using portfolios of student work in instruction and assessment.* Portland, OR: Northwest Regional Educational Laboratory.

Arthur, M., Bochner, S., & Butterfield, N. (1999). Enhancing peer interactions within the context of play. *International Journal of Disability, Development and Education, 46* (3), 367–381.

Athey, I. (1984). Contributions of play to development. In T. D. Yawkey & A. D. Pellegrine (Eds.), *Child's play: Developmental and applied* (pp. 9–28). Hillsdale, NJ: Erlbaum.

Au, K. H., & Kawakami, A. J. (1991). Culture and ownership. *Childhood Education, 67,* 280–284.

Axline, V. (1947). *Play therapy.* New York: Ballantine Books.

Ayres, J. (1978). Learning disabilities and the vestibular system. *Journal of Learning Disabilities, 11,* 18–29.

Ayres, J. (1981). *Sensory integration and the child.* Los Angeles: Western Psychological Services.

Azrin, N. H., & Armstrong, P. M. (1973). The "minimeal"—A method for teaching eating skills to the profoundly retarded. *Mental Retardation, 11,* 9–13.

Azrin, N. H., Sneed, T. J., & Foxx, R. M. (1973). Dry bed: A rapid method of eliminating bedwetting (enuresis) of the retarded. *Behavior Research and Therapy, 11,* 427–434.

Bagnato, S. J., & Neisworth, J. T. (1990). *System to Plan Early Childhood Services (SPECS).* Circle Pines, MN: American Guidance Service.

Bagnato, S. J., & Neisworth, J. T. (1991). *Assessment for early intervention: Best practices for professionals.* London: Guilford.

Bagnato, S. J., & Neisworth, J. T. (2000). Assessment is adjusted to each child's development. *Birth–5 Newsletter, 1* (2), 1.

Bagnato, S. J., Neisworth, J. T., & Munson, S. M. (1989). *Linking developmental assessment and early intervention: Curriculum-based prescriptions* (2nd ed.). Rockville, MD: Aspen.

Bagnato, S. J., Neisworth, J. T., & Munson, S. M. (1997). *Linking assessment and early intervention: An authentic curriculum-based approach.* Baltimore: Paul H. Brookes.

Bailey, D. B. (1987). Collaborative goal setting with families: Resolving differences in values and priorities for services. *Topics in Early Childhood Special Education, 7,* 59–71.

Bailey, D. B. (1996). An overview of interdisciplinary training. In D. Bricker & A. Widerstrom (Eds.), *Preparing personnel to work with infants and young children and their families* (pp. 3–22). Baltimore: Paul H. Brookes.

Bailey, D. B., Blasco, P. M., & Simeonsson, R. J. (1992). Needs expressed by mothers and fathers of young children with disabilities. *American Journal on Mental Retardation, 97,* 1–10.

Bailey, D. B., Harms, T., & Clifford, R. M. (1983). Matching changes in preschool environments to desired changes in child behavior. *Journal of the Division for Early Childhood, 7,* 61–68.

Bailey, D. B., & Nabors, L. A. (1996). Tests and test development. In M. Bailey & M. Wolery (Eds.), *Assessing infants and preschoolers with special needs,* (pp. 23–43). Englewood Cliffs, NJ: Prentice-Hall.

Bailey, D. B., Simeonsson, R. J., Yoder, D. E., & Huntington, B. S. (1990). Infant personnel preparation across eight disciplines: An integrative analysis. *Exceptional Children, 57,* 26–35.

Bailey, D. B., Jr., Skinner, D., Rodriguez, P., Gut, D., & Correa, V. (1999). Awareness, use and satisfaction with services for Latino parents of young children with disabilities. *Exceptional Children, 65* (3), 367–381.

Bailey, D. B., & Wolery, M. (1984). *Teaching infants and preschoolers with handicaps.* Columbus, OH: Merrill.

Bailey, D. B., & Wolery, M. (1992). *Teaching infants and preschoolers with disabilities.* Englewood Cliffs, NJ: Prentice-Hall.

Baker, B. L., & Brightman, A. J. (1997). *Steps to independence: Teach everyday skills to children with special needs.* Baltimore: Paul H. Brookes.

Baker, E., Wong, M., & Walberg, H. (1995). The effects of inclusion on learning. *Educational Leadership, 52* (4), 33–35.

Ball, E., & Blachman, B. (1988). Phoneme segmentation training: Effect on reading readiness. *Annals of Dyslexia, 38,* 297–225.

Barkley, R. A. (2000). Genetics of childhood disorders: XVII. ADHD, part 1: The executive functions and ADHD. *Journal of the American Academy of Child and Adolescent Psychiatry, 39* (8), 1064–1068.

Barnett, W. S. (1995). Long-term effects of early childhood programs on cognitive school outcomes. *The Future of Children; Long-Term Outcomes of Early Childhood Programs, 5* (3), 25–50.

Barrera, I. (2000). Honoring differences: Essential features of appropriate ECSE services for young children from diverse sociocultural environments. *Young Exceptional Children, 3* (4), 17–24.

Batshaw, M. L. (2001). How a young child develops. In M. L. Batshaw (Ed.), *When your child has a disability. The complete sourcebook of daily and medical care.* (2nd ed.) (pp. 35–55). Baltimore: Paul H. Brookes.

Batshaw, M. L., & Perret, Y. M. (1986). *Children with handicaps: A medical primer.* Baltimore: Paul H. Brookes.

Batshaw, M. L., & Rose, N. C. (1997). Birth defects, prenatal diagnosis, and prenatal therapy. In M. L. Batshaw (Ed.), *Children with disabilities* (pp. 35–52). Baltimore: Paul H. Brookes.

Baylcy, N. (1968). Behavioral correlates of mental growth: Birth to thirty-six years. *American Psychology, 23,* 1–7.

Bazyk, S. (1990). Factors associated with the transition to oral feeding in infants fed by nasogastric tubes. *American Journal of Occupational Therapy, 43,* 723–728.

Bearcrane, J., Dodd, J. M., Nelson, J. R., & Ostwald, S. W. (1990). Educational characteristics of Native Americans. *Rural Educator, 11,* 1–5.

Beckman, P. J., Robinson, C. C., Jackson, B., & Rosenberg, S. A. (1986). Translating developmental findings into teaching strategies for young, handicapped children. *Journal of the Division for Early Childhood, 10,* 45–52.

Becvar, D. S., & Becvar, R. J. (1993). *Family therapy: A systematic approach.* Boston: Allyn and Bacon.

Behrman, R. (1995). Statement of purpose. *The Future of Children: Long-Term Outcomes of Early Childhood Programs, 5,* i.

Bender, B. G. (1999). Learning disorders associated with asthma and allergies. *School Psychology Review, 28* (2), 204–214.

Bennett, J., & Grimley, L. K. (2001). Parenting in the global community: A cross cultural/international perspective. In M. J. Fine & S. W. Lee (Eds.), *Handbook of diversity in parent education: The changing faces of parenting and parent education* (pp. 97–133). San Diego: Academic Press.

Bergman, P., & Escalona, S. (1949). Unusual sensitivities in young children. *Psychoanalytic Studies of Young Children*, 332–352.

Berns, R. M. (1993). *Child, family, community.* New York: Harcourt Brace Jovanovich.

Bernstein, V. J. (1989). Dramatic responses in a safe space: Helping parents to reach difficult babies. *Zero to Three, 9,* 1–5.

Bernthal, J. E., & Bankson, N. W. (1998). *Articulation and phonological disorders.* Boston: Allyn and Bacon.

Berrueta-Clement, J., Schweinhart, L., Barrett, S., Epstein, A., & Weikert, D. (1984). *Changed lives.* Ypsilanti, MI: High Scope Educational Foundation.

Berry, J. O., & Zimmerman, W. W. (1983). The stage model revisited. *Rehabilitation Literature, 44,* 275–278.

Bettelheim, B. (1967). *The empty fortress.* New York: Macmillan Free Press.

Bettelheim, B. (1987, March). The importance of play. *Atlantic Monthly,* 35–46.

Beukelman, D. R., & Mirenda, P. (1998). *Augmentative and alternative communication: Management of severe communication disorders in children and adults.* Baltimore: Paul H. Brookes.

Bigge, J. L. (1991). *Teaching individuals with physical and multiple disabilities.* Englewood Cliffs, NJ: Prentice-Hall.

Blachman, B. (1989). Phonological awareness and word recognition: Assessment and intervention. In A. G. Kamhi & H. W. Catts (Eds.), *Reading disabilities: A developmental language perspective* (pp. 133–158). Boston: College-Hill.

Blasco, P. M. (2001). *Early intervention services for infants, toddlers, and their families.* Boston: Allyn and Bacon.

Block, M. E. (1994). *A teacher's guide to including students with disabilities in regular physical education.* Baltimore: Paul H. Brookes.

Bloom, B. S. (1976). *Human characteristic and school learning.* New York: McGraw-Hill.

Blosser, J. L., & DePompei, R. (1994). *Pediatric traumatic brain injury.* San Diego: Singular Publishing.

Blue-Manning, M. J., Turnbull, A. P., & Pereira, L. (2000). Group action planning as a support strategy for Hispanic families: Parent and professional perspectives. *Mental Retardation, 38* (3), 262–275.

Bobath, K., & Bobath, B. (1972). Cerebral Palsy. In P. H. Peterson & C. E. Williams (Eds.), *Physical therapy services in the developmental disabilities* (pp. 31–185). Springfield, IL: Charles C. Thomas.

Bondurant-Utz, J. A. (1994). An overview of the assessment process: Introduction. In J. A. Bondurant-Utz and L. B. Luciano, (Eds.), *A practical guide to infant and preschool assessment in special education* (pp. 3–13). Boston: Allyn and Bacon.

Bondurant-Utz, J. (2002). *Practical guide to assessing infants and preschoolers with special needs.* Upper Saddle River, NJ: Merrill/Prentice-Hall.

Bondurant-Utz, J. A., & Luciano, L. B. (1994). *A practical guide to infant and preschool assessment in special education.* Boston: Allyn and Bacon.

Bowe, F. (1995). *Birth to five: Early childhood special education.* New York: Delmar.

Bowlby, J. (1969). *Attachment.* New York: Basic Books.

Bowlby, J. (1973). *Separation: Anxiety and anger.* New York: Basic Books.

Bowlby, J. (1980). *Attachment and loss: Vol. 3. Loss, sadness and depression.* New York: Basic Books.

Brandenburg-Ayres, S. (1990). *Working with parents* (Bilingual/ESOL Special Education Collaboration and Reform Project). Gainesville: University of Florida.

Bredekamp, S. (Ed.). (1987). *Developmentally appropriate practice in early childhood programs serving children from birth through age 8.* Washington, DC: National Association for the Education of Young Children.

Bredekamp, S. (1993). The relationship between early childhood education and early childhood special education: Healthy marriage or family feud? *Topics in Early Childhood Special Education, 13* (3), 258–273.

Bredekamp, S., & Copple, C. (Eds.) (1997). *Developmentally appropriate practice in early education programs* (rev. ed.). Washington, DC: National Association for the Education of Young Children.

Bredekamp, S., & Rosegrant, T. (1992). *Reading potentials: Appropriate curriculum and assessment for young children* (Vol. 1). Washington, DC: National Association for the Education of Young Children.

Bricker, D. D. (1986). *Early education of at-risk and handicapped infants, toddlers, and preschool children.* Glenview, IL: Scott Foresman.

Bricker, D. D. (1993). Then, now, and the path between: A brief history of language intervention. In A. P. Kaiser & D. B. Gray (Eds.), *Enhancing children's communication: Research foundations for intervention* (pp. 11–31). Baltimore: Paul H. Brookes.

Bricker, D. D. (1995). The challenge of inclusion. *Journal of Early Intervention, 19* (3), 179–194.

Bricker, D. D. (1996). Assessment for IFSP development and intervention planning. In S. J. Meisels & E.

Fenichel (Eds.), *New visions for the developmental assessment of infants and young children* (pp. 169–192). Washington, DC: Zero to Three National Center for Infants, Toddlers, and Families.

Bricker, D. D. (1998). *An activity-based approach to early intervention.* Baltimore: Paul H. Brookes.

Bricker, D. D., & Cripe, J. (1992). *An activity-based approach to early intervention.* Baltimore: Paul H. Brookes.

Bricker, D. D., & Widerstrom, A. (1996). *Preparing personnel to work with infants and young children and their families.* Baltimore: Paul H. Brookes.

Briggs, M. H. (1993). Team talk: Communication skills for early intervention teams. *Journal of Childhood Communication Disorders, 15,* 33–40.

Brinker, R. P., Frazier, W., & Baxter, A. (1992). Looking beyond family systems to societal systems. *OSERS News in Print, 4* (3), 8–17.

Bronfenbrenner, U. (1977). Toward an experimental ecology of human development. *American Psychologist, 32,* 513–531.

Bronfenbrenner, U. (1979). *The ecology of human development: Experiments by nature and design.* Cambridge, MA: Harvard University Press.

Brookins, G. H. (1993). Culture, ethnicity, and bicultural competence: Implications for children with chronic illness and disability. *Pediatrics, 91,* 1056–1062.

Brooks, V. B. (1986). *The neural basis of motor control.* New York: Oxford University Press.

Brown, C. W. (1992). Summary of selected education reform bills: Implications for early childhood. *DEC Communicator, 18* (3), 4.

Brown, C. W., & Rule, S. (1993). Personnel and disciplines in early intervention. In W. Brown, S. K. Thurman, & L. F. Pearl (Eds.), *Family-centered early intervention with infants and toddlers: Innovative cross-disciplinary approaches* (pp. 245–268). Baltimore: Paul H. Brookes.

Brown, C. W., & Seklemian, P. (1993). The individualized functional assessment process for young children with disabilities: Lessons from the Zebley Decision. *Journal of Early Intervention, 17* (3), 239–252.

Brown, W. H., & Conroy, M. A. (2002). Promoting peer-related social-communicative competence in preschool children. In H. Goldstein, L. Kaczmarek, & K. M. English (Eds.), *Promoting social communication* (pp. 173–210). Baltimore: Paul H. Brookes.

Bruder, M. B. (1995). The challenge of pediatric AIDS: Framework for early childhood special education. *Topics in Early Childhood Special Education, 15,* 83–89.

Bruder, M. B., Anderson, R., Schutz, G., & Caldera, M. (1991). Project profile. *Journal of Early Intervention, 15,* 268–277.

Bruder, M. B., & Bologna, T. (1993). Collaboration and service coordination for effective early intervention. In W. Brown, S. K. Thurman, & L. F. Pearl (Eds.), *Family-centered early intervention with infants and toddlers* (p. 103–128). Baltimore: Paul H. Brookes.

Bruner, J. (1990). *Acts of meaning.* Cambridge, MA: Harvard University Press.

Bukatko, D., & Daehler, M. W. (1992). *Child development: A topical approach.* Boston: Houghton Mifflin.

Burd, L., & Moffatt, M. (1994). Epidemiology of fetal alcohol syndrome in American Indians, Alaskan Natives, and Canadian Aboriginal Peoples: A review of the literature. *Public Health Reports, 109,* 688–693.

Burgess, D. M., & Streissguth, A. P. (1992, September). Fetal alcohol syndrome and fetal alcohol effects: Principles for educators. *Phi Delta Kappan,* 24–29.

Buscemi, L., Bennett, T., Thomas, D., & Deluca, D. (1996). Head Start: Challenges and training Needs. *Journal of Early Intervention, 20* (1), 1–13.

Buysse, V., & Wesley, P. (1993). The identity crisis in early childhood special education: A call for professional role clarification. *Topics in Early Childhood Special Education, 13* (4), 418–429.

Calhoun, M. L., & Rose, T. L. (1988). Promoting positive parent-child interactions. *Teaching Exceptional Children, 21* (4), 44–45.

Call, G., & Ziter, F. A. (1985). Failure to thrive in Duchenne muscular dystrophy. *Journal of Pediatrics, 106,* 939–941.

Camarata, S. (1995). A rationale for naturalistic speech intelligibility intervention. In N. E. Fey, J. Windsor, & S. G. Warren (Eds.), *Language intervention: Preschool through elementary years* (pp. 63–84). Baltimore: Paul H. Brookes.

Campbell, P. H. (1995). Supporting the medical and physical needs of students in inclusive settings. In N. Haring & L. Romer (Eds.), *Welcoming students who are deaf-blind into typical classrooms* (pp. 277–305). Baltimore: Paul H. Brookes.

Campbell, P. H. (1999). Establishing motor competence: A new frontier? *Journal of Early Intervention, 22* (1), 22–24.

Campbell, P. H. (2000). Promoting participation in natural environments by accommodating motor disabilities. In M. E. Snell & F. Brown (Eds.), *Instruction of students with severe disabilities.* Upper Saddle River, NJ: Prentice-Hall.

Campbell, P. H., & Bailey, K. (1991). Issues in health care in the education of students with the most severe disabilities. In M. C. Wang, M. Reynolds, & H. Walberg (Eds.), *Handbook of special education, Vol. 4* (pp. 143–160). Oxford, England: Pergamon Press.

Capara, G. V. Barbaranelli, C., Pastorelli, C., Bandura, A., & Zimbardo, P. G. (2000). Prosocial foundations of children's academic achievement. *Psychological Science, 11* (4), 302–306.

Carey, W. B. (1970). A simplified method for measuring infant temperament. *Journal of Pediatrics, 77,* 188–194.

Carnegie Corporation. (1994). *Starting points: Meeting the needs of our youngest children.* New York: Author.

Carta, J. J. (1994). Developmentally appropriate practices: Shifting the emphasis to individual appropriateness. *Journal of Early Intervention, 18* (4), 342–343.

Carta, J. J. (1995). Developmentally appropriate practice: A critical analysis as applied to young children with disabilities. *Focus on Exceptional Children 27* (8), 1–14.

Carta, J. J., Atwater, J. B., Schwartz, I. S., & McConnell, S. R. (1993). Developmentally appropriate practice and early childhood special education: A Reaction to Johnson and McChesney Johnson. *Topics in Early Childhood Special Education, 13* (3), 243–254.

Carta, J. J., Schwartz, I. S., Atwater, J. B., & McConnell, S. R. (1991). Developmentally appropriate practice: Appraising its usefulness for young children with disabilities. *Topics in Early Childhood Special Education, 11,* 1–20.

Case-Smith, J. (2000). Effects of occupational therapy services on fine motor and functional performance in preschool children. *American Journal of Occupational Therapy, 54* (4), 372–380.

Cavallaro, C. C., Haney, M. & Cabello, B. (1993). Developmentally appropriate strategies for promoting full participation in early childhood settings. *Topics in Early Childhood Special Education, 13* (3), 292–307.

Center for Disease Control. (1993, April). *HIV/AIDS surveillance report.* Atlanta, GA: Author.

Center for Innovations in Special Education. (1999). *First steps—Transitions to early childhood special education. A helpful guide for parents* (rev. ed.). Colombia: University of Missouri. (ERIC Document Reproduction Service No. ED 436 891).

Chan, J. B., & Sigafoos, J. (2000). A review of child and family characteristics related to the use of respite care in developmental disability services. *Child & Youth Care Forum, 29* (1), 27–37.

Chan, S. (1990). Early intervention with culturally diverse families of infants and toddlers with disabilities. *Infants and Young Children, 3,* 78–87.

Chapman, J. K., & Elliott, R. N. (1995). Preschoolers exposed to cocaine: Early childhood special education and head start preparation. *Journal of Early Intervention, 19,* 118–129.

Chasnoff, I. (1989). Drug use and women: Establishing a standard of care. *Annals of New York Academy of Sciences, 562,* 208–210.

Chess, S., & Thomas, A. (1986). *Temperament in clinical practice.* New York: Guilford.

Children's Defense Fund. (1990). *Latino youths at a crossroads.* Washington, DC: Author.

Chira, S. (1994). Study confirms worst fears on U.S. children. *New York Times,* April 12, pp. A1, A11.

Chomsky, N. (1976). On prelinguistic prerequisites of speech. In R. V. Campbell & P. T. Smith (Eds.), *Recent advances in the psychology of language* (pp. 242–256), New York: Plenum.

Cohen, E. G. (1994). *Designing groupwork: Strategies for the heterogeneous classroom.* New York: Teachers College Press.

Cohen, E. G. (1994). Restructuring the classroom: Conditions for productive small groups. *Review of Educational Research, 64* (1), 1–35.

Cohen, L. G., & Spenciner, L. J. (1994). *Assessment of young children.* White Plains, NY: Longman.

Cohen, L. G., & Spenciner, L. J. (1998). *Assessment of children and youth.* New York: Longman.

Cohn, E. (2001). Parent perspectives of occupational therapy using a sensory integration approach. *American Journal of Occupational Therapy, 55* (3), 285–294.

Cole, K. N. (1995). Curriculum models and language facilitation in the preschool years. In M. E. Fey, J. Windsor, & S. F. Warren (Eds.), Language intervention: Preschool through elementary years (pp. 39–62). Baltimore: Paul H. Brookes.

Cole, K. N., Mills, P., Dale, P., & Jenkins J. (1991). Effects of preschool integration for children with disabilities. *Exceptional children, 58,* 36–45.

Cole, M. L., & Cole, J. T. (1989). *Effective intervention with the language impaired child.* Gaithersburg, MD: Aspen.

Coleman, M. (1987). The search for neurobiological subgroups in autism. In E. Schopler & G. Misibov (Eds.), *Neurobiological issues in autism* (pp. 163–179). New York: Plenum.

Coleman, M. (1989). Young children with autism or autistic-like behavior. *Infants and Young Children, 1* (4), 22–31.

Conroy, M. A., & Davis, C. A. (2000). Early elementary–aged children with challenging behaviors: legal and educational issues related to IDEA and assessment. *Preventing School Failure, 44* (4), 163–168.

Cook, R. E., Tessier, A., & Klein, M. D. (1992). *Adapting early childhood curricula for children with special needs.* New York: Macmillan.

Cook, R. E., Tessier, A., & Klein, M. D. (1996). *Adapting early childhood curricula for children in inclusive settings.* Englewood Cliffs, NJ: Macmillan.

Cook, R. E., Tessier, A. M., & Klein, M. D. (1999). *Adapting early childhood curricula for children in inclusive settings.* Englewood Cliffs, NJ: Prentice-Hall.

Cook, R. E., Tessier, A., & Klein, M. D. (2000). *Adapting early childhood curricula for children in inclusive settings.* Upper Saddle River, NJ: Prentice-Hall.

Copeland, A. P., & White, K. M. (1991). *Studying families.* Newbury Park, CA: Sage.

Copeland, M. E., & Kimmel, J. R. (1989). *Evaluation and management of infants and young children with disabilities.* Baltimore: Paul H. Brookes.

Craft, D. H. (1994) Inclusion: Physical education for all. *Journal of Physical Education, Recreation and Dance, 65*, 23–55.

Cratty, B. J. (1988). *Adapted physical education in the mainstream.* Denver: Love.

Crockenberg, S., Lyons-Ruth, K., & Dickstein, S. (1993). The family context of infant mental health: II. Infant development in multiple family relationships. In C. H. Zeanah (Ed.), *Handbook of infant mental health.* New York: Guilford.

Cummins, J. (1989). A theoretical framework for bilingual special Education. *Exceptional Children, 56*, 111–120.

Davis, M. D., Kilgo, J. L., & Gamel-McCormick, M. (1998). *Young children with special needs: A developmentally appropriate approach.* Boston: Allyn and Bacon.

Davis-McFarland, E. (2000). Language and oral-motor development and disorders in infants and young toddlers with human immunodeficiency virus. *Seminars in Speech and Language, 21* (1), 19–34.

Deal, A. G., Trivette, C. M., & Dunst, C. J. (1988). Family functioning style scale. In C. J. Dunst, C. M. Trivette, & A. G. Deal (Eds.), *Enabling and empowering families: Principles and guidelines for practice* (pp. 175–184). Cambridge, MA: Brookline Books.

DEC (Division for Early Childhood). (1993). *DEC recommended practices: Indicators of quality in programs for infants and young children with Special Needs and Their Families.* Reston, VA: Council for Exceptional Children.

DEC (Division for Early Childhood). (1994). Position statement on inclusion. *Illinois Subdivision for Early Childhood Newsletter, 1*, 1–2.

DEC (Division for Early Childhood). (2000). *DEC recommended practices in early childhood special education.* Reston, VA: Council for Exceptional Children.

Deci, E. L., & Ryan, R. M. (1990). A motivational approach to self: Integration in personality. In R. Dienstbier (Ed.), *Nebraska symposium on motivation* (Vol. 38). Lincoln: University of Nebraska Press.

Delgado, M. R., & Combes, M. (1999). Management of motor impairment: Approaches for children with cerebral palsy. *Exceptional Parent, 29* (6), 42–45.

Demchak, M. A., & Drinkwater, S. (1992). Preschoolers with severe disabilities: The case against segregation. *Topics in Early Childhood Special Education, 11*, 70–83.

Denier, P. L. (1993). *Resources for teaching children with diverse abilities: Birth through eight.* Fort Worth, TX: Harcourt Brace.

DeSantis, L. D., & Thomas, J. T. (1994). Childhood independence: Views of Cuban and Haitian immigrant mothers. *Journal of Pediatric Nursing, 9*, 258–267.

Devlin, B. K., & Reynolds, E. (1994). Child abuse: how to report. *American Journal of Nursing, 21*, 26–31.

Dewey, J., & Dewey, E. (1962) *Schools of tomorrow.* New York: Dutton.

Diamond, K. E., Hestenes, L. L., & O'Connor, C. E. (1994). Integrating young children with disabilities in preschool: Problems and promise. *Young Children, 49*, 68–75.

Dickinson, D., & McCabe, A. (2001). Bringing it all together: The multiple origins, skills and environmental supports of early literacy. *Learning Disabilities Research and Practice, 16* (4), 186–202.

Diffily, D., & Fleege, P. O., (1993). *Sociodramatic play: Assessment through portfolio.* (ERIC Document Reproduction Service No. ED 354 079).

Donahue-Kilburg, G. (1992). *Family-centered intervention for communication disorders.* Gaithersburg, MD: Aspen.

Donnellan, A. M. (Ed.). (1985). *Classic readings in autism.* New York: Teachers College Press.

Downing, J. E. (1999). *Teaching communication skills to students with severe disabilities.* Baltimore: Paul H. Brookes.

Dowrick, P. W., & Raeburn, J. M. (1995). Self-modeling: Rapid skill training for children with physical disabilities. *Journal of Developmental and Physical Disabilities, 7*, 25–37.

Driscoll, A., & Nagel, N. G. (2002). *Early childhood education.* Boston: Allyn and Bacon.

Duchan, J. F. (1995). *Supporting language learning in everyday life.* San Diego: Singular Publishing.

Duchan, J. F. (1997). A situated pragmatics approach for supporting children with severe communication disorders. *Topics in Language Disorders, 17* (2), 1–18.

Duhaney, L. M. G., & Duhaney, D. C. (2000). Assistive technology: Meeting the needs of learners with disabilities. *International Journal of Instructional Media, 27* (4), 393–401.

Dunlap, L. L. (1997). *An introduction to early childhood special education.* Boston: Allyn and Bacon.

Dunst, C. J. (1999). Placing parent education in conceptual and empirical context. *Topics in Early Childhood Social Education, 20,* 96–104.

Dunst, C. J. (2000). Revisiting "rethinking early intervention." *Topics in Early Childhood Special Education, 20* (2), 95–104.

Dunst, C. J., Bruda, M., Trivette, C., & McLean, M. (2001). Natural learning opportunities of infants, toddlers and preschoolers. *Young Exceptional Children, 4* (3), 18–25.

Dunst, C. J., & Bruder, M. B. (1999). Increasing children's learning opportunities in the context of family and community life. *Children's Learning Opportunities Report, 1* (1).

Dunst, C. J., & Deal, A. G. (1992). Training Part H early intervention practitioners to work effectively with families. *OSERS News in Print, 5* (1), 25–28.

Dunst, C. J., Hamby, D., Trivette, C. M., Raab, M., & Brudrer, M. B. (2000). Everyday family and community life and children's naturally occurring learning opportunities. *Journal of Early Intervention, 23* (3), 151–164.

Dunst, C., Horby, D., Trivette, C., Raabl, M., & Bruda, M. (2000). Everyday family and community life and children's naturally occurring learning opportunities. *Journal of Early Intervention, 23* (3), 151–164.

Dunst, C. J., & Trivette, C. M. (1994). Aims and principles of family support programs. In C. J. Dunst, C. M. Trivette, & A. G. Deal (Eds.), *Supporting and strengthening families.* (pp. 30–48). Cambridge, MA: Brookline Books.

Dunst, C. J., Trivette, C. M., Davis, M., & Cornwell, J. C., (1994). Characteristics of effective help-giving practices. In C. J. Dunst, C. M. Trivette, & A. G. Deal (Eds.), *Supporting and strengthening families* (pp. 171–186). Cambridge, MA: Brookline Books.

Dunst, C. J., Trivette, C. M., & Deal, A. G. (1988). *Enabling and empowering families: Principles and guidelines for practice.* Cambridge, MA: Brookline Books.

Dunst, C. J., Trivette, C., & Deal, A. G. (1994a). Enabling and empowering families. In C. J. Dunst, C. M. Trivette, & A. G. Deal (Eds.), *Supporting*

*and strengthening families* (pp. 2–11). Cambridge, MA: Brookline Books.

Dunst, C. J., Trivette, C. M., & Deal, A. G. (1994b). Resource-based family-centered intervention practices. In C. J. Dunst, C. M. Trivette, & A. G. Deal (Eds.), *Supporting and strengthening families* (pp. 140–151) Cambridge, MA: Brookline Books.

Dunst, C. J., Trivette, C. M., & Mott, D. W. (1994). Strengths-based family centered intervention practices. In C. J. Dunst, C. M. Trivette, & A. G. Deal (Eds.), *Supporting and strengthening families: Vol. 1: Methods, strategies, and practices.* Cambridge, MA: Brookline Books.

Dyson, L. L. (1997). Fathers and mothers of school-age children with developmental disabilities: Parental stress, family functioning and social support. *American Journal on Mental Retardation, 102* (3), 267–279.

Edmonds, P., Martinson, S. A., & Goldberg, P. F. (1990). *Demographics and cultural diversity in the 1990's: Implications for services to young children with special needs.* Washington, DC: Special Education Programs (ED/OSERS). (ERIC Document Reproduction Service No. ED 325 555).

Egan, R. W. (1989). *Transition needs assessment for younger special education children.* Chicago: The Illinois Planning Council on Developmental Disabilities.

Emde, R. N., & Harmon, R. J. (Eds.). (1982). *The development of attachment and affiliative systems.* New York: Plenum Press.

Engel, A. L. (2000). Finding the right early intervention and education programs. In M. D. Powers (Ed.), *Children with autism* (2nd ed.) (pp. 181–212). Bethesda, MD: Woodbine House.

Epilepsy Foundation of America. (n.d.) *Information for teachers and providers of day care to young children* (Poster). 4351 Garden City Drive, Landover, MD: Author.

Erikson, E. (1963). *Childhood and society.* New York: Norton.

Erickson, M. F., & Kurz-Reimer, K. (1999). *Infants, toddlers and families: A framework for support and intervention.* New York: Guilford Press.

*Fact Sheet: Families and the Workplace.* Retrieved April 24, 2002, from http://www.preventchildabuse.org/research_ctr/fact_sheets/families_workplace.pdf

Fahey, K. R. (2000a). Language acquisition problems exhibited in classrooms. In K. R. Fahey & D. K. Reid (Eds.), *Language development, differences, and disorders* (pp. 247–296). Austin, TX: Pro-Ed.

Fahey, K. R. (2000b). Speech problems in classrooms. In K. R. Fahey & D. K. Reid (Eds.), *Language development, difference, and disorders* (pp. 297–322). Austin, TX: Pro-Ed.

Faine, M. P. (1994). Dental nutrition concerns of children with developmental disabilities. *Infant-Toddler Intervention, 4,* 11–24.

Fallon, M. A. (1996). Case-study teaching: A tool for training early interventionists. *Infants and Young Children, 8* (4), 59–62.

Fantuzzo, J W., Stoltzfus, J., & Lutz, M. N. (1999). An evaluation of the special needs referral process for low–income preschool children with emotional and behavioral problems. *Early Childhood Research Quarterly, 14* (4), 465–482.

Farlow, L. J., & Snell, M. E. (2000). Teaching basic self-care skills. In M. E. Snell & F. Brown (Eds.), *Instruction of students with severe disabilities* (pp. 331–380). Upper Saddle River, NJ: Prentice-Hall.

Farran, D. C. (1990). Effect of intervention with disadvantaged disabled children: A decade review. In S. J. Meisels & J. P. Shonkoff (Eds.), *Handbook of early childhood intervention* (pp. 501–539). New York: Cambridge University Press.

*Federal Register,* 1989, P.L. 99-457: 20 U.S.C., Sec. 1471(b)(1)(3).

Feuerstein, R. (1980). *Instrumental enrichment: An intervention program for cognitive modifiability.* Baltimore: University Park Press.

Field, T., & Sostek, A. (1983) *Infants born at risk.* New York: Grunc and Stratton.

Fink, D. B. (1992). The Americans with Disabilities Act: How will it impact your center. *Child Care Information Exchange, 85,* 43–46.

Finnie, N. R. (1975). *Handling the young cerebral palsied child at home.* New York: Dutton.

Finucane, B., & Cronister, A. (2000). The genetic aspects of Fragile X Syndrome and genetic counseling. In J. D. Weber (Ed.), *Children with Fragile X Syndrome: A parents' guide* (pp. 67–91). Bethesda, MD: Woodbine House.

Fisher, A., Murray, E., & Bundy, A. (1991). *Sensory integration: Theory and practice.* Philadelphia: F. A. Davis.

Fisher, K., & Lays, J. (Eds.). (1995). *Children, youth, and family issues. 1995 State Legislative Summary* (Item No. 6135). Denver, CO: National Conference of State Legislatures. (ERIC Document Reproduction Service No. ED 392 543).

Fitzgerald, M. (1999). Criteria for Asperger's disorder. *Journal of the American Academy of Child and Adolescent Psychiatry, 38* (9), 1071.

Flavel, J. H. (1982). *Cognitive Development.* Englewood Cliffs, NJ: Prentice-Hall.

Fletcher, J. M., & Foorman, B. R. (1995). Issues in definition and measurement of learing disabilities: The need for early intervention. In G. R. Lyon (Ed.), *Frames of reference for the assessment of learning disabilities.* (pp. 185–200). Baltimore: Paul H. Brookes.

Folsom-Meek, S. L., & Gillam, R. B. (1992). *Effects of a motor development training program on child care providers with children in integrated settings.* Indianapolis, IN: Annual Convention of the American Association of Health, Physical Education, Recreation and Dance. (ERIC Document Reproduction Service No. ED 351 301).

Foorman, B., Francis, D., Beeler, T., Winkates, D., & Fletcher, J. (1997). Early intervention for children with reading problems: Study designs and preliminary findings. *Learning Disabilities: A Multidisciplinary Journal, 8* (1), 63–72.

Foorman, B., & Torgesen, J. (2001). Critical elements of classroom and small-group instruction promote reading success in all children. *Learning Disabilities Research and Practice, 16* (4), 203–212.

Forgan, J. (1996). *Developmentally appropriate software for young children.* Presentation of the Council for Exceptional Children Annual Conference. Orlando, Florida.

Forman, G. (1996). A child constructs an understanding of a water wheel in five media. *Childhood Education, 72* (5), 269–273.

Fowler, S. A., Chandler, L. K., Johnson, T. E., & Stella, M. F. (1988). Individualizing family involvement in school transitions: Gathering information and choosing the next program. *Journal of the Division for Early Childhood, 12,* 208–216.

Fowler, S. A., Donegan, M., Lueke, B., Hadden, D., & Phillips, B. (2000). Evaluating community collaboration in writing interagency agreements on the age 3 transition. *Exceptional Children, 67* (1), 35–50.

Fowler, S. A., Haines, A. H., & Rosenkoetter, S. E. (1990). The transition between early intervention services and preschool services: Administrative and policy issues. *Topics in Early Childhood Special Education, 9* (4), 55–65.

Fox, L., Hanline, M. F., Vail, C. O., & Galant, K. R. (1994). Developmentally appropriate practice: Applications for young children with disabilities, *Journal of Early Intervention, 18* (3), 243–257.

Fradd, S. H. (1990). *A cultural workbook for starting your own cultural expedition.* Gainesville, FL.: Institute for Advanced Study of the Communication Process.

Fraiberg, S. (1959). *The magic years.* New York: Scribner.

Fredericks, H. D., Baldwin, V., Grove, D. N., & Moore, W. G. (1975). *Toilet training the handicapped child.* Monmouth, OR: Teaching Research.

Freud, A. (1966). *Writings of Anna Freud: Vol. 6: Northality and Pathology in Childhood.* New York: International Universities Press.

Froebal, F. (1896). *The education of man.* New York: Appleton & Co.

Furth, H., & Wachs, H. (1975). *Thinking goes to school.* New York: Oxford University Press.

Furuno, S., O'Reilly, K. A., Hosaka, C. M., Inatsuka, T. T., Zeisloft-Falbey, B., & Allman, T. (1988). *Hawaii early learning profile checklist.* Palo Alto, CA: VORT.

Gabor, L. M., & Farnham, R. (1996). The impact of children with chronic illness and/or developmental disabilities on low-income single parent families. *Infant-Toddler Intervention: The Transdisciplinary Journal, 6* (2), 167–180.

Gallagher, J. (1989). A new policy initiative: Infants and toddlers with handicapping conditions. *American Psychologist, 44,* 387–391.

Gallagher, J., Maddox, M., & Edgar, E. (1984). *Early childhood interagency transition model.* Bellevue, WA: Edmark.

Gandini, L. (1993). Fundamentals of the Reggio Emelia approach to early childhood special education. *Young Children, 49* (1), 4–8.

Gardner, H. (1993). *Multiple intelligences: The theory in practice.* New York: Basic Books.

Gardner, H. (1999). *Intelligence reframed: Multiple intelligence for the 21st century.* New York: Basic Books.

Gersten, R., Brengeleman, S., & Jimenez, R. (1994). Effective instruction for culturally and linguistically diverse students: A reconceptualization. *Focus on Exceptional Children, 27* (1), 1–16.

Gesell, A., & Amatruda. (1947). *Developmental diagnosis.* New York: Paul B. Holder.

Gesell, A., and Ames, L. (1937) *The Education of Man.* New York: Appleton and Co.

Gesell, A., & Ilg, F. L. (1940). *The first five years of life: A guide to the study of the preschool child.* New York: Harper and Row.

Gesell, A., & Ilg, F. L. (1943). *The infant and child: The culture of today.* New York: Harper and Brothers.

Gesell, A., Ilg, F. L., & Ames, L. B. (1977). *The child from five to ten.* New York: Harper and Row.

Getch, Y. Q., & Neuharth-Pritchet, S. (1999). Children with asthma: Strategies for educators. *Teaching Exceptional Children, 31* (3), 30–36.

Getz, M. (1993). *Pervasive Developmental Disorders (PDD).* Park Ridge, IL: Lutheran General Hospital, Department of Pediatrics.

Gilkerson, L., & Stott, F. (2000). Parent-child relationships in early intervention with infants and toddlers with disabilities and their families. In C. H. Zeanah, Jr. (Ed.), *Handbook of infant mental health* (2nd ed.) (pp. 457–471). New York: Guilford Press.

Glasgow, J. H., & Adaskin, E. J. (1990). The West Indians. In N. Waxler-Morrison, J. Anderson, & E. Richardson (Eds.), *Cross-cultural caring: A handbook for health professionals in Western Canada* (pp. 214–244). Vancouver, BC: University of British Columbia Press.

*Goals 2000: Educate America Act* (P.L. 103-227), March 31, 1994.

Goddard, H. H. (1916). *Feeblemindedness: Its causes and consequences.* New York: McMillan & Co.

Goldstein, H., Kaczmarek, L. A., & English, K. M. (2002). *Promoting social communication.* Baltimore: Paul H. Brookes.

Goldstein, H., & Strain, P. S. (1994). Peers as communication agents: Some new strategies and research findings. In K. G. Butler (Ed.), *Early intervention: Working with parents and families* (pp. 110–122). Gaithersburg, MD: Aspen.

Goleman, D. (1995). *Emotional intelligence.* New York: Bantam Books.

Gomby, D. S., Larner, M., Stevenson, C., Lewit, E., & Behrman, R. (1995). Long-term outcomes of early childhood programs: Analysis and recommendations. *The Future of Children, 6* (3), 6–24.

Gopnick, A., Meltzoff, A., & Kuhl, P. (1999). *The scientist in the crib: Minds, brains, and how children learn.* New York: William Morrow & Co.

Grandin, T. (1984). My experiences as an autistic child and review of the literature. *Journal of Orthomolecular Psychiatry, 13,* 144–174.

Grandin, T. (2000). Foreword to the second edition. In M. D. Powers (Ed.), *Children with autism* (2nd ed.) (pp. xi–xii). Bethesda, MD: Woodbine House.

Green, C. (1996). ADHD in the under-fives—Survival Psychology. CH.A.D.D. Eighth Annual Conference, November 14–16, 1996. Chicago, IL. Presenter Handouts, pp. 66–71.

Greenberg, R. (2000). Substance abuse in families: Education issues. *Childhood Education, 76* (2), 66–69.

Greenspan, S. I. (1992). *Infancy and early childhood: The practice of clinical assessment and intervention with emotional and developmental challenges.* Madison, CT: International University Press.

Greenspan, S. I. (1992). Reconsidering the diagnosis and treatment of very young children with autistic spectrum or pervasive developmental disorder. *Zero to Three, 13* (2), 1–9.

Greenspan, S. I. (1999). Working with children who have processing problems. *Scholastic Early Childhood Today, 13* (5), 19–20.

Greenspan, S. I. (1999). Working with children who show attention problems. *Scholastic Early Childhood Today, 13* (2), 24–25.

Greenspan, S. I. (2000). Working with children who have social/emotional disorders. *Scholastic Early Childhood Today, 14* (5), 22–23.

Greenspan, S. I. (2000a). Working with children who are physically challenged. *Scholastic Early Childhood Today, 14* (7), 24–25.

Greenspan, S. I. (2000b). Working with children who have chronic illnesses. *Scholastic Early Childhood Today, 15* (2), 22–23.

Greenspan, S. I. (2001c). Working with children who have motor difficulties. *Scholastic Early Childhood Today, 15* (4), 20–21.

Greenspan, S. I. (2000d). Working with children who have perceptual problems. *Scholastic Early Childhood Today, 14* (4), 26–27.

Greenspan, S. I., & Greenspan, N. T. (1985). *First feelings: Milestones in the emotional development of your baby and child.* New York: Viking.

Greenspan, S. I., & Meisels, S. J. (1996). Toward a new vision for the developmental assessment of infants and young children. In S. J. Meisels & E. Fenichel (Eds.), *New visions for the developmental assessment of infants and young children* (pp. 11–26). Washington, DC: Zero to Three National Center for Infants, Toddlers, and Families.

Greenspan, S. I., & Weider, S. (1998). *The child with special needs: Encouraging intellectual and emotional growth.* Reading, MA: Addison-Wesley.

Greenspan, S. I., & Wieder, S. (1999). A functional developmental approach to autism spectrum disorders. *The Journal of the Association for Persons with Severe Handicaps, 24* (3), 147–161.

Gregory, E. (1997). *One child, many worlds: Early learning in multicultural communities.* New York: Teachers College Press.

Griffer, M. R. (1999). Is sensory integration effective for children with language-learning disorders? A critical review of the evidence. *Language, Speech and Hearing Services in Schools, 30* (4), 393–400.

Griffith, D. R. (1988). The effects of perinatal cocaine exposure on infant neurobehavior and early maternal-infant interactions. In I. J. Chasnoff (Ed.), *Drugs, alcohol, pregnancy and parenting* (pp. 105–113). Boston: Kluwer.

Groce, N. (1990). Comparative and cross-cultural issues. *Disability Studies Quarterly, 10,* 1–39.

Groce, N. E., & Zola, I. K. (1993). Multiculturalism, chronic illness, and disability. *Pediatrics, 91,* 1048–1055.

Guess, D., & Noonan, M. J. (1982). Curricula and instructional procedures for severely handicapped students. *Focus on Exceptional Children, 14,* 1–12.

Guidry, G., Van den Pol, J., Keeley, E., & Neilson, S. (1996). Augmental traditional assessment and information: The video share model. *Topics in Early Childhood Special Education, 16* (1), 51–65.

Guiliani, C. A. (1991). Current theoretical issues in motor control. *Proceedings of the II Step Conference.* Norman, OK.

Guralnick, M. (Ed.). (1997). *The effectiveness of early intervention: Discussions for second generation research.* Baltimore: Paul H. Brookes.

Guralnick, M. J. (1990). Major accomplishments and future directions in early childhood mainstreaming. *Topics in Early Childhood Special Education, 10,* 1–17.

Guralnick, M. J. (1994). Mother's perceptions of the benefits and drawbacks of early childhood mainstreaming. *Journal of Early Intervention, 19* (2), 169–183.

Guralnick, M. J., & Bricker, D. D. (1987). The effectiveness of early intervention for children with cognitive and general developmental delays. In M. J. Guralnick & F. C. Bennett (Eds.), *The effectiveness of early intervention for at-risk and handicapped children* (pp. 115–173). New York: Academic Press.

Hagerman, R. J. (2000). What is Fragile X Syndrome? In J. D. Weber (Ed.), *Children with Fragile X Syndrome: A parents' guide* (pp. 1–32). Bethesda, MD: Woodbine House.

Haines, A. H. (1992). Strategies for preparing preschool children with special needs for the kindergarten mainstream. *Journal of Early Intervention, 16,* 320–333.

Haines, A. H., Rosenkoetter, S. E., & Fowler, S. A. (1991). Transition planning with families in early intervention programs. *Infants and Young Children, 3* (4), 38–47.

Hallahan, D., & Kauffman, J. (1994). *Exceptional children: Introduction to special education.* Boston: Allyn and Bacon.

Hamblin-Wilson, C., & Thurman, S. K. (1990). The transition from early intervention to kindergarten: Parental satisfaction and involvement. *Journal of Early Intervention, 14,* 55–61.

Hancock, T. B., & Kaiser, A. P., (1996). Siblings' use of milieu teaching at home. *Topics in Early Childhood Special Education, 16* (2), 168–190.

Hanft, B., Burke, H., & Swenson-Miller, K. (1996). Preparing occupational therapists. In D. Bricker & A. Widerstrom (Eds.), *Preparing personnel to work with infants and young children and their families* (pp. 115–134). Baltimore: Paul H. Brookes.

Hanft, B., & Striffler, N. (1995). Incorporating developmental therapy in early childhood programs: Challenges and promising practices. *Infants and Young Children, 8* (2), 37–47.

Hanline, M. (1988). Making the transition to preschool: Identification of parent needs. *Journal of the Division for Early Childhood, 12,* 98–107.

Hanline, M. F. (1991). Transitions and critical events in the family life cycle: Implications for providing support to families of children with disabilities. *Psychology in the Schools,* (1), 53–59.

Hanline, M. F. (1993). Learning within the context of play: Providing typical early childhood experiences for children with severe disabilities. *Journal of the Association of Persons with Severe Handicaps, 18,* 121–129.

Hanline, M. F. (1999). Developing a preschool play–based curriculum. *International Journal of Disability, Development and Education, 46* (3), 289–305.

Hanline, M. F., & Knowlton, A. (1988). A collaborative model providing support to parents during the child's transition from infant intervention to preschool special education public school programs. *Journal of the Division for Early Childhood, 12,* 116–125.

Hanson, M. J. (1999). *Early transitions for children and families: Transitions from infant/toddler services to preschool education.* Reston, VA: ERIC Clearinghouse on Disabilities and Gifted Education, Council for Exceptional Children. (ERIC Document Reproduction Service No. ED 434 436).

Hanson, M. J., & Harris, S. R. (1986). *Teaching the young child with motor delays.* Austin, TX: Pro-Ed.

Hanson, M. J., & Lynch, E. W. (1989). *Early intervention: Implementing child and family services for infants and toddlers who are at risk or disabled.* Austin, TX: Pro-Ed.

Hanson, M. J., & Lynch, E. W. (1995). *Early intervention: implementing child and family services for infants and toddlers who are at risk or disabled.* Austin, TX: Pro-Ed.

Hanson, M. J., & Widerstrom, A. H. (1993). Consultation and collaboration: Essentials of integration efforts for young children. In C. A. Peck, S. L. Odom, & D. D. Bricker (Eds.), *Integrating young children with disabilities into community programs* (pp. 149–168). Baltimore: Paul H. Brookes.

Harbin, G. L., Danaker, J., Bailer, D., & Eller, S. (1991). *Status of states' eligibility policy for preschool children with disabilities.* Chapel Hill, NC: Carolinas Policy Studies Programs.

Harbin, G. L., Gallagher, J. J., & Terry, D. V. (1991). Defining the eligible population: Policy issues and challenges. *Journal of Early Intervention, 15,* 13–20.

Harbin, G. L., & McNulty, B. A. (1990). Policy implementation: Perspectives on service coordination and interagency cooperation. In S. L. Meisels & J. B. Shonkoff (Eds.), *Handbook of early intervention* (pp. 700–722). Cambridge: Cambridge University Press.

Harbin, G. L., McWilliam R. A., & Gallagher, J. J. (2000). Services for young children with disabilities and their families. In J. P. Shonkoff & S. J. Meisels (Eds.), *Handbook of early childhood intervention* (2nd ed.) (pp. 387–415). New York: Cambridge University Press.

Harmin, M. (1994). *Inspiring active learning: A handbook for teachers.* Alexandria, VA: Association for Supervision and Curriculum Development.

Harris, K. R., & Graham, S. (1996). Constructivism and students with special needs: Issues in the classroom. *Learning Disabilities Research and Practice, 11,* 134–137.

Hartup, W. W., & Moore, S. G. (1990). Early peer relations: Developmental significance and prognostic implications. *Early Childhood Research Quarterly, 5,* 1–17.

Hasselbring, T., & Glazer, C. (2000). Use of computer technology to help students with special needs. *The Future of Children: Children and Computer Technology, 10* (2), 102–122.

Hatton, C. (1998). Whose quality of life is it anyway? Some problems with the emerging quality of life consensus. *Mental Retardation, 26,* 104–115.

Hauser-Cram, P., Upshur, C. C., Krauss, M. W., & Shonkoff, J. P. (1988). *Implications of Public Law 99-457 for early intervention services for infants and toddlers with disabilities* (Social Policy Report). Washington, DC: Society for Research in Child Development.

Head Start Bureau. (1993). *Head Start performance standards on services for children with disabilities.* Office of Human Developmental Services, Administration for Children, Youth and Families. Washington, DC: U.S. Government Printing Office.

Head Start Bureau. (2000). Washington, DC: U.S. Department of Health & Human Services.

Healy, A., Keese, P., & Smith, B. (1987). *Early services for children with special needs: Transactions for family support.* Baltimore: Paul H. Brookes.

Henderson, L. W., & Meisels, S. J. (1994). Parental involvement in the developmental screening of their young children: A multiple-source perspective. *Journal of Early Intervention, 18* (4), 368–379.

Hendrick, J. (1984). *The whole child*. St. Louis: Mosby/ Times Mirror.

*HIV/AIDS surveillance report*. Atlanta, GA: Author.

Hoge, D. R., & Parette, H. P. (1995). Facilitating communicative development in young children with disabilities. *Infant-Toddler Intervention, 5*, 113–130.

Hohmann, M., Banet, B., & Weikart, D. P. (1979). *Young children in action*. Ypsilanti, MI: High/Scope Educational Research Foundation.

Holland, B. V. (1992). *The right stuff: Developmentally appropriate physical education for early childhood preschool through grade two for all children*. Indianapolis, IN: Annual Convention of the American Association of Health, Physical Education, Recreation, and Dance. (ERIC Document Reproduction Service No. ED 347 784).

Holvoet, J., Guess, D., Mulligan, M., & Brown, F. (1980). The individual curriculum sequencing model: A teaching strategy for severely handicapped students. *Journal of the Association for Persons with Severe Handicaps, 5*, 337–351.

Honig, A. S. (1993). *Infant mental health: Implications for parenting in limited resource families*. Paper presented at the Plight of Young Children Conference, College Station, TX. (ERIC Document Reproduction Service No. ED 356 059).

Horn, E. M. (1991). Basic motor skills instruction for children with neuromotor delays: A critical review. *Journal of Special Education, 25*, 168–197.

Horn, E. M. (1993). In DEC Task Force on Recommended Practices (Ed.). *DEC recommended practices: Indicators of quality in programs for infants and young children with specials needs and their families* (pp. 84–89). Reston, VA: Council for Exceptional Children.

Horn, E. M. (1996). Interventions to promote adaptive behavior skills. In S. L. Odom & M. E. McLean (Eds.), *Early intervention/early childhood special education: Recommended practices* (pp. 259–285). Austin, TX: Pro-Ed.

Horn, E. M., & Childre, A. (1996). Assessing adaptive behavior. In M. E. McLean, D. B. Bailey, & M. Wolery (Eds.), *Assessing infants and preschoolers with special needs* (pp. 462–490). Upper Saddle River, NJ: Merrill/Prentice-Hall.

Houts, A. C., & Liebert, M. W. (1984). *Bedwetting: A guide for parents and children*. Springfield, IL: Charles C. Thomas.

Howard, V. F., Williams, B. F., Port, P. D., & Lepper, D. (1997). *Very young children with special needs*. Columbus, OH: Merrill.

Hoy, C., & Gregg, N. (1994). *Assessement: The special educator's role*. Pacific Grove, CA: Brooks/Cole.

Huettig, C., & O'Connor, J. (1999). Wellness programming for preschoolers with disabilities. *Teaching Exceptional Children 31* (3), 12–17.

Hunt, J. M. (1961). *Intelligence and Experience*. New York: Ronald Press.

Hunt, N., & Marshall, K. (2002). *Exceptional children and adults*. Boston: Houghton Mifflin.

Hupp, S. (1989). *Exploring the world through play: Use of mastery behaviors by young children with developmental delays*. Minneapolis: University of Minnesota, Institute for Disabilities Studies.

Huttenlocher, P. (1991). *Neural plasticity*. Paper presented at the Brain Research Foundation, Women's Council University of Chicago, Chicago September 26.

Illinois State Board of Education. (1986). *Early intervention state plan*. Springfield, IL: Early intervention State Plan Grant, Department of Special Education.

Innocenti, M. (1987). *Parent handbook*. Logan: Utah State University, Outreach and Developmental Division (Preschool Transition Project, Developmental Center for Handicapped Persons, Utah State University, Logan, UT 84322).

Innocenti, M., Rule, S., & Fiechtl, B. (1987). *Helping parents to be informed advocates for their children: Planning materials for four meetings to provide information and support*. Logan: Utah State University, Outreach and Developmental Division (Preschool Transition Project, Developmental Center for Handicapped Persons, Utah State University, Logan, UT 84322).

Jambunathan, S., Burts, D. C., & Pierce, S. (2000). Comparisons of parenting attitudes among five ethnic groups in the United States. *Journal of Comparative Family Studies, 31* (4), 395–408.

Janney, R., & Snell, M. E. (2000). *Modifying schoolwork*. Baltimore: Paul H. Brookes.

Jernberg, A. M., & Booth, P. B. (1999). *Theraplay* (2nd ed.). San Francisco: Jossey–Bass.

Jessee, P. O., Wilson, H., & Morgan, D. (2000). Medical play for young children. *Childhood Education, 76* (4), 215–218.

Johnson, D. W., & Johnson, R. (1995). *Teaching students to be peacemakers*. Edina, MN: Interaction Book Company.

Johnson, D. W., & Johnson, R. (1997). *Joining together: Group theory and group skills*. Boston: Allyn and Bacon.

Johnson, D. W., & Johnson, R. (1998). Teaching students to manage conflicts in diverse classrooms. In J. W. Putnam (Ed.), *Cooperative learning and strategies for inclusion* (pp. 167–184). Baltimore: Paul H. Brookes.

Johnson, L. (Ed.). (1992). *Forward. Policy issues: Creating a unified vision.* Proceedings. (pp. i–ii). Columbus: The Ohio Early Childhood Special Education: Higher Education Consortium.

Jones, C. B. (1996). *ADD in early childhood.* CH.A.D.D. Eighth Annual Conference, November 14–16. Chicago: Presenter Handouts. pp. 194–199.

Jones, H. A., & Rapport, M. J. N. (1997). Research-to-practice in inclusive early childhood education. *Teaching Exceptional Children*, 57–61.

Jones, K., Smith, W., Ulleland, C., & Streissguth, A. (1973). Pattern of malformation in offspring of alcoholic women. *Lancet, 1*, 1267–1271.

Kaiser, A. P. (1993). Parent-implemented language intervention: An environmental systems perspective. In A. P. Kaiser & D. B. Gray (Eds.), *Enhancing children's communication: Research foundations for intervention* (pp. 63–84). Baltimore: Paul H. Brookes.

Kaiser, A. P., Hancock, T. B., & Hester, P. P. (1998). Parents as cointerventionists: Research on applications of naturalistic language teaching procedures. *Infants and Young Children, 10* (4), 46–55.

Kaiser, A. P., Hemmeter, M. L., Ostrosky, M. M., Fischer, R., Yoder, P., & Keefer, M. (1996). The effects of teaching parents to use responsive interaction strategies. *Topics in Early Childhood Special Education, 16* (3), 375–406.

Kamhi, A. G. (1996). Linguistic and cognitive aspects of specific language impairment. In M. D. Smith & J. S. Damico (Eds.), *Childhood language disorders* (pp. 97–116). New York: Thieme Medical Publishers.

Karnes, M. (Eds.). *Early intervention for infants and children with handicaps* (pp. 145–158). Baltimore: Paul H. Brookes.

Karnes, M., Johnson, L., Cohen, T., & Schwedel, A. (1985). Facilitating school success among mildly and moderately handicapped children by enhancing task persistence. *Journal of the Division for Early Childhood, 9* (2), 136–150.

Karr, J. A., & Landerholm, E. (1991). *Reducing staff stress/burnout by changing staff expectations in dealing with parents.* (ERIC Document Reproduction Service No. ED 351 128).

Kastenbaum, R. J. (1986). *Death, society, and human experience.* Columbus, OH: Merrill.

Katims, D. S., & Pierce, P. L. (1995). Literacy-rich environments and the transition of young children with special needs. *Topics in Early Childhood Special Education, 15*, 219–234.

Katz, L. (1990). Impressions of Reggio Emilia Preschools. *Young Children, 45*, 4–10.

Kelly, J. F., & Barnard K. E. (2000). Assessment of parent-child interaction: Implications for early intervention. In J. P. Shonkoff & S. J. Meisels (Eds.), *Handbook of early childhood intervention* (2nd ed.) (pp. 258–289). New York: Cambridge University Press.

Keogh, B. (2000). Risk, families and Schools. *Focus on Exceptional Children, 38* (4), 1–10.

Kephart, N. C. (1963). *The brain-injured child in the classroom.* Chicago: National Society for Crippled Children and Adults.

Kephart, N. C. (1971). *The slow learner in the classroom.* Columbus: OH: Merrill.

Kirk, S. A. (1958). *Early education of the mentally retarded.* Urbana: University of Illinois Press.

Kirk, S. A. (1965). Diagnostic, cultural, and remedial factors in mental retardation. In Sonia F. Osler & R. F. Cooke, (Eds.), *Biosocial basis of mental retardation.* Baltimore: Johns Hopkins Press.

Kirsch, I. S., Jungeblut, A., Jenkins, L., & Kolstad, A. (1993) Adult literacy in America: *A first look at the results of the national adult literacy survey.* Princeton, NJ: Educational Testing Service.

Klaus, M. H., & Robertson, M. O. (Eds.). (1982) *Birth, interaction and attachment.* Skillman, NJ: Johnson & Johnson.

Klein, E. R., & Stull, J. (2000). Efficacy of the multidisciplinary evaluation for preschoolers with suspected developmental delays. Philadelphia: Temple University Center for Research in Human Development and Education. (ERIC Document Reproduction Service No. ED441 035).

Klein, M. (1952). In J. Rivere (Ed.), *Developments in pscho-analysis.* London: Hogarth Press.

Kleinhammmer-Tramill, Rosenkoetter, S., & Tramill, J. (1994). Early intervention and secondary/transition services: Harbingers of change in education. *Focus on Exceptional Children, 27* (2), 1–15.

Knight, D., & Wadsworth, D. (1993). Physically challenged students: Inclusion classrooms. *Childhood Education, 69*, 211–215.

Koenig, K., Rubin, E., Klin, A., & Volkmar, F. R. (2000). Autism and the pervasive developmental disorders. In C. H. Zeanah, Jr. (Ed.), *Handbook of infant mental health* (2nd ed.) (pp. 298–310). New York: Guilford Press.

Kolberg, J., Gustafson, K., & Ekblad, A. (1999). *Early childhood special education for children with disabilities, ages three through five: Transition.* Bismark: North Dakota State Department of Public Instruction, Division of Special Education. (ERIC Document Reproduction Service No. ED 443 225).

Kontos, S., & File, N. (1993). Staff development in support of integration. In C. A. Peck, S. L. Odom, & D. D. Bricker (Eds.), *Integrating young children with disabilities into community programs* (pp. 169–186). Baltimore: Paul H. Brookes.

Koplow, L. (Ed.). (1996). *Unsmiling faces: How preschools can heal.* New York: Teachers College, Columbia University.

Kopp, C. B., Baker, B. L., & Brown, K. W. (1992). Social skills and their correlates: Preschoolers with developmental delays. *American Journal on Mental Deficiency, 96,* 357–366.

Koppenhaver, D. A., Pierce, P. L., Steelman, J. D., & Yoder, D. E. (1995). Contexts of early literacy intervention for children with developmental disabilities. In M. E. Fey, J. Windsor, & S. F. Warren (Eds.), *Language intervention: Preschool through elementary years* (pp. 241–276). Baltimore: Paul H. Brookes.

Kostelnik, M. J., Soderman, A. K., & Whiren, A. P. (1999). *Developmentally appropriate curriculum: Best practices in early childhood education.* Upper Saddle River, NJ: Prentice-Hall.

Kostelnik, M. J., Stein, L. C., Whiren, A. P., & Soderman, A. K. (1998). *Guiding children's social development: Classroom practices.* Albany, NY: Delmar.

Kübler-Ross, E. (1969). *On death and dying.* New York: Macmillan.

LaBoskey, V. K. (2000). Portfolios here, portfolios there . . . searching for the essence of educational portfolios. *Phi Delta Kappan, 81* (8), 590–595.

Lagrander, J. M., & Reid, D. K. (2000). Language acquisition and usage: Multicultural and multilingual perspectives. In K. R. Fahey & D. K. Reid (Eds.), *Language development, differences and disorders* (pp. 177–211). Austin, TX: Pro-Ed.

Lambie, R. (2000). Working with families of at-risk and special needs students: A systems change model. *Focus on Exceptional Children, 32* (6), 1–22.

Lambie, R., & Daniels-Mohring D. (2000). *Family systems within education contexts: Understanding students with special needs.* Denver, CO: Love.

Lamorey, S., & Bricker, D. D. (1993). Integrated programs: Effects on young children and their parents. In C. A. Peck, S. L. Odom, & D. D. Bricker (Eds.), *Integrating young children with disabilities into community programs* (pp. 249–270). Baltimore: Paul H. Brookes.

Langley, M. B. (1996). Screening and assessment of sensory functions. In M. McLean, D. B. Bailey, & M. Wolery (Eds.), *Assessing infants and preschoolers with special needs* (pp. 123–164). Columbus, OH: Merrill.

La Paro, K. M., Pianta, R. C., & Cox, M. J. (2000). Teachers' reported transition practices for children transitioning into kindergarten and first grade. *Exceptional Children, 67* (1), 7–20.

Lavoie, R. D. (1995). Life on the waterbed: Mainstreaming on the homefront. *Attention!, 2* (1), 25–29.

Layton, T. L., & Davis-McFarland, E. (2000). Pediatric human immunodeficiency virus and acquired immunodeficiency syndrome: An overview. *Seminars in Speech and Language, 21* (1), 7–17.

Layton, T. L., & Scott, G. S. (2000). Language development and assessment in children with human immunodeficiency virus: 3 to 6 years. *Seminars in Speech and Language, 21* (1), 37–47.

Lazar, I., & Darlington, R. (Eds.). (1982). Lasting effects of early education: A report from the consortium for longitudinal studies. *Monograph for the Society for Research in Child Development, 27* (2-3, Serial No. 195). Summary report, DHEW Publication No. OHDS 80-30/79.

Lazzari, A. M., & Kilgo, J. L. (1989). Practical methods for supporting parents in early transitions. *Teaching Exceptional Children, 22* (1), 40–43.

Leff, P. T., & Walizer, E. H. (1992). *Building the healing partnership.* Cambridge, MA: Brookline Books.

Lennenberg, E. (1967). *Biological foundations of language.* New York: Wiley.

Lequerica, M. (1993). Stress in immigrant families with handicapped children: A child advocacy approach. *American Journal of Orthopsychiatrics, 63,* 545–552.

Lerner, J. W. (2000). *Learning disabilities: Theories, diagnoses, and teaching strategies.* Boston: Houghton Mifflin.

Lerner, J. W. (2003). *Learning disabilities: Theories, diagnosis, and teaching strategies.* Boston: Houghton Mifflin.

Lerner, J., Lowenthal, B., & Egan, R. (1998). *Preschool children with special needs: Children at-risk and children with disabilities.* Boston: Allyn and Bacon.

Lerner, J., Lowenthal, B., & Lerner, S. (1995). *Attention Deficit Disorders: Assessment and treatment.* Pacific Grove, CA: Brooks/Cole.

Lerner, J., Mardell-Czudnowski, C., & Goldenberg, D. (1987). *Special education for the early childhood years.* Englewood Cliffs, NJ: Prentice-Hall.

Lewis, R. (1998). Assistive technology and learning disabilities: Today's realities and tomorrow's promises. *Journal of Learning Disabilities, 31* (1), 16–26.

Lidz, C. S. (1991). *Practitioner's guide to dynamic assessment.* New York: Guilford Press.

Lieber, J., Beckman, P. J., & Strong, B. N. (1993). A longitudinal study of the social exchanges of young children with disabilities. *Journal of Early Intervention, 17,* 116–128.

Lieberman, A. (1993). *The emotional life of the toddler.* New York: Free Press.

Lin, S. L. (2000). Coping and adaptation in families of children with cerebral palsy. *Exceptional Children, 66* (2), 201–218.

Linder, T. W. (1990). *Transdisciplinary play-based assessment.* Baltimore: Paul H. Brookes.

Linder, T. W. (1993). *Transdisciplinary play-based assessment: A functional approach to working with young children* (2nd ed.). Baltimore: Paul H. Brookes.

Lipson, M., & Wixson, B. (1991). *Assessment and instruction of reading disabilities: An interactive approach.* New York: HarperCollins.

Little, L. (1999). *Early developments.* Chapel Hill: University of North Carolina. (ERIC Document Reproduction Service No. ED 443 564).

Lonigan, C. J., Bloomfield, B. G., & Anthony, J. L. (1999). Relations among emergent literacy skills, behavior problems, and social competence in preschool children from low– and middle–income backgrounds. *Topics in Early Childhood Special Education, 19* (1), 40–53.

Losardo, A., & Notari-Syverson, A. (2001). *Alternative approaches to assessing young children.* Baltimore: Paul H. Brookes.

Lovaas, O. I. (1987). Behavioral treatment and normal educational and intellectual functioning in young autistic children. *Journal of Consulting and Clinical Psychology, 55,* 3–9.

Lowenthal, B. (1989). Optimizing rapport in diagnosis. *ICEC Quarterly, 38* (3), 13–18.

Lowenthal, B. (1991). Techniques for family assessment by the early interventionist. *ICEC Quarterly, 40* (1), 12–18.

Lowenthal, B. (1992a). Assessment of young children in the mainstream. *Early Child Development and Care, 79,* 39–45.

Lowenthal, B. (1992b). Functional and developmental models: A winning early intervention combination. *Infant-Toddler Intervention, 2,* 161–168.

Lowenthal, B. (1995). Naturalistic language intervention in inclusive environments. *Intervention in School and Clinic, 31,* 114–118.

Lowenthal, B. (1996). The use of community resources by families of young children with special needs. *Learning Disabilities: A Multidisciplinary Journal, 7* (1), 37–41.

Lowenthal, B. (1997). Useful early childhood assessment: Play-based, interviews, and multiple intelligences. *Early Child Development, 129,* 43–49.

Lowenthal, B. (1999). Effects of maltreatment and ways to promote children's resiliency. *Childhood Education, 75* (4), 204–209.

Lowenthal, B. (2001). *Abuse and neglect: The educator's guide to the identification and prevention of child maltreatment.* Baltimore, MD: Paul H. Brookes.

Lowenthal, B. (2001). *Child maltreatment: The teacher's role in identification, prevention, and intervention.* Baltimore: Paul H. Brookes.

Lowenthal, B. (2002). *Abuse and neglect: The educator's guide to the identification and prevention of child maltreatment.* Baltimore: Paul H. Brookes.

Lowenthal, B., & Lowenthal, M. (1995). The effects of asthma on school performance. *Learning Disabilities, 6,* 41–46.

Luby, J. L. (2000). Depression. In C. H. Zeanah, Jr. (Ed.), *Handbook of infant mental health* (2nd ed.) (pp. 382–396). New York: Guilford Press.

Lucariello, J. (1994). Freeing talk from the here and new: The role of event knowledge and maternal scaffolds. In K. G. Butler (Ed.), *Early intervention I: Working with infants and toddlers* (pp. 79–94). Gaithersburg, MD: Aspen.

Luria, A. R. (1980). *Higher control functions in man.* New York: Plenum.

Lynch, E. W., & Hanson, M. J. (1992). *Developing cross-cultural competence.* Baltimore: Paul H. Brookes.

Lynch, E. W., & Hanson, M. J. (1998). *Developing cross-cultural competence.* Baltimore: Paul H. Brookes.

Lyon, G. R., Alexander, D., & Yaffee, S. (1997) Progress and promise in learning disabilities. *Learning Disabilities: A Multidisciplinary Journal, 8* (1), 1–6.

Maag, J. W. (1999). *Behavior management: From theoretical implications to practical applications.* San Diego, CA: Singular.

Magnusson, C. J., & Justen, J. E. (1981). Teacher made adaptive and assistive aids for developing self-help skills in the severely handicapped. *Journal for Special Educators, 17,* 389–400.

Mahoney, G. (1999). Moving toward a new motor intervention paradigm. *Journal of Early Intervention, 22* (1), 19–21.

Mahoney, G., Finger, I., & Powell, A. (1985). Relationship of maternal behavioral style to the development of organically impaired mentally retarded infants. *American Journal of Mental Deficiency, 90,* 296–302.

Mahoney, G., & Neville-Smith, A. (1996). The effects of directive communications on children's interactive engagement: Implications for language development. *Topics in Early Childhood Special Education, 16* (2), 236–249.

Mahoney, G., & Powell, A. (1988). Modifying parent-child interaction: Enhancing the development of handicapped children. *Journal of Special Education, 22,* 82–96.

Mahoney, G., Robinson, C., & Powell, A. (1992). Focusing on parent-child interaction: The bridge to developmentally appropriate practices. *Topics in Early Childhood Special Education, 12,* 105–120.

Mahoney, G., & Wheatley, A. P. (1994). Reconceptualizing the individual education program: A constructionist approach to educational practice for young children with disabilities, In P.L. Safford, B. Spodel, & O. N. Saracho (Eds.), *Early childhood education* (pp. 118–141). New York: Teachers College Press.

Main, M., & Solomon, J. (1986). Discovery of an insecure disorganized/disoriented attachment pattern: Procedures, findings, and implications for the classification of behavior. In T. B. Brazelton & M. Yogman (Eds.), *Affective development in infancy* (pp. 95–124). Norwood, NJ: Ablex.

Mallach, R. S. (1993). *Cultural responsive services for children.* Bernalillo, NM: Southwest Communication Resources.

Mallory, B. (1992). Convergent models for early intervention practice. *Topics in Early Childhood Special Education, 14,* 1–12.

Malone, D. M. (1999). Contextual factors informing play–based program planning. *International Journal of Disability, Development and Education, 46* (3), 307–324.

Mann, V. (1993). Phoneme awareness and future reading ability. *Journal of Learning Disabilities, 26* (4), 259–269.

Marcovitch, H. (1994). Failure to thrive. *British Medical Journal, 308,* 35–38.

Marshall, J. (2000). Critical reflections on the cultural influences in identification and habilitation of children with speech and language difficulties. *International Journal of Disability, Development and Education, 47* (4), 355–369.

Martinson, M. C. (1982). Interagency services: A new era for an old idea. *Exceptional Children, 48,* 389–395.

Marvin, C., & Miranda, P. (1993). Home literacy experiences of preschoolers enrolled in Head Start and special education programs. *Journal of Early Intervention, 17,* 351–367.

Marvin, C., & Miranda, P. (1994). Literacy practices in Head Start and early childhood special education classrooms. *Early Education and Development, 5,* 289–300.

Mauer, D. M. (1999). Issues and application of sensory integration theory and treatment with children with language disorders. *Language, Speech, and hearing Services in Schools, 30* (4), 383–392.

May-Benson, T. (2000). "I can't do it . . ." Examining coping skills in children with SI dysfunction. *OT Practice, 5* (23), 12–15.

Mayer, M. (1996). Children who are deaf or hard of hearing. In E. L. Meyen (Ed.), *Exceptional children in today's schools* (pp. 315–350). Denver, CO: Love.

Mayes, L. (1999). Developing brain and in utero cocaine exposure: Effects on neural ontogeny. *Development and Psychopathology, 11* (4), 685–714.

Mayes, L., Granger, R., Bornstein, M., & Zuckerman, B. (1992). The problem of prenatal cocaine exposure: A rush to judgement. *Journal of the American Medical Association, 267,* 406–408.

Mayes, L., Volkmar, F., Hooks, M., & Chicchetti, D. (1993). Differentiating pervasive developmental disorder not otherwise specified from autism and language disorders. *Journal of Autism and Developmental Disorders, 23,* 79–90.

McCall, R. (1994). An inclusive preschool physical education program. *Journal of Physical Education, Recreation, and Dance, 35,* 45–47.

McCann, D. (1996). *Brief overview of Fetal Alcohol Syndrome and effects.* (CreaConInc@aol.com; fasfi-idm@accessone.com)

McCardle, P., Cooper, J., Houle, G., Karp, N., & Paul-Brown, D. (2001). Emergent and early literacy: Current Status and Research Directions— Introduction. *Learning Disabilities Research and Practice, 16* (4), 183–185.

McCollom, J. A., & Stayton, V. D. (1996). Preparing early childhood special educators. In D. Bricker & A. Widerstrom (Eds.), *Preparing personnel to work with infants and young children and their families: A team approach* (pp. 67–90). Baltimore: Paul H. Brookes.

McConnell, S. R., & Odom S. L. (1999). A multimeasure performance–based assessment of social competence in young children with disabilities. *Topics in Early Childhood Special Education, 19* (2), 67–74.

McCubbin, M. A., McCubbin, H. I., & Thompson, A. I. (1987). Family hardiness index. In H. I. McCubbin, & A. I. Thompson, (Eds.), *Family assessment inventories for research and practice.* (pp. 125–130). Madison: University of Wisconsin.

McDermott, D. (2001). Parenting and ethnicity. In M. J. Fine & S. W. Lee (Eds.), *Handbook of diversity in parent education: The changing faces of parenting and parent education* (pp. 73–96). San Diego: Academic Press.

McGonigel, M. J., Woodruff, G., & Roszmann-Millican (1994). The transdisciplinary team: A model for family-centered early intervention. In L. Johnson, J. Gallagher, & M. L. LaMontagne (Eds.), *Meeting early intervention challenges* (pp. 95–132). Baltimore: Paul H. Brookes.

McLane, J. B., & NcNamee, G. D. (1990). *Early Literacy.* Cambridge, MA: Harvard University Press.

McLane, J. B., & NcNamee, G. D. (1991). The Beginnings of Literacy. *Zero to Three, 12* (1) 1–8.

McLean, L. N., & Cripe, J. W. (1997). The effectiveness of early intervention for children with communication disorders. In M. J. Guralnick (Ed.), *The effectiveness of early intervention* (pp. 349–428). Baltimore: Paul H. Brookes.

McLean, M. (1996). Assessment and its importance in early intervention/early childhood special education. In M. McLean, D. B. Bailey, & M. Wolery (Eds.), *Assessing infants and preschoolers with special needs* (pp. 1–21). Englewood Cliffs, NJ: Prentice-Hall.

McLean, M., Bailey, D. B., and Wolery, M. (1996). *Assessing infants and preschoolers with special needs.* Englewood Cliffs, NJ: Merrill.

McWilliam, R. A., Lang, L., Vandiviere, P., Angell, R., Collins, L., & Underdown, G. (1995). Satisfaction and struggles: Family perceptions of early intervention services. *Journal of Early Intervention, 19,* 43–60.

Meisels, S. J. (1989). Can developmental screening tests identify children who are developmentally at-risk? *Pediatrics, 83,* 578–585.

Meisels, S. J. (1996). Charting the continuum of assessment and intervention. In S. J. Meisels & E. Fenichel (Eds.), *New Visions for the developmental assessment of infants and young children* (pp. 27–52). Washington, DC: Zero to Three National Center for Infants, Toddlers, and Families.

Meisels, S. J., & Provence, S. (1989). *Screening and assessment: Guidelines for identifying young disabled and developmentally vulnerable children and their families.* Washington, DC: Zero to Three: National Center for Infants, Toddlers, and Families.

Meyer, C. A. (1992). What's the difference between authentic and performance assessment? *Educational Leadership, 49* (8), 39–40.

Meyer, D., Vadasy, P., & Fewell, R. (1981). *Living with a brother or sister with special needs: A book for sibs.* Seattle: University of Washington Press.

Meyer, D., Vadasy, P., Fewell, R., & Schell, G. (1985). *A handbook for the fathers' program.* Seattle: University of Washington Press.

Miller, J. E. (2000). The effects of race/ethnicity on early childhood asthma prevalence and health care. *American Journal of Public Health, 90* (3), 428–430.

Miller, L. T., & McNulty, B. A. (1996). A values-based model of infant and toddler assessment. In S. J. Meisles & E. Fenichel (Eds.), *New visions for the developmental assessment of infants and young children* (pp. 347–360). Washington, DC: Zero to Three National Center for Infants, Toddlers, and Families.

Miller, N. B. (1994). *Nobody's perfect: Living and growing with children who have special needs.* Baltimore, MD: Paul H. Brookes.

Miller, R. (1996). *The developmentally appropriate inclusive classroom in early educations.* Albany, NY: Delmar.

Miller, S. E. (1999). Balloons, blankets and balls: Gross-motor activities to use indoors. *Young Children, 54* (5), 58–63.

Minuchin, S. (1974). *Families and family therapy.* Cambridge, MA: Harvard University Press.

Mirenda, P. (1999). Augmentative and alternative communication techniques. In J. E. Downing (Ed.), *Teaching communication skills to students with severe disabilities* (pp. 119–138). Baltimore: Paul H. Brookes.

Montessori, M. (1967). *The Absorbent Mind.* New York: Holt, Rinehart and Winston.

Morgan, S. R. (1987). *Abuse and neglect of handicapped children.* Boston: College Hill/Little, Brown.

Morris, S., & Klein, M. D. (1987). *Pro-feeding skills: A comprehensive resource for feeding development.* Tucson, AZ: Therapy Skill Builders.

Morsink, C. V., & Lenk, L. (1992). The delivery of special education programs and services. *Remedial and Special Education, 13* (6), 33–43.

Moses, K. (1987). The impact of childhood disability: The parent's struggle. *Ways* (Spring), 6–10.

Myer, D., Vadasy, P., Fewell, R., & Schell, G. (1985). *A handbook for the fathers program.* Seattle: University of Washington Press.

Myers, B., Olson, H. C., & Kaltenbach, K. (1992). Cocaine exposed infants: Myths and misunderstandings. *Zero to Three, 13,* 1–5.

National Assessment of Educational Progress (NAEP). (1996). Tips for teachers. Developed under funding from the U.S. Office of Special Education Programs (OSEP). *Learning to Read/Reading to Learn.* ERIC Clearinghouse on Disabilities and Gifted Education.

National Assessment of Educational Progress (NAEP). (1996). Learning to Read: Reading to Learn. ERIC Clearinghouse on Disabilities and Gifted Education. http://www.cec.sped.org.ericec.htm.

National Association for the Education of Young Children (NAEYC). (1987). Position statements on developmentally appropriate practice in early childhood programs. *Young Children, 41,* 3–29.

National Association for the Education of Young Children and National Association of Early Childhood Specialists in State Departments of Education. (1991). Guidelines for appropriate curriculum content in programs serving children ages 3 through 8: A position statement. *Young Children, 46,* 21–38.

National Association for the Education of Young Children (NAEYC). (1997). *Developmentally appropriate practice in early childhood programs.* Washington, DC: National Association for the Education of Young Children.

National Center for Educational Statistics. (1994). *Language characteristics and schooling in the United States: A changing picture, 1979–1989.* Washington DC: U.S. Department of Education, Office of Educational Research and Improvement.

National Center for Educational Statistics. (1999). *NAEP 1998 readings: A report card for the nation and the states.* Washington, DC: National Center for Educational Statistics.

National Commission of Children. (1991). *Beyond rhetoric: A new American agenda for children and families.* Washington, DC: Government Printing Office.

National Information Center for Children and Youth with Disabilities. (1999). *Traumatic brain injury.* Fact Sheet Number 18. Washington, DC: National Information Center for Children and Youth with Disabilities. (ERIC Document Reproduction Service No. 307 243).

National Reading Panel. (2000). Washington, DC: National Institute of Child Health and Human Development.

Nelson, C. A. (2000). The neurobiological bases of early intervention. In J. P. Shonkoff & S. J. Miesels (Eds.), *Handbook of early childhood intervention.* (2nd ed.) (pp. 204–227). New York: Cambridge University Press.

Nelson, J. R., Smith, D. J., & Dodd, J. M. (1991). Understanding the cultural characteristics of American Indian families: Effective partnerships under the Individualized Family Service Plan (IFSP). *Rural Special Education Quarterly, 11,* 33–38.

Nelson, N. W. (1994). Curriculum-based language assessment and intervention across the grades. In G. P. Wallach & K. G. Butler (Eds.), *Language learning disabilities in school-age children and adolescents* (pp. 104–131). Boston: Allyn and Bacon.

Nelson, N. W. (1998). *Childhood language disorders in context: Infancy through adolescence.* Boston: Allyn and Bacon.

Neuman, G. (1998). *Helping your kids cope with divorce the Sandcastles way.* New York: Times Books.

New, R. (1991). Early childhood teacher education in Italy: Reggio Emilia's master plan for master teachers. *The Journal of Early Childhood Teacher Education, 12,* 3.

Newman, S., & Dickinson, D. (Eds.). (2001). *Handbook on early literacy.* New York: Guilford.

Noonan, M. J., & McCormick, L. (1993). *Early intervention in natural environments: Methods and procedures.* Pacific Grove, CA: Brooks/Cole.

Noonan, M. J., & Ratokalau, N. B. (1991). PPT: The Preschool preparation and transition project. *Journal of Early Intervention, 15,* 390–398.

Oakley, G. P. (1998). Folic-acid-preventable spina bifida and anencephaly. *Bulletin of the World Health Organization, 76,* (2), 1–3.

Odom, S. L. (1994). Developmentally appropriate practice, policies, and use for young children with disabilities and their families. *Journal of Early Intervention, 18,* 346–348.

Odom, S., & Brown, W. (1993). Social interaction skills interventions for young children with disabilities in integrated settings. In C. A. Peck, S. I. Odom, & D. I. Bricker (Eds.), *Integrating young children with disabilities into community programs* (pp. 39–64). Baltimore: Paul H. Brookes.

Odom, S. L., & Diamond, N. E. (1998). Inclusion of young children with special needs in early childhood education: The research base. *Early Childhood Research Quarterly, 13* (1), 3–25.

Odom, S. L., & McEvoy, M. A. (1990). Mainstreaming at the preschool level: Potential barriers and tasks for the field. *Topics in Early Childhood Special Education, 10,* 48–61.

Odom, S. L., & McLean, M. E. (1996). *Early intervention/early childhood special education: Recommended Practices.* Austin, TX: Pro-Ed.

Odom, S. L., McLean, M. E., Johnson, L. J., & Montagne, M. J. (1995). Recommended Practices in early childhood special education: Validation and current use. *Journal of Early Intervention, 19* (1), 1–17.

O'Donnell, P. A. (1969). *Motor and haptic learning.* Belmont, CA: Dimensions/Fearon.

Okimoto, A. M., Bundy, A., & Hanzlik, J. (2000). Playfulness in children with and without disability: Measurement and intervention. *American Journal of Occupational Therapy, 54* (1), 73–82.

Olson, J., & Esdaile, S. (2000). Mothering young children with disabilities in a challenging urban environment. *American Journal of Occupational Therapy, 54* (3), 307–314.

Olson, B. H., Larsen, A. S., & McCubbin, H. I. (1983). Family strengths. In D. H. Olson, H. I. McCubbin, H. L. Barnes, A. S. Larsen, M. L. Muxen, & M. A. Wilson (Eds.), *Families: What makes them work?* (pp. 261–262). Beverly Hills, CA: Sage.

Orelove, F. P., & Sobsey, D. (1987). *Educating children with multiple disabilities: A transdisciplinary approach.* Baltimore: Paul H. Brookes.

Orelove, F. P., & Sobsey, D. (1996). *Educating children with multiple disabilities.* Baltimore: Paul H. Brookes.

Orr, M. E. (1997). *Nutrition.* In P. A. Potter & A. G. Perry (Eds.), *Fundamentals of nursing: Concepts, process, and practice* (pp. 1089–1127). St. Louis: Mosby.

Osborn, J., Sherwood, D., & Cole, K. (1991). *Mediated learning program.* Seattle: University of Washington Press.

Owens, R. E., Jr. (1996). *Language development: An introduction.* Boston: Allyn and Bacon.

Palinscar, A. S., & Brown, A. L. (1994). Reciprocal teaching of comprehension-fostering and monitoring activities. *Cognition and Instruction, 1,* 117–175.

Parten, M. B. (1932). Social participation among preschool children. *Journal of Abnormal and Social Psychology, 27,* 243–269.

Paul, J. L., & Simeonsson, R. J. (1993). *Children with special needs.* New York: Harcourt Brace Jovanovich.

Paul, R. (1994). Profiles of toddlers with slow expressive language development. In K. G. Butler (Ed.), *Early intervention II: Working with parents and families* (pp. 65–78) Gaithersburg, MD: Aspen.

Peck, C., Odom, S., & Bricker, D. (Eds.). *Integrating young children with disabilities into community programs: Ecological persepectives on research and implementation.* Baltimore: Paul H. Brookes.

Pestalozzi, J. H. (1990). *How Gertrude teaches her children.* (L. E. Holland & E. C. Turner, Trans.). Syracuse, NY: Bardeen.

Peterson, N. (1987). *Early intervention for handicapped and at-risk children.* Denver: Love.

Peterson, N. L. (1991). Interagency collaboration under Part H: The key to comprehensive multidisciplinary, coordinated infant/toddler intervention services. *Journal of Early Intervention, 15,* 89–105.

Peterson, N. L., Barber, P. A., & Ault, M. M. (1994). Young children with special health care needs. In P. L. Safford, B. Spodek, & O. Saracho (Eds.), *Early childhood special education* (pp. 165–191). New York: Teachers College Press.

Peterson, N. L., & Mantle, J. A. (1983). Interagency collaboration: Applications in early intervention for the handicapped. In E. M. Goetz & N. E. Allen (Eds.), *Early childhood education: Special environmental, policy, and legal considerations* (pp. 209–259). Rockville, MD: Aspen.

Peuschel, S. M. (1985, January–February). Atlantoaxial instability in children with Down's syndrome. *Down Syndrome News.*

Phelps, L. (1995). Psychoeducational outcomes of Fetal Alcohol Syndrome. *School Psychology Review, 24,* 200–212.

Phillips, C. B. (1994). The movement of African-American children through sociocultural contexts: A case of conflict resolution. In B. L. Mallory & R. S. New (Eds.), *Diversity and developmentally appropriate practices* (pp. 137–154). New York: Teachers College Press.

Piaget J. (1952). *The origins of intelligence in children.* (M. Cook, Trans.). New York: International University Press.

Piaget, J. (1954). *The construction of reality in the child.* New York: Basic Books.

Piaget, J. (1962). *The language and thought of the child.* New York: World Publishing.

Piaget, J. (1970). *The science of education and psychology of the child.* New York: Grossman.

Piaget, J. (1971). *Biology and knowledge.* Chicago: University of Chicago Press.

Plotkin, H., Rauch, F., Bishop, N. J., Montpett, K., Ruck-Gibis, J., Travers, R., & Glorieux, F. H. (2000). Pamidronate treatment of severe osteogensis imperfecta in children under 3 years of age. *Journal of Clinical Endocrinology and Metabolism, 85* (5), 1846–1850.

Powers, M. D. (2000). What is autism? In M. D. Powers (Ed.), *Children with autism.* (2nd ed.) (pp. 1–44). Bethesda, MD: Woodbine House.

Pratt, B. (1999). Making it work: Using technology in a classroom for young children with multiple disabilities. *Learning and Leading with Technology, 26,* (8), 28–31.

Premack, D. (1959). Toward empirical behavior law, I; *Psychological Review, 66,* 219–223.

Prenatal exposure to alcohol. (2000). *Alcohol Research & Health, 24* (1), 32–41.

Project Head Start. (1965). Economic Opportunity Act of 1965.

Puckett, M. B., & Black, J. K. (2000). *Authentic assessment of the young child: Celebrating development and learning.* Upper Saddle River, NJ: Prentice-Hall.

Pugach, M. C., & Johnson, L. J. (1995). *Collaborative practitioners: Collaborative schools.* Denver, CO: Love.

Quill, K. A. (2000). *Do-watch-listen-say: Social and communication intervention for children with autism.* Baltimore: Paul H. Brookes.

Quindlen, A. (1991). Teaching kids early enough to make a difference. *Chicago Tribune,* Section 1, June 11.

Raffi (singer). (1986). *A children's sampler of singable songs.* Willowdale, Ontario: Shoreline Records, a division of Troubadour Records Ltd. (cassette).

Ratner, V., & Harris, L. (1994). *Understanding language disorders: The impact on learning.* Eau Claire, WI: Thinking Publications.

Rao, S. S. (2000). Perspectives of an African American mother on parent-professional relationships in special education. *Mental Retardation, 38* (6), 475–488.

Raskin, M., & Higgins, E. (1998). Assistive technology in the homes of children with learning disabilities: An exploratory study. *Learning Disabilities: A Multidisciplinary Journal, 9* (2), 33–56.

Raver, S. A. (1991). *Strategies for teaching at-risk and handicapped infants and toddlers: A transdisciplinary approach.* New York: Merrill.

Raver, S. (Ed.). (1998). *Intervention strategies: Infants and toddlers with special needs.* Columbus, OH: Merrill Prentice-Hall.

Reamer, F. G. (1990). *Ethical dilemmas in social services.* New York: Columbia University Press.

Reid, D. K (2000). Epilogue. In K. R. Fahey & D. Kim Reid (Eds.), *Language development, differences, and disorders* (pp. 481–489). Austin, TX: Pro-Ed.

Rekate, H. L., Theodore, N., Sonntag, V. K. H., & Dickamn, C. A. (1999). Pediatric spine and spinal cord trauma. State of the art for the third millennium. *Child's Nervous System, 15* (11–12), 743–750.

Resnick, L., & Klopfer, L. (1989). Toward the thinking curriculum: An overview. In L. Resnick & L. Klopfer (Eds.), *Toward the thinking curriculum: Current cognitive research* (pp. 1–18). Alexandria, VA: Association for Supervision and Curriculum Development.

Riccio, C., Hynd, G., Cohen, M., & Gonzalez, J. (1993). Neurological basis of attention deficit hyperactivity disorder. *Exceptional Children, 60,* 118–124.

Rice, M. L. (1995). The rationale and operating principles for a language-focused curriculum for preschool children. In M. L. Rice & H. A. Wilcox (Eds.), *Building a language-focused curriculum for the preschool classroom: Foundation for lifelong communication* (pp. 27–38). Baltimore: Paul H. Brookes.

Richarz, S. (1993). Innovations in early childhood education: Models that support the integration of children of varied developmental levels. In C. A. Peck, S. L. Odom, & D. D. Bricker (Eds.), *Integrating young children with disabilities into community programs* (pp. 83–108). Baltimore: Paul H. Brookes.

Richek, M., Jennings, J., Caldwell, J., & Lerner, J. (2002). *Reading problems: Assessment and teaching strategies.* Boston: Allyn and Bacon.

Richey, D. D., & Wheeler, J. J. (2000). *Inclusive early childhood education.* Albany, NY: Delmar.

Richmond, J. (1990). Low-Birth Weight Infants. *JAMA (Journal of the American Medical Association), 263* (22), 3069–3070.

Rizzo, T. L., Davis, W. E., & Toussaint, R. (1994). Inclusion in regular classes: Breaking from traditional curricula. *Journal of Physical Education, Recreation, and Dance, 65,* 24–27.

Rodger, S., & Ziviani, J. (1999). Play-based occupational therapy. *International Journal of Disability, Development and Education, 46* (3), 337–365.

Rogers, S. J. (1982). Cognitive characteristics of handicapped children's play. In R. Pelz (Ed.), *Developmental and clinical aspects of young children's play.* Monmouth, OR: Westar Series Paper, No. 17.

Romeo, F. F. (2000). The educator's role in reporting the emotional abuse of children. *Journal of Instructional Psychology, 27* (3), 183–186.

Romski, M. A., & Sevcik, R. A. (1996). *Breaking the speech barrier: Language development through augmentative means.* Baltimore: Paul H. Brookes.

Rosenberg, S. A., & Robinson, C. C. (1990). Assessment of the infant with multiple handicaps. In E. D. Gibbs & D. M. Teti (Eds.), *Interdisciplinary assessment of infants* (pp. 177–190). Baltimore: Paul H. Brookes.

Rosenkoetter, S. E. (1992). Guidelines from recent legislation to structure transition planning. *Infants and Young Children, 5* (1), 21–27.

Rosenkoetter, S. E., & Squires, S. (2000). Writing outcomes that make a difference for children and families. *Young Exceptional Children, 4* (1), 2–8.

Rossetti, L. M. (1996). *Communication intervention.* San Diego, CA: Singular.

Rous, B., Hemmeter, M. L., & Schuster, J. (1999). Evaluating the impact of the STEPS model on development of community-wide transition systems. *Journal of Early Intervention, 22* (1), 38–50.

Rousseau, J. J. (1911). *Emile.* (B. Foxley, Trans.). London: Dent. (Originally published in 1762).

Rule, S., Fiechtl, B. J., & Innocenti, M. S. (1990). Preparation for transition to mainstreamed postpreschool environments: Development of a survival skills curriculum. *Topics in Early Childhood Special Education, 9* (4), 78–90.

Rule, S., Losardo, A., Dinnebeil, L. A., Kaiser, N., & Rowland, C. (1998). Research challenges in naturalistic intervention. *Journal of Early Intervention, 21,* 283–293.

Rutter, M., & Schopler, E. (1992). Classification of pervasive developmental disorders: Some concepts and practical considerations. *Journal of Autism and Developmental Disorders, 22,* 459–482.

Saland, S. J., & Taylor, L. (1993). Working with families: A cross-cultural perspective. *Remedial and Special Education, 14,* 25–32.

Salisbury, C. L. (1993). Mainstreaming during the early childhood years. *Exceptional Children, 58,* 146–155.

Salisbury, C. L., & Vincent, L. J. (1990). Criterion of the next environment and best practices: Mainstreaming and integration 10 years later. *Topics in Early Childhood Special Education, 10,* 78–89.

Salvia, J., & Ysseldyke, J. E. (1998). *Assessment.* Boston: Houghton Mifflin.

Sameroff, A. J. (1987). The social context of development. In N. Eisenberg (Ed.), *Contemporary topics in developmental psychology* (pp. 273–291). New York: Wiley.

Sameroff, A. J., & Emde, R. N. (Eds.). (1989). *Relationship disturbances in early childhood.* New York: Basic Books.

Sameroff, A. J., & Fiese, B. H. (1990). Transactional regulation and early intervention. In S. J. Meisels & J. P. Shonkoff (Eds.), *Handbook of early childhood intervention* (pp. 119–149). New York: Cambridge University Press.

Sandall, S., McLean, M., & Smith, B. (Eds.). (2000). *DEC recommended practices in early intervention/early childhood special education.* Denver, CO: Division for Early Childhood (DEC) of the Council for Exceptional Children (CEC).

Sandall, S. R. (1993). Curricula for early intervention. In W. Brown, S. K. Thurman & L. E. Pearl (Eds.), *Family-centered early intervention with infants and toddlers: Innovative cross-disciplinary approaches* (pp. 129–151). Baltimore: Paul H. Brookes.

Sattler, J. M. (1992). *Assessment of children.* San Diego, CA: Jerome M. Sattler.

Schaefer, C. E., & Digeronimo, T. F. (1997). *Toilet training without tears.* New York: Signet Books.

Schopler, E. (1985). Parents of psychotic children as scapegoats. In A. M. Donnellan (Ed.), *Classic readings in autism.* New York: Teachers College Press.

Schwartz, I. S., & Olswang, L. B. (1996). Evaluating child behavior change in natural settings: Exploring alternative strategies for data collection. *Topics in Early Childhood Special Education, 16,* 82–101.

Schwartz, I. S., & Swinth, Y. (1994). Physical and occupational therapists in naturalistic early childhood settings: Challenges and strategies for training. *Topics in Early Childhood Special Education, 14,* 333–349.

Schweinhart, L. J., Barnes, H. V., & Weikart, D. B. (1993). *Significant benefits: the High/Scope Perry Preschool study through age 27.* Monographs of the High/Scope Educational Research Foundation. No. 10. Ypsilanti, MI: High/Scope Press.

Schweinhart, L. J., & Weikart, D. B. (1980). *Young children grow up: The effects of the Perry Preschool Program on youths through age 15.* Ypsilanti, MI: The High/Scope Press.

Schweinhart, L. J., & Weikart, D. B. (1988). The High/Scope Perry Preschool Program. In R. H. Price, E.L Cowen, R. P. Lorion, & J. R. McKay (Eds.), *14 ounces of prevention* (pp. 53–65). Washington, DC: American Psychological Association.

Segal, M., & Weber, N. T. (1996). Nonstructured play observation: Guidelines, benefits, and caveats. In S. J. Meisels & E. Fenichel (Eds.), *New visions for the developmental assessment of infants and young children* (pp. 207–230). Washington, DC: Zero to Three National Center for Infants, Toddlers, and Families.

Seligman, M., & Darling, R. B. (1989). *Ordinary families: Special children.* New York: Guilford.

Sewell, T. J., Collins, B. C., Hemmeter, M. L., & Shuster, J. W. (1998). Using simultaneous prompting within an activity-based format to teach dressing skills to preschoolers with developmental delays. *Journal of Early Intervention, 21,* 132–142.

Shea, T. M., & Bauer, A. M. (1991). *Parents and teachers of children with exceptionalities.* Boston: Allyn & Bacon.

Shelov, S. P., & Hannemann, R. E. (Eds.). (1998). *Caring for your baby and young child* (rev. ed.). New York: Bantam.

Sherman, C. (2000). Sensory integration is controversial Dx. *Family Practice News, 1013,* 40.

Shotts, C. K., Rosenkoetter, S. E., Streufert, C. A., & Rosenkoetter, L. I. (1994). Transition policy and issues: A view from the states. *Topic in Early Childhood Special Education, 14* (3), 395–411.

Shriver, M. D., Anderson, C. M., & Proctor, B. (2000). Evaluating the validity of functional behavior assessment. *School Psychology Review, 30* (2), 180–192.

Silberman, R. K. (1996). Children with visual impairments. In E. L. Meyen (Ed.), *Exceptional children in today's schools* (pp. 351–398). Denver, CO: Love.

Simeonsson, N., Lorimer, M., Shelley, B., & Sturtz, J. (1995). Asthma: New information for the early interventionist. *Topics in Early Childhood Special Education, 15* (1), 32–43.

Singh, D. K. (2000). *Families of Head Start children: What do we know?* Niagra, NY: Niagra University. (ERIC Document Reproduction Service No. ED 445 779).

Skeels, H. (1942). A study of the effects of differential stimulation on mentally retarded children: A follow-up study. *American Journal of mental deficiency, 46*, 340–350.

Skeels, H. (1966). *Adult studies of children and contrasting life experiences.* Monograph of the society for Research in Child Development, No. 31. Chicago: University of Chicago Press.

Skeels, H., & Dye, H. (1939, November). *A study of the effects of differential stimulations on mentally retarded children.* Proceedings and Address of the Annual Session of the American Association on Mental Deficiency.

Skinner, B. F. (1957). *Verbal behavior.* New York: Appleton-Century-Crofts.

Skinner, B. F. (1959). *Verbal behavior* (2nd ed.). New York: Appleton-Century-Crofts.

Sloman, L. (1991). Use of medication in pervasive developmental disorders. *Psychiatric Clinics of North America, 14*, 165–181.

Smeriglio, V. L., & Wilcox, H. C. (1999). Prenatal drug exposure and child outcome. Past, present, future. *Clinical Perinatology, 26* (1), 1–16.

Smith, B. K., & Hill, E. W. (1990). The development of a motor curriculum for preschool children with visual impairments. *Peabody Journal of Education, 67* (2), 41–53.

Smith, D. D., & Lukasson, R. (1995). *Introduction to special education: Teaching in an age of challenge.* Boston: Allyn & Bacon.

Smith, M. M. (1989). NAEYC–confronting tough issues. *Young Children, 44*, 32–37.

Smith, S., Fairchild, M., & Groginsky, S. (1995) *Early childhood care and education: An investment that works.* Denver, CO: National Conference of State Legislatures.

Smith, T., Groen, A. D., & Wynn, J. W. (2000). Randomized trial of intensive early intervention for children with pervasive developmental disorder. *American Journal on Mental Retardation, 105* (4), 269–285.

Snell, M. E. (1987). *Systematic instruction of persons with severe handicaps.* Columbus, OH: Merrill.

Snell, M. E., & Brown, F. (2000). *Instruction of students with severe disabilities.* Upper Saddle River, NJ: Prentice-Hall.

Sonag, J. C., & Schacht, R. (1994). An ethnic comparison of parent participation and information needs in early intervention. *Exceptional Children, 60*, 422–433.

Spiegel-McGill, P., Reed, D. J., Konig, C. S., & McGowan, P. A. (1990). Parent education: Easing the transition to preschool. *Topics in Early Childhood Special Education, 9* (4), 66–77.

Stayton, V. D., & Miller, P. S. (1993). Combining general and special early childhood standards in personnel preparation programs: Experiences from two states. *Topics in Early Childhood Special Education, 13* (3), 372–387.

Stein, M. A., Efron, L. A., Schuman, W., Blum, N., & Glanzmann, M. (in press). *Attention–deficits and hyperactivity.*

Stern, D. (1977). *The first relationship: Infant and mother.* Cambridge, MA: Harvard University Press.

Stinnett, N., & DeFrain, J. (1985). Family strengths inventory. In N. Stinnett & J. DeFrain (Eds.), *Secrets of strong families.* (pp. 180–182). New York: Berkley Books.

Strain, P. S. (1990). LRE for preschool children with handicaps: What we know, what we should be doing. *Journal of Early Intervention, 4*, 291–296.

Strain, P. S., & Hoyson, M. (2000). The need for longitudinal, intensive social skill intervention: LEAP follow–up outcomes for children with autism. *Topics in Early Childhood Special Education, 20* (2), 116–122.

Strain, P. S., Jamieson, B., & Hoyson, M. (1986). Learning experiences: An alternative program for preschoolers and parents. In C. J. Meisel (Ed.), *Mainstreaming handicapped children: Outcomes, controversies, and new directions* (pp. 251–269). Hillsdale, NJ: Erlbaum.

Straka, E., & Bricker, D. (1996). Building a collaborative team. In D. Bricker & A. Widerstrom (Eds.), *Preparing personnel to work with infants and young children and their families: A team approach* (pp. 321–345). Baltimore: Paul H. Brookes.

Stremel, K. (2000). Recommended practices in technology applications. In S. Sandall, M. McLean, & B. Smith (Eds.), *DEC recommended practices in early intervention/early childhood special education* (pp. 55–64). Denver, CO: Division for Early Childhood (DEC) of the Council for Exceptional Children (CEC).

Summers, J., Steeples, T., Peterson, C., Naig, L., McBride, S., Wall, S., Liebow, H., Swanson, M., & Stowitschek, J. (2001). Policy and management supports for effective service integration in early Head Start and Part C Programs. *Topics in Early Childhood Special Education, 21* (1), 16–32.

Svejda, M. J., Pannabecker, B. J., & Emde, R. N. (1982). Parent-to-infant attachment. In R. N. Emde & R. J. Harmon, (Eds.), *The development of attachment and affiliative systems.* New York: Plenum Press.

Swan, W. W., & Morgan, J. L. (1993). *Collaborating for comprehensive services for young children and their families.* Baltimore: Paul H. Brookes.

Szatmari, P. (1992). The validity of autistic spectrum disorders: A literature review. *Journal of Autism and Developmental Disorders, 22*, 583–600.

Tabors, P. O. (1997). *One child, two languages: A guide for preschool educators of children learning English as a second language.* Baltimore: Paul H. Brookes.

Tabors, P. O. (1998). What early childhood educators need to know: Developing effective programs for linguistically and culturally diverse children and families. *Young Children, 53* (6), 20–26.

Taulbee, D. R. (1988). *Curriculum for the special education early childhood center.* Jackson County, MI: Jackson County Intermediate School District.

Tefft, D., Guerette, P., & Furumasu, J. (1999). How important is mobility for your child? *Exceptional Parent, 29* (4), 40–45.

Tenbrink, T. D. (1999). Assessment. In J. M. Cooper (Ed.), *Classroom teaching skills* (pp. 308–348). Boston: Houghton Mifflin.

Thomas, A., & Chess, S. (1977). *Temperament and development.* New York: Bruner/Mazel.

Thomas, A., Chess, S., Birch, H. G., Hertzig, M. E., & Korn, S. (1963). *Behavioral individuality in early childhood.* New York: New York University Press.

Thorp, E. (1997). Increasing opportunities for partnership with culturally and linguistically diverse families. *Intervention in School and Clinic, 32,* 261–269.

Thorp, E. K., & McCollum, J. A. (1994). Defining the infancy specialization in early childhood special education. In L. Johnson, R. J. Gallagher, & M. L. LaMontagne (Eds.), *Meeting early intervention challenges* (pp. 167–184). Baltimore: Paul H. Brookes.

Tiegerman-Farber, E., & Radziewicz, C. (1998). *Collaborative decision making: The pathway to inclusion.* Upper Saddle River, NJ: Prentice-Hall.

Tomey, H. A. (1992, March 5). *Teaching mathematics to the adolescent with a specific learning disability.* Presentation at the annual conference of the Learning Disabilities Association, Atlanta, GA.

Torgesen, J. (1991). Learning disabilities: Historical and conceptual issues. In B. Wong (Ed.), *Learning about learning disabilities* (pp. 3–39). San Diego: Academic Press.

Trask, C. L., & Kosofsky, B. E. (2000). Developmental considerations of neurotoxic exposures. *Clinical Neurobehavioral Toxicology, 18* (3), 541–561.

Trawick-Smith, J. (2000). *Early childhood development.* Columbus, OH: Merrill/Prentice-Hall.

Trivette, C., & Dunst, C. (2000). Recommended practices in family-based practices. In S. Sandall, M. McLean, & B. Smith (Eds.), *DEC recommended practices in early intervention/early childhood special education* (pp. 39–44). Denver, CO: Division for Early Childhood (DEC) of the Council for Exceptional Children (CEC).

Tronick, E. Z., & Beeghly, M. (1999). Prenatal cocaine exposure, child development, and the compromising effects of cumulative risk. *Clinics in Perinatology, 26* (1), 151–171.

Turnbull, A. P., Turbiville, V., & Turnbull, H. R. (2000). Evolution of family-professional partnerships: Collective empowerment as the model for the early twenty-first century. In J. P. Shonkoff & S. J. Meisels (Eds.), *Handbook of early childhood intervention* (2nd ed.) (pp. 630–650). New York: Cambridge University Press.

Turnbull, A. P., & Turnbull, H. R. (1990). *Families, professionals, and exceptionality: A special partnership.* Columbus, OH: Merrill.

Turnbull, A. P., & Turnbull, H. R. (1997). *Families, professionals, and exceptionality.* Upper Saddle River, NJ: Merrill/Prentice-Hall.

Turnbull, A. P., & Turnbull, H. R. (2001). *Families, professionals and exceptionality: A special partnership.* Columbus, OH: Merrill.

U.S. Department of Education. (1933). *Educating young children prenatally exposed to drugs and at risk* (ISBN Publication No. 0-16-041868-2). Washington, DC: U.S. Government Printing Office.

U.S. Department of Education. (1994). *To assure the free appropriate public education of all children with disabilities.* Sixteenth annual Report to Congress on the Implementation of the Individuals with Disabilities Act. Washington DC: U.S. Government Printing Office.

U.S. Department of Education. (1995). *To assure the free appropriate public education of all children with disabilities.* Seventeenth Annual Report to Congress on the Implementation of the Individuals with Disabilities Act. Washington DC: U.S. Government Printing Office.

U.S. Department of Education. (1996). *To assure the free appropriate public education of all children with disabilities.* Eighteenth Annual Report to Congress on the Implementation of Individuals with Disabilities Act. Washington, DC: U.S. Government Printing Office.

U.S. Department of Education. (2000). *To assure the free appropriate public education for all children with disabilities.* Report to Congress on the Implementation of the Individuals with Disabilities Education Act. Washington, DC: Government Printing Office.

U.S. General Accounting Office. (1995). *Early childhood centers: Services to prepare children for school often limited.* GAO/HEHS-95-21. Washington, DC: DHHS.

Umansky, W., & Hooper, S. R. (1998). *Young children with special needs.* Upper Saddle River, NJ: Prentice-Hall.

Umbreit, J. (1996a). Functional analysis of disruptive behavior in an inclusive classroom. *Journal of Autism and Developmental Disorders, 22,* 483–492.

Umbreit, J. (1996b). Functional analysis of disruptive behavior in an inclusive classroom. *Journal of Early Intervention, 20,* 18–29.

Vaughn, S., Reiss, M., Rothlein, L., & Hughes, M. T. (1999). Kindergarten teachers' perceptions of instructing students with disabilities. *Remedial and Special Education, 20* (3), 184–191.

Vincent, L. J., & Beckett, J. A. (1993). Family participation. In DEC Task Force on Recommended Practices, *DEC recommended practices: Indicators of quality in programs for infants and young children with special needs and their families* (pp. 19–29). Reston, VA: Council for Exceptional Children.

Volkmar, F. R. (1992). Three diagnostic systems for autism: DMS-III, DSM III-R, and ICD-10. *Journal of Autism and Developmental disorders, 22,* 483–492.

von Bertalanffy, L. (1968). *General systems theory.* New York: Braziller.

Vygotsky, L. S., (1962). *Thought and language.* Cambridge, MA: MIT Press.

Vygotsky, L. S. (1978a). *Thought and language.* Cambridge, MA: MIT Press.

Vygotsky, L. S. (1978b). In M. Cole, V. John-Steiner, S. Scribner, & Souberman (Eds.), *Mind in society: The development of higher psychological processes.* Cambridge, MA: Harvard University Press.

Walker, H. M., Schwarz, I. E., Nippold, M. A., Irvin, L. K., & Noell, J. W. (1994). Social skills in school-age children and youth: Issues and best practices in assessment and intervention. *Topics in Language Disorders, 14* (3), 70–82.

Walker, J. E., & Shea, T. M. (1988). *Behavior modification: A practical approach for teachers* (4th ed.). Columbus, OH: Charles E. Merrill.

Walter, V., & Petr, C. (2000). A template for family-centered interagency collaboration. *Families in Society: The Journal of Contemporary Human Services, 8* (5), 470–479.

Wanzer, P. (1999). Obstacle courses: Challenging brain food. *Exceptional Parent, 29* (4) 54–57.

Warren, S. F., & Yoder, P. J. (1994). Communication and language intervention: Why a constructivist approach is insufficient. *The Journal of Special Education, 28,* 248–258.

Warren, S. L., Emde, R. N., & Sroufe, L. A. (2000). Internal representations: Predicting anxiety from children's play narratives. *Journal of American Academy of Child and Adolescent Psychiatry, 39* (1), 100–107.

Washington, K., Schwartz, I. S., & Swinth, Y. (1994). Physical and occupational therapists in naturalis-

tic early childhood settings: Challenges and strategies for training. *Topics in Early Childhood Education, 14,* 333–349.

Weber, J. D. (2000). Introduction. In J. D. Weber (Ed.), *Children with Fragile X Syndrome: A parents' guide* (pp. 67–91). Bethesda, MD: Woodbine House.

Wehman, T., & Gilkerson, L. (1999). Parents of young children with special needs speak out: Perceptions of early intervention services. *Infant Toddler Intervention: The Transdisciplinary Journal, 9* (2), 137–157.

Weissbourd, B. (1993). Family support programs. In C. Zeanah (Ed.), *Handbook of infant mental health* (pp. 402–413). New York: Guilford Press.

Wesson, K. A. (2001). The "Volvo Effect": Questioning standardized tests. *The Journal of the National Association for Education of Young Children, 36,* (2), 16–18.

Wetherby, A. M., & Prizant, B. M. (1996). Toward earlier identification of communication and language problems in infants and young children. In S. J. Meisels & E. Fenichel (Eds.), *New visions for the developmental assessment of infants and young children* (pp. 289–312). Washington, DC: Zero to Three National Center for Infants, Toddlers, and Families.

Wetherby, A. M., & Prizant, B. (1993). Profiling communication and symbolic abilities in young children. *Journal of Childhood Communication Disorders, 15,* 23–32.

Wetherby, A. M., & Prizant, B. (1998). *Communication and symbolic behavior scales, developmental profile, research edition.* Chicago: Applied Symbolix.

Wetherby, A., & Prizant, B. (1999). Enhancing language and communication development in autism: Assessment and intervention guidelines. In D. Berkell Zagor (Ed.), *Autism: Identification, education, and treatment* (pp. 141–174). Mahwah, NJ: Lawrence Erlbaum.

Wetherby, A. M., Prizant, B. M., & Hutchinson, T. (1998). Communicative, social-affective, and symbolic profiles of young children with autism and pervasive developmental disorder. *American Journal of Speech-Language Pathology, 7,* 79–91.

Whipple, E. E. (1999). Reaching families with preschoolers at risk of physical child abuse: What works? *Families in Society, 80* (2), 148–160.

Whitbread, N. (1972). *The evolution of the nursery-infant school: A history of infant and nursery education in Britain, 1800–1972.* London: Routledge & Kegan Paul.

Widerstrom, A., & Bricker, D. (1996). Into the 21st Century. In D. Bricker & A. Widerstrom (Eds.), *Preparing personnel to work with infants and young children* (pp. 347–354). Baltimore: Paul H. Brookes.

Widerstrom, A. H., Mowder, B. A., & Sandall, S. R. (1991). *At-risk and handicapped newborns and infants: Development, assessment, and intervention.* Englewood Cliffs, NJ: Prentice-Hall.

Williams, D. F. (1999). The child who stutters: Guidelines for the educator. *Young Exceptional Children, 2* (3), 9–14.

Williams, L. (1994). Developmentally appropriate practice and cultural values: A case in point. In B. L. Mallory & R. S. New (Eds.), *Diversity and developmentally appropriate practice* (pp. 155–182). New York: Teachers College Press.

Windsor, J. (1995). Language impairment and social competence. In M. E. Fey, J. Windsor, & S. Warren (Eds.), *Language intervention: Preschool-through the elementary years.* Baltimore: Paul H. Brookes.

Winton, P. J. (1993). Providing family support in integrated settings: Research and recommendations. In C. A. Peck, S. L. Odom, & D. D. Bricker (Eds.), *Integrating young children with disabilities into community programs* (pp. 65–80). Baltimore: Paul H. Brookes.

Winton, P. J., & Bailey, D. B. (1988). The family-focused interview: A collaborative mechanism for family assessment and goal setting. *Journal of the Division for Early Childhood, 3,* 195–207.

Winton, P. J., & Bailey, D. B. (1994). Family-centered practices in early intervention for children with hearing loss. In J. Roush & N. Matkin (Eds.), *Infants and toddlers with hearing loss: Identification and family-centered intervention* (pp. 23–42). Parkton, MD: York Press.

Witt, J. C., Elliot, S. N., Kramer, J. J., & Gresham, F. M. (1994). *Assessment of children: Fundamental methods and practices.* Dubuque, IA: Grown and Benchmark.

Wolery, M. (1983). Evaluating curricula: Purposes and strategies. *Topics in Early Childhood Special Education, 2,* 15–24.

Wolery, M. (1996). Using assessment information to plan intervention programs. In M. McLean, D. B. Bailey, & M. Wolery (Eds.), *Assessing infants and preschoolers with special needs* (pp. 519–527). Englewood Cliffs, NJ: Prentice-Hall.

Wolery, M. (2000). Recommended practices in child-focused interventions. In S. Sandall, M. McLean, & B. Smith (Eds.), *DEC recommended practices in early intervention/early childhood special education* (pp. 29–38). Denver, CO: Division for Early Childhood (DEC) of the Council for Exceptional Children (CEC).

Wolery, M., & Dyk, L. (1984). Arena assessment: Description and preliminary social validity data. *The Journal of the Association for the Severely Handicapped, 9,* 231–235.

Wolery, M., & Fleming, L. A. (1993). Implementing individualized curricula in integrated settings. In C. A. Peck, S. L. Odom, & D. D. Bricker (Eds.), *Integrating young children with disabilities into community programs: Ecological perspectives on research and implementation* (pp. 109–132). Baltimore: Paul H. Brookes.

Wolery, M., & Smith, P. D. (1989). Assession self-care skills. In D. B. Bailey & M. Wolery (Eds.), *Assessing infants and preschoolers with handicaps* (pp. 447–477). Columbus, OH: Merrill.

Wolery, M., & Strain, P. (1992). Applying the framework of developmentally appropriate practice to children with special needs. In S. Bredekamp & T. Rosegrant (Eds.), *Teaching potentials: Appropriate curriculum and assessment for 3–8 year olds.* Washington, DC: National Association for Education of Young Children.

Wolery, M., Werts, M., & Holcombe, A. (1994). Current practices with young children who have disabilities: Placement assessment, and instruction issues. *Focus on Exceptional Children, 6* (26), 1–12.

Wolery, M., & Wilbers, J. (1994). *Including children with special needs in early childhood programs.* Washington, DC: NAEYC.

Wolfensberger, J. L. (1972). *The principles of normalization in human services.* Toronto: National Institute of Mental Retardation.

Wood, M. M., Combs, C. C., Grunn, A., & Weller, D. (1986). *Developmental therapy in the classroom* (2nd ed.). Austin, TX: Pro-Ed.

Yoder, P. J., Kaiser, A. P., Goldstein, H., Alpert, C., Mousetis, L., Kaczmarek, L., & Fischer, R. (1995). An exploratory comparison of milieu teaching and responsive interaction in classroom applications. *Journal of Early Intervention, 19,* 218–242.

Yoshikawa, H. (1995). Long-term effects of early childhood programs, on social outcomes and delinquency. *The Future of Children: Long-term Outcomes of Early Childhood Programs, 6* (3), 51–75.

Young, E. (1993). The NICU and early transitional care. In M. Krajicek & R. Thompkins (Eds.), *The medically fragile infant* (pp. 13–23). Austin, TX: Pro-Ed.

Zabel, M. K. (1991). *Teaching young children with behavioral disorders: CEC mini-library.* Reston, VA: ERIC Clearinghouse on Handicapped and Gifted Children. (ERIC Document Reproduction Service No. ED 333 657).

Zeanah, C. H., Boris, N. W., & Lieberman, A. F. (2000). Attachment disorders of infancy. In A. J. Sameroff,

M. Lewis, & S. M. Miller (Eds.), *Handbook of developmental psychopathology* (2nd ed.) (pp. 293–307). New York: Kluwer Academic/Plenum.

Zervigon-Hakes, A. (1995). Translating research findings into large-scale public programs and policies. *The Future of Children: Long-term Outcomes of Early Childhood Programs, 6* (3), 175–191.

Zigler, E., Hopper, P., & Hall, N. W. (1993). Infant mental health and social policy. In C. H. Zeanah,

(Ed.), *Handbook of infant mental health.* New York: Guilford Press.

Zuckerman, B. (1990). In perspective: Crack-exposed babies come of school age. *The Brown University Child Behavior and Development Letter, 6* (9), 1–2.

Zuckerman, B., & Brown, E. R. (1993). Maternal substance abuse and infant development. In C. Zeanah (Ed.), *Handbook of infant mental health* (pp. 143–158). New York: Guilford Press.

# Author Index

Aase, J. M., 155
Abbeduto, L., 223
Abbott, C. F., 55
Ainsworth, M. D., 189, 191
Allen, L., 44
Aller, S. K., 165
Allport, G. W., 193
Amatruda, 140
Ames, L. B., 24, 139, 140
Anderson, C. M., 208
Anderson, P. P., 63, 282
Anderson, R., 44
Andrews, K. B., 201
Angell, R., 51
Anthony, J. L., 197, 206
Armstrong, D. M., 177
Arter, J. A., 88
Arthur, M., 197
Atwater, J. B., 41, 126
Au, K. H., 42
Ault, M. M., 101
Ayres, J., 141
Azrin, N. H., 176, 177

Bagnato, S. J., 73, 75, 82, 89
Bailey, D. B., 8, 34, 61, 63, 75,
    76, 78, 81, 84, 89, 90, 91, 104,
    130, 143, 144, 148, 161, 171,
    179, 180, 182, 248
Baker, B. L., 174, 175, 197
Baker, E., 102
Bandura, A., 205
Barbaranelli, C., 205
Barber, P. A., 101
Barkley, R. A., 198, 200
Barnard, K. E., 51
Barnes, H. V., 7, 17, 27, 28, 246
Barnett, W. S., 7, 8, 247
Barrera, I., 13, 14, 15

Batshaw, M. L., 146, 147, 150,
    228
Bauer, A. M., 49
Bayley, N., 24
Bazyk, S., 180
Beckman, P. J., 196
Becvar, D. S., 49
Becvar, R. J., 49
Begghly, M., 153, 155
Behrman, R., 4, 10
Bender, B. G., 157
Benner, J., 63
Bennett, T., 7, 37
Bergman, P., 24
Berns, R. M., 60, 205
Bernstein, V. J., 191
Berry, J. O., 54
Bettlheim, B., 201, 202
Beukelman, D. R., 234
Bigge, J. L., 147, 148, 149, 160
Birch, H. G., 194
Bishop, D. J., 149
Black, J. K., 79, 81, 84, 88
Blasco, P. M., 129, 228
Blehar, M., 191
Block, M. E., 164
Bloom, B. S., 26
Bloomfield, B. G., 197, 206
Blue-Manning, M. J., 62, 63
Blum, N., 201
Bochner, S., 197
Bologna, T., 109, 110
Bondurant-Utz, J. A., 78, 80,
    171
Boris, N., 191
Bornstein, M., 153
Bowe, F., 152, 177
Bowlby, J., 190
Brandenburg-Ayres, S., 43

Bredekamp, S., 41, 79, 82, 91, 97,
    125
Bricker, D. D., 54, 80, 97, 102,
    110, 114, 116, 124, 127, 128,
    129, 130, 135, 230, 232, 246,
    247, 249
Briggs, M. H., 104
Brightman, A. J., 174, 175
Bronfenbrenner, U., 48, 49, 50,
    270
Brooks, V. B., 144
Brown, A. L., 87
Brown, C. W., 78, 99
Brown, E. R., 155
Brown, F., 174, 175, 178
Brown, K. W., 197
Brown, S. W., 102
Brown, W. H., 233, 234
Bruda, M., 12
Bruder, M. B., 44, 96, 97, 100,
    102, 103, 106, 107, 109, 110,
    152
Bruner, J., 221
Bukato, D., 50, 62, 143, 205
Bundy, A., 62, 141, 196
Burd, L., 154
Burgess, D. M., 153
Burke, H., 110
Buscemi, L., 7, 37
Butterfield, N., 197

Cabello, B., 83
Caldera, M., 44
Caldwell, J., 256, 257
Call, G., 148
Campbell, P. H., 161, 163, 179,
    180, 182
Capara, G. V., 205
Carta, J. J., 41, 126

Case-Smith, J., 141
Cavallaro, C. C., 83
Chan, J. B., 43, 44, 67
Chandler, L. K., 278
Chapman, J. K., 152
Chasnoff, I., 152, 153
Chess, S., 193, 194
Childre, A., 171, 178
Chira, S., 4
Chomsky, N., 220
Cohen, L. G., 76, 78, 80, 81, 90, 118
Cohn, E., 141
Cole, K. N., 88, 232
Collins, B. C., 172, 181, 182
Collins, L., 51
Combes, M., 161
Conroy, M. A., 187, 208, 233, 234
Cook, R. E., 60, 63, 82, 97, 104, 160, 161, 178, 180, 233
Cooper, J., 253
Copeland, M. E., 177, 178
Copple, C., 41, 79, 91, 97, 125
Cornwall, J. C., 107
Correa, V., 63
Cox, M. J., 13, 273
Craft, D., 164
Cratty, B. J., 164
Cripe, J. W., 228, 246, 249
Crockenberg, S., 64, 66
Cronister, A., 202

Daehler, M. W., 50, 62, 143, 205
Danaker, J., 8, 34
Darling, R. B., 64, 66
Darlington, R., 27, 28
Davis, C. A., 187, 208
Davis, M. D., 99, 105, 107, 118, 124, 126, 130, 134
Davis, W. E., 164
Davis-McFarland, E., 152
Deal, A. G., 19, 52, 57, 58, 90, 97
Deci, E. L., 186
DeFrain, J., 52
Delgado, M. R., 161
Deluca, D., 7, 37

Demchak, M. A., 102
Denier, P. L., 66
DeSantis, L. D., 42
Devlin, B. K., 59
Dewey, E., 24
Dewey, J., 24
Diamond, K. E., 102
Dickenson, D., 253
Dickstein, S., 64, 66
Dinnebeil, L. A., 103
Dodd, J. M., 42
Donahue-Kilburg, G., 224
Donegan, M., 13,
Donnellan, A. M., 201, 202
Downing, J. E., 214, 234
Dowrick, P. W., 181
Drinkwater, S., 102
Driscoll, A., 122, 125
Duchan, J. F., 222
Duhaney, D. C., 163
Duhaney, L. M., 163
Dunlap, L. L., 126
Dunst, C. J., 12, 19, 39, 41, 52, 58, 90, 96, 97, 100, 102, 103, 106, 107
Dye, H., 26
Dyson, L. L., 54

Edgar, E., 8, 280
Edmonds, P., 62, 63, 64
Efron, L. A., 201
Egan, B., 124, 230
Egan, R. W., 275, 276, 279, 283
Eller, S., 8, 34
Elliot, S. N., 92
Elliott, R. N., 152
Emde, R. N., 189, 197
Engel, A. L., 203
Erickson, M. F., 48, 58
Erikson, E., 48, 58, 124, 192–193, 207
Escalona, S., 24
Esdaile, S., 58

Fahey, K. R., 226, 228
Faine, M. P., 183
Fairchild, M., 8
Fantuzzo, J. W., 187, 188

Farlow, L. J., 171, 173, 174, 175, 180
Farnham, R., 138
Fenichel, E. S. 63, 282
Feuerstein, R., 87
Fewell, R., 65, 66
Fiechtl, B., 281
Field, T., 191
Fiese, B. H., 19, 189
Finnie, N. R., 158, 161
Finucane, B., 202
Fischer, R., 232
Fisher, A., 62, 141
Fisher, K., 62
Fleming, L. A., 114
Fletcher, J. M., 8
Foorman, B., 8, 253
Forgan, J., 263
Forman, G., 123
Fowler, S. A., 109, 278, 279, 280
Fox, L., 82, 118
Foxx, R. M., 176, 177
Fredericks, H. D., 176
Freud, S., 192, 195, 207
Froebel, F., 24, 128
Furumasu, J., 163

Gabor, L. M., 138
Galant, K. R., 118
Gallagher, J., 8, 280
Gamel-McCormick, M., 99, 105, 118, 124, 126, 130, 134
Gandini, L., 123
Gardner, H., 84
Gesell, A., 24, 122, 140, 167
Getch, Y. Q., 157
Getz, M., 201
Gilkerson, L., 55
Glanzmann, M., 201
Glorieux, F. H., 149
Goddard, H. H., 26
Gold, S., 55
Goldberg, P. F., 62, 63, 64
Goldenberg, D., 161
Goldstein, H., 214
Goleman, D., 84, 85
Gomby, D. S., 4,
Gopnick, A., 6, 8

Graham, S., 221
Grandin, T., 204
Granger, R., 153
Green, C., 197, 198
Greenberg, R., 153
Greenspan, N. T., 188
Greenspan, S. I, 75, 124, 145, 187, 203
Gregg, N., 88
Gregory, E., 74, 91
Gresham, F. M., 92
Griffer, M. R., 141
Griffith, D. R., 152
Grimley, L. K., 63
Groce, N., 43
Groen, A. D., 203
Groginsky, S., 8
Guerette, P., 163
Guidry, G., 88
Guiliani, C. A., 144
Guralnick, M. K., 6, 7, 8, 41, 101, 206
Gut, D., 63

Hadden, D., 13
Haines, A. H., 109, 175
Hall, N. W., 59
Hallahan, D., 188, 206
Hamblin-Wilson, C., 278
Hamby, D., 12, 19, 41, 52, 58, 90, 96, 97, 100, 102, 103, 106, 107
Hancock, T. B., 229, 232
Haney, M., 83
Hanft, B., 110
Hanline, M. F., 82, 118, 195, 197, 270, 275, 276, 278
Hanson, M. J., 43, 74, 83, 91, 97, 109, 114, 123, 134, 143, 145, 146, 147, 148, 150, 157–160, 163
Hanzlik, J., 196
Harbin, G. L., 8, 34
Harris, S. R., 143, 145, 146, 147, 150, 157, 158, 159, 160, 163, 221
Hartup, W. W., 190
Hatton, C., 171

Hemmeter, M. L., 172, 181, 182, 278
Henderson, L. W., 78
Hendrick, J., 62
Hertzig, M. E., 194
Hestenes, L. L., 102
Hester, P. P., 229, 232
Honig, A. S., 189
Hooper, S. R., 123, 124, 126, 128, 177, 206
Hopper, P., 59
Horn, E. M., 170, 171, 178
Houle, G., 253
Howard, V. F., 41, 102, 107
Hoy, C., 88
Hughes, M. T., 275
Hummeter, M. L., 232
Hunt, N., 26, 226, 228
Hupp, S., 196
Hutchinson, T., 227

Innocenti, M., 281
Irvin, L. K., 189

Janney, R., 179
Jenkins, L., 38
Jennings, J., 256, 257
Jessee, P. O., 196
Johnson, D. Q., 118
Johnson, L. J., 7, 37, 104
Johnson, R., 118
Johnson, T. E., 278
Jones, H. A., 102
Jungeblut, A., 38
Justen, J. E., 177

Kaiser, A. P., 229, 232
Kaiser, N., 103
Kaltenbach, K., 152
Kamhi, A. G., 221
Karp, N., 253
Karr, J. A., 55
Kastenbaum, R. J., 54
Kauffman, J., 188, 206
Kawakami, A. J., 42
Keefer, M., 232
Keeley, E., 88
Kelly, J. F., 51

Keough, B., 4, 6
Kephart, N., 141–142, 186
Kilgo, J. L., 99, 105, 118, 124, 126, 130, 134, 279
Kimmel, J. R., 177, 178
Kirk, S. A., 27
Kirsch, I. S., 38
Klein, E. R., 145, 207
Klein, M. D., 82, 97, 104, 178, 179, 233
Kleinhammer-Tramill, 25
Klin, A., 200
Klopfer, L., 17
Knight, D., 164
Koenig, K., 200
Kolstad, A., 38
Konig, C. S., 270
Kontos, S., 110
Koplow, 62
Kopp, C. B., 197
Korn, S., 194
Kosofsky, B. E., 153
Kostelink, M. J., 84, 88, 122, 126, 127, 130
Kramer, J. J., 92
Kübler-Ross, E., 52, 54
Kuhl, P., 6, 8
Kurz-Reimer, K., 48, 58

La Paro, K. M., 13, 273, 274
LaBoskey, V. K., 88
Lagrander, J. M., 224
Lamorey, S., 102
Landerholm, E., 55
Lang, L., 51
Larner, M., 4
Larsen, A. S., 52
Lavoie, R. D., 18
Lays, J., 62
Layton, T. L., 152
Lazar I., 27, 28
Lazzari, A. M., 279
Lennenberg, E., 143
Lepper, D., 41, 102, 107
Lequerica, M., 43
Lerner, J. W., 34, 87, 124, 135, 161, 198, 200, 222, 230, 247, 256, 257, 259, 260

Lewis, R., 40
Lewit, E., 4
Lidz, C. S., 88
Lieber, J., 196
Lieberman, A. F., 190, 191
Lin, S. L, 146
Linder, T. W., 86, 128, 129, 220
Lonigan, C. J., 197, 206
Lorimer, M., 156
Losardo, A., 74, 82, 88, 89, 103, 104
Lovaas, O. I., 203
Lowenthal, B., 19, 59, 61, 89, 106, 156, 157, 224, 230
Lowenthal, J., 124, 198, 230
Luby, J. L., 205
Lucariello, J., 221
Lukasson, R., 150
Luria, A. R., 87
Lutz, M. N., 187
Lynch, E. W., 43, 74, 83, 91, 97, 114, 123, 134
Lyons-Ruth, K., 64, 66

Maag, J. W., 123, 232
MacMillan, M., 25
MacMillan, R., 25
Maddox, M., 8, 280
Magnusson, C. J., 177
Mahoney, G., 51, 122, 125, 126, 157, 230
Majidi-Ahi, S., 44
Mallach, R. S., 44
Malone, D. M., 195
Mardell-Czudnowski, C., 161
Marshall, J., 63
Marshall, K., 226, 228
Martinson, S. A., 62, 63, 64
Mauer, D. M., 141
May-Benson, T., 141
Mayes, L. C., 145, 153, 202
McCabe, A., 253
McCall, R., 164
McCann, D., 155
McCardle, P., 253
McCollum, J. A., 110
McConnell, S. R., 41, 126, 186, 206

McCormick, L., 96, 174, 182
McCubbin, H. I., 52
McCubbin, M. A., 52
McDermott, D., 282
McEvoy, M. A., 41
McGowan, P. A., 270
McLean, M., 12, 39, 41, 74, 75, 76, 78, 79, 81, 84, 89, 90, 228
McNulty, B. A., 76
McWilliam, R. A., 51
Meisels, S. J., 73, 75, 77, 78, 79, 81
Meltzoff, A., 6, 8
Meyer, D., 65, 66, 88
Miller, J. E., 54
Miller, L. T., 76
Miller, N. B., 66
Miller, R., 100, 101, 102, 104, 156
Miller, S. E., 161
Mirenda, P., 234
Moffatt, M., 154
Montessori, M., 24, 25
Montpett, K., 149
Moore, S. G., 190
Morgan, D., 196
Morgan, J. L., 110
Morris, S., 179
Moses, K., 52
Mott, D. W., 52
Mowder, B. A., 48
Murray, E., 62, 141
Myers, B., 152

Nabors, L. A., 81
Nagel, N. G., 122, 125
Neilson, S., 88
Neisworth, J. T., 73, 75, 82, 89
Nelson, J. R., 42
Nelson, N. W., 42, 143, 220–222, 226, 230, 232
Neuharth-Pritchet, S., 157, 201
Neuman, G., 62
Neveille-Smith, A., 230
Nippold, M. A., 189
Noell, J. W., 189
Noonan, M. J., 96, 174, 182
Notari-Sylerson, A., 74, 82, 88, 89, 104

O'Donnell, P. A., 142
O'Connor, C. E., 102
Odom, S. L., 41, 102, 126, 186, 203, 206, 247
Okimoto, A. M., 196
Olson, B. H., 52
Olson, H. C., 152
Olson, J., 58
Orelove, F. P., 177, 178, 180, 181
Orr, M. E., 180
Osborn, J., 88
Ostrosky, M. M., 232
Owens, R. E., 222

Palinscar, A. S., 87
Pannabecker, B. J., 189
Parten, M. B., 195
Pastorelli, C., 205
Paul, J. L., 48
Paul-Brown, D., 253
Peabody, E., 24
Peck, C., 102, 247
Pereira, L., 62, 63
Perret, Y. M., 146, 147, 150, 228
Peterson, N. L., 38, 101, 109
Peuschel, S. M., 160
Phillips, C. B., 13, 43
Piaget, J., 17, 24, 122, 140, 141, 157, 220–221, 240, 242–244, 245
Pianta, R. C., 13, 273
Plotkin, H., 149
Port, P. D., 41, 102, 107
Powell, A., 125, 126
Pratt, B., 165
Premack, D., 208
Prizant, B. M., 89, 226, 227, 230, 231
Proctor, B., 208
Provence, S., 77
Puckett, M. B., 79, 81, 84, 88
Pugack, M. C., 104

Quill, K. A., 230

Raab, M., 12, 19, 41, 52, 58, 90, 96, 97, 100, 102, 103, 106, 107

Raeburn, J. M., 181
Rao, S., 63
Rapport, M. J., 102
Rauch, F., 149
Raver, S. A., 55, 63
Reamer, F. G., 61
Reid, D. K., 220, 224, 270
Reiss, M., 275
Resnick. L., 17
Reynolds, E., 59
Rice, M. L., 214
Richarz, S., 115
Richek, M., 256, 257
Richey, D. D., 97, 101, 115–116, 127
Rizzo, T. L., 164
Robinson, C., 126
Rodriquez, P., 63
Romeo, F. F., 61
Romski, M. A., 228
Rose, N. C., 228
Rosegrant, T., 82
Rosenkoetter, S. E., 25, 109, 134, 273, 278, 279, 280, 282
Rossetti, L. M., 124, 227, 232
Rothlein, L., 275
Rous, B., 278
Rousseau, J.-J., 23
Rowland, C., 103
Rubin, E., 200
Ruck-Gibis, J., 149
Rule, S., 99, 103, 281
Ryan, R. M., 186

Saland, S. J., 4
Salisbury, C. L., 101
Salvia, J., 79, 81
Sameroff, A. J., 19, 189
Sandall, S. R., 39, 41, 48, 100, 114, 123
Sattler, J. M., 81, 84
Schell, G., 65
Scholpler, E., 202
Schuman, W., 201
Schurz, M., 24
Schuster, J., 278
Schutz, G., 44
Schwartz, I. S., 41, 126, 138, 189

Schweinhart, L. J., 7, 17, 27, 28, 246
Scott, G. S., 152
Seklemian, P., 78
Seligman, M., 64, 66
Sewell, T. J., 172, 181, 182
Shea, T. M., 149
Shelley, B., 156
Sherman, C., 141
Sherwood, D., 88
Short-Meyerson, K., 223
Shotts, C. K., 278
Shriver, M. D., 208
Shuster, J. W., 172, 181, 182
Sigafoos, J., 67
Simeonsson, N., 156, 157
Simeonsson, R. J., 48
Singh, D. K., 63
Skeels, H., 26, 27
Skinner, B. F., 17
Skinner, D., 63
Sloman, L., 203
Smeriglio, V. L., 153
Smith, B., 39, 41
Smith, D. J., 42
Smith, D. D., 150
Smith, S., 8
Smith, T., 203
Sneed, T. J., 176, 177
Snell, M. E., 173, 174, 175, 178, 179
Sobsey, D., 177, 178, 180, 181
Soderman, A. K., 84, 88, 122, 126, 127, 130
Solano, T., 165
Sostek, A., 191
Spandel, Y., 88
Speigel-McGill, P., 270, 273, 278
Spenciner, L. J., 76, 78, 80, 81, 90
Squires, S., 134
Stayton, V. D., 110
Stein, M. A., 201
Stella, M. E., 278
Stern, D., 190
Stevenson, C., 4
Stinnett, N., 52
Stoltzfus, J., 187
Strain, P. S., 214

Straka, E., 110
Streissguth, A. P., 153
Stremel, K., 40
Strong, B. N., 196
Stroufe, L. A., 197
Struefers, C. A., 278
Stull, J., 145
Sturtz, J., 156
Summers, J., 38
Svecik, R. A., 228
Svejda, M. J., 189
Swan, W. W., 110
Swenson-Miller, K., 110
Swinth, Y., 138

Taulbee, D. A., 125
Taylor, L., 44
Tefft, D., 163
Tenbrink, T. D., 135
Terry, D., 1991
Tessier, A., 82, 97, 104, 233, 178
Thomas, A., 194, 194
Thomas, D., 7
Thomas, J. T., 42
Thompson, A. I., 52
Thurman, S. K., 278
Torgesen, J., 253, 259
Toussaint, R., 164
Tramill, T., 25
Trask, C. L., 153
Travers, R., 149
Trawick-Smith, J., 220, 221, 224
Trivette, C., 12, 19, 39, 41, 52, 57, 58, 90, 96, 97, 100, 102, 103, 106, 107
Tronick, E. Z., 153, 155
Turbiville, V., 58
Turnbull, A. P., 51, 58, 60, 61, 62, 63
Turnbull, H. R., 51, 58, 60, 61

Umansky, W., 123, 124, 126, 128, 177, 206
Umbreit, J., 206
Underdown, G., 51

Vadasy, P., 65, 66
Vail, C. O., 82, 118

Van den Pol, J., 88
Vandiviere, P., 51
Vaughn, S., 275
Vincent, L. J., 101
Volmar, F. R., 200
Vygotsky, L. S., 19, 87, 221

Wadsworth, D., 164
Walberg, H., 102
Walker, H. M., 189
Wall, S., 191
Wanzer, P., 161
Warren, S. L., 197, 232
Washington, K., 138
Waters, E., 191
Weber, J. D., 202
Wehman, T., 55
Weider, S., 124, 203
Weikart, D. B., 17, 27, 28, 246
Weissbourd, B., 58, 59
Wesson, K. A., 78

Wetherby, A. M., 89, 226, 227, 230, 231
Wheatley, A. P., 122
Wheeler, J. J., 97, 101, 115–116, 127
Whipple, E. E., 59
Whiren, A. P., 84, 88, 122, 126, 127, 130
Whitbread, N., 25
Widerstrom, A. H., 48, 104, 109
Wilbur, J., 102
Wilcox, H. C., 153
Williams, D. F., 44, 228
Willias, B. F., 41, 102, 107
Wilson, H., 196
Windsor, J., 227, 232
Winton, P. J., 41, 90
Witt, J. C., 92
Wolery, M., 61, 63, 75, 76, 78, 80, 81, 82, 84, 89, 90, 91, 102,

104, 114, 130, 143, 144, 148, 161, 171, 179, 180, 182, 248
Wong, M., 102
Wynn, J., 203

Yoder, P. J., 229, 232
Yoshikawa, H., 8
Young, E., 270
Ysseldyke, J. E., 79, 81

Zabel, M. K., 187
Zeanah, C. J., 191
Zervigon-Hakes, A., 4, 5
Zier, F. A., 148
Zigler, E., 59
Zimbardo, P. G., 205
Zimmerman, W. W., 54
Zola, I. K., 43
Zuckerman, B., 153, 155, 156

# Subject Index

Abstract thinking, 141
Abuse and neglect:
  abuse, defined, 59
  effects of, 61
  ethical dilemmas, 61
  National Child Abuse Hotline, 60
  reporting, 60
Accommodation, 244
Acquired Immune Deficiency Syndrome (AIDS),
  151–152
Active engagement of students and parents, 122
Activity-based instruction, 127
  and language development, 233
Adaptive behavior:
  defined, 169–170
  in preschool curriculum, 170–171
  principles of, 171–173
  role of the family, 171
  toileting skills, 173–176
Adaptive skills (see Adaptive behavior)
Aggressive behavior, 205
Alternative-form reliability, 81
American Academy of Pediatrics, 7
American Sign Language (ASL), 234
Americans with Disabilities Act (ADA), 36, 165
Anecdotal records, 83
Arthrogryposis multiplex congenita, 149
Articulation disorders, 227
Asperger's disorder, 205
Assessment:
  alternative methods, 82–90
  checklists, 84
  multiple intelligence, 84–85
  observation, 83–84
  rating scales, 84
  authentic, 88–89
  child-find process, 75–76
  cognitive, 72
  criterion-referenced/curriculum-based tests, 82

  defined, 70
  development of rapport, 92
  developmental screening, 77–78
  diagnosis, 78–79
  dynamic, 87–88
  ecological factors, 73–74
  eligibility for special services, 74
  of the family, 51, 89
  fine motor, 72
  functional behavioral, 208
  gross motor, 71–72
  individualized planning of programs and
    intervention, 79–80
  instruments, 80–82
  judgment-based, 89
  language-expressive, 72
  language-receptive, 72
  methods for obtaining information, 70–73
  of motor delays and disabilities, 145
  nondiscriminatory, 91
  norm-referenced tests, 81–82
  performance, 88–89
  monitoring, 80
  performance, 88–89
  personal-social/self-help skills, 72
  play-based, 86–87
  portfolio, 88
  process, 71–72
  program evaluation, 80
  psychoeducational, 71
  purposes of, 70
  referral, working with parents, 55
  scaffolding, 87
  special considerations for young children, 90–92
  stages of the process, 75
  standardized tests, 78
  testing preschoolers, 91
  tests, 81–82
  transdisciplinary play-based, 72

Assimilation, 244
Assistive technology, 32, 40
Asthma, 156–157
Atlanto-Axial Instability, 160
Attachment, 189
Attention deficit hyperactivity disorder (ADHD),
        197–201
    defined, 198
    subtypes, 198–199
Auditory activities, 20
Auditory processing dysfunctions and language
        development, 226
Augmentive communicative systems, 234
Authentic assessment, 88–89
Autistic disorder (autism), 201–205, 226
    defined, 226
    characteristics of, 202
    educational approaches, 203
    etiology, 201–202
    Fragile X syndrome, 202
    intervention, 202–203
    and language development, 226–227
    parents of children with, 202
    pharmacological intervention, 203
    treatment, 202

Beach Center on Families and Disability at the
        University of Kansas, 51
Behavior recording, 209
Behavioral approach to intervention, 207–209
Behavioral curriculum, 121, 123
Behavioral psychology, 17, 18
Behavioral techniques and language development,
        232
Bladder control (*see* Toileting skills)
Bodily/kinesthetic intelligence, 84–86
Bonding, 189
Brain development of children at risk, 6
Brittle bones (osteogenesis imperfecta), 149

Cerebral palsy, 146–147, 150, 228
    causes, 146
    nonspastic, 147
    spastic, 147
Child abuse (*see* Abuse and neglect)
Child-find process and assessment, 75
Childhood arthritis, 149
Childhood disintegrative disorder, 205

Children at risk, 25–26
    biological factors, 4, 5
    brain development, 6
    early intervention, 5, 6–8
    eligibility for special services, 74
    environmental factors, 4, 5, 9
    established risk conditions, 4, 5
    Head Start, 4
    legislation and programs, 29, 36–39
    Head Start, 37
    Title I: Compensatory Education Programs,
        38
    low-birth-weight infants, 5
    programs, 25–26
    transition, 273
Children with disabilities/special needs:
    cautions for working with, 160
    cultural diversity, 13–15
    diagnosis, 78
    educational environments, 10–13
    eligibility for special services, 74
    family acceptance of, 53–54
    home instruction, 12
    hospital environment, 12
    inclusion, 11
    least restrictive environment, 11
    legislation affecting (table), 29
    legislation and programs, 28–36
    medical, 151–157
    Acquired Immune Deficiency Syndrome
        (AIDS), 151–152
    asthma, 156–157
    crack/cocaine, prenatal exposure to, 152
    Down syndrome, 160
    feeding, 160
    Fetal Alcohol Syndrome/Effect, 153–156
    handling, 159
    intervention strategies, 157–164
    positioning, 158
    play environment, 128
    preschoolers, 10
    residential facilities, 12
    resource rooms, 12
    separate classes, 12
    special services, 9–10
    teaching language skills to, 233
Cognitive curriculum, 121, 122
Cognitive delays and language development, 226

Cognitive development, 239–267
  abilities, 240
  cognitive activities, 20, 247
  and computer technology, 262–263
  curriculum development, 245, 248–250
  early literacy, 253–262, 264–267
  High/scope project, 245
  intervention activities, 247–253
  Piaget's stages of growth, 243–244
  teaching activities, 250–253
  theories of, 242–246
  transactional approach, 245
Cognitive skills, 241
Cognitive-interactionist theory of language,
    220–221
Communication (*see* Language development)
Community self-sufficiency, 170
Compensatory education programs, 38
Computer-based technology, 40
  and cognitive development, 262–263
Concrete operations, 141
Constructive learning, 122
  and cognitive development, 245
Constructivist curriculum, 121, 122–123 (*see also*
    Reggio Emilia approach)
Content validity, 82
Contingency contracting, 208
Continuum of alternative placements, 99
Continuum of care, 108
Conventional IQ, 85
Convulsive disorder, 150
Cooperative learning, 118
Council for Exceptional Children, 106
Crack/cocaine, prenatal exposure to, 152
Criterion-referenced/curriculum-based
    instruments, 82
Cultural and linguistic diversity (CLD), defined, 13
Cultural diversity, 13–15
  additive responses, 15
  appropriate practices, 14
  beliefs about disabilities, 43
  child-rearing practices, 14, 42
  and children with special needs, 13–15
  communication styles, 43
  cultural and linguistic mediation, 15
  early intervention and, 62–64
  establishing rapport, 15
  establishing trust, 63

families, 62–64
  interaction styles, 44
  interpreters, use of, 43
  interventionists, 44
  law and policy, 42–44
  needs assessment, 63
  nondiscriminatory assessment, 91
  second language acquisition, 224–225
  and transition, 282
Curriculum development, 113–135
  activity-based approach, 246, 249
  adaptive behavior in preschool curriculum,
      170–171
  cognitive-oriented approach, 246, 248–250
  content, 115
  cooperative learning, 118–120
  daily schedule, 117
  defining the curriculum, 114
  early intervention, 115, 116
  evaluation of, 115–116
  IEP, 130
  IFSP, 130, 131
  inclusive curriculum, guidelines, 115
  learning centers, 117, 118, 119
  naturalistic philosophy, 118
  play, role of, 128
  routines and schedules, 117
  social relationships, 115
  types of curricula, 120–128
  behavioral, 123
  cognitive, 122
  constructivist, 122–123
  developmental, 122
  developmentally appropriate practice (DAP),
      113, 124–127
  ecological/functional, 123
  natural approach, 124
  psychosocial, 124
  Reggio Emilia approach, 122–123
Custody issues, 61–62

Department of Health and Human Services, 37
Developmental communication, 217
Developmental curriculum, 121, 122
Developmental delay:
  defined, 74
  and eligibility for services, 98
  and IDEA, 34

Developmental milestones, 142–143, 295–300
Developmental motor theory, 140
Developmental screening, 77–78
Developmental theories, 15–17
Developmental therapy, 204
Developmentally appropriate practices (DAP),
      113, 121, 124–127
Diagnosis of children with special needs, 78
Direct instruction, 123
Division for Early Childhood (DEC), 11, 39, 78,
      79, 92, 97, 102, 104, 105, 126
   in the Council for Exceptional Children, 126
   recommended practices, 39, 126, 127
Divorce issues, 61–62
Down syndrome, 147
Dressing skills, 180–182
Duchenne muscular dystrophy, 148
Dynamic systems theory, 143, 144

Early Childhood Amendments to IDEA,
      PL 102-119, 29
Early childhood transition model, 280
Early education:
   behavioral theories, 17–18
   children at risk, 25–26
   cognitive theories, 17
   constructive learning, 17
   developmental theories, 15–16, 18
   historical perspective, 23–24
   intervention, 25
   problem solving, 17
   social theories, 18
   special education, 24
   theoretical foundations, 15–20
Early Education Program for Children with
      Disabilities (EEPCD), 29, 35–36
Early intervention (*see* Intervention)
Early Intervention Program for Infants and
      Toddlers with Disabilities, 32 (*see also*
      Individuals with Disabilities Education Act
      of 1997)
Early literacy, 253–262, 264–267
   activities, 260
   development, 254
   importance of, 253–254
   Learn to Read/Read to Learn document,
      257–259

phonological awareness, 259–262
precursers of reading and writing, 255
in reading, 256
strategies for teachers, 264–267
in writing, 255
Eating skills:
   adaptive equipment, 178–179
   behavioral techniques, 176
   gavage feedings, 180
   positioning techniques, 178
   systematic instruction, 177
   therapeutic feeding, 177
   typical development of, 177
Ecological framework and diagnosis, 78
Ecological/functional curriculum, 121, 123
Ecologically based evaluation, 83
Economic Opportunity Act of 1965, 37
Education for All Handicapped Children Act
      (EHA), PL 98-199, 29
Education of Handicapped Children's Act
      Amendments, 29
Education of the Handicapped Act
      Amendments, 29
Educational Amendments, PL 93-389, 29
Educational environments (*see also* Learning
      environments):
   defined, 10
   for children with special needs, 10–13
   homebound instruction, 12
hospital environments, 12
   inclusion, 11
   infants, 12
   residential facilities, 12
   resource rooms, 12
   separate classes, 12
   toddlers, 12
Emergence of words, 218
Emotional behavior disorder, 188
Emotional development (*see* Social and emotional
      development)
Emotional disturbance (ED), 187
   and language development, 227
Emotional intelligence, 84
Emotional IQ, 85
Empowerment of the family, 56, 57
Enablement of the family, 56
Enabling model of service coordination, 106

Epilepsy, 150
Ethnic diversity (*see* Cultural diversity)
Event sampling, 84
Expansion and language development, 230
Extrinsic reinforcement, 18

Failure to thrive, 191
Families:
    assessment of, 51, 89
    and intervention, 41
    cultural diversity in, 14, 62–64
    defined, 47–48
    and transitions, 274–275
Family (*see* Family systems; Families)
Family Enablement Project, 57
Family Functioning Style Scale, 52
Family Hardiness Index, 52
Family Infant and Preschool Program, 58
Family Strengths Inventory, 52
Family Strengths Scale, 52
Family systems:
    abuse and neglect, 59–61
    acceptance and grief, 52–54
    adaptive behavior, 171
    assessment of, 51, 55
    cultural diversity, 14, 62–64
    custody issues, 61–62
    defined, 19
    divorce, 61–62
    early education, theory of, 18–19
    early intervention, 54–59
    empowerment of the family, 56
    enablement of the family, 56
    family, defined, 47–48
    fathers, 64–66
    framework, 49
    model of, 50
    need for adult, 48–49
    referral for assessment, 55
    siblings, 66–67
    support programs/groups, 58–59, 293–294
    model, 50–51
    poverty, 64
    respite care, 67
    recognition in the law, 49
    systems analysis, 49
Father-child interaction, 64

Fetal Alcohol Syndrome/Effect, 153–156
    characteristics in affected children, 154
    symptoms, 155
Fine motor activities, 19
Fluctuating tone, 148
Fluency problems, 228
Folic acid, 149
Follow-Through education program, 38
Fragile X syndrome, 202
Functional behavioral assessment, 208

Gavage feedings, 180
General case method, 124
General education classes, 10
Grand mal seizure, 151
Grooming skills, 182–183
Gross motor activities, 19
Guided learning, 118

Handicapped Children's Early Education Act
    (HCEEP), 29
Head and spinal cord injury, 150
Head Start, 7, 9, 11,24, 26, 29, 27, 37
    Early Head Start Program, 38
Head Start Expansion and Quality Improvement
    Act, PL 101-501, 29
Hearing loss and language development, 225
High/Scope Educational Research Foundation of
    Ypsilanti, Michigan, 28, 125, 126, 245
Home Start, 38
Hypertonicity, 147
Hypotonicity, 147

Identifying correct response, 232
IEP (*see* Individualized education program)
IFSP (*see* Individualized family service plan)
Improving America's Schools Act, 38
Incidental teaching, 118
Inclusion, 11, 101, 164
    guidelines, 115
    settings, 10, 41 (*see also* General education
        classes)
Individualized education program (IEP), 11, 31,
    40, 51, 65, 113, 134, 157, 281
    components, 134
    formulating goals and objectives, 134
    sample, 132–133

Individualized family service plan, 11, 33, 40, 42, 51, 65, 89, 98, 105, 113, 131, 134, 157, 281

Individuals with Disabilities Act of 1977 (IDEA), 3, 9, 12, 26, 28, 29, 30, 31, 32, 34–35, 36, 41, 49, 89, 97, 99, 105, 107, 108, 187, 208, 273, 283
  categories, 35
  developmental delay, 34
  mediation, 35

Infant programs for children with special needs, 8–9

Infant/Toddler program eligibility, 33

Innatist theory of language, 220

Integrated therapy, 105

Interactional view of development, 140

Interagency collaboration, 33, 107–110
  guidelines for facilitating, 109–110
  procedures to establish, 108–109

Interdisciplinary teams, 104

Interpersonal intelligence, 84–86

Interscorer reliability, 81

Intervention:
  behavioral approach, 207
  and cognitive development, 250–253
  curriculum for children with special needs, 115
  early, 25
  curriculum models, 121
  interdisciplinary teams, 104
  multidisciplinary teams, 103
  referral for assessment, 55
  transdisciplinary teams, 104
  participation of the family, 54–59
  early studies, 26–27
  humanistic approach, 206
  language development:
  activities, 234–237
  activity-based, 233
  behavioral techniques, 232
  classroom, 233
  milieu teaching, 229–230
  naturalistic teaching, 229
  parents, 232
  peer-mediated, 233
  responsive interaction, 230
  longitudinal studies, 27–28
  participation of the family, 54–59
  psychodynamic approach, 206

and social and emotional development, 206–211
  strategies, 209–210
  for children with medical disabilities, 157–164
  time out, 209

Intrapersonal intelligence, 84–86

IQ:
  conventional, 85
  emotional, 24, 25,

Kindergarten, 24, 25, 128
  defined, 24
  Froebel model, 24

Language development, 212–238
  behavioral theory, 219–220
  cognitive-interactionist theory, 220–221
  communication, defined, 214
  difficulties, 224–228
  auditory processing dysfunctions, 226–227
  autism and pervasive development disorder, 226–227
  cognitive delays, 226
  cultural diversity, 224–225
  emotional disturbances, 227
  hearing loss, 225
  injury, 228
  intervention, 228–237
  milieu teaching, 229–230
  motor dysfunction, 228
  second language acquisition, 224–225
  speech disorders, 227–228
  structural abnormality, 228
  visual impairments, 225–226
  innatist theory, 220
  intervention activities, 235–237
  language, defined, 215
  linguistic systems, 222–223
  social-interactionist theory, 221
  speech, defined, 215
  stages of, 215–219
  theories of, 219–222

Language-culture mediators, 15

Laws and policies:
  assistive technology, 40
  children at risk, 29 (table), 36–39
  children with disabilities 29 (table)
  computer-based technology, 40

and cultural diversity, 42–44
early childhood education, 23–25
historical perspectives, 23–26
inclusive settings, 41
intervention, family, 41
learning environments, 97–99
mediation, 24
recognition of the family, 49
special education laws, 35–36
the Technology Act, 40
transition, 273–274
Lead agency, 33
Learn to Read/Read to Learn document, 257–259
Learning centers, 117, 118, 119
Learning environments, 95–110
center-based, 97
combined home- and center-based, 97
early intervention teams, 103–105
establishing physical environment, 130
home-based, 96–97
inclusion, 101
integration, 99–103
interagency collaboration, 107–110
guidelines for facilitating, 109–110
procedures to establish, 108–109
interdisciplinary teams, 104
law and policy, 97–99
mainstreaming, 101
multidisciplinary teams, 103
natural environments, 102
placement options, 99
for preschoolers with disabilities, 100
service coordination, 95, 105–107
transdisciplinary teams, 104
Least restrictive environment (LRE), 11, 100
Leave No Child Behind Act (LNCB), 29
Legislation (*see* Laws and policies)
Linguistic diversity (*see* Cultural diversity; Second language acquisition)
Linguistic intelligence, 84–86
Linguistic mediation, 15
Literacy (*see* Early literacy)
Logical-mathematical intelligence, 84–86
Low-birth-weight infants, 5

Mainstreaming, 101
Maternal Behavior Rating Scale, 51

Mediated Learning Program, 88
Mediation, and Individuals with Disabilities Act, 35
Mental retardation, 202
and Fetal Alcohol Syndrome, 153
Milieu teaching and language development, 229–230
Modeling, 208
Morphology, 222
Motor delay, 145
Motor development:
activities for, 161–162
atypical, 144–146
cognitive development, 139
delays and disabilities, 144–146
Acquired Immune Deficiency Syndrome (AIDS), 151–152
adaptive equipment, 162
arthrogryposis multiplex congenita, 149
assessment of, 145
asthma, 156–157
cerebral palsy, 146–147
classifications, 146
Down syndrome, 160
effects of, 144
feeding, 160
Fetal Alcohol Syndrome/Effect, 153–156
folic acid, 149
handling, 159
head and spinal cord injury, 150
intervention strategies, 157–164
medical, 151–157
multiple disabilities, 150
muscle tone problems, 147
muscular dystrophy, 145, 148
occupational therapy, 163
osteogenesis imperfecta (brittle bones), 149
peripheral nerve injuries, 148
physical therapy, 163
positioning, 158
progressive diseases, 148
spina bifida, 145, 148–149
spinal cord injuries, 148
static central nervous system anomalies, 146
structural defects, 149–150
theories of, 140–143
types of, 146–151

Motor development *(continued)*
  developmental motor theory, 140
  dynamic systems theory, 143, 144
  fine motor skills, 143
  gross motor skills, 143
  inclusion, 164
  milestones in, 142–143
  motor programs theory, 143, 144
  normal growth and development, 139–144
  perceptual-motor learning, 141
  physical education, 164
  plasticity of the brain, 143
  reflexes, 143
  sensory integration, 141
  sensory-motor learning, importance of, 140
  sequence of, 142
Motor programs theory, 143, 144
Movement education, 161
Multidisciplinary services, 33
Multidisciplinary teams, 103
Multiple intelligence, 84–86
Muscle tone problems, 147
Muscular dystrophy, 145, 148,
Musical intelligence, 84–86

National Assessment of Educational Progress, 257
National Association for the Education of Young
      Children (NAEYC), 97, 121, 125, 195, 196
National Association of Early Childhood
      Specialists in State Departments of
      Education, 1991, 125
National Child Abuse Hotline, 60
National Organization for Rare Disorders, 165
National Reading Panel, 260
Natural approach curriculum, 121, 124
Natural environment, 41, 102
Naturalistic intelligence, 84, 86
Naturalistic philosophy, 118
  and language development, 229
Needs assessment and transition, 282
Negative reinforcement, 18
Neglect *(see* Abuse and neglect)
Noncategorical identification, 33
Nursery school, 23, 24

Occupational therapy, 163
Orphan disease, 166

Orphan drug, 166
Osteogenesis imperfecta (brittle bones), 149

Parallel talk and language development, 230
Parent and Child Centers education program,
      38
Parents and language development, 232
Peer-mediated intervention and language
      development, 233
Perceptual-motor learning, 141
Performance assessment, 88–89
Peripheral nerve injuries, 148
Perry Preschool Program, 27, 28, 38
Personal/social responsibility, 170
Pervasive development disorder, 188, 201–205
  characteristics of, 202
  educational approaches, 203
  Fragile X syndrome, 202
  intervention, 202–203
  and language development, 226–227
  parents of children with, 202
  pharmacological intervention, 203
  treatment, 202
Petit mal seizure, 151
Phonemes, 222, 259
Phonemic awareness *(see* Phonological
      awareness)
Phonological awareness, 259–262, 264–265
  activities to develop, 260
  assessing, 261
Phonology, 222
Physical education and motor development,
      164
Physical therapy, 163
Piaget, J., 245, 122, 140, 157, 17, 220, 221, 24,
      240, 242–244
  abstract thinking, 141
  accommodation, 244
  assimilation, 244
  cognitive curriculum, 242
  cognitive growth, stages of, 243–244
  concrete operations, 141
  constructivist theory, 125
  preoperational thought, 141
  schemata, 244
  sensory-motor learning, importance of, 140
  sensory-motor period, 140

stages of development, 141
theory of sensory integration, 140
PL 92-424, 29
PL 93-389, 29
PL 98-199, 29
PL 99-457, 30, 49, 51, 89, 97, 105, 107
PL 101-218, 29
PL 101-476, 29
PL 101-501, 29
PL 102-119, 105
PL 102-119, 29, 30, 49, 89, 97
PL 105-17, 29, 32, 49
Play:
   assessment based on, 86–87
   and children with special needs, 128
   importance of, 128
   role of in curriculum, 128
   in social and emotional development, 195
   stages of, 196
Play therapy, 130, 207
Policy (*see* Laws and policies)
Portfolio assessment, 88–89
Positive reinforcement, 18
Pragmatics, 223
Predictive validity, 82
Prelinguistic behavior, 216
Premack principle, 208
Preoperational thought, 141
Prepared environment, 25
Preschool Learning Assessment Device, 88
Preschooler programs for children with special
   needs, 8–9
Project Head Start (*see* Head Start)
Prompting, 123, 232
Psychomotor seizure, 151
Psychosocial curriculum, 121, 124
Public Law (*see* PL)
Punishment, 208

Rating scales, 84
Reading stories and literacy development, 256
Reggio Emilia approach, 121, 122–123
Regular class, 100
Reinforcement, 18, 208
Reliability, 81
Residential facility, 100
Resource room, 12, 100

Respiratory Distress Syndrome, 139
Responsive interaction and language
   development, 230
Role transition, 104–105
Running record, 84

Scaffolding, 87, 221, 244
Schedules of reinforcement, 209
Second language acquisition, 224–225
Section 504 of the Rehabilitation Act, 35
Seizure disorder, 150, 151
Self-care skills, 170 (*see also* Self-help skills)
Self-concept development activities, 19
Self-help skills:
   assessment of, 72
   dressing, 180–182
   eating, 176–180
   grooming, 182–183
   toileting, 173–176
Self-talk and language development, 230
Semantics, 222–223
Sensory deficits, 202
Sensory integration, 140, 141
Sensory-affective interaction, 191
Sensory-motor learning, importance of, 140
Separate class environment, 100
Separate school environment, 100
Sequenced Transition to Education in the Public
   Schools (STEPS) model, 278
Service coordination:
   continuum of care, 108
   enabling model, 106
   family-centered, 106
   and learning environments, 105–107
   responsibilities of the service coordinator, 33,
      95, 105
   transition in providers, 275–276
Shaping, 123, 208, 232
Siblings, 66
Social activities, 20
Social adjustment, 170
Social and emotional development:
   bonding and attachment, 189–192
   defining problems, 187–188
   emotional disturbance, 187
   play, 195
   problems in young children, 197–206

Social and emotional development *(continued)*
  aggressive behavior, 205
  intervention, 206–211
  pervasive developmental disorders, 201–205
  socialization, 206
  withdrawn behavior, 205–206
  temperament, 193
  theories of, 189–197
Social theories and early education, 18
Social-interactionist theory of language, 221
Spatial intelligence, 84–86
Special education:
  historical perspective, 24, 25
  laws regarding, 35–36
Special needs:
  activities and curriculum for children, 19–20
  defined 3–6, 25
Special services for children with disabilities, 9–10
  eligibility for, 74
Specimen record, 84
Speech:
  defined, 215
  disorders, 227–228
Spina Bifida, 145, 148–149
Spinal cord injuries, 148
Split-half reliability, 81
Standardized tests, 78
Static central nervous system anomalies, 146
STEPS model, 286
Stuttering, 228
Substance abuse, prenatal exposure, 152, 154
System to Plan Early Childhood Services
        (SPECS), 89
Systematic instruction and eating skills, 177
Systems analysis and the family, 49

Tactile defensiveness, 141
Task Force on Recommended Practices for the
        Division for Early Childhood of the
        Council for Exceptional Children, 169
Teaching activities to foster cognitive
        development, 250–253
Technology Act, 29, 40
Temperament:
  and social and emotional development, 193
  ten factors of, 194
Test-retest reliability, 81

Tests, 81–82
  criterion-referenced/curriculum-based, 82
  norm-referenced, 81–82
  reliability, 81
  validity, 81–82
Therapy, 207
Time out, 209
Title 1: Compensatory Education Programs, 38
Toddler programs for children with special needs,
        8–9
Toileting skills, 172, 173–176
  at night, 175–176
  distributed practice, 174
  methods of training, 173–174
  prerequisite skills, 173
  rapid method, 175
  timed toileting, 174
Transactional Intervention Program (TRIP), 125,
        126
Transdisciplinary approach, 104
Transdisciplinary play-based assessment (TPBA),
        86
Transdisciplinary teams, 104
Transition, 12–13, 32, 270–286
  affect on children, 277
  for children at risk, 273
  communication issues, 281
  coordinator, role of, 283
  defined, 272–273
  factors affecting, 278–282
  families, 274–275
  interagency agreements, 274
  interagency coordination, 280
  and the law, 273–274
  legal rights, 282
  multicultural considerations, 282
  needs assessment, 282
  planning, 282
  research on, 277
  role of administrators, 277
  service providers, 275–276
  stages in coordinating, 284–286
  STEPS model, 286
  testing and placement issues, 281
  transportation, 289
Traumatic brain injury (TBI) and language
        development, 228

Universal precautions, 152

Validity, 81–82
Vestibular stimulation, 141
Visual activities, 20
Visual impairments and language development,
    225–226
Voice disorders, 227

Vygotsky, L., 19, 87, 221
    theory of cognitive development, 244–245
    zone of proximal development (ZPD), 221, 245

Whole-child theory, 16
Withdrawn behavior, 205–206

Zone of proximal development (ZPD), 221, 245